FREEDOM, POWER, AND DEMOCRATIC PLANNING

INTERNATIONAL LIBRARY OF SOCIOLOGY
AND SOCIAL RECONSTRUCTION

Editor: Dr. Karl Mannheim

FREEDOM, POWER
& DEMOCRATIC
PLANNING

BY

KARL MANNHEIM

Author of IDEOLOGY AND UTOPIA,

MAN AND SOCIETY IN AN AGE OF RECONSTRUCTION, ETC.

Edited by

HANS GERTH and ERNEST K. BRAMSTEDT

LONDON

ROUTLEDGE & KEGAN PAUL LTD

BROADWAY HOUSE: 68-74 CARTER LANE, E.C.4

First published in England 1951

© *Oxford University Press, Inc. 1950*

*No part of this book may be reproduced
in any form without permission from
the publisher, except for the quotation
of brief passages in criticism*

Second impression 1965
Third impression 1968

SBN 7100 3292 7

*Printed in Great Britain by
Compton Printing Ltd
London and Aylesbury*

Foreword

○

When Karl Mannheim died early in 1947 in his fifty-third year, he left a number of unpublished manuscripts in varying stages of completion. At the invitation of Dr. Julia Mannheim, the author's widow and lifelong collaborator, I assisted in forming an editorial team, selected from Mannheim's friends and former students, for the purpose of making at least part of this material available to the wider public. We were united in the conviction that not only do the ideas laid down in these writings form an essential key to the full understanding of Mannheim's work, but they contain a most important and topical contribution to social theory as well as impetus for social action.

The present book is the first of the posthumous volumes. The editorial work on it was performed by Dr. Hans Gerth, of Madison, Wisconsin, and by Dr. Ernest K. Bramstedt, in close co-operation with Dr. Agnes Schwarzchild, both of London, England. Dr. Julia Mannheim's participation was essential in every phase of the work. The section on 'Control of the Economy,' in Chapter 5, had to be rewritten completely; the responsibility for its present form is mine. The final draft was re-checked against the original manuscript by both editors. The bibliographic and other documentary material was added mainly by Hans Gerth, who must be regarded as primarily responsible for the text as it now stands. The Rockefeller Foundation generously awarded a grant to the Institute of World Affairs of the New School for Social Research for the work of preparing the various manuscripts for publication.

Probably, had the author lived to revise it, he would have changed and supplemented the text in many directions. But what could still be preserved is a work, complete in itself, that may well be considered his political testament.

Adolph Lowe

April 1950
Institute of World Affairs
New School for Social Research
New York, N. Y.

A Note on the Work of Karl Mannheim

Q

In common with great sociologists of the past, such as Comte and Spencer, Marx and Max Weber, Mannheim engaged in sociological study as a response to the challenging present. For him sociology was a specifically modern way of thought which contributes to the rational self-orientation of man in industrial society. By raising us to a new level of self-awareness, the intellectual tools that the sociologist forges open up for us an insight into the dangerous process of the modern world with its drift toward social upheavals and world wars.

In many ways the present book rounds out Mannheim's attempts at analyzing the contemporary crisis. Originally departing from abstract philosophical concerns, he addressed himself, during his German period, primarily to the intellectual constellation of modern society. The main fruit of these studies was *Ideology and Utopia,* first published in German in 1929 and issued in an enlarged English edition in 1936. In it, following the tradition of Max Weber and Max Scheler, Mannheim fully developed what has come to be known as *Wissenssoziologie* or sociology of knowledge.

The main thesis of this approach to social thought is that ideas emerge and develop in response to, and are determined by, the social-historical situation in which intellectual skill groups find themselves. And not only do such social-historical factors account for the particular political expectancies and demands that representative thinkers elaborate, but social determination reaches into the most intimate recesses of man's mind. The basic categories that inform one's view of social reality, the vision of past and future, especially the conception of human freedom, are shown to be bound up with the thinker's basic political stand and group identification. Even where the social observer is careful to control his personal bias, to argue 'objectively' by not indulging in special pleading and subjective value preferences, his social-historical background can be shown to condition his ways of thought.

For Mannheim, thinking about social reality means first to 'see' something, to bring facts into 'perspective,' and by so doing possibly to 'overlook' and bypass other things. Thus social thought is necessarily 'perspectivist' thought, and derives from a standpoint located in the historical and social context. Thinkers of comparable rank and stature may 'view' the identical object from different standpoints and then reach from divergent perspectives apparently opposite conclusions. But what becomes of truth if this is the basic intellectual situation? Mannheim sought to implement the quest for objectivity by assessing the angle of vision in which social reality presents itself to men in different social and historical situations. Since the waning of the Middle Ages, social thought has manifested itself in competition—social and intellectual. Ever broader groups have awakened to the fact that history is made by man, and have, with varying success, claimed to enter ever broader decision-making processes. They have found representative spokesmen, skilled in elaborating and justifying their aspirations and outlook.

Mannheim presented in *Ideology and Utopia* the panoramic procession of Western social thought in terms of the politically oriented, socially rooted ideas that were advanced by the intellectual elites of the past in an increasingly pluralist universe of discourse. Capitalizing on Marx's and Nietzsche's discovery of socially and psychologically determined forms of 'false consciousness' and 'rationalizations,' Mannheim aimed at piercing through outmoded ways of thought which stop short of meeting present reality. These he called 'ideologies.' His earlier monograph on conservative thinking contained a classic analysis of the way in which feudal and preindustrial social strata and their spokesmen in Germany 'reacted' at the beginning of the nineteenth century against the advent of liberalism and the middle class. In *Ideology and Utopia* he demonstrated how a conservative 'style of thought' emerged out of unreflective traditionalist attitudes all over Europe and competed alongside the liberal-democratic style of thought for the 'definition of the situation.' With the advent of the modern factory worker an additional social position offered the opportunity for elaborating a further way of thought in critical opposition to all others: Marxian socialism as the modern form of 'utopian' thought.

Both ideological and utopian thought fail to meet social reality adequately. The former lags behind reality, misrepresenting it in obsolete concepts, while the latter projects the hope of the disadvantaged for the good society into the present. Hence much of contemporary thought is to the piercing critic a confusion of tongues, a combat of political theologies, which threaten to drown rationally sober discussion and thus disrupt the stability of society itself. Where the pursuit of special interests becomes universal and the major intellectual currents gravitate toward rigidly embattled pressure groups inflamed by ideologies or utopias, social breakdown seems unavoidable. Is there no one who cares for the whole and thus rises to a comprehensive perspective? But can a stratified and dynamic society offer the elevated social position necessary for a more than partial view?

Mannheim in 1929 placed his hope on the 'socially unattached intelligentsia,' as Alfred Weber has called this interstitial stratum of modern society. Mentally and socially highly mobile, emancipated from the fetters of the feudal patronage system, not enrolled in the bureaucratic structures and machines of metropolitan society, they appeared to Mannheim as the 'predestined advocates of the intellectual interests of the whole.' The very competition in ideas might inspire them to gradual syntheses of partial perspectives, and thus lead them to a progressively comprehensive and rational understanding of reality, which is the prerequisite of a scientific approach to politics and social change. 'Thus they might play the part of watchmen in what otherwise would be a pitch-black night.' [1]

[1] *Ideology and Utopia, An Introduction to the Sociology of Knowledge* (London, New York, 1936), p. 143.

II

Mannheim's emigration to England in 1933 proved to be much more than a change in physical location. His German writings reflect the critical detachment of the Continental scholar of that epoch, who had not committed himself beyond his trust in the socially unattached intelligentsia. Now the Nazi counter-revolution and the growing international tension confronted him with the crisis of Western society in an all too concrete form. At the same time, he found himself in a new intellectual and emotional climate, gradually experiencing social forces of stability and cohesion alien to the bureaucratic societies in which he had spent the first forty years of his life.

In the eighteenth century, Voltaire had come to early industrial England from an absolutist state where one social stratum in alliance with one Church wielded unlimited power. What then impressed him was the peaceful pluralism of England's political and religious groups which in no way seemed to threaten the stability of the social order. Two centuries later, Mannheim, too, could not find in an England now fully industrialized any trace of that tendency toward artificial conformity which dominated totalitarian Central Europe. But he was even more surprised by the absence of that chaotic diversity of hostile groups that had destroyed the Weimar Republic. He discovered that spontaneous conformity could coexist with the freedom of many experimenting groups; genuine tolerance toward a wide variety of political attitudes and critical evaluations seemed to draw its very strength from the nationwide acceptance of certain ultimate principles.

From that time on, Mannheim's sociology became a progressive attempt at integrating the findings of his past thinking with the experience gained in a new environment. Ever ready to learn, Mannheim enriched his conceptual framework by a subtle blend of Anglo-American with German and French sociological traditions. But the leading question and basic concern of Mannheim's vision of the contemporary crisis might be expressed in Max Weber's question: How are freedom and democracy in the long run compatible with the development of capitalism?

Uncontrolled capitalism itself was more and more viewed

critically by Mannheim. Its dynamic social and economic technology, its urbanization and mobilization of uprooted masses, its steeply graded income pyramids, massive pressure-group movements, and class struggles, its uneven developmental rhythms of economic and national expansion raise the threat of social and personal disintegration. 'The chief difficulty of modern society lies not so much in its vastness as in the fact that the liberal method of organization has not reached the stage where it can produce the *organic articulation* [*Gliederung*] which a vast and complex society needs.' [2] Social cohesion and integration depend, above all, upon the proper balance of the rational and irrational factors dominant in industrial mass society. But as the result of a process of 'fundamental democratization,' the older type of restrictive democracy of propertied and educated elites has been increasingly displaced by a democracy of emotionalized masses. 'In a society in which the masses tend to dominate, irrationalities which have not been integrated into the social structure may force their way into political life. This situation is dangerous because the selective apparatus of mass democracy opens the door to irrationalities in those places where rational direction is indispensable. Thus, democracy itself produces its own antithesis and even provides its enemies with their weapons.' [3]

Fully appreciative of the political, social, and ethical traditions of the older Western democracies which have so far blocked inroads of anti-democratic and irrational fanaticisms from the extreme right and left, Mannheim nevertheless saw the disintegrative forces that swept over Central Europe everywhere at work. They are stimulated by a dangerous culture lag between those spheres of social organization which require management on the level of planning, and our ways of thinking and conduct which have remained on historically backward levels. The central issue of our time is therefore characterized by him as the transition toward a planned society. Only a strategy of gradual reform toward over-all planning of society can lead us out of the dilemmas that oppose the professed belief in the

---

[2] Karl Mannheim, *Man and Society in an Age of Reconstruction: Studies in Modern Social Structure* (New York, 1940), p. 106.

[3] Ibid. p. 63.

dignity of the individual to the leveling processes of actual
standardization, the affirmation of equal opportunities for all
to the reality of unregulated competition among economic giants
and dwarfs, the infinite stimulation of consumers' wants to the
sharp inequalities of income, the ethic of hard work to the
recurring mass unemployment, the perfection of our means of
mass communication and techniques of popularization to the
low levels of taste and mass intelligence.

III

The present volume is another decisive step in the direction of
'sociology for life.' It had been initiated by his wartime essay
Diagnosis of Our Time,[4] in which educational and moral-
religious problems play the dominant role. Now a comprehensive
theory of contemporary civilizations is presented by a thinker
to whom 'thinking' more and more meant the unity of diagnosis
and therapy. The detached critical observer has grown into the
political and social strategist who tries to understand so that
others may be able to act.

The book begins by restating the fateful issues of our time.
A combination of major social forces is heading for disaster
unless these forces are brought under control. Bureaucratic
monopoly capitalism dominates the scene. It is justified by its
beneficiaries in terms of the eighteenth-century ideas of classical
liberalism. Essentially preindustrial revolutionary conceptions,
these ideas have been transformed into a conservative ideology
through the change of meaning and function they undergo in
a plutocratic environment. At the same time industrialization,
urbanization, and bureaucratization have created their own
antidote: the development of new social techniques of large-scale
and long-range control. But for lack of co-ordination, these
techniques have so far only served to strengthen the disintegrative forces, national and international. Subject to
competition among unequals, to opaque power processes beyond
their control, and to the uprooting effects of metropolitan life,
the lower strata lose their stake in the social order. Mass frustra-

---

[4] London and New York, 1943.

tions, apathy, and various compensatory mechanisms drive them into what Erich Fromm has called 'escape from freedom.'

In this critical moment of history the strategic position is held by England and America. Living on a deeply ingrained democratic and religious-moral tradition, these Western societies have gradually followed the continental European states in developing a bureaucratic administration alongside their traditional two-party systems. They hold, in Mannheim's view, the key to the new social order of 'planning for freedom.' There, responsible administrative agencies with enlarged jurisdiction and centralized power can develop in accord with the legacy of a democratic way of life and the age-old experience of constitutional government. The middle classes, whose existence is bound up with a 'third way' between reaction and revolution, supplemented by free-lancing groups of intellectual elites and skill groups of expert planners, are the spearheads of the transition toward the new society. A democratically selected planning elite can work out the optimum balance between centralized authority and delegation of power to local and regional agencies. A bold social education for life and the reconstruction of the ruling elites by the planned admixture of socially ascending groups are to pave the way toward the good society.

However, in pondering the problems of a truly democratic process of planning, Mannheim did not stop at the external prerequisites for a new society. Certainly full employment and social security, genuine economic and educational opportunity, and the balance of a peaceful world order must serve as the institutional foundations of the future. But, as he had stated in his *Diagnosis of Our Time,* no society can survive unless basic values, institutions, and· education are integrated with one another. Thus it is only natural that a large section of the present volume, Part III, 'New Man—New Values,' should be devoted to a systematic theory of the democratic personality, its formation and conditioning.

The concept of 'integration,' always essential to Mannheim's thinking, serves well to illustrate the development of his ideas about the relation between the nature of man and the institutions of society. Originally, integration was for him a scientific concern, namely, the task of the sociologist in bringing together the isolated findings of the different social sciences, psychology, history, economics, etc., so that a comprehensive view of society and its dynamics may gradually evolve. But with Mannheim's growing emphasis on social strategy and reform, integration becomes his central concept of social action, which aims at reuniting the departmentalized spheres of life—such as politics and economics, or work and leisure—and assigning a legitimate place to the disfavored strata of society. From there he develops in accord with modern psychology the concept of 'integrating behavior' as the ideal pattern of a democratic community expressing co-operative attitudes, as opposed to the domineering pattern prevailing in an authoritarian society.

The final step is taken when in his last writings Mannheim assigns to religion, freed from authoritarian and superstitious admixtures, the task of an ultimate integration of all human activities. This is indeed a far cry from his German period, when his interest in religious manifestations was confined to discovering their relations with social history. In a spirit of extreme rationalism he had, at that time, interpreted intellectual development as moving from theology through philosophy to sociology. It is true that up to his last day he expected from sociology, 'perhaps the most secularized approach to the problems of human life,' the answer to 'how far the variability of social phenomena including the prevailing evaluations are functions of a changing process.'[5] But at the moment when he had arrived at a penetrating social pathology of the Self, the limits to social analysis had become obvious to him, and he had gained a new insight into the archaic regions of the human mind and into certain basic experiences beyond the realm of *ratio* and science.

It was a very practical issue that first brought him up against the significance of the human aspect of planning. As early as 1935, in the German edition of *Man and Society in an Age of Reconstruction,* he was haunted by the ancient idea: *quis custodiet ipsos custodes?* In gradually evolving the outlines of the answer to 'who is to plan the planners,' which is laid down in the present book, he was deeply influenced by a group of

[5] *Diagnosis of Our Time,* p. 126.

prominent Christian thinkers, among them T. S. Eliot, J. Middleton Murry, and J. H. Oldham. Over many years he met with this group for periodic discussions, he himself playing an outstanding part in reorienting the ideas of its members. Then and there he became convinced that sociology and social philosophy cannot afford to remain 'religion blind' any more than a truly religious concern with the world can remain 'society blind.'

In conclusion, we should like to draw the reader's attention to Mannheim's rare gift of assimilating and co-ordinating diverse trends of thought. Mannheim the analyst followed in the footsteps of Marx, Max Weber, and Mead in recognizing the conditioning power of social structures and institutions not least for thought and volition. And Mannheim the educator strongly believed in the creative potentialities of man in accordance with Rousseau's democratic and humanist legacy in modern psychology and pedagogy.

In a similar manner, he tried to reconcile tendencies of pragmatism with the insights gained by the psychology of the unconscious. At the same time he took strong exception to those who claimed to have solved the problem of 'right behavior' by the postulate of successful adjustment. 'Given values can always be interpreted both as a means of adjustment to real situations, and as types of adjustment which are directed by a particular *Weltanschauung* . . . justification of a type of behavior as being an efficient piece of adjustment to a given situation does not yet determine its being right or wrong from a Christian or a non-Christian point of view.' [6] The history of mankind is for Mannheim more than a story of continuous readjustment. It reflects for him also the cumulative impact of major paradigmatic experiences. The new society can come to life only as the creation of men who are willing to readjust themselves once again—but under the lodestar of genuine values.

Ernest K. Bramstedt
Hans Gerth

[6] *Diagnosis of Our Time*, pp. 145 and 148.

Preface

○

This is a book on the principles of a society that is planned yet democratic—a society strictly organized in some of its basic spheres yet providing all the more freedom where freedom is essential. We propose to *plan for freedom;* therefore we endeavor to define its content and find the way that leads to it.

This is a book dealing with the shape of society beyond *Laissez-Faire* or Total Regimentation on the one hand, and beyond the alternatives of Fascism or Communism on the other: it proposes a Third Way incorporating the painful experiences of the last decades into a new pattern of Democracy. We set out to show a way through reform and peaceful change, but a way that will demand serious sacrifices from all. Planning the transition needs to be as decisive as mapping out a distant future.

This book gives no blueprints; it is neither a list of abstract desiderata for the philosopher nor a detailed program for the administrator. The last bitter decades have taught us that one can neither conceive of a Good Society without reference to the actual state of affairs nor reconstruct a whole social order by piecemeal administrative reforms. But we can very well lay down principles to convey the general vision of the kind of society we want to build. These principles will serve as the measuring-rod and should help the administrator to assess the merits of single reforms and decisions.

In times of slow change one can proceed more or less by intuition without constantly consulting principles. But in a postwar social landslide, when greater upheaval takes place in a month than in normal decades, awareness of the social significance of events is prerequisite to survival. We are concerned with the social implications of the transformation of society which had its roots in the last war, but is only now coming into full play. No departmental or sectional changes are considered by themselves but only in their interdependence. Without underrating the significance of the economic structure we shall show that without corresponding alterations on the political and cultural level no reform is satisfactory. Increasingly it is recognized that real planning consists in co-ordination of institutions, education, valuations and psychology. Only one who can see the important ramifications of each single step can act with the responsibility required by the complexity of the modern age. Under these circumstances a book on the essentials of democratic planning has as its theme social life in its totality: new institutions, new men, new values.

Of course, in a short treatise like this only some crucial changes can be examined. But at times it is more important to view the general lay of the land than to lose oneself in minor details. At this historic moment nothing is certain—all is in flux—any proposal may be cancelled by tomorrow's events. At best one may aspire to an understanding of the general trend and the nature of real problems. The merits of any concrete solution are open to debate and some or even all proposals may have to be changed in detail. Yet if they are to the point, it can be only because the analysis has laid a finger on the sore spot of society. We present this general view for the discussion of those vital issues facing all of us in the hope that the reader may join us in working toward a new society. This task is the responsibility not of a remote happy few but of all of us, for such is the essence of democracy.

The United Nations are called upon to make history, but they may fail if they set the developmental stage in the wrong spirit. Then Fascism, which they set out to fight by force of arms, might creep in through the new institutional framework. On the other hand, genuine and effective co-operation may be thwarted by a strong, Moscow-sponsored Communist drive that would draw a dividing line between the nations.

Now, more than ever, mere drift would be fatal and would certainly lead to a dictatorship of the Right or the Left. No generation ever faced such a hard and onerous task; but never in human history have rulers and decision-makers accumulated such great power to do the right thing.

It is the good fortune of the Anglo-Saxon peoples, with their long and profound democratic heritage, to be able to set the pattern of reorganization and lay the foundations for a New World.

It is a good fortune, a privilege, but also a tremendous responsibility.

K. M.

January 1947
London

Contents

○

PART I

Diagnosis of the Situation

1

Main Symptoms of the Crisis

○

For centuries it has been the Anglo-Saxon procedure to amend and remodel institutions whenever a new course becomes unavoidable. Like the ancient cathedrals that man has built, enlarged, and reconstructed down the centuries, adding new aisles in the new style of the age but never tearing up the old, the social structure has been overhauled and renewed by a process of additions, emendations, and alterations of institutions. Without compunction, Gothic builders added their lofty arches to the sterner Norman vaults, and later periods added decorations and features to their taste, yet the cathedral still remains one whole and the various styles fit together. The break was visible only to the historian who began dividing the centuries into stylistic periods; he undertook, as it were, to analyze the principles upon which the various parts were built. Following the pattern of organic growth, the British, unconscious of changed principles and methods, have modified the social structure by remaking institutions inherited from the past. This method of reform without fanfare has been the strength of Britain's policy —but there are junctures in history when the mere conversion of a structure is not enough. The change has come either so rapidly or so profoundly that the builder must stop to analyze the principle of what he finds and visualize what he wants to achieve.

The present trust in the British tradition of 'muddling through,' just because former generations have been fortunate enough to switch over at the right moment, is a liability. Diagnosis of the situation will show that basic social change can no longer be met by mere repairs and institutional patchwork. We must consciously assess our objectives to get us out of the rut: this requires thoroughgoing comprehension of the new trend, of social change.

At times the wagon of history moves along a straight and open road, at others it has to turn a sharp corner. On the smooth highway little or no steering is necessary, nor need the map be consulted. But at the sharp corner, careful and alert driving is necessary, lest the precious load of tradition, culture, and worldly goods be upset. At the crossroads of history we must look for reorientation, consult the map, and ask ourselves: Where do the roads lead, where do we want to go?

It is at such crucial crossroads of history that we find ourselves. No lament for the age is needed, no nostalgic moan about deterioration, but a critical analysis of what has engendered it.

If one wishes to build a social system, one must have a guiding idea of the new system, an awareness of shortcomings in the existing one and of what causes current maladjustments. Eventually one may ask for ways and means to change the social mechanism. A diagnosis of the situation must precede any statement of new aims and proposed means.

Most symptoms of maladjustment in modern society can be traced to the fact that a parochial world of small groups expanded into a Great Society in a comparatively short time. This unguided transformation caused manifold disturbances and unsolved problems throughout social life. They can be set right only with due attention to the circumstances surrounding the calamities.

Unguided, unplanned transition does not cause major disturbances where the social units are small and when sufficient time is allowed for adjustment by trial and error. Even then maladjustments occur through the occasional inexpediency of a prevailing pattern of action or thought in an unforeseen situation. Usually, however, a new adjustment is made with no hiatus in the process of socially co-ordinated living. The case is quite different when society develops on a large scale unguided. Here, too, innumerable efforts are made to replace obsolete patterns of behavior and organization by new ones; but either no new pattern can be found on the level of blind experimentation, or, if such a new solution emerges at last, there is a hiatus in which no satisfactory reaction is forthcoming. In such cases we shall speak of social disintegration.

While there is much talk of disintegration, the term is often used too vaguely to convey any meaning. Surely we should not speak of disintegration if a social order cherished by the observer were to vanish and be replaced by another. This is social change indeed, but not social disintegration. The cardinal point is a gradual weakening of the prevailing social structure and of the forces that sustain it, without the simultaneous growth of a new order. It is true, there are borderline cases where we are uncertain whether the lack of a new solution is a symptom of transition only or whether a serious void threatens. But by and large we know the difference. Everyone knows that occasional unemployment of a few people is just a gap in adjustment, whereas recurrent unemployment, which in its cumulative effects upsets the working of a whole social order, should be considered a symptom of disintegration. The same applies to the moral sphere. People may occasionally be uncertain about what is right or wrong and this may be taken as a matter of course. But when mass anxieties prevail, because the general ideological upheaval leaves no sound basis for common action, and when people do not know where they stand or what they ought to think about the most elementary problems of life, then again we may rightly speak of the spiritual disintegration of society.

While we attempt to show in the following pages that we are living in such an age of disintegration, we of course do not mean that disintegration is ever total. Were this the case, we could no longer go on living. Even in a disintegrating society there are self-healing processes and spontaneous adjustments that make life somehow bearable. Still, even under conditions of comparative tranquillity, the sociologically trained eye can see the gaps in the social fabric, the void in the individual intellectual, moral, and emotional make-up. In a given situation, once the cumulative effects of disintegration get out of hand, implicit chaos becomes apparent to all. There are a number of traditional answers to the threat of modern social integration.

The alternatives of capitalism *versus* socialism, dictatorship *versus* democracy, secular *versus* Christian society are such traditions in group thinking. Yet, however representative of important group forces these alternatives may be, they are less diagnosis than therapeusis, and our therapeutic choice may depend on our preference for different values. But before we choose on the basis of such preference, we must ascertain whether in fact the disturbances in our social body may be thus treated. Our diagnosis must detect the symptoms and causes of social disintegration; only then can we consider the pros and cons of different treatments.

I. NEW SOCIAL TECHNIQUES MAKING FOR MINORITY RULE

In our present analysis we take it for granted that the mere numerical increase of modern societies is a fundamental cause of our difficulties. This growth is primarily due to the astounding increase in population since the Industrial Revolution—itself the product of the machine technique.[1] For a long time we have been aware that the widespread use of machinery carries its own social implications. Thus it is well-known that the transition from the handloom to the mechanical loom revolutionized the division of labor and created factory life with its mechanized and rationalized work. But this is only one aspect of technological change following population growth. The economic inventions that provided the masses with food, clothing, and shelter have often received due attention, whereas the development of other techniques, likewise in consequence of population growth, have almost been overlooked. We have in mind 'social techniques' in the sphere of politics, education, warfare, communication, propaganda, and so on. Their true nature has come to light only during the last few decades.[2]

By social techniques * I refer to all methods of influencing human behavior so that it fits into the prevailing patterns of social interaction and organization. The existence of social techniques

* In all my writings on modern society I have emphasized the significance of social techniques as well as other points to be mentioned in the present diagnosis. In order to weight them properly, I cannot avoid referring to them again. Here, however, they are not dealt with merely casually but form part of a more comprehensive and systematic survey of the factors making for disintegration.

is especially evident in the Army, where efficiency rests mainly upon stringent organization, training, and discipline, specific forms of self-control and obedience. Not only in the Army, but also in so-called civilian life people have to be conditioned and educated to fit into prevailing patterns of social life. Factory work requires specialized training of skill, behavior, and habits, a specific form of discipline and rank, a well-defined division of labor and controlled interrelations between people and their jobs. The dominant pattern may be democratic or authoritarian; education serves both systems. At the same time it is only one of the social techniques aimed at the creation of the desired type of citizen.

In order to solve the problem of mass organization, modern society had to improve and extend these social techniques as well as those of the machine. Social inventions are made daily, and though little is heard of them they are nonetheless important sociologically. But the main thing about such improved social techniques today is not only their greater efficiency, but that such efficiency favors minority rule. Modern military technique, for instance, allows a much greater concentration of power in a few hands than did the techniques of any previous period. A man with a rifle could threaten a handful of people, a man with a Tommy gun or the dive bomber can intimidate a hundred, and the atom bomb, millions. Centralized control in the field of government and administration is made equally easy by such inventions as the telephone, radio, and air communications. Vast industrial empires could not be held together without these modern means of rapid communication. Yet these very same techniques also make for dictatorship.

As long as society was regulated by a natural interplay between small self-contained units, mutual controls could work. One individual could control the other, or one group the other, or the group the individual. Just as in economic life where huge combines with their monopolies replace free competition between small enterprises, so in other spheres complex social units arise that are too arbitrary to reorganize themselves, and must be governed from a center. News service, for instance, is handled by a few agencies, and scientific research is also increasingly controlled either by the State or by big industry. Large bureaucracies appear everywhere, and where formerly individuals made independent decisions according to their own best knowledge and experience, the majority now must follow instructions, and only a few departmental heads are in a position to form comprehensive judgments and a policy of their own.

Similar concentration can be observed in the methods of education and of molding public opinion. Mechanized mass production of ideas through press and radio propaganda works in the same direction. Education tends to become part of the new art of manipulating human behavior and can develop into an instrument for suppression of the many by the few. Even social work, which was formerly the sphere of private charity or the individual reformer, has been handed over to trained professionals. Its misuse can only end in constant meddling with private affairs, with little freedom from central interference or scope for living a life of one's own.

The feature common to all these examples is a tendency to establish key positions from which central decisions are made. The very existence of key positions automatically makes for minority rule.

The end of *laissez-faire* and the necessity for planning are unavoidable consequences of the present situation and the nature of modern techniques. All of us might have preferred living as cultured gentlemen of leisure in ancient Athens or as daring pioneers in the eighteenth and nineteenth centuries. But it is not given to us to choose the epoch in which we live or the problems we are called upon to solve. The concentration of all kinds of controls—economic, political, psychological, and mechanical —has gone so far (and the last war has so enormously accelerated this trend) that the question is only who shall use these means of control for what end. For used they will certainly be.

The alternatives are no longer 'planning or *laissez faire*' but 'planning for what?' and 'what kind of planning?'

II. THE NEW TECHNIQUES AND THE POWER COMPLEX

From the very beginning modern techniques were associated with the power complex. Much knowledge was acquired to increase power. Technology, both economic and social, has been developed as an instrument for seeking and increasing personal power. The capitalist pioneer, the industrialist, the financier, and the inventor are children of the same spirit. They sought knowledge or financed it in the interest of expansion and exploitation. They were interested in nature or in man only in so far as these promised profits and power; and they were interested in other countries only as markets, colonies, and military bases.[3] As Lewis Mumford[4] puts it, they stepped from the walled horizon of the medieval city into the limitless world only to bring home quick profits, and cared nothing for the wasted landscape they left on their trail. The fruits of their spoils included the destruction of tribal customs, semistarvation, tuberculosis, and soil erosion. The exclusive emphasis on power, the neurotic complex of an age rather than a character trait, destroys the world's equilibrium just as it upsets our whole mental balance. The disgraceful slums on the outskirts of our cities, built speculatively without regard to human needs, the skyscrapers erected centrally in towns not in answer to economic need but as beacons of prestige and power-display—both are expressions of the same malignant growth.

So long as modern capitalist society was an expanding system with undeveloped countries to absorb men, capital, and energies, there was always an outlet for the misuse of power and extreme forms of exploitation.[5] The liberal revolutionaries of 1848 were defeated by the reactionary powers of their countries, but there were still other worlds for them and they found a new existence and new scope for action elsewhere. Men like Mazzini, Kossuth, and Marx continued their work in England, and Karl Schurz[6] made a distinguished career in the United States. By now, however, Imperialism, the cause of recurrent international friction and economic upheaval, seems to have reached a point of saturation. The world is divided; there are no more open spaces with free homesteads for immigrants, and the backward peoples have been awakened through communication with, and education by, their rulers or trading partners. A new distribution of wealth is taking place and for European powers this will be, in contrast to the past three or four centuries, a process of contraction rather than of expansion. At least such are the prospects, so long as power is the main driving force, and expansion for the sake of exploitation is the organizing principle.

C

In the domestic pageant the social groups and classes tend to become more rigid and sharply stratified. No longer is social ascent easy for the enterprising nor are the chances of rapid success the same for the small owner. The more refined the techniques and division of labor, the less flexible the social pattern seems.

Striving for power in society is not a constant factor but grows with the opportunities. In earlier stages, this urge was still more or less controlled; the inventions and techniques it set in motion even promoted public welfare. In the final stage nothing remains but megalomanic passion, terror, and extermination,[7] a drama no one of us can watch any longer dispassionately.

III. FROM COMMUNAL ECONOMY THROUGH FREE COMPETITION TO MONOPOLIES

Just as technology in its aspects of expansion and profiteering corresponds to the old spirit of conquest and exploitation, so the whole economic system of free competition and private ownership of the means of production corresponds to one historical phase—an intermediary phase between two planned economies. At the one end was the local, self-sufficient, nonprofit economy of agrarian and handicraft communities [8]—at the other we envisage a planned economy over vast areas with international exchange and integration based upon highly developed techniques.

If we look at early capitalism and liberalism from this point of view it becomes obvious that their 'sacrosanct' institutions— the free market and free competition, based on the absolute concept of private property [9] with no external intervention—were the products of a unique and transient situation. They exactly correspond to the stage in economic development when expansion could no longer be carried out by tribal or local units, which were too small and too parochial in outlook. Later economic expansion took the form of individual penetration on the part of 'pioneers,' men with an intrepid spirit of enterprise and venture. The right to absolute disposal of individual property, as upheld against the older notion of family and corporate property and as a defense against state interference, can be fully understood as the only adequate stimulus for these individual entrepreneurs. The concept of private property operated as a dynamic force in the individual's mind, continually spurring him to risk his capital, to save the profits for further accumulation and investment, to give up leisure and pleasure for power and profits.

The picture changed when the scale of these independent economic enterprises increased more and more, while their numbers declined. Then free competition in its true sense disappeared, the scope of individual initiative began to shrink, and a new business bureaucracy [10] took the place of the independent owner. This new managerial class develops its own administrative technique, as well as new key positions. It almost invisibly creates new dependencies. With this the concept of absolute private ownership and unrestricted *laissez-faire* loses its functional justification, since it is no longer indispensable for the development and maintenance of the economic system. Not only are the newly created power positions abused in monopolistic practices, but the growing immobility of the system turns competition into a positive danger to stability. What once claimed to promote the best interests of all now abandons the employment and income of the masses to the vagaries of the business cycle.[11]

This utterly chaotic state of affairs is well known to all of us from the cruel experience of many years. For most people the crisis of the age is more evident in its economic symptoms than in other terms. But economic patterns only repeat the very same tendencies of disintegration leading to chaos in all spheres of society, though no other symptom except war spreads so widely and deeply as mass unemployment.

IV. DISPLACEMENT OF SELF-REGULATING SMALL GROUPS

Uncontrolled growth in the economic system is, as we have said, just one aspect of uncontrolled growth in modern society at large. Society is gradually becoming a conglomeration of smaller and larger groups, very often held together only by administrative agencies replacing the older small organic groups.[12] By organic we mean that self-regulating power which is characteristic of small groups but gradually vanishes in large ones. There is nothing mysterious about this self-regulating power which guarantees a certain evenness, balance, and continuity in development so long as the size of the community is limited and everybody can see approximately how things will work out. There is no mystery about correlating supply and demand in a household economy where the decision about the goods to be produced and consumed is in the same hands. Nor is there mystery in correlating supply and demand when the craftsman works for a certain number of customers whom he knows personally and whose wishes he can foresee. There is even no special mystery about the self-regulating powers of the market as long as small units compete.

The phenomenon of self-regulation in small groups has been studied more extensively in the economic sphere, but the same self-regulation takes place in other spheres. Limited size allows everyone to understand what is required of him and what to expect from the group. In direct everyday contacts with other group members, each can discover for himself the causes of success or failure and seek collective remedies when things go wrong. The *Agora* of the Greek city, the market place of the medieval town, where the church, the guildhall, and the market stalls were close to one another, enabled the citizen to take in the whole orbit of his world at a glance. Differentiation of human activities and growth of the corresponding social types happened along the lines of gradually expanding co-operation. Everybody knew his function since he could clearly see how the village supplied the town and the town, the village; how the different occupations served and balanced each other and regulated their mutual relationships. Yet among the members not only were the formal relations of social hierarchy and function clearly defined but the whole edifice of growing society was still supported by the basic institutions of family, neighborhood, and community.

All this is not said in the spirit of eulogy. The narrow outlook, the inescapable limitations, would probably have made life in such a world unbearable for us. All we want to emphasize is the nature of an integrated social pattern which is now vanishing. The most adequate expression of this evanescence is the mushroom growth of the metropolis where the last traces of organic cohesion are fading away and the principle of common living, functional interdependence, and clarity of common purpose are completely destroyed.

V. DISINTEGRATION OF TRADITIONAL GROUP CONTROLS

Another important aspect of the same process is the disintegration of ancient forms of social control.

As long as the self-regulating powers of small groups remain undisturbed, action and thought are controlled by common sense and the rules fixed by custom and precedent. Traditions are ultimately the accumulated experience of successful adjustment. Acting on the basis of tradition has the advantage of saving the individual the trouble of making a choice, or of inventing new ways where the old are capable of solving the difficulty. But tradition and custom maintain their power to control events only so long as certain conditions prevail, and it is important to enumerate at least some of these. The tasks must be simple and recurrent, needing only limited organization for their performance. Only in these circumstances does the established pattern apply; as variety increases, tasks grow too complex. Rational analysis is necessary to divide the whole into its component parts, creating new combinations and transgressing precedents.

Tradition works only so long as transformation is slow and gradual and the home, the market, the church, and the city do not represent entirely different and even antagonistic influences; or if they do, there is time to reconcile these differences and to assimilate discordant habits. Thus, as long as growth is gradual, traditions will act as controls safeguarding the amount of conformity without which co-operation is impossible. You can act only if you can base your conduct upon reasonable expectation of how people will react. People can be united in war and peace only if certain basic values are tacitly accepted by the community. So long as the group is more or less homogeneous and people live in roughly the same sort of social and cultural surroundings, and so long as there is not too much rise and fall in the social scale, customary habits will remain stable.

Historically, not only have we passed from the stage of neighborhood community to the Great Society in a relatively short time, but this growth has frequently been by fits and starts. Technical development in itself undermined those conditions that were the mainstay of tradition. Whole groups were eradicated at times, as were the old English aristocracy in the Wars of the Roses or the rural workers during the Industrial Revolution; others were driven to emigrate by economic, political, or ecclesiastic forces.

This rapid, spasmodic transformation contributed to the disintegration of ancient group controls. We can scarcely maintain that we have been able to substitute adequately for them. Undoubtedly we have succeeded in inventing a few patterns of large-scale organization, like that of the Army, the Factory, the Civil Service. But none of these has developed the elasticity and responsiveness to human needs of the small group. We still take it for granted that large-scale organizations should be abstract, arbitrary, and dehumanizing, in emulation of the first great pattern of large-scale organization, the Army.[13] Today, after shattering experiences, we can see that the controls which prevail in the Army and the Factory have, in themselves, a demoralizing effect. In the long run treating men like the cogs and wheels of a machine can only lead to deliberate inefficiency or sabotage. The equation—natural controls in small groups, mechanical devices in large-scale organizations—no longer holds. For we know that the greatest demoralization of the individual arises from overformalization.[14] The raw material for chaos is not the undisciplined barbarian but the overdisciplined factory worker or soldier who in consequence loses vitality whenever the plant closes down or when there is no one to give commands.

VI. FAILURE OF LARGE-SCALE CO-ORDINATION

As for special controls, an added irritant in modern society is the lack of successful co-ordination between different large-scale organizations. Developed as business enterprises, as state bureaucracies, or as voluntary associations, they frequently overlap in function. Unco-ordinated institutions cancel each other's effectiveness. It was quite different in medieval society where, for example, the medieval guild was an elaborate system of well-defined functions, privileges, and prohibitions. Not only were the formal relationships between the members, their social hierarchy, and their functions within the community clearly established, not only were all aspects of their life, work, leisure, culture, and worship clearly shaped and determined by the purposes of the community, but the corporations themselves were co-ordinated. They constituted the medieval city and thus differed essentially from modern employers' associations or trade unions which have only segmental functions and are hardly controlled by the community. Admitting that a large-scale society cannot continue without a certain co-ordination of its institutions does not mean a plea for corporations either in the medieval or the fascist sense. But it is equally impossible to go on conceiving of individuals as millions of abstract atoms without considering the educational and moral significance of their associations.

As long as the various social functions represented by the associations remain unco-ordinated and the associations are not considered as an organic part of the community, it is too easy to manipulate the individual by these means. In a hundred ways the modern shrewd technician of influence can reach the individual, as employer or employee, as consumer, student, radio listener, sportsman, or holiday-maker, in days of health or sickness. The result is general disorientation.[15]

The weakening and passing of controls also implies the weakening and passing of liberty. There is no real freedom in the abstract. There are only liberties. Certain types of freedom and restriction belong with each control. The soldier's freedom is different from that of the monk; the teacher's freedom is different from that of the pupil; the father's freedom within his family is different from that in his business relations; and the civil servant's freedom different from that of a free-lance artist or journalist. As long as society functions properly, all are bound by different rules and commitments, but they are also free within the framework of these commitments. What appears as unbridled behavior or license from the point of view of one control may reveal itself as bondage from some other. Where freedom begins for one person, a new type of responsibility exists for another. At first glance, the artist and free-lance journalist seem freer than the soldier or civil servant. But more thorough investigation may reveal that once the soldier and civil servant leave their strictly regulated work they are free of further responsibility and can relax. On the other hand, the artist who seems outwardly free may be bound by the higher responsibilities of his art, and the journalist by his professional code.[16] Qualitative freedom exists only in relation to qualitatively defined commitments. Absolute freedom exists only in anarchy; but this indeed proves that when the laws regulating behavior lose their power of control, freedom, too, is disappearing.

VII. DISINTEGRATION OF CO-OPERATIVE CONTROLS

The waning power of small communities also results in the vanishing of techniques once so characteristic of them, those of co-operative control.

In any social situation there are two forms of group control. One is the authoritative pattern of command and obedience, the other the pattern of development and guidance of action through co-operation. All the complicated forms of political and social organization on a higher level are derivations of these two original patterns. They are alternative methods for achieving division of labor and differentiation of social functions. The first method, that of command and obedience, very often attains great efficiency but is in most cases detrimental to the individuals concerned. The alternative of co-operation represents a creative principle. This method of shared control is one of the most significant inventions in the field of social techniques. In its conception of a common purpose which can be realized under conditions of shared responsibility, it represents, ancient as it may be, a great advance over the method that forces everyone blindly to follow the commands of one man. Allocation of different tasks in a way that enables everybody to contribute his best should be a comparatively easy division of labor; it is somewhat more difficult to develop co-operative forms of thinking, as in a debate. But in a large-scale society it is extremely difficult to find a co-operative method of creating consensus and sharing common power. Indeed, one of the greatest problems of modern Democracy is to project patterns for establishing consensus and sharing common power in large communities.

In a small sect or community of limited size one can expect all members to sense the spirit of the meeting and find through discussion how much unconscious agreement exists in their minds. However, when the growth of society produces surroundings indicative of class as well as spatial distinctions, with conflicting mental climates, and when the structure of society produces vested interests with organized pressure groups, it becomes increasingly difficult to adhere to the same methods of creating consensus. Those that worked fairly well in the simpler stages of democratic organization scarcely seem adequate now.

The democratic technique of voting tried to replace consensus and the shared responsibility of simpler groups. The institution of voting originated in primitive forms of acclamation, which later became counting of heads and finally led to various schemes of representation, developed with particular skill during the nineteenth century. But those who consider voting and the present system of suffrage the fundamental weapon of democratic control overlook the fact that democratic procedure is vitiated in many ways by manipulated opinion, organized parties, and pressure groups. Moreover, they fail to see that sharing of control is essential not only in the sphere of voting but in all functions and all sections of the community; and we have not yet succeeded in finding methods of sharing controls adequate to the demands of a Great Society.

VIII. DISRUPTIVE EFFECTS OF CLASS ANTAGONISM

Left to itself modern society develops a specific kind of disruptive effect from class distinctions and the psychological factors intensifying class antagonisms.

This aspect of modern society has often been discussed and tends to overshadow other causes of disorganization in our social system. It is, indeed, a very significant disruptive force and surely if allowed to develop uncontrolled will lead to class wars and destroy the preconditions of freedom and democratic agreement.

Contrary to the fatalistic belief in the 'class struggle,' we must emphasize that having developed methods of control that could check growing class differences, we could use them if only we wanted to do so. The obstacles to their application are considerable but essentially no more so than the other disruptive factors discussed. The first step toward mastering this sort of disintegration is to forego the negativist attitude of fatalism and to weigh the pros and cons of a reformist and a revolutionary solution. We shall return to this problem presently.

IX. DISINTEGRATION OF PERSONALITIES

Today we know that we cannot consider separately the disintegration of the primary patterns of co-operation and common life, the deterioration of social controls, the failure to co-ordinate large-scale organizations, and so on. These are not just institutions gone astray, which some objective procedure of 'institutional reconstruction' will set right. Today we know that human conduct and personality formation depend to a large extent on these same institutions. Their disintegration means the disintegration of personality. We expect disorganization of personality where institutions disintegrate because today we know that behavior and character are not abstract entities in themselves but develop primarily out of the context of activities and, to a large extent, out of the institutionalized patterns of co-operative action. That is, if the pattern of co-operation loses its regulative powers, controls are no longer acceptable. They lose their vitality and prestige: accordingly, behavior is bound to disintegrate.

A man who follows traditional patterns unquestioningly is at a complete loss if his belief in tradition is shattered and no new pattern of conduct is at hand to adopt. The same applies when there is a hiatus in the co-ordination of institutions immediately affecting human behavior.

Most of the commands we obey are supported and sanctioned by groups. There are the army code, professional codes, business codes, and moral codes governing neighborly relations. In modern society, if large organizations fail to develop their own standards, if there are no adequate ethics of industrial relations, no thorough education for citizenship bringing home the virtues of communal responsibility and, finally, if in international relations the law of the jungle prevails, then these lapses will be reflected in the conduct and character of the individuals concerned. People will still behave decently where some remnants of the family code or of the professional code are valid, but will feel lost where the old prescriptions vanish without being replaced by new ones, or where new spheres of life develop that are not yet subject to the moral consciousness of the community. The broader these spheres of lawlessness the more they disintegrate personality, until we reach a stage that Durkheim called *anomie* (*nomos*, law; *a-nomos*, lawlessness).[17] And this is the real state in which people live in a mass society that took the idea of *laissez-faire* literally, not realizing that with the disappearance of older controls, man would be left without orientation. Such a society is morally 'undermined.'

If we have not yet reached the *anomic* state, it is because the existing undercurrent of tradition and still working and expanding techniques allow agreement on day-to-day issues. But it could be seen how flabby both social conduct and moral character had become, when the first shocks of upheaval came in the shape of war, economic crisis, and inflation. Then the latent perplexity and moral insecurity of the little man came to the fore, and whole nations answered with the desperate cry for 'security,' the demand for something to hold on to. People considered anybody who promised anything resembling security a prophet, a savior, and a leader whom they would follow blindly rather than remain in a state of utter instability and lawlessness.

X. DISINTEGRATION OF CONSENSUS AND OF RELIGIOUS BONDS

If our observation is limited to how conduct deteriorates in the context of action, we have not yet fully perceived the disintegration of behavior and personality. By analyzing the causes of social disintegration, we realize that in properly integrated societies there is an additional process at work over and above the formation of conduct and character in action. It is the integrating function of ideological or spiritual inspiration chiefly represented by religion.

When speaking of Religion, the sociologist does not mean this or that creed or denomination, but a basic institution which is fairly well expressed in the word 'religion' itself. By derivation *re-ligere* means to 'bind closely' whatever you do to a supreme cause. Human activity in the context of living is first woven into a pattern through habits and conventions. But this primary integration is not enough. Man craves a more fundamental oneness relating all his scattered activities to a common purpose. If this commonly accepted purpose disappears, the social machine continues for a while to work as usual since the mutual dependencies and obligations arising from the division of labor do not allow people just to run away. But, whenever a major crisis occurs, it becomes apparent that mutual obligations are only valid if they are rooted in conscience; and conscience, although the most personal experience in man, is a guide to common life only if a moral and religious interpretation of commonly experienced events is accepted and assimilated by the members of that community.

Religion in this sense means linking individual actions and responsibilities to a broader stream of common experience. Religion, therefore, integrates once more on a deeper plane what has already been integrated for limited utilitarian purposes on the more pragmatic level of daily activity.

When religion ceases to be the deeper integrating force in human affairs, the change becomes socially apparent. Until the dissolution of medieval society, religion was alive because it was not only a creed but also a social control inspiring patterns of behavior and ideals of the good life. When this influence was first withdrawn, allowing the state, industry, and other sections of life to take care of themselves, religion lost vigor, and social life found no substitute. First Nationalism, then Socialism tried to fill this gap. In an age awaiting for world integration the self-defeating tendency and harmful influence of Nationalism, especially when it becomes an instrument of aggression, are beyond question. Certainly for a time Socialism and Communism had the power to bind human activities to a higher purpose—that of building a society based upon social justice. But this much is clear: they cannot mean religion for a great part of mankind and thus split instead of uniting men for the next great venture of building a co-operative world society.

The great paradox of any fundamental integration on the plane of *re-ligere* at the present historical juncture is that the so much needed unification of larger communities is too often achieved by antagonism against other religious creeds. These seem to create the kind of zeal and intolerance that with the help of the present perfected tools of warfare can only lead to the extinction of nations.

As long as the world consisted of several units which could develop side by side, religious zeal, time and again, resulted in wars. But those struggles of bygone days seem relatively innocent maneuvers compared with the two world wars, and even more so, in contemplation of the destructive potentialities of wars to come. The criterion of any future spiritual revival as a creative force will be its ability to integrate men without antagonizing them. The fact that this has hardly happened yet cannot be accepted as conclusive by those who believe in the creative powers in man. For in the past man has often shown that he could meet the challenge of an entirely changed environment through the emergence of a completely new mental attitude.

As we contemplate the chaotic state of unregulated capitalist society, one thing becomes quite clear: the present state of society cannot last long. We have seen that social chaos may remain latent so long as no major crisis occurs. But whenever mass unemployment or war brings the tension to a climax, new solutions must be found. By this time the world has learned that such crises are not chance, but that both mass unemployment and wars are inherent in the system. Thus the two basic evils will not disappear without a conscious and systematic attack on them. This of itself indicates that the age of *laissez-faire* is over and that only through planning can catastrophe be avoided.

2

Alternative Responses to the Situation

○

The situation just described became apparent in Central Europe even earlier than in the Western democracies. That part of the world was faced with the quandary of out-and-out chaos long before the victor countries of World War I were aware of any fundamental change. The Allies were for many years kept from realizing what was going on, owing to their greater wealth, their assured international standing, and their tradition of democratic habits and institutions. Even so, many felt that these more fortunate countries would still have to stand the test of open conflict between the forces of antagonism inherent in the social fabric. The policies adopted by Germany and Italy in internal and foreign affairs between the wars can only be understood if one realizes that these countries were already grappling with the new situation that has since become no less vital to us in one form or another. However reprehensible their responses to the challenge, at least they made an attempt to deal with the situation, whereas we have tried only traditional means of coping with the crisis. Even now, we are inclined to gloss over social problems rather than reorient ourselves to major changes in modern society. A new approach to politics can be found only if we look upon the various new social and political systems as experiments by nations faced with new evils of the age. Different approaches will then be judged on their merits as responses to the challenges presented by the changed social structure. So far only two reactions to disintegration have emerged:

(1) Totalitarian planning with its two variants, Fascism and Communism;

(2) Democratic planning gradually evolved by the progressive policies of the democracies. The basic valuations, techniques, and whole pattern, however, have not yet been clearly stated and developed. It is the object of this book to draw the outlines, to state the essentials of democratic planning.

I. TOTALITARIAN RESPONSES

The totalitarian answers can to a certain extent be characterized as those of the panic-stricken mind to a novel problem—an escape into the methods of command, pressure, coercion, and genocide. It is generally the method of societies in which the tradition of the military pattern prevails, where organization is primarily strict regimentation. The totalitarian response should be studied carefully because, in spite of its brutality, it clearly portrays the situation with which these societies had to deal, even though their concrete measures for the most part attempt to cure one evil by inflicting another and greater one.

In this sense it will be useful to see what the main features of totalitarian response are and how Communism and Fascism differ. Both realize that economic chaos creates recurrent unemployment and that this cannot in the long run be cured by palliatives only. Both realize that the right to work is a fundamental right of the citizen which the State ought to ensure. Both realize that basic security, keeping the citizen from falling below a certain level, and stability are equally concerns of the community. Likewise they recognize that basic psychological security is a public concern, and that a society cannot go on unless it deliberately acknowledges the psychological implications of stability. The morale of a community in a mass society does not develop spontaneously; it needs conscious guidance. In one word, the totalitarians realized that in the Great Society, planning in the economic, social, and moral spheres is necessary.

Another similarity between Communism and Fascism is that both conceived of planning as an all-pervasive process which was to regulate everything. Both regarded planning as centralized procedure emanating from a few key positions.

Finally the two are alike in so far as both carry through planning by dictatorship. This means absolute concentration of power in the hands of a few, through a monopolistic party. In concrete terms, it involves suspension of nearly all the rights of the free citizen. It means complete control of the press and all other organs for forming public opinion as well as complete control of the educational system. It means irresponsible use of power by official and semiofficial gangs; it means concentration camps, spying, and terrorism of all kinds. Though in their dictatorial methods there is little to choose between Fascism and Communism, it is wrong to consider the two systems identical just for that reason. We do not wish to minimize the significance of dictatorial elements and totalitarian overregimentation; we see that even the positive virtues of socialist planning are sapped. It makes, however, a great difference whether a dictatorship serves the unbridled power complex of a few party bosses, industrialists, and army leaders, or whether it aims ultimately at raising the standard of living of the many. Nobody can doubt that poverty and illiteracy have been reduced in Russia on an unprecedented scale, whereas the Nazis lowered both living and educational standards in Germany. Surely it was a great achievement on Russia's part to build a creative policy of national minorities by establishing their cultural autonomy rather than mobilize them against one another and systematically instigate feelings of alleged national and racial superiority.[1]

Both Communism and Fascism have a dictated culture,[2] but with the difference that one aims at general enlightenment of the populace and stops short only if this clashes with the official ideology. Although in Soviet Russia this ideology affects many spheres of thought, it does not aim at primitivism as Nazi education did. The Nazi ideal was the barbarian not yet humanized by Western classical and Christian values. They aimed at the inculcation of a cult of fertility and 'race' and at the deification of their own nation. It was the systematic inculcation of a creed to perpetuate struggle, conflict, and mutual extinction. Rationalist elements in Russian propaganda and education account for the overthrow of pre-industrial habits and formulae, and this was necessary to a modern industrialized society. But it should not blind us to the fact that by adopting only the rationalist tradition of Western civilization, the Russians sacrificed the wealth of thought and human experience embodied in the other traditions of European culture. Historical materialism is a sociological and philosophical doctrine that has great value only as one among the many systems of scientific hypotheses. The hostile attitude to Christianity and everything beyond the narrow bounds of historical materialism, the deliberate avoidance of nonrational values must imply sacrifice hardly acceptable to nations with a complex culture and a more diverse spiritual inheritance. To be aware that reactionary movements often make use of the nonrational forces in our culture as a weapon for their own purposes, or as camouflage for vested interests, does not justify the theorem that religion is camouflage of backwardness, a tool of reaction. In England, for instance, the deepest drive for social progress was firmly rooted in religious experience.[3]

II. THE PESSIMISTIC VIEW OF FASCISM

One of the fundamental differences between Communism and Fascism is that Fascism does not believe in the perfectibility of man and has no real utopian vision of bettering social organization and human relations. Therefore in their actions the Fascists are never guided by the idea of basic improvement of world affairs. This leads them to reckless exploitation of the immediate chances to benefit a minority, either their ruling class or their race. If, for instance, the disorganization of the economic system makes it desirable that a new order be planned on a worldwide scale, but in the transition stage pure autarchy pays better, the Fascists will throw their full weight on the side of autarchy and exploit its possibilities—even though they know that from the broader point of view it means the ruin of mankind.

While others rack their brains for ways to improve the living standard of all classes and nations, the Fascist believes only in exploitation. The best thinkers of the age worry over possible means of removing the constant threat of war, whereas the Fascist takes it for granted that war is rooted in human nature and that his 'race' stands to gain from this fact by turning out the most efficient soldiers and the most ruthless conquerors. While publicists, educators, and politicians realize the tremendous power of suggestion and emotional propaganda but are

D

reluctant to use it for fear of paralyzing the power of judgment in the next generation, the Fascist ruthlessly uses these methods in all human relations. He not only replaces the methods of political discussion by organized propaganda, but even transforms education and all important human relations into compartments of propaganda. Nor does he except personal relationships or the exploitation of leisure and communal enjoyment for his own purposes. Of course, this also applies to a large extent to Soviet Russia and to some other countries in eastern Europe, but they at least are on the defensive about such tactics; their whole educational policy, they claim, is aimed not at emotionalism but at rational thinking and analysis of human relations, however narrow its scope.

Though mankind strived most strenuously to eliminate the methods of command and suppression wherever possible, the Fascist assumes that man wants to be guided and will turn that quest for guidance into a principle of political and social organization. Thus all the democratic experiments, the fruits of centuries, can be destroyed in a few years.

In all these examples the restrictive tendency in the fascist mentality comes to the fore. The Fascist is against growth and improvement because he does not believe in the basic creative powers of man. With this pessimism and skepticism it is possible to use efficient techniques only for further exploitation. The fact that he believes in biological determinism—the inherent and unalterable quality of 'race'—is only another expression of cynical fatalism. Neither social justice in one's own country nor collaboration among nations regarded as equals is possible: and the *sacro egoismo* of the dominant race—the *Herrenvolk*—follows of necessity. This philosophy is so alarming that even if all power rested with the Fascists there would necessarily be continual ferment and rebellion, and eventually mutual destruction.

III. THE UTOPIAN HOPE OF MARXISM

Where the Fascist has too little, the Communist has rather too much. He starts with a fanatical belief in the perfectibility of human nature and of the social order. Even this unlimited faith in the potential improvement of human affairs would do no

harm were he not thereby beguiled into underestimating difficulties of the transitional stage. Being critical and often even over-
critical of the existing state of affairs, the Communist is ready to
scrap everything and make an entirely new start. The danger in
this is obvious. In diagnosing the inevitability of class war, the
Communist takes part in creating it.[4] Through relentless emphasis on the proposition that society can be essentially transformed
only by violence, he shatters the environment in which gradual
reform could be carried out. By destroying the hopes of the reformers he creates a situation in which nothing can survive but
extremist revolutionary or extremist reactionary mentality. This
acute tension and absolute antagonism is the desideratum of
revolutionary theory. At the time when it was conceived there
was some sense to it despite the ruthlessness, but nowadays this
attitude creates a situation favoring the revolutionary's defeat
and the reactionary's victory.

Modern revolutionary theory [5] was conceived at an early stage
of Capitalism, in a world of scarcity and ruthless exploitation,
when one could think only of a life-and-death struggle between
rich and poor in which the poor had nothing to lose but his
chains.[6] Since then a situation has developed in advanced industrialist countries where there are too many people who could
lose only by revolution. They would therefore prefer to see a
peaceful transformation toward a more enlightened social organization.[7] Apart from this, the early revolutionary diagnosis
erred on three points: (1) In a highly differentiated industrial
society the extreme Left has little chance of getting and holding
power unless there is profound disintegration of society. (2) The
anti-middle-class bias of the Marxist doctrine [8] is bound to alien-
ate considerable parts of the population in whom the main
chance of Fascism resides. (3) Furthermore, and this is the most
important factor, not only has the supposedly 'transitional' dictatorship in Soviet Russia not withered away, but we can presuppose that it never would in any social experiment based upon
dictatorship. This is true because, given modern social techniques, a minority will never hand over power to an unarmed
majority. Revolution against any totalitarian power, once en-
trenched, is nearly hopeless. No established totalitarian régime,
whatever its political creed, can be broken from within; it takes

an external war to unseat it.[9] It follows that the utopian hopes of the Communists that their dictatorship would gradually fade away are even more visionary than many of their other over-optimistic expectations.

This Marxian hope for a transient dictatorship was an unconscious projection of real experiences from the past, but it no longer holds true. The generation of Marx could look back on history to times when revolutions against Absolutism had succeeded or when Absolutism had gradually yielded to Democracy. But at that time the main weapon was the rifle: every man represented one rifle, every rifle one man, and ten thousand or a hundred thousand men, especially after a lost war, could turn against the tyrant. This was the real root of Democracy.[10] Today with completely different weapons, the private or semiofficial armies of the dictator, together with a centralized government and a vast network of spies, constitute a stronghold against which in peace time thus far no resistance has ever succeeded. It is most dangerous optimism to believe that this sort of power, once established, will ever abdicate for ideological reasons or for the love of freedom.

The only chance for the ideal of freedom to remain relevant in the minds of rulers lies in the continuance of free institutions and their support. The dangerous fallacy in the communist argument is that its champions promise to pay for every inch of lost freedom in the intermediary period of dictatorship with an undated check on a better future. But by now we have learned that every improvement is worth infinitely more if won gradually under conditions of freedom and democratic agreement than if it has to be paid for by sacrificing free institutions and the freedom-loving mind that goes with them. Once these have disappeared, they can hardly be regained under present conditions of social technique. Once a dictatorial system, whatever its social content, seizes the educational apparatus, it does everything to obliterate the memory and need of free thought and free living; it does its utmost to transform free institutions into tools of a minority.[11]

IV. TOWARD DEMOCRATIC PLANNING

If the whole weight of the argument just presented is accepted, then the social and political problem of our age can be formulated. Our task is to build a social system by planning, but planning of a special kind: it must be *planning for freedom,* subjected to democratic control; *planning, but not restrictionist* so as to favor group monopolies either of entrepreneurs or workers' associations, but 'planning for plenty,' i.e. full employment and full exploitation of resources; *planning for social justice* rather than absolute equality, with differentiation of rewards and status on the basis of genuine equality rather than privilege; *planning not for a classless society* but for one that abolishes the extremes of wealth and poverty; *planning for cultural standards* without 'leveling down'—a planned transition making for progress without discarding what is valuable in tradition; *planning that counteracts the dangers of a mass society* by co-ordination of the means of social control but interfering only in cases of institutional or moral deterioration defined by collective criteria; *planning for balance* between centralization and dispersion of power; *planning* for gradual transformation of society *in order to encourage the growth of personality:* in short, *planning but not regimentation.*[12]

It is important to enumerate these requirements even if on first glance it seems to be a list of desiderata that includes an element of paradox. It is our contention that these ideas seem incompatible to us only because we take existing alternatives for granted. We take it for granted that planning can only be dictatorial, because both fascist and communist planning is dictatorial. We take it for granted that liberty is the price to be paid for planning, because the fascist and communist planners wipe out all opposition by violence and terror. We think that a democratic society is bound to become restrictive and monopolist, because unconsciously we identify democracy with the latest phase of oligarchy and monopolist capitalism. We take it for granted that there is no choice in the moral world between chaos and cage, because in our *laissez-faire* democratic societies all elements of moral conformity gradually disappear, and to date no remedy has been found other than the enforcement of a common mind through dictatorial indoctrination.

But it would be short-sighted fatalism to put up with the existing disintegration and responses as final and inevitable. Our generation would be lacking in imagination if it regarded chance developments as inexorable and allowed the next generation to go on struggling to preserve types of societies unsatisfactory in themselves. It is not worth dying either for a sham democracy that favors only restriction and extremes of poverty and plutocratic wealth, or for a sham planned society in which all human freedom vanishes forever. Everything, therefore, depends on our imagination and intellectual effort. We must neither accept the existing deterioration of our democratic system as irreversible nor embrace the first chance experiments of reorganization in totalitarian states as the only possible course. Even in politics the *status quo* is instructive only if the analytic mind can disentangle (a) which features have come about through the exigencies of the changing basic structure of society and (b) which are arbitrary answers to a challenge that might be met in some other manner.

Creative politics does not differ from creative science. The latter begins where the mind moves away from established patterns; the scientist freely invents tools that do not yet exist as such in nature, although in principle they are based on nature. If we think of a planned democracy that is free, we set ourselves a goal that is not yet realized—a combination of desiderata with as yet no corresponding reality. It does not follow that so long as we observe how cause and effect work in society, we cannot influence current trends so as to reach the envisaged goal. As we constantly influence the trend of social events (and are bound to do so in the future to an ever-increasing extent), it is all the more important that we should be ever aware of the necessities of our age. In this sense true vision of the essentials of Democracy is absolutely imperative, even though our list of desiderata seems at first utopian. Experiments may miscarry, but improvement is possible only if the experimenter can clearly state what he wants; he can only try again if he knows exactly what he wanted and why he failed before.

Therefore, it is not in the least certain that what appears at first sight utopian will prove to be so in the long run. Every new vision of improving social institutions has seemed utopian to those who took the established order for granted. One might go even further and say that at least in the present situation the pattern of a society based upon democratic planning is far from being utopian, since a great many converging lines in Britain as well as in the United States move in the direction of the eight points mentioned. Without a clear vision of the purpose, however, the right moment might pass by without the desired effect.

Before undertaking to discuss the chances and agenda for a system of planned freedom in the Anglo-Saxon countries, it might be worth while to make a brief inventory of the characteristic elements of life in these democracies, cultural as well as institutional, political as well as economic. For no attempt at reforming a given society can succeed without recognizing certain of its basic characteristics.

Let us begin with Great Britain. While Russia built her new world upon the clean slate of total revolution, Britain has many elements in her tradition that should not be wiped out recklessly, because fortunately they represent a valuable heritage that may help to smooth over the difficult transition to a new social order. Making the transition smoother does not, of course, mean glossing over the difficulties or sacrifices demanded, for no birth is without suffering, no growth without pain, and no education without effort and discipline. It is true that some British characteristics are ambivalent or, by historical usage, have almost lost their meaning, e.g. the principle of majority rule; such symbols may become the tools of totalitarian abuse or mere dead-weights holding back any change. Others still have great vitality and it is certain that democratic traditions and formulae, methods and institutions, will be utilized, brought up-to-date as vehicles for the emerging needs of the present age.

Britain is more fortunate than countries that have had to undergo the hectic convulsions of a belated hasty growth of modern industrialism. She can look back on the longest and hence the most gradual development both of her rich economic resources and her political institutions. She had achieved nationhood before the disintegrating forces of modern capitalism and urbanism made their fatal impact, so that even the most incisive social and moral dislocations caused by the industrial and agricultural revolutions of the eighteenth century did not disrupt the national homogeneity. When in the course of the next fifty years the nation threatened to fall asunder into the 'two nations,' political reforms managed to re-establish basic consensus, while at the same time economic expansion provided outlets for otherwise frustrated energies. The assumption of eventual agreement on common aims has ever since remained the linchpin of the working of British parliamentary democracy. This tradition, this common experience which has held British political life together, is one of the great hopes for eventual acceptance and feasibility of democratic planning for Britain. Soviet Russia, and to a certain degree even the ill-fated German Republic, had to educate peoples with limited practical experience of free political institutions or the expression of free political will. Britain, however, fortunately possesses both—some well-tried and still flexible methods and the inherited social discipline of political discussion and compromise. Her political parties in the parliamentary system have been recognized as alternative, not mutually exclusive, solutions. Parties do not represent totalitarian organizations of particular social strata; party lines are not the only or the essential dividing lines through the entire life of the nation, as was the case, for example, in Germany after 1870, when people frequently played chess or football according to their political affiliations and seldom met on any common ground. Whether Britain will succeed in her present great experiment of a democratically planned order will depend mainly on her capacity for adapting the methods and institutions of buoyant democratic response to a basically new situation, and upon whether the spirit of common tradition is still strong enough to overcome the increasing emphasis on separate and disintegrating interests. Of course, this is more than a matter of good will and we should not blind ourselves to the immensity of the problem.

It might seem unrealistic to expect to transfer the spirit of a mid-nineteenth-century democracy (corollary to the economic expansion of a practically homogeneous middle-class society) into the infinitely more complex situation at the end of this epoch. New techniques are at work within new limitations since two wars have turned the main creditor nation of the world into a debtor nation, to mention only one of the crucial trends of world economic development. But Britain is not only fortunate in possessing a legacy of political experience to prepare her for planned agreement; her economic structure likewise shows features that, if rightly understood, may become steppingstones to an order planned for plenty, freedom, and social justice. British industries are probably somewhat less highly concentrated than those of other countries with a similar development of capitalism. And although Britain has no antitrust legislation (doubtful in effectiveness in any event) monopolies play a less striking part than, for instance, in pre-Nazi Germany or the United States. The preponderance of industries producing for mass consumption, such as cotton goods, might prepare Britain better for a system of planning toward a rising standard of living. Indeed, it is realized increasingly that British prosperity can exist only in a world which plans, if necessary by temporary sacrifice, for a higher standard of living all over the world. Obviously it would be absurd to expect a system to be democratically acceptable to all, that aimed at plenty abroad but condoned scarcity at home:

Another economic fact that may equip Britain better for peaceful reform is the long undisturbed growth of national wealth that helped the British people to preserve an equanimity that few other countries were able to enjoy. Awareness of the critical situation and the seriousness of the task before us may, so we can hope at least, prevent the drift into economic, intellectual, and psychological chaos that offers such tempting bait to all dark elements thriving on insecurity, neglect, and despair. Furthermore, a certain experience in public enterprise in Britain preserves the pattern of co-operative controls within a world of private unco-ordinated interests. War-time organization and public regulation of some aspects of private ownership may also serve as an introduction to planning, especially if certain features are at the same time recognized as warning signals.

Finally a rapid glance at the cultural and spiritual spheres would show many features that may make the change in Britain from *laissez-faire* to a democratically planned order more than the pious hope of well-meaning optimists afraid of facing the true dimensions of a gigantic task. The religious and moral sense of communal responsibility is still a reality in spite of the decadence of pre-industrial society. What is needed for real mobilization of these forces for a democratically planned state is, first, the will to adjust social life in all spheres to the demands of the new techniques; and thereafter, redefinition of basic moral values to fit emerging needs of the order desired. For a nation to whom compromise does not mean weakness and subjection to the rule of force, but acceptance of the human value of uniting fellowmen in a common responsibility, it should not be entirely novel to agree on a commonly acceptable order run by the many, not the few; for plenty, not for scarcity; for a common life, not for destruction and death. Moral forces should be the more ready to answer this appeal as the dangers of refusal are only too obvious.

V. THE EMERGING NEW PATTERN

Now, it is in the nature of a democratically adopted change that it cannot be extremist. It cannot be so radical that only those gain by it who have little to lose in the present state of society; nor can it be so conservative that it bolsters up the vested interest of any minority. Reform as opposed to revolution looks to balanced progress and therefore derives its dynamic impetus from the middle groups of society. It has been most successful when, as has often been the case in England, progressive conservatives took up the plea for reform, even though the initial drive has come from more radical groups guided by intellectual critics.

At the same time the lesson of past experience has its limitations. The new reform policy can no longer be a hit-or-miss compromise on disconnected issues, but concerns the whole of society. Five- or ten-year plans demanding prior agreement not only on the starting point but on the sequence of subsequent steps have become the pattern of social change.

This being so, it cannot be denied that there is a certain affinity between the idea of planning and the one-party system. Since the formulation and execution of a consistent plan requires a unified political will, the totalitarian systems for all their crudeness contain an element related to the historical situation today. This is what makes the challenge to democracy so serious. And contemporary democratic systems will be able to meet this challenge only if they discover new methods of creating a unified political will by voluntary agreement on the part of rival social groups. Either democracy must invent in the shortest possible time such new techniques, or some form of totalitarianism will win.

It is often said that in the various forms of representative government democracy has already developed a satisfactory method for reaching agreement. However, in examining customary legislative practice, we cannot help realizing that very little co-ordination exists in the framing even of fundamental bills. We are used to legislating on, say, military affairs, or education, or economic policy, without giving much thought to the interdependence of these matters. It was the merit of Dicey's book on representative government and public opinion [18] that it showed how a coherent system can evolve even from the haphazard methods of democratic legislation. Referring to the social reform of mid-nineteenth-century England, Dicey demonstrated that it was unified public opinion, based on the utilitarian social philosophy, that not only stimulated parliamentary activity but also achieved the intrinsic consistency of the bills enacted.

The time has passed when political will can thus be spontaneously fused by public opinion. In order to achieve democratic agreement on long-range issues today we are in need of a more elaborate method of consciously creating consensus. Of course—and this will always distinguish Democracy from Totalitarianism—the creative force of the Opposition must under no circumstances be suppressed. Constructive criticism will, if anything, become more important. But the channels through which it operates, the form in which it is presented, and the time when it is aired may undergo a change.

The new function of the Opposition becomes clear if we compare the political with the economic order. The democratic system of the pre-planning period resembled in many ways the free market. Each group fought with a good conscience for its sectional interest, trusting that the uncontrolled interplay of political forces would eventually produce harmony. But just as large-scale organization and vested interests obstruct self-regulation of the modern industrial market, so democratic societies cannot survive if their political parties stress competition at the expense of co-operation.

Experience has clearly shown that an excessively competitive party system leads straight into Fascism. There rival social forces from which Democracy draws its dynamic impulse are deliberately paralyzed without genuine integration. What spurious representation of sectional interests is preserved serves only the will of the dictator. By contrast, Democracy in an age of planning is confronted with an almost paradoxical task. On the one hand, the dynamic and critical powers of the party system are to be strengthened. On the other hand, the parties must become aware of their collective responsibility and of the limits to opposition within any comprehensive plan of social reform.

To command agreement or at least 'loyal opposition' in the sense discussed, any plan has to fulfil certain objective preconditions:

(1) The plan must be consistent. Under simpler conditions incompatible political measures naturally caused friction. But adjustment was brought about by the spontaneous forces of everyday life. Now that we have to decide on mass problems such as stability of employment, social security, equality of opportunity, et cetera, in the context of a highly organized social structure, any friction threatens to become cumulative.

(2) The plan must be acceptable to a majority. As we have pointed out already, such a majority can be found only in the center, excluding both reactionaries who do not want to move at any price, and radicals who think the millennium is just around the corner. Naturally these center groups allow for different shades of opinion. But it is in the light of these that co-operation on basic issues can be postulated. Whatever their differences on concrete issues, they agree, on the one hand, on the direction of reform and, on the other hand, on the peaceful method of change. Therefore they should be able to compromise on any actual program or, at least, to submit to majority decision.

This does not mean that fundamental issues are to be dodged in public discussion. The contrary will be true if we think of election campaigns in a planned democracy. There the various parties will fight one another on the comprehensive issues of alternative plans and of alternative methods of their realization.

Of necessity this will direct political discussions toward the fundamental problems of society. Such discussion requires great improvement in the political judgment of the average person, and this is possible only if the issues at stake can be made comprehensible to him. Though expert knowledge in the technical sense cannot be expected of him, genuine understanding of essentials is indispensable for the future voter. It is the task of political thinkers to reduce the complexities of the contemporary situation to such simple terms.

The following exposition is a modest beginning in this major undertaking. It attempts to clarify the alternatives facing the democratic citizen of today when he seeks to interpret sociopolitical issues in terms of the Third Way. To this end we shall examine some strategic problems in our present economic, social, political, and cultural situation with a view to discovering

(1) faults in the present manner of functioning
(2) appropriate methods of planning more perfect functioning
(3) safeguards to assure the democratic nature of any planned intervention.

PART II

Democratic Planning and Changing Institutions

3

On Power [1]*—A Chapter in Political Sociology*

○

The sociologist who sets out to understand contemporary political change must necessarily define 'government,' 'state,' 'society,' in terms of social organization and view them in historical perspective.

Politically significant organizations are not necessarily components of what we are used to call the *state*. This word has existed only since the Italian Renaissance, when men referred to *lo stato*.[2] The term and its meaning were innovations. Neither feudalism nor the Greek city-state can be described adequately in terms of this concept, which is bound to be increasingly incongruous with developments in the near future. The alternatives of state and society, as we think of them today, are of even later origin. The essence and implications of the concepts are derived from the Age of Liberalism. Although many of the underlying elements have changed, the connotation of the terms has remained unaltered.

The Age of Liberalism took for granted the antagonism between bureaucracy and business, usually identified with society at large. As the absolute ruler, the king, lost his prerogatives or disappeared entirely, the state became more and more identified

---

* This sub-section was planned as an independent chapter entitled *A New Approach to Political Science,* and its methodological exposition is relevant not only to the discussion of power but applies equally to the other chapters of Part II.

with bureaucratic government. Then came the influence of jurists and law courts with their legal terminology and concept of the state as an impersonal entity that could be sued or sue individuals. This legal fiction may serve the purposes of law, but contributes little to our understanding of systems prior to the formation of the modern state or to clarifying new beginnings. Hence we shall use the term 'body politic.' The broad scope of this concept permits us to view as a purely historical phenomenon the identification of the bureaucracy—including the army and judiciary—with the state. It keeps us from disregarding the political relevance of other groups and their leaders with similar sociological functions [3] in other historical periods, which are likely to reappear in the future.

By 'body politic' we shall therefore understand all groups and leaders who play an active role in the organization of society. They may be self-appointed entrepreneurs or elected magistrates, high trade-union functionaries or feudal lords of the past. Our concept comprises those political elements *par excellence* that concentrate in their hands administrative functions, military power, and social leadership.[4] The body politic, sociologically understood, inheres in all these political and politically relevant units. When we use the expression 'politically relevant' the word political stands for 'public.' It includes matters of family or employment, only as they become public concerns in a given society. The task for the political sociologist is to describe the forms of co-ordination between all political groups prevailing in a given social structure, and the sociological problem, the relations between groups and their regulation, which can be hierarchical, federative, or co-ordinating in a democratic sense.

Our definition has two advantages. It allows political sociology to pay due attention to those social forces which are not state regulated in the traditional sense and not bureaucratically controlled, yet may integrate the political processes of governing, organizing, leading, co-ordinating, and so on. Furthermore, the obsolete dual conception of 'state' and 'society,' which has little basis in fact today, can be discarded. This dualism usually equates state with bureaucracy, and society with the conglomeration of vigorous organizations that successfully claim the epithets 'free and private.' Besides, our terminology checks the idea that freedom is threatened only by state power, as if other organizations of society were not equally dangerous and out to encroach on man's life, i.e. to expand beyond their legitimate sphere of activity. It is meaningless to assert that the fight for freedom consists in hampering central authorities as much as possible, and to call this goal freedom regardless of the possible chaos resulting from the unhampered action of lesser social units.

The old dualism between bureaucracy and free society became obsolete when their boundaries increasingly overlapped as the Age of Free Enterprise waned partly as a result of the following changes:

1. Among private interests bureaucracies have developed that sometimes equal the central bureaucracies in strength and power.[5]

2. The clear distinction between elected, appointed, or self-appointed (so called 'independent') management personnel tends to become vague.

3. There is no longer a clear distinction between private management directors, who owe their function to appointment and pursue a definite career, and publicly elected or appointed leaders.. Besides, both public and private corporations perform functions that are politically relevant (that is, concern the public interest); many issues are settled by self-regulation which formerly were thought to be managed best by the Civil Service. On the other hand, there are advisory bodies of experts attached to the Civil Service that are nonbureaucratic in character.[6]

4. Many business units, labor, and other voluntary associations have public significance; their co-ordination is no longer a matter of private decisions.[7]

5. The State acts in several countries as a partner in 'private' business corporations. Hence the old boundary lines between private and public enterprise no longer hold.[8]

6. Finally, and least explored, a new personality type has developed through these combinations in certain sections of the bureaucracy. This type of man blends the initiative of the free entrepreneur with the tradition of the civil servant to think primarily in terms of public welfare.[9]

In the light of these developments the old dispute regarding bureaucracy or no bureaucracy seems merely ideological for private bureaucracy is no better in itself than state bureaucracy. Both can be improved if adequate measures are taken, so that the real question becomes: What form of organization is best adapted to solve the problems in a given situation? When, where, and to what extent shall we centralize or decentralize, when and where shall we admit or encourage private enterprise, where shall we favor delegation of powers or self-government by small governing bodies?

Our decisions will not be guided by bias for or against civil-service rule, but by considerations of the rank, size, and nature of the organization, its make-up, functions, situation, promise of optimal efficiency, accountability, and ease of democratic control. Finally, we shall have to consider the single group and its organization with regard to its place in the whole body politic and its relation to the general plan. Gaetano Mosca's words are still pertinent today:

> From our point of view there can be no antagonism between *state* and *society*. The state is to be looked upon merely as that part of society which performs the political function. Considered in this light, all questions touching interference or noninterference by the state come to assume a new aspect. Instead of asking what the limits of state activity ought to be, we try to find out what the best type of political organization is, which type, in other words, enables all the elements that have a political significance in a given society to be best utilized and specialized, best subjected to reciprocal control and to the principle of individual responsibility for the things that are done in the respective domains.
>
> When people contrast state management with private initiative, they are often merely comparing work done by a bureaucracy with work that might be done by other directing elements in society. The latter may, in fact, in some cases actually have an official status without necessarily being paid employees.[10]

Once we free ourselves of the bogey that whatever the state and its bureaucracy do is wrong and contrary to freedom, and that whatever others do is efficient and synonymous with freedom, we can squarely face the true issue. Reduced to a single phrase, the issue is that in our modern world everything is political, the state is everywhere, and public responsibility is interwoven in the whole fabric of society. Freedom consists not in denying this interpenetration but in defining its legitimate uses in all spheres, setting limits and deciding the pattern of penetration and, last but not least, in safeguarding public responsibility and shared control over decisions. From this follows the importance of institutional control for a strategy of reform in a democratically planned society, and the need for a theory of power based on democratic principles.

II. TOWARD A DEMOCRATIC THEORY OF POWER *

There is much wavering between the extremes of anarchism (abolition of all forms of power) and hard-boiled power politics. Normally a middle course is pursued. Without consistent principles, however, our political policies appear opportunist, mere expedients of the hour.

Democracy, rightly understood, implies a theory of power aimed at defining ways of distributing and controlling communal power for maximum security, efficiency, and freedom.[11] The theory appropriate for the Third Way will not preach with Gandhi abstention from all power, or succumb to the blind power worship of Nazism, nor will it represent the 'golden mean' appropriate to the 'timotropic' society, as it has rightly been called.[12] This type of society pursues the acquisition of wealth as the *summum bonum,* thinking to avoid the use of power by exerting economic pressure either overtly or covertly. Obviously, no society can exist without some form of power. A meaningful theory is less concerned with the abstract question of power or no power than with its actual forms and their social setting. It observes the transmutations of power with structural changes of society; it asks what kind and amount of power goes to different members and agents of society; finally it detects and condemns abuses of power and cruelty.

Our statement anticipates the solution in general terms. There is a great difference between functional and arbitrary power. Any society, however, may rightly be called despotic which permits ruling groups and individuals to wield more power than their functions require or allows them to use power arbitrarily.

We shall next elaborate and illustrate our proposition. A democratic theory of power must be comprehensive. Power

* This and the following parts of the chapter on Power were written in Summer 1946.

means not merely violence, the use of brute force by the army or police. Nor do we mean to restrict our concept of power to political power. We speak of economic and administrative power as well as of the power of persuasion working through religion, education, and media of mass communication such as the press, motion picture, and radio. Power is present whenever and wherever social pressures operate on the individual to induce desired conduct. The means of inducing 'obedience to pressures' are significant, but of secondary importance. The pressures may be overt or they may be inherent in the socio-economic system or any established pattern of social roles.

With H. Goldhamer and E. Shils [13] we would distinguish various forms of power, and speak of *domination* and *manipulation*. The former refers to relations in which the power-holder expresses his wishes by giving commands, the latter to relations in which the power-holder exercises influence without stating the expected behavior.

This comprehensive definition of power allows for the analytical reduction of various forms of constraint to a common denominator, and thus permits answering the question which types and combination of pressures are at work in any given system and how a new system substitutes new pressures for old. Such a concept of power will enable us to interpret society at the level of planning when control of all social forces is at issue; politics is no longer a separate compartment, and the use of violence is no longer considered the only means upholding a social order.

This new approach also discards as fallacy the economic theory of Liberalism. The socialists rightly repudiated the alleged 'freedom' of the modern worker to sell his labor in any market he liked. If freedom and constraint are clearly defined, he is not free but subject to pressure disguised as free choice. The issue is not that of freedom *versus* power but of alternate forms of pressures exerted by social power. Having said this, we depart from the socialist argument by emphasizing the different nature of pressures, human or inhuman, demanding co-operation or imposing regimentation.

Social change does not move from absolute domination to absolute freedom but goes through transmutations of different power structures. Forms of power, i.e. various forms of pressure, change because the nature of the action sought and the techniques of their social control change. A few examples may serve to illustrate the point.

An agrarian economy with poor means of communication and an army of self-equipped and fortified cavalry or charioteers will favor the development of decentralized feudalism. Personal pressures combine with ecclesiastic power and contractual relations to create stable loyalties—the power of tradition rather than legal enactments regulates human relations.[14]

In contrast, a society with highly developed techniques of production, efficient means of communication, and strict division of labor will be run from a few centers according to general rules. The machinelike interdependence of the parts will lend itself to specific forms of pressure. A person may be kept in his place not so much by direct command as by the fear of losing his job and status. He may protect himself against this threat and pressure by joining a trade union which seeks to establish counterpressures by the power of large-scale organization.

Once the structure of society changes, its pressures and means of control will change concomitantly. Accordingly a new type of authority will be established, using new sanctions against the non-conformist. This is not all. The selection and education of those who command and maneuver pressures will vary just as much as the training for conformity and obedience.

Despite the scope of these variations, barely analyzed thus far, no society can dispense with controls altogether. Society like nature abhors a vacuum, though the process of substituting one set of controls for another usually involves a crisis. The problem of our age is not so much, as many people would like to assume, to abolish capitalist controls at all costs, to get rid of the pressures of the market and the self-balancing of forces in as many spheres of life as possible; the real task is rather to substitute new controls for ineffectual ones in order to eliminate waste, restore efficiency, give scope to foresight—eliminating *inter alia* cyclical unemployment—and to do all this without inhuman regimentation or needless interference with the normal aspirations of the citizenry.

III. THE THREE BASIC FORMS OF POWER

Manifestations of power differ according to their means of control. Hence we may profitably distinguish between three basic forms of power: free sway, organized destruction, and institutionalized or canalized power.

(a) *Free sway* of uncontrolled violence on the part of individuals or groups leads to chaos, anarchy, and *anomie*. The closest analogy to free sway in power relationships is electricity in its natural unmastered form. Fitful flashes of lightning during a thunderstorm may be downright destructive, whereas the same energy brought under technological control obediently serves human ends.

The free sway of emotional energy sweeps everything before it like a hurricane, representing a borderline state of socialization, the minimum. Outbreaks of panic or senseless rage are the horror of responsible men. We try by all manner of means to avoid such outbreaks of naked passion. We have a *horror vacui* in society lest such crowd emotion get out of hand. The contagion of emotion, the disappearance of social control and self-control, characterize its manifestation and lead to mob action such as pogroms and lynchings.[15]

(b) *Organized destruction,* such as wars, revolutions, et cetera, show external forms of organization, but their violent methods and destructive aims tend toward free sway.

Control of both sorts of power—of violence, revolution, chaos, and even war—offers no major problem. It rests primarily upon the use of armed forces in defense of a given order. Hence we shall say no more about it, but turn to the main theme of political sociology.

(c) *Canalized power,* as we wish to term it, is vested in institutions and produces orderly patterns of human interaction subject to norms, codes, and rules. Power is controlled and in turn controls conduct. Its various forms will be discussed presently. Institutionalized power may be dangerous when either too lax or too rigid. The freedom it admits may mean a drift toward *laissez-faire* without leadership, or at the opposite extreme may suppress all self-expression and become unbearable.

Most of our ideas about canalized power and control are limited for two reasons: Our crucial experiences and our terminology of power—'legitimate power,' 'suppression,' 'freedom'—are modeled on internalized personal relations. Further, the operations of power and its controls have been scrutinized only in small groups. The transfer of these experiences to large organizations and their projection to society at large is for the most part taken for granted. But it is doubtful whether what we may expect of small group relationships will hold good for large-scale organizations, as it is questionable whether the kind of freedom we are used to in personal relationships or small groups can be enjoyed in large organizations.

Next we may proceed to discuss the transformation of canalized power and its control. We shall need to differentiate between various phases in the institutionalization of power and to relate them to their concomitant phases of socialization.

IV. POWER IN PERSONAL RELATIONSHIPS

However complex its derivatives, the archetype of power-experience is the personal feeling of strength in making another person bow to our will. Psychic coercion, as practiced in magic, is modeled on this primary experience. From the first, man's feeling of power has been joined with control of other people's behavior. Hence any discussion of power is associated with that of control. Our power is measured by the extent and degree of our control over our fellowmen (including their services); and our power, in turn, is controlled to the extent that our fellowmen check our will to control them.

Although power and control primarily mean coercion, the use of the words soon broadens, since we do not control other men by commands and threats alone, but often through kindness and persuasion. Hence power is present no matter how we induce people to comply with our wishes. Interaction in power relations is not based on fear alone but on mutual response, which is perhaps the more fundamental and general source of human control.[16]

In personal relations mutual control prevails. Its intensity and forms vary with the personal qualities of the participants and with their relationship, whether ephemeral acquaintance, friendship, courtship, or whatever it may be. The operation of power

in personal relations directly reflects the 'weight' of the respective personalities involved. In purely personal relations power
is diffuse and controls are casual.

A certain hardening, a first step toward an institution of
power, occurs when behavior in personal relations becomes patterned. This occurs swiftly, since even the most private personal
relationship is part of the continuous social process and subject
to established or emergent forms, following precedent or molding new patterns of intimacy.[17] Transition from a state of fluidity begins in the folkways, as Sumner [18] calls the conventionalized forms of expedient conduct through which the past rules
the present. Folkways may assume one of two forms: they may
be usages merely practiced without emphasis, or mores hallowed
by the moral code of religion. Here social pressures begin to
operate, which no longer derive from personal power relationships. At this stage of culture individual behavior reflects and is
subject to norms and values sanctioned by groups and corporate
bodies, priesthoods, et cetera. Thus *A* may rebuke *B* for not
doing things properly, his censure conveying the misgivings of
a community mainly concerned with perpetuating its established
way of life and controlling behavior from a point quite outside
the sphere of person-to-person relationships.

Sanctions connected with folkways—whether positive, i.e. ap-
proving certain behavior, or negative, i.e. disapproving and cen-
suring it—are merely casual. For although they have their locus
outside personal relationships, they are not yet fully integrated
into the social fabric since they result from diffuse power. Integration finally occurs when power is turned over to an institution by organized sanctions. This change is fundamental.

'Anyone may lift his brow at a departure from accepted usage,
or join with his neighbor in ostracizing someone who has violated the mores. Only the proper officers or functionaries may
undertake the sanctioned procedures of an institution.' [19] Institutions follow recognized rules, formal procedure. The most advanced form of institutionalized control is the law as interpreted
and enforced by the courts and police power. The transition
from diffuse power and casual controls to organized ones is
significant because it leads in a curious way to the reification of
the purely personal pressures of the social process. In terms of

social behavior, law enforcement may be said to consist of a carefully thought out interplay of pressures exerted by various individuals performing their established roles according to well-defined rules. When we say that society exerts institutional pressures, the abstract noun 'society' stands for the co-ordinated behavior of many individuals, none of whom singly (as in personal relations) elicits the desired behavior on the part of the controlled individual. Ideas of jurisdiction and authority develop at this stage. Now, the law defines who can decide when, what kind of, and what amount of pressure should be applied against whom.

Institutional sanctions coexist with folkways and mores, and societies vary in their definition of behavior subject to organized and diffuse sanctions, to law and to mores. Anglo-Saxon societies prefer to regulate a maximum of conduct by convention and are inclined to believe that only behavior regulated by folkways and mores is free. By contrast, societies influenced by the tradition of Roman law lean toward statutory regulation, where definitions are clear-cut and the sources of pressure are explicit and visibly organized.

V. POWER CONCENTRATION IN FUNCTIONS

A different and equally important phase of the transmutation of person-to-person controls into social ones may be observed when the survival of the group demands organized co-operation. A tribal hunting team, for instance, is organized around the social objective of providing food. Regulation and pressure not only serve to maintain an established way of life but effectively guarantee fulfilment of this collective function. Provision for such necessary functions is the external source and motive for regulation in contrast to mere person-to-person relationships. The collective responsibility calls for recurrent and lasting functions, including that of leadership. The leader may give orders to the subordinate members of his team and on occasion use physical or psychological pressures. In so doing he links his personal, physical, and mental strength to an objective function. He acts not so much on behalf of the community and its generalized ways of doing things as for the sake of successful performance. In this situation a strange metamorphosis occurs: the 'archaic' experience of purely personal power is linked to and, so to speak, transfused into the social function. This may possibly explain why we speak equally of 'power' whether an individual controls another in a personal relationship or controls him on behalf of society for a functional objective. We may go further and say that power is vested in the function. The metamorphosis is also significant because it demarcates the beginning of the process that substitutes the control of man by institutions and organizations for that of man by man. Organized controls, as we know, have their own dynamic and require activities that none of the original partners may have foreseen or intended.

This transmutation of personal into functional power leads to ramifications which merit close attention:

1. The progressive detachment of functional power from the personal qualities of the user leads to increasing identification of power with a role. From now on the role will of itself determine the nature of challenge and response, whereas originally the leader owed his functional superiority to purely personal qualities in the fulfilment of a socially recognized function.

2. This identification of power as a function stabilizes the various roles such as those of leader and followers. The kind and degree of power vested in roles and functions can, for instance, be transferred to a successor to leadership by designation, election, or inheritance (primogeniture) more or less regardless of personal abilities. To be sure, there is a difference between what a strong man and a weak man will make of a job; yet once leading roles are outlined they define and confer the degree and form of available power to the incumbent.

3. Most significant at this stage is the dawn of differentiation between essential function and arbitrary personal power. The concept of purely personal power depending on the strength of one individual influencing another in the social process gives way to the concept of power as social control serving collective aims.

4. Social control is exercised in expanding communities by means of special social techniques discussed in our text. In simple face-to-face relations in small groups the techniques of social control are undifferentiated. In the course of social development, however, their range and degree increase. Physical

strength can be implemented by arms. Psychic strength develops means of psychic coercion through magical devices, techniques of persuasion, tricks of shrewdness, deception, sex appeal through charms and coquetry, and a vast array of suggestive devices. In small groups such as mutual acquaintances, these devices may be simple and transparent. For the control of expanding masses inhabiting large territories, following specialized occupational pursuits in complex organizations, highly refined techniques and tools of control have been developed.

Not only do time and space shrink before man equipped with modern means of communication but varied cultures evolved through different traditions tend to merge into one interdependent world-wide civilization. They tend to become standardized in the process of common exposure to similar means of control and appeal.

It is important to this argument that every discovery of a major novel social technique demands a new type of organization, which in turn becomes a new power center with peculiar characteristics and independent power dynamics. The tendency toward organizational autonomy in the exercise of power was quite visible in the long struggle between ecclesiastic and secular authorities, Pope and Emperor of the medieval Occident—a struggle that can be sociologically understood as a conflict between an organization intent on monopoly of the means of spiritual and psychic coercion and one of professional warriors, a conflict of the chalice against the sword.

In modern society the machinery of formal education, including adult education, is one of the most powerful organizations for fashioning men's minds. Organized public persuasion is also gaining in strength. Functions formerly fulfilled by the priesthood alone are now shared by the educator, administrator, political propagandist, journalist, and public relations counselor. All of them use modern means of mass communication and reproduction, press, radio, film, television, mimeographs, phonographs, photographs, and the like, to implement policies of their own. They are partly co-ordinated and partly conflicting.

Besides, we have social techniques to influence economic behavior. Positive and negative sanctions of all sorts are used to make producers, distributors, and consumers play their parts.

The development of economic technology is stupendous in agricultural and industrial production, in transportation and distribution, and it implements powerful corporate organizations. Their policies represent generally a compromise between the promotional activities of special interest groups and the demands of the community as a whole.

The transmutation of power in the social process may be analyzed in another way. The various spheres of action and the organized interests of society have a differential impact upon man's behavior and this impact may vary with the changing social structure. In one age economic organization may be most powerful; in another, military organization may predominate. Such changes and differentials in influence, however, apply also to institutions such as schools. The United States, for instance, has made greater use of schools in modern times than European countries. It was largely due to education that the assimilation and Americanization of millions of immigrants throughout the nineteenth century was accomplished in America. In the United States the school system plays a larger part in the creation and transmission of national loyalty than in England, where loyalties to the nation result from a more widely dispersed set of controls.[20] The German educational structure under the Weimar Republic could not withstand the pressure of divided loyalties from antidemocratic parties and their youth organizations of the Right and Left.[21]

VI. SIGNIFICANT LESSONS

The distinctions made plain above should help us to steer clear of debating power as such or in general. They should make concrete observation of the power process, its variations and transmutations, an easy matter. Hence the question how to master the process may be stated more specifically.

1. The master control of the power process must necessarily be total. This does not mean that identical methods of control should be used everywhere and all the time. Rather, means and measures of control need to be co-ordinated and interrelated. Each form of power at whatever level of social interaction and organization it may occur will have to be dealt with appropriately on its respective ground. Finally, 'no control,' 'leave alone,'

may often serve best, if the place of such behavior patterns in the power structure of society is recognized and agreed upon.

2. Some examples may serve to illustrate the proposition that varied power processes must be dealt with by appropriate means on their respective levels.

Purely personal relationships, such as those of parents and children, pupils and teachers, playmates, lovers, or friends, cannot be created or helped by organizational measures which have no part in them. Such relationships are not sectional; total personalities are engaged in interaction, and the situation can be changed only by changing the personalities concerned. Of course, this is not to say that good laws and organizations are irrelevant, or that one might not provide better and indispensable opportunities for such personal relationships. But in enacting and planning organizations, one should not lose sight of the central aim—to facilitate personal relationships.

On the other hand personal influence cannot substitute for bad organization. The personal approach does not replace the organizational one. Controlling men without controlling institutions is doomed to failure. In eliminating or reducing the effects of the profit motive, it is better to establish co-operatives or enact an 'excess profit tax' than to preach the virtues of service and condemn acquisitive vices.

Given, however, a new legal organizational framework within which the service motive can operate, as for instance in the Civil Service, individual training and moral education will help to mold personalities fit to serve.

3. Our definitions can further teach us that institutional controls *per se* are not always dehumanizing. It is false romanticism to assume that new devices for increasing regulation of society are necessarily changes for the worse. Recalling the distinction we have made between functionally justified power and arbitrary power and realizing that all organized social life involves distribution of power, we may seek to establish moral criteria for legitimate power differentials and search for an objective measure for legitimate use of power. Thus far no objective measure has been found other than the amount and kind of power required for the performance of objective functions. Without being able to gauge precisely the amount of power requisite for cer-

tain functions, for all practical purposes we usually know the minimum and maximum power required for standard functions. In the Army, in a factory, or in police work we know roughly what man-power, weapons, or service personnel is required for efficient performance and management.[22] The functional appraisal of power would seem to provide a basis for establishing moral criteria for its use,[23] central to our theory.

4. Our distinctions permit us likewise to enquire into the concentration and distribution of power. Whether or not and how much power should be centralized depend, of course, on the nature of the function concerned and its setting. Democratic sentiment, inclined to minimize power differentials and eager to broaden participation in the decision-making process, would fear undue concentration of power as leading to minority rule and despotism. For the sake of efficiency it should beware of the dangers of unlimited dispersion of power: anarchy and chaos.

VII. POWER CONCENTRATION IN GROUPS

Power centers not only around functions and functional groups or associations such as the tribal hunting team, ecclesiastic bodies, economic corporations, or the Army, but around organic groups as units of communal life, so-called communities. Communal life, embracing nearly all aspects of human activities, responding to all needs and ambitions, tends to develop its own solidarity. Unless challenged by outsiders members of the community will take their oneness for granted and share an unconscious 'we-feeling.' Under certain conditions communal groups tend to become conscious of their common values and distinctiveness. This consciousness may first express itself as ethnocentricity, i.e. differential treatment of in-group and out-group members. *Nationalism* is a modern form of such sentiments on the part of large communities organized in states or aspiring to such organization. Conscious emphasis on tradition and culture, a tendency toward independent regulation of group affairs, and finally a desire for sovereignty, a sense of a special mission, political and/or cultural, feed this sentiment of nationalism.

The functional units already described may or may not coincide with the boundaries of these communities, since the latter result from the interplay of historical forces and changes which lend them peculiar features. The functional unit, 'international cartel,' for instance, does not coincide with the territory of any nation or state, whereas the Army does.

Communities may expand, small communities may merge into larger ones, and we may list a series of communities by size, from tribal and local communities to regional and national communities. The largest unit existing at a given time may be called the 'frame group.' At present the national unit is the real frame group [though the Soviet Union represents a multi-nationality-state basing its solidarity on special patriotism to the Soviet. Also the British Empire as a Commonwealth of Nations would seem to constitute an exception to the rule.—Ed.] The Great Powers since the advent of modern imperialism are engaged in expanding their spheres of economic, cultural, and political influence competitively. Their striving for hegemony among groups of weaker states is likely to lead to a pattern of regional solidarity and consciousness. The main world regions will probably be polarized between an Anglo-Saxon orbit and a Russian orbit.*

The place and nature of this community-centered power differ from those of functional power. The same holds for the calamities produced by these two types of power complexes and their possible mastery.

The most conspicuous difference between functional and communal power units is the greater rationalism of the former. Although economic mass associations such as trade unions, cooperatives, et cetera, may boast of their size for reasons of prestige, their predominant motive is rational interest, and their aims can be, and mostly are, clearly defined. This is why, once an equilibrium of power is reached, reasonable compromise emerges spontaneously in spite of mutual antagonisms, and there is always a latent tendency to draw a line between functional and arbitrary uses of power. In the long run this criterion may well gain recognition and ascendancy. Psychologically speaking, a process of sublimation may take place among bargaining functional units and lead from purely egoistic calculation through compromise to mutual consideration and fair play. This development is partly supported by the implicit mutuality of all cooperation along functional lines. It may become predominant if

* This passage was already written in 1946. [Ed.]

F

circumstances such as national emergency bring it to the fore. Last but not least, educational efforts tend to emphasize mutuality and co-operation as against conflict of interests; hence they promote rationality.

This tendency toward greater rationality is not yet visible in the concentration of power around communal units of various sizes. This is probably due to their different purposes and origins. They emerged chiefly in response to emotional needs, and their territorial expansion made for peculiar emotional changes.

Communal units serve primarily the need to belong somewhere. A tribe, a village, a county, a region, a nation may develop from a network of functions based on the division of labor (and in this sense on rational needs); but they become communities only to the extent that the members develop 'we-feelings,' setting them apart from outsiders and making them behave differently. Therefore nation-states do not always coincide with 'natural' economic areas.[24] The solidarity of nation-states rests on a 'we-feeling' which as such constitutes power. Power based on communal interest is distinct from that based on functional integration. Man motivated by his allegiance to functional power units behaves differently than when motivated by his loyalty to the nation.[25]

The we-feeling emanating from communities of whatever origin contributes greatly to defining man's place in the world, and his desire for status may often prevail over rational interest. The we-feeling is not sectional in operation; it affects not merely one center of man's interests but permeates his entire personality. A person whose place and status feeling is mainly determined by that of his community may be said to live on 'borrowed prestige' —on the prestige of his community. He may therefore be convinced that his own growth depends on the expansion and status of his community in the world.[26] Power that lives on tribalism, regionalism, and nationalism usually rouses more fear than power that works through economic interest alone. The latter is sectional and rationally assessable; the former is scattered and unpredictable.

Another factor makes for greater irrationality in the feeling of communal interest: it spreads through contagion and emotional fusion. In playing one's role in the economic game, in fulfilling one's special function, one remains at a certain distance from one's partner. Antagonism and mutuality both presuppose separate identity. In communal solidarity, however, more and more people feel united by sharing the common we-feeling. Once established, it develops its own dynamic. However powerful it may be and however harmful its irrationality when contributing to Imperialism, the sociologist has no reason to assume that this force defies rational analysis and social mastery. Max Weber once correctly observed that irrational behavior was more predictable in its course than rational.[27]

The behavior of an hysterical person, for instance, lends itself more easily to prognosis than responses of normally calculating persons aiming at expedient adjustment. The latter may more often reach unexpected conclusions than people acting under the compulsion of psychopathological or irrational drives. Their conduct shows a cycle that can be analyzed, evaluated, and dealt with in its various phases.

Similarly, the mastery of aggressive nationalism, often emanating from or leading up to an inflated we-feeling, will require skilful analysis with regard to its mainsprings. Only by such analysis may we hope to bring disturbing outbreaks under control by suitable measures and checks.[28]

VIII. THE NATURE AND POWER OF COMMUNAL SENTIMENT

Power inherent in the we-feeling of communal solidarity may be characterized as follows:

1. Communal sentiment is not always expansive and aggressive. Militant nationalism, for example, is a modern product, although differential treatment of insiders and outsiders (ethnocentrism) is ancient. Furthermore, smaller countries, such as Sweden, Norway, Holland, Portugal, and Switzerland, which once were expansive and aggressive, have settled down to the peaceful conduct of their affairs. Similarly, British expansionism reached a point where it ceased to be militant, owing to saturation or to a psychological mutation.

Only carefully prepared comparative investigations of changes on all levels—economic, military, psychological, and educational —will yield satisfactory explanations of the rise and decline of aggressive nationalism. The sequence, direction, and tempo of changes, and the interplay of measures on various planes will have to be observed.

2. Requisite to such a study is a sound classification of psychological needs finding satisfaction in both balanced and aggressive communal solidarity.

The former seems desirable as it satisfies among other things the individual's craving for belonging and security, for status and self-esteem.

Common-sense observations show that educational measures greatly influence desires and their means of gratification. It makes all the difference in child rearing whether we encourage self-esteem and controlled self-assertion balanced by respect for others or whether we encourage, or at any rate tolerate, self-aggrandisement and provocative, so-called 'manly' behavior. The same applies with certain modifications to education for group behavior. As in personal relations, so in international relations one may encourage *sacro egoismo*, self-seeking expansionism, as Italian Fascism has done, or one may teach and encourage mutual regard and co-operation.

Though not the sole deciding factor for the growth of communal or national consciousness educational measures are highly significant in this field. Methods of education for personal and group honesty do exist. The difficulty, however, is how to win resolute co-operation for co-ordinated educational efforts all over the world. It goes without saying that the real task of UN and especially of UNESCO is to promote such unity.

3. Communal sentiment is not simply imposed from on high but results from complex historical processes. Its gradual expansion neutralizes militant aggressiveness in smaller sub-units. In other words: fusion of smaller units absorbs or at least mitigates the aggressive tendencies of the previously autonomous units.

The Nation-State is after all the best example of absorption of units previously striving for autonomy. Feudal barons and independent cities surrendered their claims and subordinated themselves to the more comprehensive scheme of the Nation-State. Jealousies may survive for a long time, but as the process of fusion goes on, the desire for autonomy and sovereignty is transferred to the Nation-State and its organs. One way of liquidating aggressive group sentiment is therefore fusion of smaller units with a concomitant transfer of group aggressiveness to the new larger unit. It is mainly a matter of social guidance to what sort of more comprehensive unit this transfer will be directed.

Often hesitancy and uncertainty can be observed during an interim period in regard to which larger units loyalty should be attached. In such cases historical events (threats of war, warfare and its outcome, political alliances, power hegemony, etc.) push emotions in different directions, and the conscious political manipulation of leaders strongly influences the direction of integration. Needless to say, if UN fails to focus loyalties on the new world organization, the development of rival regional 'we-feelings,' and militant at that, will be unavoidable.

4. There exist, however, other natural (unplanned) tendencies of expanding group solidarity. Between the two world wars the Socialists and Communists showed that they could bring about solidarity along class lines through guidance, education, and manipulation of public opinion—a loyalty often superseding that of national solidarity. The same has been demonstrated by the Roman Catholic Church. They could frequently focus basic loyalty on their international common interest, and for many members this proved to be stronger than their national allegiance.[29] Hence, not only do different loyalties prevail at times in the same individual, but the direction of communal solidarity can be manipulated at certain junctures of history. Generally speaking, we are living in an epoch that is equally open to national, international, or sectional integration ('Workers of the World, unite!') and open to fusions larger than national units. As we have pointed out, apparently one or the other tendency periodically prevails, and we may assume that countries such as Germany, Spain, and Italy, which did turn Fascist, might equally well have turned Communist. In present-day France an unstable equilibrium of forces exists so that events, social forces, manipulative and educative efforts may well decide the outcome.

The main reason for these tensions seems to be that the expanding process of emotional fusion becomes ever more detached from the locale of origin. Such detachment releases certain emotions in the individual, paving the way for loyalty and fusion which seek for some fixation (*kathexis*) on objects or causes.

These objectives, however, are not simply determined from on high, as has happened more or less in the past, but are more open to personal choice. In a tribal community, in villages, in regions, in the period of awakening nationalism, the place of birth largely determined man's fate. For a few individuals or a minority there existed a limited range of choice. Here, the emergence of 'divided loyalties' (to the Church—or to the Emperor) can be observed. Yet, the historically developed areas of basic solidarity on the whole defined everybody's place and held a grip on the people.

Greater social mobility, however, improved means of transportation and communication, motion pictures, radio, press and the various forms of propaganda loosen the old intense loyalties. They may shift from one objective to another and hence allegiance can be manipulated to a greater extent. A few words may serve to evaluate this process.

5. In addition to the previously mentioned processes, urbanization and its ramifications undermine the primary forms of solidarity, especially to the community. In a huge metropolitan area, with its suburbs, satellite cities, lodging houses and tenements,[30] with the separation of office and factory from home, communal solidarity means less and less to more and more people. Neither the place or country of birth, nor the nation in which they happen to live means much to them. We usually call this process uprooting, and the pejorative sense of the term is justified in so far as with most people loss of identification with a definite locale and nonparticipation in community life lead to disintegration of character. This detachment from a locale of one's own leaves a feeling of belonging somewhere either undeveloped or unfulfilled. It makes for mental insecurity and unattached emotional states, leaving people easy prey to propaganda. Uprooted men may become shiftless migrants, criminals, often cynics with no conviction or stability.

What we see as character disintegration or loss of personality in the individual appears as 'atomization' of society when observed as a mass phenomenon. Communities turn into crowds when this uprooting occurs, the deeper side of the self loses ground, surface reactions predominate, and the propagandist enters on the scene as skilful manipulator.[31] The mental state produced by these conditions is one of the dangers of modern times. Its prevention through various measures must be our main concern, as such states give rise to suggestibility, leading to outbreaks of panic, despair, and atrocities.[32]

The situation, however, is complicated by the fact that what we pejoratively call 'uprooting' has its positive aspects both for personality formation and the construction of a world-community. Uprooting, viewed positively, might be called emancipation. Hardly anybody will doubt that the establishment of larger communities—possibly a world-wide community—is possible only if people overcome the state of unconditional subservience to the power demon of national sovereignty and aggressive nationalism. Partial uprooting, emancipation, is therefore necessary and is indeed achieved by progressive men.

We may call a person 'emancipated' who does not think in terms of 'my country—right or wrong,' who is not a chauvinist expecting his parish church to be the most magnificent in the world. He achieves emancipation by partial uprooting, by selecting for personal identification only certain traditions and values of his community. In so doing he does not shut out the character-forming influences of community participation, nor does he sacrifice his right to independent thought and personal development. He is emancipated because he is always ready to move toward a more comprehensive integration of the world but he does so without turning cosmopolitan by denouncing his solidarity with his nation. The emancipated person shares the fate of his country but his vision reaches beyond the *sacro egoismo* of modern nationalism. An increasing number of emancipated citizens in all camps can help to bring about an integrated world for all.

6. In view of the emancipation process we have to redefine the function of the intelligentsia at the present juncture. The emancipated intellectuals are those who are capable of extricating themselves mentally from the pressures both of outlived folkways and of manipulative attacks of propagandists who try to impose upon them doctrines and artificial ideologies of nationalism. The intelligentsia try to resist this ideological pressure even at the price of being called unreliable by aggressive nationalists.

Seen from this angle, the intelligentsia represents considerable power. Once we admit that power does not rest in guns, airplanes, money, or functional units alone, but in guidance and integration of community sentiment, the intelligentsia holds as important a key position as do the chiefs of the Army or big businessmen. This holds especially for an age when ideas and ideologies help to bring about solidarity and mere emotional contagion does not suffice. The special significance of the intelligentsia in the power process can be appreciated even more fully in view of the fact that the simpler forms of community loyalties tend to become more lax.[33] What psychologists call the 'motivation' of a person can therefore be operated upon according to plan.

By motivation we understand the possibility of influencing man's wishes and strivings socially. Motivation plays a significant role in education.[34] A pupil learns, for instance, his geography or language lesson more readily and efficiently if he knows the purpose of learning and if he identifies himself with the objective. Obviously, there is no innate wish to learn geography or foreign languages. A definite person, the educator (parent or teacher) induces the desire. Thus in every society there are always motivated and motivating individuals. In simple cultures motivation is all-pervasive and dispersed. The values of the community motivate the individual. Before he embarks on action society has already defined for him worthwhile ends and undesirable ends. Thus, his choice is limited. The more flexible society becomes, the less frequently are values and motivations induced unconsciously from outside. Values no longer are inherent in things, as for instance when people think of women as inferior, or of foreigners as slaves, or of the poor as lesser human beings. Values are no longer taken for granted as facts. Greater social mobility creates flexible minds, everything becomes subject to discussion, preferences and purposes are questioned, and justification is necessary if we wish to motivate people along certain lines. In this process the motivating individuals are generally intellectuals. They hold a key position in social change as specialists in the invention and diffusion of ideas, and although in the short-range view they may seem to be powerless, they are more effectual in the long run than the visible holders of power-commanding guns, airplanes, et cetera. Political thinkers such as Rousseau, Marx, Pareto, Adam Smith, Mill, exerted great influence when their hour came. Apart from the fact that the producers and disseminators of ideas have gained in significance since folkways weakened, the permanence of their influence is due to the fact that ideas are peculiarly evasive. Guns can be located and destroyed, not so ideas. You can kill their advocates as heretics and prophets, yet the ideas may survive and spread. Thus, ideas represent power, especially manifest when in the form of sabotage. Totalitarian dictators, however great their power, fear nothing more than sabotage. They know that organized power can be disintegrated, not necessarily first by direct action, such as revolution, but by subversive propaganda, sapping the loyalties of men to whom weapons are entrusted and who have to do the work in fields and factories.

IX. FUNCTIONAL AND COMMUNAL POWER AT VARIANCE

The mastery of power concentrated in groups differs from that vested in functions. The latter has a rational nucleus. It may be covered up by emotion and it is usually associated with vested interests, yet its rational element may serve as a point of departure for a humanizing and socializing power process. The inherent function may serve those who wish to neutralize gradually harmful aggressive emotions, and to control or absorb sectional vested interests into a communal scheme.

The struggle for intelligent control of predatory power and irrational impulse may be solidly based on helpful criteria of functional *versus* nonfunctional power elements. It can be proved, for instance, that it is against the welfare of the community for conservative-minded owners to run a mill with obsolete machinery. The technological backwardness of many British mines until their recent nationalization and the blocking of technological change in the American building trades are cases in point. One can likewise prove that self-seeking monopolies should be checked by impartial authorities.

By contrast it is more difficult to establish criteria for various types of communal cohesion and of national sovereignty. Nevertheless there are ways and means of dealing rationally with these issues. In the past an ever-changing balance of power settled problems as they arose. The mighty suppressed the weak with varying success. Similarly, smaller social units fought continuously for the allegiance of individuals to expand their competitive jurisdictional control, as is obvious in the struggle between State and Church, interdenominational rivalries, political party strife, and the competition of schools of philosophy. Our own age increasingly subjects irrational factors of communal cohesion to rational analysis and criteria. Those who aim at peaceful world co-operation may play on two promising tendencies:

1. Sentiments of communal cohesion, such as nationalism, are no longer considered good or evil. We have to distinguish between undoubtedly harmful features, such as chauvinist aggressiveness and functionally significant traditions of the community, whatever their content. Certain elements of national sentiment are indispensable for defining the status of peoples in the world and for assuring mental balance. Political and educational leaders should aim at eradicating the harmful features of nationalism which block peaceful world co-operation. They should be tolerant toward such traditional elements as language, mores, and culture, which implement communal cohesion without preventing international co-operation.

This division of the issue of power into one half subject to comprehensive regulation, and the other half left to autonomous group definition is the great contribution inherent in the idea of federalism. It distinguishes the United States and the Anglo-Saxon world in general that they have made federalism the backbone of their political organization; it is the distinguishing mark of the U.S.S.R. that it has adopted the federalist principle in the organization of its multinationality state.

2. The same division of the power issue is posed in view of the peculiar entanglement of functional units and interest groups in the present world situation.

Functional units, such as a hunting team, a factory, or an industrial combine tend to grow and accumulate power. So do units of communal cohesion, such as tribes, villages, regions, nations, et cetera. In the past functional units developed for the most part within the confines of communal groups and hence were ultimately ruled by group authorities. Business establishments and entire industrial systems grew into the mold of communal units, first of a town or a region, later of a nation. The same holds for armies, bureaucracies, organizations built around the ever-expanding means of communication and transport.

In the past such patterns of growth were fairly transparent to man. Handicraft and small-scale industry combined with poor means of communication to keep expansion within the geographical boundaries of 'territories' as nuclei of communal integration. Later the need of defense against rival expanding units, administrative and police requirements, made the State appear the 'embodiment' and 'protective organization' of communal fusion on a national scale. These nation-states characteristically promoted a 'we-feeling' which permeated the functional units of their territory. These units were experienced by the citizenry as organic parts of national growth and its concomitant common spirit.

Yet to conceive the two aspects as part of the same process is a failing of the short-range view which cannot discern the laws of growth and the different principles implementing the expansion of communal and functional units. From a broader point of view the two tendencies reinforce one another only during the epoch of the nation-state. Then functional units, such as the system of business enterprise, indeed serve the nation-state, which in turn promotes industries within its boundaries. The economic policies of the so-called 'successor states' to the Austro-Hungarian Empire between the two world wars may serve as a typical illustration. But this state of fusion did not prevent the gradual rise of two serious problems.

On the one hand, the autonomous growth of the functional units often caused the unit of communal cohesion to expand, as is characteristic of economic imperialism. Aggressiveness in this case does not primarily result from communal interest *per se*, but from national we-feelings put to the service of the power promoters of industrial and commercial interests. Functional organizations become dangerous when inflated with national pride. The cure in this case is control of both factors and of their interaction on the plane of organization and education.

On the other hand, functional units may expand beyond the boundaries of communal group cohesion. Frequently boundaries are considered a handicap to their optimal performance. The functional units then begin to apply pressure against the walls of the restrictive mold. This happened, for instance, during the Middle Ages when trade and commerce expanded beyond city limits and thus laid the foundations of an economic system on a territorial, and later national, scale around which national sentiment could grow.

Today the same process seems to be repeating itself on a larger scale. Our functional units, due to mass production and improved means of communication, tend to push against the walls of the nation-state and to develop international organizations.

This growth of functional units beyond national boundaries and their ability to develop an interdependent and functional system on an international scale may lead to new types of power combinations, which are as yet unstable and shapeless but which may one day mediatize and progressively impair the sovereignty of nation-states.[35] Such obsolescence of the national power state serves the proper end whenever interdependent, world-wide functions cannot be exercised satisfactorily in terms of the single nation-state. Maladjustments, economic, social, or political, would often seem amenable to solution if supernational and functional organizations could handle them. Instead crises arise in the unco-ordinated attempts of nations to deal with such problems independently and often in competition with one another. The most blatant case in point is the attempt of one nation to transfer to other countries the burden of functional unemployment arising from opposition to methods of planning. In such a case the nation in question exports its unemployment by underselling the domestic producers of other countries. This may well become a method of domination practiced by the United States if no agreement to combat unemployment can be achieved on a world-wide basis.

The same broad maladjustment with its concomitant injustice is involved in large-scale population transfers from one country to another in order to solve economic, social, or psychological problems of the 'mother country.' Again, a world-wide, or at least regional, settlement of the underlying maladjustments and causes would offer greater opportunities for readjustment and an equitable distribution of the 'burden.'

Similarly, a psychological campaign for international tolerance cannot be launched by a single nation. The dangerous prestige sentiments of obsolete national units can only be dissipated if overlapping functional integrations act as solvents. They offer greater security in a rational and comprehensive scheme of functional world organization.

In the same manner national frustrations due to lack of markets, raw materials, and job opportunities can be overcome if the disfavored nation is integrated into the more comprehensive network of world trade and made to participate in educational and intellectual efforts to build a peaceful social order. Obviously, large-scale problems can only be solved in a broad setting, and our future depends on the control of those internationally overlapping key positions on which rests the transformation of nation-states into networks of wider range.

X. BASIC POWER PATTERNS OF TODAY

Our problem is how to gain control over the diverse centers of arbitrary power, how to co-ordinate and weld them into a more comprehensive pattern, how to discipline them gradually to function in the service of the community.

Techniques of democratic control originating in small groups will have to be adapted to today's large-scale units, both in regard to internal organization and external interrelations. This is no easy task, as small units are not always democratically controlled and large-scale units present peculiar difficulties.

As a rule the internal power pattern of nations and their domestic problems are dominated by issues raised during the transition from an unplanned to a planned society.[36] Major differences seem to result from the goal of a partially as against a totally planned society, a mixed as against a totalitarian social structure.

In the Soviet Union central authorities wield absolute power over society and even under a benevolent government democracy and freedom in their Western interpretation are absent. The dangers of this would seem to lie in the inefficiency and indifference of masses excluded from the decision-making process. Where things move in a reactionary direction, the Nazi solution is most probable: total planning for the benefit of gangster groups allied to the most reactionary forces in society.

The United States appears to be vacillating between the survival of 'rugged individualism' and piecemeal conceptions of preventive planning. Instead of taking the lead in planning, Federal authorities seem to act as arbitrator, compensating for the defects and abuses arising out of the competitive economy dominated by big monopolies.[37]

The British pattern comes closest to what we call 'planning for freedom.' There a government-steered economy tends toward balance between free and managed sectors. The danger is a lack of realization of this, which may disturb the delicate equilibrium and result in governmental controls being expropriated by a ruling group.

In the United States the main danger would seem to be that experimental readjustments in the face of another potential economic crisis might prove ineffectual. In a deep and lasting depression, sweeping and swift changes of attitude may lead to mass insurgence and overt or covert dictatorship.

In systems such as the Russian one, devolution, decentralization, and democratization in the Western sense might possibly establish a mixed system. These democratic techniques could be introduced even though the key positions would be firmly held by a central authority guaranteeing basic functions. The American and British systems also offer prospects for the emergence of halfway systems. There vigilance must focus on those special interest groups and organizations which try to establish themselves between the individual and his government, and which seek to turn over-all planning into sectional planning.

XI. BASIC POWER PATTERNS IN INTERNATIONAL RELATIONS

The war may be said to have brought one great advance. The great number of competing nations with exaggerated national pride and imperialist aspirations has been superseded by a free though still uneasy balance of power concentrated in and radiating from the U.S.A. and the U.S.S.R. It is less likely now that local tensions and conflicts will lead to world conflagration unless the great powers wish for it.

Just as cartels and syndicates of once independent business units in the economic sphere do not eliminate undercover competition so in the sphere of politics their counterparts, the world powers, will continue to compete for hegemony. Yet, their ex-

panded spheres of interest may well provide sufficient scope for
development, and once an equilibrium is attained by bargaining, imperialist pressures may subside for some time, because the
two world powers are sufficiently strong to guarantee the new
legal order. Such bipolar equilibrium might at any rate be more
stable and enduring than the unstable equilibrium of many
powers, which established the League of Nations. The old League
was possibly more democratic on paper, but it lacked 'realism'
and, having no 'teeth,' hampered rather than developed efficient
measures of ensuring a peaceful international order.

To be sure, small nations may well be favored or underprivileged according to their roles as partners or pawns in the game
of power competition under cover of agreements. Our main hope
rests in tenacious insistence on fair play on the part of political
forces spread all over the world, who are truly interested in and
stand for the transformation of present-day imperialism into a
peaceful order.

The regional power system may, of course, lead to a dangerous revival of the Westphalian Peace formula: *Cuius regio, eius
religio*. Various cultures, various political systems, openly or
more or less surreptitiously, will seek to impose their schemes of
value upon the peoples under their regional jurisdiction. Thus,
the great powers may widen the breach between their regions,
thereby heading for a final struggle for world domination. Increasing cultural cleavage in that event would foster emotional
tension and breed mutual fears and suspicions, and World War
III might be upon us for no better reason than the blind drifting
characteristic of modern society.

XII. ABUSES OF POWER AND THEIR PREVENTION

Democracy seeks to control power, whatever its forms. Our
analysis of master positions in the present world resulted in the
demand for their integration into a unified world authority able
to co-ordinate the subordinate power centers. This co-ordination should, however, beware of turning the emerging power
center into the most devastating giant in world history, which
might arbitrarily devour its own children. The problem of democratic control arises at all levels of social organization, and most
urgently at the top.

Obviously, one can hardly anticipate tactical details of a final world-wide integration, yet one may reasonably venture to discuss problems of democratic control in the near future. A balance sheet of liabilities and assets, of risks and opportunities for the control of possible abuses of power in the present age may suitably conclude this chapter.

Let us begin by listing our main dangers and risks:

1. As we have seen, an unheard-of concentration of power resulting from the centralization of new social techniques should properly head the list of danger spots.

2. The increasing physical and mental defenselessness of the average citizen is a further liability in the struggle against abuses of power. This impotence of the man in the street in the face of great powers based on correlated social techniques is, as it were, the reverse side of the medal. Turned into a mere cog in the vast social machinery, the average citizen is left in a mental state approaching apathy or agony.[38]

3. Apathy may become paralyzing if the mentally disarmed citizen is suddenly obsessed with anxiety likely to develop into mass anxiety as a result of the frightening nature of modern social crises. So long as it functions smoothly, large-scale society dispels the uncertainties of life like a sheltering mother. Once its dynamic forces get out of hand, however, and chaos prevails, social life becomes even more frightening than the blind elemental forces of nature—volcanoes, tempests, fire, and flood. Fear of uncertainty and mutual distrust, primary fruits of chaos, may lead to arbitrary exercise of power and anarchy.

4. Furthermore, latent insecurity may be systematically exploited and manipulated by men in control. Play on fear is detrimental in personal relations, highly dangerous in intergroup relations, and devastating in the competition of great power blocks. Hitler conspicuously developed the technique of arbitrary terrorism and, for a time, gained astounding concessions from a policy of appeasement. Then the inevitable happened. Unfortunately, this ancient technique for gaining the upper hand continues beyond the threshold of the Atomic age.

5. Playing with fire is the more dangerous as the momentum of organization and cumulative events in modern society keeps us from halting organized destruction—war—at short notice.

Once the course is set, organizations are set up, orders are given, emotions roused, and the great drift gets under way toward all-out destruction.

6. The dilemma of our age may be restated as follows: Our anxieties push us to extremes; lack of control leads to chaos—stringent controls confine us to a caged-in existence. Ultimately the solution depends on our insight and wisdom. Most of our technology can be used both for good and evil. The release of atomic energy is the paramount case in point. Its destructive use leads to the annihilation of man and his civilization; its constructive use may usher in the age of plenty. The same holds for most of our technological means and skills.

Now, what are the main assets and opportunities of our age?

1. Scientific advance is so rapid in the psychological as well as the technological field that an integrated science of man may enable us to understand clearly the causes of maladjustments, the sources and forms of the abuses of power. Genuine democracy is allied to rational science and the diffusion of knowledge which is greatly facilitated by excellent means of mass communication and highly developed educational skills. Swift dissemination of knowledge and information necessary for the control of power and modern debunking techniques should serve efficiently to check the hide-and-seek of power. Not every citizen need know all the ins-and-outs of jobbing and lobbying operations. If key men in the opposite camp and versatile and watchful journalists are in the know, the mere threat of public exposure often acts as a deterrent. For this reason the maintenance of civil liberties, of free speech and free assembly, acts as a catalyst even if the public is politically not yet fully mature. Abuses can be efficiently controlled even in the monopolist phase of capitalism so long as civil liberties are effectively guaranteed; whereas even under a benevolent and, let us assume, highminded dictator, deterioration is bound to take its course for want of controls.

2. The possibility of implementing democracy by the use of efficient social techniques is a further asset. Once democratic consensus in favor of democratic planning is achieved, a realistic reform policy can be inaugurated simultaneously on all levels, and arbitrary power in all its forms and ramifications can be brought under control.

G

3. But improved techniques by themselves do not solve problems such as the control of power, the redirecting of human wishes and energies. A moral and religious awakening must accompany technological knowhow. Hence it is pertinent to evaluate such of our opportunities and external conditions as are ripe for a moral revival, even though this must come from within.

Thinking in terms of humanity as a whole is no longer chimerical dreaming, but the demand of the hour. This vision may still be beyond the reach of many of our self-styled 'hard-boiled' realists whose 'realism' consists in thinking and acting according to the ideas of a bygone age. Yet, once it is realized that we cannot afford a third world war and that we must stop tyranny wherever it shows its ugly head, the vision of mankind as a whole lies open.

4. These three ideas should serve to implement a new sense of undivided and collective responsibility. It is no longer a hollow phrase to assert that we are all in the same boat. The interdependence of modern society makes one nation's famine or economic ruin a menace to others. There is little opportunity for worship of power in a society based on the indispensable contributions—material, physical, and intellectual—of millions of highly educated citizens.

5. Once this collective responsibility is realized, commonly accepted tensions may well subside all around, tensions that go with the latent-power philosophy of the old order. Power politics flourish only so long as stress and strain in the social and psychological spheres intimidate people into submitting to the domination of cliques, interest groups, parties, and nations. Any relaxation of the general stress and strain reduces anxieties, encourages people to resist suppression in workaday life and to substitute everywhere patterns of mutual deference and cooperation for those of domination and submission.

This sense of collective responsibility applies primarily to internal, though little by little also to external relations of nations. Realization of our interdependence should help to reduce the need for autarchy and protectionist economic policies. As soon as international exchange of goods and services becomes profitable, the desire for the—after all risky—enterprise of war diminishes. This psychological lesson at least we can learn from those states which for geographical and historical reasons have had opportunities for creating wealth through peaceful industry and trade. The once violent aggressiveness of their citizenries could relax and they enjoyed increasing security and higher standards of living. The more primary needs are satisfied peacefully, the more psychological tensions subside, anxiety over food and security will diminish, and people will be less inclined to power politics. This taming quality of prosperity may be illustrated not only by these historical examples, but also by the small and prosperous democracies of the Scandinavian countries, Switzerland, and so on.

Relaxation of strain and stress is facilitated by our immense productive capacity, by our means of transportation and communication, and by our systems of rational administration. Even if we cannot count on 'one world,' greatly expanded regions allow for a more equitable distribution of strains and stress among the plurality of nations than was the case within the limited bounds of protectionist nation-states. Food can be shipped from surplus regions to famine areas, credits can reduce the uneven tempo of economic development among the countries of a world region, the migration of populations can be regulated in spite of local economic or psychological states of tension. Similarly upheavals of social disintegration can first be localized, then taken care of, if the hegemony concerned should wish to stop such rivalry. Just as the Roman Empire established its *Pax Romana* among formerly bellicose peoples, so the rule of the great powers may spare us the guerrilla wars of small brigand states.

This venture in creating order and security for a long period to come and over a widespread area would diminish aggression, even were the superpowers to undertake it for the usual reasons of mere expediency. Still, the emerging peaceful order would be stronger and more constructive if such measures were part of a policy deliberately planned as an experiment in transforming bellicose domineering mentalities into peaceloving ones.

6. An additional factor that may help to diminish tension, dissipate power monopolies, and lessen the power complex is the new means and techniques of warfare.

The new weapons greatly reduce the military significance of national boundary lines. It does not, of course, disappear completely, but it is diminished to the extent that airpower makes space shrink and atom bombs threaten to carry warfare anywhere.[39] Countries can now be attacked from afar. Long-distance attack requires only bases for naval and airpower which may be remote from their target areas. This new military threat makes Maginot lines or any closed lines of attack and defense more and more obsolete.

Britain's military policy in the Middle and Far East may serve to illustrate the new tendencies. The occupation or direct domination of entire countries such as Egypt or India can be dispensed with in favor of free co-operation under the guarantee that bases remain in reliable hands. The new spatial concepts of security for the United States have led to the establishment of a far-flung system of naval and air bases in seemingly 'outlying' areas. The new range of military power promotes mutual defense agreements of vast world regions under the hegemony of the great powers.

This tendency might be stronger if the superstates did not suspect one another. Not only would the tensions between them be eased but also those within their regions. The age-old justification for imperialism was the fear of actual or presumed external aggression. Were this fear to be reduced, increased armaments, excessive police powers, and dictatorship could hardly be justified.

The elimination of superannuated conflicts from international relations will, of course, not eradicate all at once domineering aggressiveness and fears. Psychology teaches us that fears may survive their original causes. This holds all the more for century-old sentiments. Still a re-educational campaign co-ordinated with the relaxation of stress and strain could achieve much in a relatively short time. A law which I propose calling the 'law of condensation and co-ordination of operations' might prove effective. By this I mean that social change can be achieved swiftly by constant co-ordinated efforts in the desired direction. The Nazis and the Russians have developed this technique and achieved in a relatively short time changes that otherwise might have taken centuries. They used these techniques for their particular ends. We could use them for ours, for the reduction of aggression and domination.

4

The Ruling Class in Capitalist and Communist Society [1]

c

I. THE RUSSIAN EXPERIMENT APPRAISED

One source of confusion and obstacle to the reformist transformation of society is the utopian idea of a classless society,[2] lack of clarity about the class concept, and the widespread assumption of inevitable class war. Thorough analysis of these ideas can show their interrelationship. Since these concepts are derived from the revolutionary interpretation of Marxism they are from the outset so framed as to exclude reform.

In the history of human thought the definition of basic terms usually determines the form, direction, and conclusion of the argument. It attests to Marx's powerful system of ideas that all his concepts are mutually supplementary: the reformer must have the courage to rethink and redefine his terms.

Marx was great in raising the crucial problems of society, but his answers are rooted in the expectation of inevitable class war. In our view this merely reflects an era of scarcity, a premise from which Marx drew unwarranted generalizations. Besides, techniques of social reform were still unknown and undeveloped in his time. Class struggle may be inevitable in the face of states of inordinate tension. But an alternative course is at least feasible when pressure generated by scarcity can be reduced and necessary changes can be undertaken in an atmosphere free from tension.[3]

Marx described and analyzed certain aspects of his society realistically, but advocated a utopian means-end scheme of political development without visualizing feasible alternatives. He overemphasized the destructive elements of capitalist bourgeois society and was rather optimistic in assuming that once certain institutions were removed, the good society would emerge spontaneously, maintain its internal balance, and produce rational and truly human personalities.

Our first task, then, is to analyze existing conditions realistically, to distinguish the weak from the valuable components of our society, and to examine the danger spots in contemporary planned societies. This procedure, however, should not blind us to their achievement, which would be lost to us if we adhered to the *status quo*.

Any analysis of the failure of the Russian experiment faces two alternatives. One may say that Soviet society is no socialist society, and that we hope for a better experiment, this being more or less the Trotskyist attitude. Or, with the Stalinists, one may point to the adverse circumstances of the Russian experiment, the threat of a hostile environment, the war and its ramifications. Thus, one might ascribe all shortcomings to unfavorable conditions and events, and even dismiss the unpleasant features of Soviet bureaucracy as Tsarist survivals.[4] In contrast to both points of view we shall try to steer between undesirable developments, on the one hand, which may indeed be ascribed to the unfavorable conditions of the Russian experiment, and on the other hand, those which apparently result from certain structural difficulties in a society planned on Leninist lines.

As to the success or failure of the Russian experiment in terms of its professed original purposes, one is mainly struck by the absence of a classless society. The experiment succeeded in expropriating the means of production; aside from minor qualifications no private citizen can own such means. Yet the U.S.S.R. failed to do away with inequalities of power and income. What are the reasons for these deviations from the original idea of a classless society?

II. THE PATTERN OF CAPITALIST SOCIETY

To be sure, the U.S.S.R. succeeded in eradicating the traditional type of domination, where a money economy based on competition and family inheritance evolves ruling classes whose ownership and control of the industrial machine allow them to dominate the population. Their mainstay is chiefly a broad middle class.[5] The profit system and various other mechanisms, among them primarily the educational system, offer opportunities for social ascent to members of the middle class and allow them to stabilize their acquired social positions. They are interested in preserving the existing order and function as a balance wheel between the tendencies toward upper-class excess and lower-class revolution. The middle class have a stabilizing power because they develop a psychology of balance: they are equally afraid of being suppressed by an oligarchy or wiped out by the proletariat. Given sufficient mobility between the classes, the possibility of social ascent from lower- to middle-class positions, and adequate security for the underprivileged, revolutions are unlikely. For people in a flexible society with established equilibrium are rather frightened of change, and knowing the dangers of a sudden fall, aim at avoiding the uncertainties of upheaval.

These balancing tendencies are strengthened in a capitalist society by the prevalent political and social institutions. As long as capitalism is still in the making, mass organizations are either avoided or strictly controlled. All real life is relegated to small voluntary associations. So-called 'organic groups' are favored, such as the family, the community, or voluntary associations in the nature of clubs, unions, and colleges. Economic life centers around the farm, workshop, small business firms. Despite a certain amount of social rank[6] there is interchange among the members; people depend on one another. All of them see more or less clearly the common tasks and special functions, and personalities are molded by sharing responsibilities.

This internal interchange is supplemented externally by the functional interdependence of various associations. As the modern party system evolves,[7] great care is taken not to preclude constant regrouping, even when mass parties become unavoidable. Thus fluidity and mobility remain possible. Finally, the State is not conceived as the source or creator of these groups, but as a controlling and supervisory agency. Accordingly authority is conceived not as overlordship but as the enforcement of rules emanating from association.[8]

This structural balance is ultimately the source of the political and social freedom of the individual. It keeps everyone in his place and prevents undue excesses liable to destroy this state of equilibrium.

These conditions prevail in a steadily expanding economy, free from large fluctuations between 'boom' and 'bust.' The hope of the reformer rests on the expectation that with modern techniques of social planning even the contemporary society of large-scale capitalism can be balanced. What matters is the fact that the upper and middle classes have a stake in the creation and preservation of a stable societal framework by conceding sufficient social services and social improvements to the lower classes to give the latter also a stake in the social order and make them a stabilizing element. On the basis of our modern understanding of the economic process, leaders of the middle classes must realize that only steady prosperity and an adequate rise in purchasing power for all can guarantee continuance of social equilibrium.

Thus a natural pressure in the social order, as it were, runs counter to the oligarchic tendencies of the ruling groups and makes some of them ready for farsighted compromise. Timely realization of this need for compromise is certainly a question of enlightenment. But we do not think of enlightenment as a substitute for sound economic policy or as productive *per se* of social co-operation. Enlightened policies become constructive only when implemented by modern techniques of social reconstruction.

III. THE PATTERN OF COMMUNIST SOCIETY

In fairness to the Russian experiment one may evaluate as positive achievement the abolition of traditional private ownership of the means of production and the end of hereditary transmission of power along class lines. Inherited privilege has been replaced largely by reward of merit. The Russians also made great strides in linking status to function and in promoting local and occupational mobility, though largely under administrative co-ercion.[9] Social distances seem to have been reduced, and on the whole fewer opportunities seem to exist for individuals and families to make their acquired power positions hereditary. Last but not least, nothing prevents production for use instead of for private profit, as there are no vested interests aiming at specula-tion and restriction of production. Aside from social considera-tions of accumulation there is no reason for curtailing the pur-chasing power of the masses, and steady employment seems to be assured.

Though Soviet Russia thus has remedied a number of short-comings of capitalist society, she finds herself confronted with new difficulties which the capitalist system has solved fairly satis-factorily. Her crucial problem was how to establish social stabil-ity without providing entire social strata with an economic and/or hereditary interest in preserving the *status quo*? However objectionable the system of private and hereditary property may be in the light of social justice, it fulfils one necessary function by inducing certain classes to identify their interests with the stability of society. Once this method of providing for social stability is discarded, a practicable substitute has to be found, for any social order would prove unstable and could be over-thrown at a moment's notice unless it contained groups holding a vested interest in its existence.[10]

After the downfall of the old ruling class, a leading group had to emerge with sufficient coherence and the will to identify itself with the new social system. This identification has been established mainly by political rather than economic means.

The assignment of social rank without using the traditional factors of private property and income for defining status was equally difficult. Again, political instead of economic means had to serve.

Finally, the provision of work incentives and discipline by means other than the profit motive among middle and upper level groups or the fear of starvation among the lower strata presented another major problem. Once the invisible pressure of unemployment no longer threatened, greater use had to be made of political means.

In other words three sets of difficulties had to be overcome:

how to produce a new ruling group fit to guarantee a stable social order, how to discover new status-defining factors other than income and property, and how to provide new work incentives.

The answers to these problems were institutions that are neither ephemeral nor fortuitous features, but meet essential requirements of Stalinist society.

The most important are, first, the One-Party-System, with its peculiar methods of integration and coercion, and, secondly, wage differentials and other graded social rewards reintroduced contrary to the original belief in social equality. Consequently, new power and status disparities have emerged in place of the old inequalities of wealth and income.

The fact that these institutions emerged as solutions of inherent difficulties of the new system does not, of course, preclude the invention of better solutions in the future. In any case these institutional features of Stalinist society should be regarded as more basic than those shortcomings that may be ascribed to the historical vicissitudes of the Russian experiment.

IV. THE VALUE OF GRADED REWARDS

The reintroduction of income differentials ranging from one to twenty, of opportunities to save and invest savings in state bonds, of hereditary personal property and of small holdings for collective farmers prove that graded rewards were necessary to stimulate individual effort. Thus, the Russians rediscovered what capitalist society knows all too well: that income differentials are still the cheapest means of gaining maximum effort from the citizenry. Soviet application of the principle does teach, however, that graded rewards are justified if they stimulate social productivity, but unjust if they merely perpetuate inherited privilege.

Besides, the Soviet government was shrewd enough to realize that social emulation for prestige, fame, success, and individual and group competition, combined with graded money rewards, add to efficiency. Thus, stimulation of effort rests not on a single inducement but on a combination of incentives. In this Soviet policy admits that, though all competition is socially rooted, different incentives and rewards appeal to different individuals.

In principle, this is not new, since in every society there have been various forms of rivalry in use. What is new is the studied combination of various rewards and bonuses and their consistent focus on social productivity. Under the Soviet the technique of group competition and the social glorification of 'heroes of labor' as symbolized by the Stakhanovites, fill the same role as graded wage rates. One may well speak of this deliberate combination as a novel technique of manipulating incentives.[11]

Wage differentials and graded rewards, however, do not serve merely as work incentives. They have also a stabilizing function in Soviet society as a substitute for the stabilizing power of inherited property under capitalism. Differential income establishes differential status and endears each position—except the lowliest one—to the person who holds it. In a society of equals nobody would take risks as each position would be equally precious or rather, equally valueless, whereas in a graded society everybody (except the humblest) jealously guards his own. Although man continuously strives for betterment, his achieved status is considered a niche guaranteed by the existing order. Thus, a bond is established between man's self-respect and self-interest and the social order.

Although this again is not a new principle, the Soviet system has excelled other societies in manipulating these social forces. It abolished private ownership of the means of production and what the Marxists call the 'private exploitation of labor,' and also free financial speculation. After some experiments, however, saving was again encouraged by way of private investment in state bonds which may be bequeathed. By these means the successful individual becomes a bondholder interested in the state as in a capitalist enterprise, without acquiring, however, the power of financial direction. He cannot speculate against the interest of the community or invest money in a line of production that might run counter to the generally accepted plan.

V. DESIRABLE AND UNDESIRABLE EQUALITY

The reintroduction of wage differentials and graded rewards in the Soviet system seems to call for reconsideration of the meaning of equality. The ideal of equality must be qualified by a distinction between desirable and undesirable equality. There is one form of equality, or rather 'leveling,' that seems connected with factory work, and especially with the increasing role of unskilled and semiskilled labor. Standardized performance and similarity of income create an impression of mechanical equality which is projected into society at large. In making this impression an ideal the propagandists have disregarded the dehumanizing effects of leveling equality and the absence of opportunities for personal distinction or for creative outlets for the power drive in man.[12]

This mechanical equality may be contrasted with the kind of equality prevalent among craftsmen and small landholders of the past. The oldtime craftsmen were roughly equal in status with only moderate gradations. In the craft guilds the individual worker not only had an opportunity to express himself creatively in his work [13] but could even gain distinction by producing a *Meisterwerk*. Varying grades in the evaluation of workmanship led to higher rank and added to the zest for life.

This craving for distinction and for the continuous approval of one's fellow workers differs from the megalomania fostered by the excessive inequalities of power and prestige of modern society. It differs also from the pride and vanity associated with inherited privilege rather than personal achievement. Handled skilfully, and within bounds, social differentiation provides a number of stimuli that operate on different individuals in different ways and thereby produce a great variety of social patterns and personality types.[14]

With regard to the formation of the personality, traditional society differs from that of the age of mass organization. The old order, despite a tendency to insist on conformity in its smaller sub-units, shows on the whole considerable diversity of motivation patterns, habits, and expectations, whereas the society of the masses tends to create standard mentalities, the mass-produced man. The greater variations in traditional society are due to greater effectiveness in personality formation on the part of small groups and associations such as the family, the artisan's workshop—ethnic, primary groups, geographic, occupational units of all sorts. When it comes to over-all integration, adjustment results from multilateral tensions in such a society of diversified conditioning processes.

The individual bred in a differentiated society hates to be subject to a simple, undifferentiated, hence 'abstract' rule. This hatred was first expressed in the struggle against the attempt of absolutism to establish greater homogeneity in its political territories. Hatred breaks out with every new wave of standardization. The man of differential conditioning prefers working out his own solution to striving for agreement among many conflicting attitudes. When integration is imperative he will at first show stubborn resistance. Once this is broken, however, he will be willing to adapt himself to co-operation with men and women of different background, status, or descent.

Thus stratification by status is not harmful but on the contrary creative and stimulating for the shaping of personalities. Social stratification becomes harmful only when it loses fluidity, freezing into a rigid hierarchy that breeds exclusiveness and segregation and turns the pressure of the upper into oppression of the lower classes.[15] Differences then harden into prejudice, hindering communication and exchange of ideas among groups. Segregated groups are compelled to develop into status-ridden cliques [16] and through this defense mechanism lose their desire and qualifications for common life or adjustment to broad social change.

To demand that proper stratification be achieved by social control is by no means asking the impossible. Societies in the past developed codes of good and bad conduct which brought home to the individual the importance of social approval. Similarly, a planned society could develop social codes to define desirable conduct patterns for group relationships. Expressions of group pretensions or of an excessive clannishness could be exposed to ridicule if the community were to set itself seriously to the task of group co-ordination and co-operation.

Once suitable methods of group co-ordination are established, combining spontaneous growth and diversity with controlled integration, society could dispense with the frequent use of administrative coercion. It could also renounce manipulation by means of mass communication from remote centers, for though this produces unity, it is likely to foster the standardized mass-mind.

VI. OVERLAPPING OF STATUS DISTINCTIONS

Group differences and their concomitant differences in attitude are politically significant in various ways. They act as a check on modern Mass-Man,[17] whose mind is prone to slogans and satisfied with oversimplified formulae. They operate as a psychological shock absorber throughout society, helping to prevent one-sided cleavages which rend society in two.

Status differences are based on a number of factors.[18] We may call the distinctions created by wealth and income primary, and those of ethnic and family background, of geographic, occupational, and educational variation, secondary distinctions. These differences show up in speech, manners, food preferences, customs, and the like. All these dissimilarities not only multiply graded distinctions, but their continuous overlap prevents the definition of a person's status in terms of a single criterion.

This overlap is significant as it provides various foci and outlets for ambition, and thus gives opportunities to all to compensate for shortcomings and inferiority feelings due to failure in a single field of endeavor. One who cannot be proud of his family background may compensate by aspiring to a good education and professional status. Another, falling short in scientific achievement, may excel in sports or civic organization, or he may pride himself upon belonging to a traditional or pioneer group.

The function of overlapping distinctions in providing compensatory opportunities for injured pride again has a stabilizing effect on the social structure as a whole. It prevents any single status from taking precedence over others. It is just as dangerous to exaggerate racial or cultural differences as political and economic differences. Every absolute breach prevents the gradual reformation of society. A jug may easily break along the line of a single crack but may last a long while with several intersecting cracks. Great variations in man's activities and alignments are the best guarantee for cohesion and continuity. Marx saw but one way to transform the capitalist economy: by revolution. Hence, it was consistent with his singlemindedness that he sought to eliminate overlapping shades and conceive of a situation in which the economic alternatives would be decisive and all-inclusive. It might seem equally consistent for advocates of reform strategy to impute paramount importance to these secondary status distinctions.

But here, too, everything depends upon proper balance. Both primary and secondary status distinctions may bring about such great and dangerous variety of modulations in individual and group aspirations as to endanger the democratic consensus necessary for co-ordination and planning. Chaos in modern society cannot be avoided by relying solely on the spontaneous balance attained by the interplay of divergent aims and volitions. The Russian planner will have to face the problem of how to keep the re-emerging status differentiation within bounds. The task of the redistributive society of the future will be to control strictly those personal and group aspirations that run counter to the agreed plan. This does not exclude, however, a marked tolerance toward some personal property, or other factors of social status differentiation, so long as these do not disturb public economic policy, but rather help people to identify themselves with a social order guaranteeing them their cherished differences, and thereby gaining necessary stability.

VII. POWER DIFFERENTIATION

Focusing our attention again on the Soviet Union, we find that not only class and status differences were reintroduced there but also inequalities of power. Order was established by a system of strictly organized social units in place of the power that in Western societies emanates from ownership and inheritance and is expressed in open class stratification aiming at balance. In the Soviet Union stability has been achieved by making mass organizations such as trade unions, co-operatives, trusts, industrial concerns, in addition to the press, the bureaucracy, and the army, the bases of the social structure. These are all placed under an equally strong organization comprising the ruling class, i.e. the Communist party.

The Russians in so doing did not invent something altogether new. Rather they pushed to its logical conclusions a development latent in all modern large-scale societies, that is, syndicalism both at the top and bottom of the social structure. Western democratic society still represents a dominant combination of innumerable small communities and groups (such as the family, the village) with a great conglomeration of voluntary associations (such as religious associations, lodges, and so on), on the one hand, and mass syndicates such as trade unions, co-operatives, etc. on the other.[19]

The Syndicalists [20] were the first to realize the significance of mass organization in modern society. They saw that organized groups held together not by ephemeral or multiple purposes but by some basic sectional interest are powerful social agents, alone capable of concerted action in the new medium of mass society.

The syndicate, e.g. trade union, focuses all its energies on its sectional interests and by this method achieves both intensity and continuity of action. This latent power becomes apparent when implemented by modern means of propaganda. It is greater still when the members adhere to a quasi-philosophical creed which keeps their minds oriented to a common end. At this point mass discipline can be developed which allows for the execution of consistent policies through the ups and downs of tactical contingencies.[21]

The Syndicalists also realized that the masses *per se* can only form a regiment and provide momentum, but that the rank and file cannot hammer out a consistent policy or take the initiative.[22] Leadership functions hence require an active minority, which in turn attains optimum efficiency only when welded into a fighting sect. This insight and method might have been borrowed from the Jesuits, who were the first order to recognize the significance of *propaganda fidei* and the efficiency of a disciplined fighting organization based upon the tenets of a creed.[23]

The totalitarian one-party-state hence represents the adaptation of a ruling class to the age of mass organization where the primary source of power no longer rests on ownership and small associations but on large-scale organization in control of the means of violence, communication, and administration.

There are but two ways of checking the power of the great syndicates. First, a new type of balance may be established between them, which I suggest calling 'block balance.' Block balance represents, not an equilibrium of countless small enterprises, communities, and voluntary associations, but the mutual toleration of the large sectional organizations which are func-

tionally interrelated and eventually come to realize their interdependence.

Secondly, a 'super-group' may be established, independent of
sectional organizations but recruiting members from, and/or in-
filtrating, all of them. By having members in all subordinate
·organizations, its influence may permeate all; being a 'super-
power,' it is bound to watch their co-operation according to an
established plan. This is obviously the Party. The totalitarian
party is the ruling class in a world of total syndicalization. The
further syndicalization advances, the more nearly we approach
the stage of the 'organized ruling class.' [24]

If this holds true, the social structure of the Soviet Union obviously does not represent a classless society but is a structure
with a new kind of upper class organized in a totalitarian party
and with mass organizations as a base. The totalitarian party
splits the people even more rigidly along class lines than is the
case in traditional societies. The decision-making groups are
sharply set off from the majority, who have no say in important
policy issues and are free to discuss means only. As all key positions in political, economic, and military organizations are held
by party members, the imposition of the party line would not
necessarily appear arbitrary. In 1936 industrial management was
entirely in the hands of party members, representing between
50 to 70 per cent of the total party membership. The key positions in labor unions, co-operatives, press and publishing establishments, and so on, were likewise held by party members.[25]

The Western and the Russian ruling classes, of course, differ
in that the former are largely hereditary in nature. Despite the
introduction of fees in Russian institutions of higher learning
and the educational privileges extended to the progeny of the
officer corps and administrative officials of all sorts, we should
remember that 70 per cent of the party members did not join
until 1929, i.e. after Stalin's victory over Trotsky, and only 8.3
per cent of the members joined the party before 1920.[26]

In comparing Western social organization with the Soviet system, we can apply Max Weber's distinction between individual
and collective appropriation of power.[27] The former is regulated
in terms of competition among the members at large of a ruling
stratum, whereas the second follows the pattern we know in our

H

defense and executive organizations. An army, for instance, represents an accumulation of power which is not to be won by free competition but through the assignment of legally and conventionally defined greater or smaller shares of that power to various officers according to their rank, which defines their jurisdictions. Whereas in Western society with its flexibly organized classes every capitalist or member of the ruling class may more or less accurately assess his personal share of power in terms of property, income, and social position open to free competition, in Russia the party and bureaucracy have collectively appropriated all positions of power and allot shares to individuals according to their respective status.[28]

This is no reflection on the Soviet system, as no large-scale society can be administered without men in power. Granted this premise, the idea of a classless society (meaning originally the negation of all inequalities of power, hence of power *per se*, and the disappearance of all class-domination) is clearly utopian.[29]

The true issue is whether the collectivist appropriation of power by an organized group or political order is preferable to individual appropriation by a loosely connected, historically developed, and gradually expanding ruling stratum. The sociological problem therefore boils down to analysis of the differences between a highly organized, dominating party and a historically integrated class composed of ruling groups. Cohesion among the latter rests not on organization but on a web of social relationships that enables them to wield power through contacts.

Collective appropriation of power with apportionment of differential shares is not new. In simpler societies the system has existed since time immemorial.[30] In certain preliterate societies the hunting team is the joint owner of the hunting ground and all members co-operate to increase the bag. The subsequent distribution follows rules of graded equity, not of equality. None goes empty, but the better hunter or rather the hunter with higher prestige gets a larger share.

In a communist society one of the main objects of distribution is power, i.e. the privilege of making important decisions, of assuming responsibilities and controlling the activities of subordinates, of winning prestige and admission to still more influential groups. In one respect this ruling group [31] is more strictly exclusive than in Western society, because 'admission to the party' is subject to certain jealously guarded selective principles. Proved efficiency is not enough; there are criteria of loyalty to the cause and of like-mindedness. It would be erroneous to think the one-party-system less exclusive than that of older ruling classes. The tendency toward segregation and the studious efforts to create an *esprit de corps* are even stronger than among Western ruling classes. The latter promote cohesion by subtle devices which operate on all levels of the mind, conscious and unconscious. The cohesion of a historical ruling class is ensured primarily by tacit consensus rooted partly in the common vested interest through ownership and inheritance, and partly in common customs, attitudes, and mores which are informally acquired and transmitted from generation to generation.

As historically developed cohesion is increasingly and covertly established on different planes, there is no need for strict indoctrination of orthodox dogmas,[32] dictatorial pressure, purges,[33] and political police.[34] An organized ruling group, however, especially one that owes its ascent to revolution, is bound to create cohesion on short notice, hence will use ruthless forms of regimentation both in admission to its ranks and in building permanent loyalties.

VIII. LESSONS OF THE RUSSIAN EXPERIMENT

Replacement of the traditional ruling class of Russia by an organized party and establishment of the new social order by fiat naturally required greater ruthlessness than the growing order that developed from established vested interests. This fact has been unduly exploited and misused by propagandists, often intent on glorifying and perpetuating the existing ruling classes of the West. While any complex society requires a ruling class, this need neither justifies the *hybris* of a particular ruling class nor exempts its members and agents from the control of society which they must serve in their ruling capacity.

Hence, if we favor the gradual remodeling of our traditional ruling classes instead of their outright replacement by a completely new social order, we may profit by the lessons of historical experiments. These lessons may be stated briefly as follows:

1. Doubtless the advent of a ruling class in the form of a totalitarian party does not represent historical progress but is at best a solution *faute de mieux* in an historical situation offering no alternative way out.

2. This stage of development is reached by a society split exclusively along lines of imbalanced sectional mass organizations. A time comes when the even stronger totalitarian party seizes the opportunity to establish block balance among the syndicates and co-ordinates them along functional lines.

3. So long as capitalist society is still in a state of transformation, development can be guided and the growth and sway of powerful syndicates can be kept in check. Although in industrial large-scale society it is impossible to forestall mass organization along class lines, it makes all the difference whether they maintain their give-and-take through bargaining under state control or whether they are allowed to control the state. Prevention of the drift toward totalitarian states demands strengthening the organic groups, voluntary small associations, and the like, as useful counterweights to sectional consolidation. The political freedom of the citizen must be carefully guarded lest he be mobilized in his sectional role [35] and lest parliament be transformed into a representation of sectional mass organizations.

4. In order to prevent the domination of sectional organizations over society at large, a broad section of people with property on a moderate scale is desirable. Their status and interest operate as stabilizing elements and they represent middle-class culture which for centuries has been basic to Western tradition. Western tradition, being dynamic, may undergo significant transformation. It still provides the best point of departure for new cultural developments. Recent decades have shown that the sudden liquidation of entire middle classes and their traditions in central Europe has resulted in a mass civilization which is rejected by high-minded men of these very same civilizations.

Thoughtful Americans too are not uncritical in face of naive 'gadget worship' and the frequent identification of technological efficiency with moral advancement. They are far from accepting the pursuit of the dollar and economic success as supreme values.[36] Similarly, thoughtful Germans detest that spirit of hyperorganization and militarization which ultimately led to Hitler.

Finally, it may not be too farfetched to suppose that admirers of the Soviet Union, though taking pride in her social progress and economic advance, yet have misgivings about her dictatorial practices and mass-mindedness. These drawbacks are usually said to be unavoidable momentarily, but hardly to be commended as the final pattern of a new civilization. Indicative of intellectual dissatisfaction may be the fact that some years ago the Soviet Union launched a new educational campaign, translating the classics of the ascending *bourgeoisie* (such as Schiller, Lessing, and so on, and honoring them as exponents of a great legacy and a source of inspiration representing a new revolutionary spirit and 'realism' in literary art. Great admiration for Shakespeare, Goethe, and Balzac is also justified on the grounds of 'realism' despite their conservative political attitudes.[37]

5. The right course for the democratic forces of the West is not blindly to attack the old ruling groups, but to remodel them into a transitional group angled toward a new type of social leadership. This can best be effected by enlarging their ranks by providing opportunities of ascent for all sections of the population, with no lower but rather higher standards of selection. Once admitted, newcomers will absorb valuable elements of upper-class traditions and skills.[38]

Whatever form the new society may develop during this period of transition, leadership functions will have to be filled by somebody. The problem of social engineering is not so much how to push mechanical equalitarianism to a dead level, but how to provide sufficient opportunities for social ascent by supporting and encouraging initiative and enterprise for the rejuvenation of traditional leadership by infusions of new blood. In our view the quality of a society should nct and cannot be evaluated by the presence or absence of a ruling class but by its methods of selecting leaders, the range of opportunities for ascent, and the social value of leadership functions in the ruling class.

IX. METHODS OF SELECTING LEADERS

We should distinguish between two ways of choosing leaders, by traditional methods or by scientific selection.

Different social orders follow different ways of selecting leadership. However varied the qualifications for leadership, they usually are not rationally designed and decreed, although rational elements may occasionally enter in.[39] In a society of warriors fighting skill will determine selection. This chief criterion, however, is generally combined with prestige by descent and kinship. A priestly caste may demand proof of magic powers as prerequisite. Feudal society added landed estates to military prowess and noble birth. With the growth of commerce and industry, the ability to make money or mere inheritance of wealth became the decisive factor.

In the unplanned society of today no hard and fast rule defines criteria for admission to the ruling groups. Some of the current criteria represent survivals of the past; others emerge with demands for social change. Medieval society required a religious bent and executive talent in the selection and education of its clerics; the seventeenth and eighteenth centuries valued intellect and erudition regardless of theological bias to meet the sudden need for a secular bureaucracy in Continental Europe.

All these traditional methods of selecting leaders, regardless of differences, have one element in common. The nature of 'success' and the traits of the 'successful man' are never explicitly defined or measured. If, for instance, people consider financial success the criterion for leadership in a plutocratic society, we do not know whether such success results from personal initiative, from speculative and imaginative foresight, from organizing ability, or from unscrupulous ruthlessness, good luck, the ability to impress other people, or a mercenary marriage. If people deem 'the struggle for life' the best means of selection, or if they cherish the belief that the gifted man will always rise to the top, they merely express their justification of the ruling classes. As Gustav Ichheiser [40] pointed out,

All our generalized statements about the nature of success, such as 'fortes fortuna adiuvat' or the opposite that 'the great thieves get away with it and the little ones are hanged' cannot be taken at their face value or as factual observations. Mostly they represent justifications of an existing social order by the successful men or they express the dissatisfaction of the underprivileged.

The current transformation of an unplanned society of group and personal competition into a planned society will result in increasingly systematic ways of selecting leaders. Instead of taking for granted that free competition will automatically bring the right man to the top, we shall become more critically aware of desirable qualities for leadership and of special talents for the performance of special functions.[41] This change will entail the development and improvement of scientific measurement of desirable personality traits and skills.

X. SCIENTIFIC SELECTION AND ITS LIMITATIONS

Scientific selection for jobs began in those fields of vocational guidance where simple skills and abilities could be isolated and measured. The growth of society demands scientific selection not only for simple routine jobs but also for more demanding posts and complex functions. Specific aptitude tests are bound to become more comprehensive. In due course they will be fashioned into reliable tools. Instead of dealing only with separate traits, special skills, and intelligence, the study of total personality will be increasingly developed.[42]

Scientific selection and supervision by means of systematic records have been developed in the schools.[43] The school population is periodically tested, and the children's development, like that of hospital patients, is subject to regular and systematic control. Modern schools, besides administering intelligence tests, keep elaborate records not only of scholastic achievement but also of character traits, and furnish over the years profiles of maturation and growth. But so far the trend to survey the entire school population is restricted largely to skills and personality traits relevant to academic progress in the conventional sense. It has been balanced by a countertendency to emphasize the individual and by case-study methods to examine the whole career of a particular student against his background and personality traits. This approach refrains from techniques of group diagnosis, emphasizing qualitative as against quantitative analysis.

Despite its qualitative nature the case-study method can counterbalance arbitrary observations of a single teacher by combining staff members into a co-operative team of trained observers. The staff is assisted by a psychologist and a psychiatrist who check the teachers' observations and interpretations. Conclusions based on qualitative case studies allegedly have 'greater predictive value than the objective tests used either singly or in combination.' [44]

Undoubtedly these still largely experimental methods promise to become efficient tools in selecting leaders. All-round observation and follow-up studies will ensure increasingly sound diagnosis and reliable prognosis. Well-staffed schools may become preliminary screening centers for future leaders. But the greater the potentialities of such 'clinical' methods of observation, the more we must guard against their potential abuse.

The British Education Act of 1944, for instance, established three types of secondary schools: the grammar, the technical, and the modern school.* One cannot but wonder whether this division and the briefs for it do not lend a pseudopsychological cloak to discrimination actually rooted in class distinctions rather than based on the alleged basic abilities and preferences of the pupils. Teachers and psychologists should make it their rule to protest against abuses of science for stabilizing and rationalizing social prejudice.

Guarded against such exploitation, scientific selection promises a method of choice more strictly according to ability and merit. It will fit the man better to his job and make the job fit the man. Generally speaking it will aid different types of men to find suitable places in an ever more differentiated society of expanding opportunities. The new techniques of job analysis should be mentioned in this connection as they reveal the combination of special aptitudes and personality traits demanded for a particular job.

The more thorough, broad application of scientific methods, however, discloses their limitation. Even a whole battery of scientific tests cannot do away with the laboratory nature of this method of selection. It serves best in selecting people for definitely prescribed tasks and routines. Despite the constant flux of social change and the vicissitudes of modern life, many such routine jobs still exist. Army life, including combat service, not to mention Civil Service and industrial management, enables us to define fairly predictable job patterns and to test differential aptitude and degrees of adaptability.

---

* The grammar school is roughly equivalent to the academic high school in the United States; the modern school, to the U.S. elementary school. [Ed.]

World War II brought with it a wide application of the new scientific techniques. The Germans were the first to apply their methods on a large scale; the War Office Selection Board in the British Army and the respective personnel selection agencies of the U.S. Armed Forces followed suit and revolutionized mass selection by extending scientific methods of selection and assignment to all ranks of their armies. Sir Ronald Adams organized and systematized the new approach in Great Britain on realizing the shortcomings of old-fashioned methods of interviewing boards when one half of their recommended candidates for commission proved to be unsuitable.

The hidden favoritism of these boards became obvious. Interviewers were primarily interested in whether or not the candidates shared their idiosyncrasies, their manners and ways of thought. Increasing distrust of the older methods of selection led to postwar adaptation of new techniques and methods also for personnel selection in British Civil Service and industry.

We should, however, beware of the assumption that actual placements in large-scale organizations, even if jobs were as rigidly defined in function and rank as in the army, coincide with organization blueprints in administrative manuals and scientific assignment schedules. In a highly competitive society, persons trained for competition will find many ways and means of carrying competitive tactics and stratagems, fair or foul, into what seem strictly planned, graded, disciplined, and methodically administered organizations. In general one may venture to say that in America more than in Europe large-scale organizations are characterized by informal cliques, flexibly competitive fields, overlapping of actual power distribution and 'blueprint' authority, and eagerness to develop charts, schedules, 'rules and regulations,' and 'scientific' devices and hurdles according to managerial plans. The U.S. Army as an army of 'civilian soldiers' may be said to illustrate characteristics of American society in extreme form.[45]

XI. CO-ORDINATED METHODS OF SELECTION

Efficiency in dynamic spheres of life requires responses and abilities that adequately meet the changing demands of the situation. Here a good case can be made for competition as a selective mechanism. Not only does rivalry measure whatever traits and skills ensure well-defined performances, but it puts persons into situations that test resourcefulness and call forth the requisite combination of latent capacities. Competition not only measures but helps to produce successful men and failures.

A planned society will indeed know fields of endeavor demanding initiative for unpredictable decisions from men who can hardly be discovered by scientific preselection. The vicissitudes of a dynamic world cannot be foreseen by a scientific selecting agency. Even a planned society will have to choose political leaders who prove and mold themselves in actual struggle and public competition for leadership, for the triumph of their respective ideas, for the trust and confidence of the citizenry. A centrally planned society without zones of free competition will have difficulty finding in the second generation qualified successors to the pioneer personality types of the original initiators. Men trained to obey and do routine tasks set for them by others are hardly men of initiative when they reach the top.

For these and similar reasons the Third Way should preserve existing fields of free competition alongside the planned sectors, just as it will have to find ways of combining scientific and other methods of selecting personnel.

The need for the coexistence of the two selective methods and of the correspondingly planned and unplanned sectors was realized when the growth of the modern Civil Service threw the issue into bold relief.[46] It has frequently been argued that the Civil Service should be led by qualified political leaders, victorious in free political competition and capable of checking and balancing the career officials who discharge their routine tasks in an environment of pre-established gradations. The country—so ran the argument—should depend upon the interplay of the two types of public servants. Hence, modern democracies in an age of bureaucratic administration already are aware of the coexistence of the two sectors of society and their respective types of leaders. Recent developments have led to a great expansion of the planned sectors and an upsurge of executive agencies outside the traditional Civil Service. The more powerful this sector becomes, the more imperative it will be to invigorate public struggle and competition for political leadership.

XII. BROADENING THE BASIS OF SELECTION (THE BRITISH SITUATION)

For some time one of the issues of Western democracy has been how to broaden the social selection of leading groups. No doubt one of the weaknesses of present-day England lies in the very narrow selection of her ruling classes. One might rather speak of an oligarchy than of a democracy when thinking of the social makeup in contrast to the constitutional form of political life.

According to the well-known investigations of Laski [47] and Nightingale,[48] England's ruling class consisted until lately of about 1000 families who held the leading positions in society.

Between 1800 and 1924 60% of the Cabinet came from the ruling class. The percentage varies from 73 in the first period to only 27 in the last period—thus showing increasing democratization. . . Seventy percent were educated in British universities, half of them in Oxford. Fifty-six percent came from leading public schools. . . The British Foreign Office: 53% belong to the aristocracy and gentry, only 40% came from business families. The aristocracy and rentier classes formed 56% of the Diplomatic Service, but only 40% of the Foreign Office. . . Bishops, Deans, Judges, Home and India Servants, Governors of Dominions, directors of banks and railways all come from the same class.[49]

Sociologically speaking England has been a political democracy run by an oligarchy which has gradually expanded its basis of selection. The basis was first the aristocracy and gentry, with the addition of successful merchants and bankers, and later of industrialists. In the present broadening of the basis the upper classes seek to absorb the more gifted members of the lower classes of society. Their ideology is perhaps best expressed in a sentence in Collingwood's *The New Leviathan:* 'The dialectic of internal politics is the conversion of a ruled class into collaborators in the art of ruling. . .' [50]

In many respects the organization of the English is a most skilful sociological product. It admirably fitted the dual purpose of enabling a minority to run a huge Empire and, at the same time, to rule the mother country, absorbing thereby all the shocks of societal change and world politics. This statement, however, is double-edged. On the one hand it implies that the system splendidly served the purpose of a traditional type of society; it also admits, however, that the system can hardly survive under present world conditions, unless the ruling stratum is considerably broadened and adjusted to the new tasks of leadership.

Traditional social selection and organization in England has produced a small group of leading men fit to rule, whose homogeneity and consensus qualified them to play the game under any circumstances and in any part of the world. The educational system with its 'public' schools and universities served to establish that tacit consensus and the 'team spirit,' which enables Englishmen wherever they meet to follow certain unwritten rules and promptly to form a co-operating team. This integration takes place on different levels: it is more concerned with producing conformist habits and a distinctive mentality than with inculcating a definite creed. The covert method of breeding co-operative attitudes enlists the help of home and neighborhood, of the educational influences of the boarding school, and, later, of professional associations, clubs, and the all-pervasive class-atmosphere. Playing fields are as important as the classics, which serve mainly to implement a basic code of values and provide a socializing substratum of knowledge. Men think of the same literary and historical models when discussing human affairs and the meaning of changing events. Textbooks and syllabi are composed not primarily for their intellectual value, but rather for their contribution to character building. The word 'character' precisely reflects the ambiguity of purpose. On the one hand it means timeless leadership abilities; on the other it implies a certain class loyalty and solidarity with the ruling team, seclusion against outsiders, a dual system of norms—one only for members of one's class, the other for outsiders.

The system excellently combined this tendency to exclusiveness and the concomitant *esprit de corps* with ascent opportunities for those best qualified of the lower social classes.[51] There was nothing new in the tacit consensus of a ruling class. This in itself is the most widespread phenomenon in history. But the ability to combine this with a readiness to assimilate newcomers from the lower classes and to do it properly was and is an exceptional virtue. It is well known that the ruling class originated with the amalgamation of the remnants of the feudal aristocracy with the mercantile classes. Thus, from the very beginning, mixed attitudes were developed. The ruling class emphasized seclusion and exclusiveness for the sake of maintaining power and standards; but it also valued versatility and bargaining skills. In an age unfamiliar with planning, the ruling class developed systematic ascent opportunities and even planned ways of social descent as in the case of the younger sons of peers. Social ascent in England followed two acknowledged avenues; one led to the ruling class, by way of success in business, administration, and politics, absorption being indicated through social contacts; the other, by way of education combined with a scholarship system for selecting the fittest.

Another exceptional quality of the English system is its power to assimilate newcomers. This works mainly through unconscious, skilful arrangements in the same selective machinery. The public schools, by removing boys from home before puberty, mold their loyalties at a critical stage in their development. They check absolute devotion to the family and use the deflected emotions for creating loyalty to the larger unit of the school. The adolescent tends in any case to shift loyalties from the family to the spontaneous associations of youth and these are important educational factors. Gangs, cliques, and their team spirit may be skilfully used for promoting and diffusing a team spirit through the entire ruling class. By learning to be loyal to one's team one learns to be loyal to one's class. Equally skilful is allowing the spontaneous fermentation of the age of puberty to grow within these gangs, while stopping short of unruliness. Loyalty to one's house, loyalty to one's school,[52] nation, and Empire constitute an interconnected pattern.[53] By training for the small unit one trains at once for the large one, and one seeks to expand this loyalty by allowing the successful individual to assume ever-greater responsibilities and to exert wider influence.

This is essentially the nineteenth-century English system, which could hardly have worked better during a time when society was not yet ready for mass democracy.[54] It provided leadership for the country and Empire, maintaining equilibrium between them. The broad social changes of recent decades, however, have obviously turned many former virtues into present-day obstacles. Neither reverence for ancient traditions and their values nor a radical, disparaging attitude aimed at making a clean sweep will avail. Only a selective attitude toward social inheritance will do, studiously eliminating what is harmful while strengthening or improving valuable tendencies that can be readjusted to the new conditions. This readjustment calls for more than unconscious trial-and-error procedures, namely a sociological diagnosis and inventory of the inheritance in the light of the changing historical situation.

XIII. SOCIAL VALUE OF FUNCTIONS PERFORMED BY THE RULING CLASS

The growth of industrial society demands more leaders than Oxford and Cambridge can supply for all the economic, political, and social functions of England. The numerical inadequacy of existing academic institutions has suddenly become obvious. To enroll more university students and graduates, the secondary school system must be changed and expanded, and more scholarships must be granted.[55] The question is how to expand and democratize the system of breeding tacit consensus.

The Russians have shown how to build cadres of leaders quickly and how to create the essential loyalties. The Russian model, however, should not be copied. Its extremist methods were possibly unavoidable in a society lacking primary stability where a new ruling class had to establish new loyalties on short notice. The Russian method combined the Army pattern with that of secret societies.[56] Their psychological technique fuses propaganda and terror: suggestion, inspiration, and control of conscience through spying, supervision, and purges. Thus, enthusiasm and fear are simultaneously at work in addition to what may be called 'organized thought,' i.e. institutionalizing a fixed doctrine which all members of the leading elite have to accept without reservation.

This method may possibly be used whenever a mass organization has suddenly to replace a historical ruling class, when large sectional associations have to be tamed, or heterogeneous groups without common traditions be merged. The pattern of the one-party system is, however, not necessarily the implement of all planned society. A traditional society embarking upon planning and having at its command a historically developed ruling class can retain the latter's virtues and thus combine conformity with great elasticity and personal freedom.

For the same reason there is no need to abandon the older institutions for creating tacit consensus. Among others, in Britain the system of 'public' boarding schools has many features which should not only be preserved but socialized. That is to say, more scholarships should facilitate the admission of an increasing percentage of pupils without diluting the valuable traditions of the 'public' schools. Should dilution threaten, new schools might be founded on the same pattern, so that not only the few but the best of the whole population, and ultimately all, might share the valuable elements of tradition. Wise democratization not only considers the numbers admitted to education, but carefully weighs the substance of what is to be transmitted. It is more important to preserve the highest forms of cultural achievement than to engage in sudden expansion. The demand for standards, rightly understood, is as democratic as that for numbers.

Not all expansion necessarily dilutes standards. On the contrary, some of the negative features of a snobbish ruling class may well be eliminated by expansion. Undue emphasis on superficial badges of rank will ultimately disappear. The more leadership becomes a matter of merit rather than birth, the less will distinction focus on expendable mannerisms and panoply, or on the 'conspicuous consumption' and 'conspicuous waste' of a leisure class, as described by Veblen.[57]

The boarding schools of a democratic community can teach co-operative living at low cost without 'conspicuous waste.' One should think of them in terms of camps, where youths of different background mingle and live together. This need not lower the quality of school life and work. On the contrary, a shade of asceticism appeals to youth. This was recognized in the older public schools, which adopted Spartan simplicity. The ascetic bent, however, was somewhat incongruous with the actual wealth of the boys' families and that of the institution, and hence remained a make-believe austerity, whereas in the camps of the future it would be genuine and truly educational.

Gradual expansion of traditional methods of creating like-mindedness alone will not do. The British system fortunately can

rely upon established capital of emotional solidarity and conformity. Survival depends, however, on its ability to incorporate
a great deal of rational awareness.

The larger the group and its membership, the greater their
social disparity and heterogeneity, and the greater the demand
for intellectual integration. Thought spreads more readily than
emotion, especially traditionally shaped sentiment. The latter
can only flourish where continuity prevails between generations
and neighborly communities—i.e. where there is time for growing habit formation and the transmission of a dense network of
personal contacts. By contrast thought is more abstract in that it
is detached from the time and place of original conception.

XIV. HUMANITIES OR SOCIAL STUDIES?

If cohesion must be established swiftly, modern methods of mass
persuasion may have to be used. Even the English, if they wish
to broaden social reform, cannot do without ideologies. In this
process British traditions, which formerly were absorbed more
or less unconsciously, will have to be ·put down in black and
white so that they can be understood by ever-widening circles.

In this connection the 'classic' tradition with its overemphasis
on 'culture' must be reconsidered. Contempt for practical vocational training is the legacy of a bygone age when slaves did the
work and the freeborn devoted themselves to the *artes liberales*.
So much for the limitations of tradition This one created an
ideal world—a dream world in which not human beings but
statues seemed to act. This classicist conception of antiquities
will have to go if the classical tradition is to mean anything to a
generation that faces broad social change and possibly chaos,
and craves for realistic understanding of social forces. Modern
scholarship is actually revising the false idealization of Mediter-
ranean antiquity as an age of solemnity and rigidity; it has discovered and stressed the completely experimental character of
Greek philosophy.

'The chief strength of the Greek lay in their freedom from
hampering intellectual tradition. They had no venerated classics,
no holy books, no dead languages to master, no authorities to
check their free speculation.' [58]

Instead of a new interpretation of the classics, social science instruction may well become the core of a curriculum destined to integrate a new ruling elite. Why approach the study of man and of his contemporary problems in a roundabout fashion? Historical studies will, broaden one's horizon, but it should be the horizon of contemporary life and its problems. How can new leaders lead without an adequately informed understanding of contemporary society and its problems, and without a social philosophy to fit an evolutionary democratic society?

XV. THE DANGER OF OVERASSIMILATION

A historical ruling class can be reconstructed by broadening its base, automatically producing an internal transformation and a new mentality through fusion with the newcomers. Formerly, under oligarchical rule, conservative groups easily absorbed and assimilated the few scholarship-holders and other successful aspirants to leadership. The ascending individuals renounced loyalty to their own class and soon conformed to the ruling group.

There are two main objections to this overassimilation in the future. First, democratic mass society can no longer be based upon mass ignorance and apathy but requires leadership on all levels of society. It has been observed correctly that the scholarship system in the past deprived the working classes of their own potential leaders.

Secondly, ready assimilation of scholarship boys and girls and of the self-made man in various walks of life has also the disadvantage that it prematurely breaks their greater vitality. People who make their way in life by self-help are frequently men of new ideas and values, men of initiative and mental alertness, whereas conservative groups, which for generations have mainly upheld and preserved what others have achieved, are less likely to produce men willing to take risks and receptive to new ideas. The self-made man making his way 'from rags to riches' often develops a keenness most desirable in a society bound to change. If these mental traits are discouraged or neutralized by overassimilation, society loses resources for change and adaptation.

XVI. FUNCTIONS OF A RECONSTRUCTED RULING CLASS

Obviously social processes such as a broader selection of leaders, the fusion of old and new elements, do not by themselves produce optimum results. In modern society such processes require direction lest they lead to sterile fermentation. From the argument above we can roughly determine two main functions for leadership in an age of planning. A reconstructed ruling class must first visualize and define, at least as clearly as any totalitarian ruling class, the principles and objectives of democracy in industrial society. Secondly, it must devise practicable ways and means to attain its ends by reforms and mass consensus.

If this holds true the new ruling class must not only transmit and safeguard the best elements of tradition, but must develop dynamic ideas, the vision of a society able to cope with contemporary crises by democratic means. This can be done if diagnosis and therapy of society truly become the concern of all in leading positions, if all members of the ruling stratum are inspired with the greatness and uniqueness of their destiny: to save both their nation and mankind in the gravest hour of history. Obviously a change of heart is needed and a new mental climate to encourage, not suppress, men of ideas and vision. In other words, a democracy on the defensive must be turned into one that is constructive and militant. Intellectual initiative, of course, can come only from men who are open to change and can view things in a new perspective.

The peculiar difficulty of militant democratic leaders, however, is that the desired peaceful transformation of society forbids fanaticism and the ruthless suppression of dissentient groups; it demands consensus and co-operation at every stage. The unity of a democratic ruling group is bound to be dialectical. The goal cannot be fully anticipated but has to be worked out at various levels in the experimental process of common endeavor. For the same reason a democratic ruling class does not maintain unity by embracing a creed but by working out solutions, testing alternative policies toward common ends and reaching temporary agreement on concrete issues. As many issues as possible are left to discretion, in order to enable varying interests and ideas again and again to be synthesized even at the stage of planning—only an indispensable minimum is defined for agreement under all circumstances. This preference for different points of view, coupled with the will to agree and cooperate with opponents on common policies, is feasible only for a group that has learned to change the traditional 'tacit concensus' into a dynamic one.

Agreement not only on appreciation of the past but on the desirability of a creative transformation must be kept constantly alive. Sociologically speaking, this blend of attitudes can only develop in a mental climate ready for reconciliation of opposing ideas on innumerable occasions in everyday life. This is possible only in a continuous social process of mutual assimilation and adaptation in working out common policies by debate while cherishing freedom above all.

5

The Reformation of Politics

❧

Coherent policies, especially economic ones, obviously cannot be implemented without affecting the political machinery. The need to adjust political machinery to social change does not imply that the present political institutions of the United States or of Great Britain should be scrapped and replaced by different ones. On the contrary, what needs to be done is to transform existing political institutions into better tools without impairing their original function of integrating the life of the nation.

Often the two purposes seem to be at variance because the administration of a changing society requires continuous readjustment of its institutions, whereas national integration calls for stability of political institutions. Usually the dilemma is solved by leaving the traditional framework intact, while allowing for experimentation in procedure, as, for example, in the case of British parliamentary institutions and governmental 'action agencies' of the United States. The strength of constitutional sentiment in the United States would not permit the Nazi Bundists or Communists 'openly to profess their aims'—as Marx did in the *Communist Manifesto*. Both Bundists and Communists overtly affirmed their loyalty to the Federal Constitution during the 'thirties, making spurious claims to leadership in realization of its aims. For the rest, the great social evolution of American society from a colonial democracy of 5 million settlers to an imperial world power of 150 millions did not entail a break with the Constitution of the 'Founding Fathers,' but rather a continuous and 'fruitful misinterpretation' of precedents in the light of new emergencies.

Without embarking on detailed proposals we should like to develop a few basic principles which are bound to change the political machinery, once planning—and especially planning for freedom—becomes the accepted goal of government.

In order to understand contemporary political developments, the political sociologist inquires into the meaning of government and defines its role in historical perspective.

Tribal organization is simple: essentially it rests on patterns of kinship. Fusion of several families and clans makes for more complex units: smaller sub-units are held together in a larger framework which regulates their interrelationship. *Politikos* originally meant 'public' as contrasted with family, kin, or occupational association. 'Public' life existed among the self-regulated and isolated sub-units and filled the interstices. 'Politics' and 'public' therefore refer primarily to interrelations of groups which for the sake of co-operation have to overcome their self-sufficiency and seclusion. This network of intergroup relations forms the 'body politic.' The nature of these intergroup regulations in many ways determines the shape of the community at large. If the sub-units are hierarchically organized, the community in turn will tend to evolve regulations dependent on rank. If the sub-units are co-ordinated as equals, a kind of federative or democratic organization will appear. The main function of government, regardless of form, is to integrate smaller groups into a scheme of special functions more comprehensive than that of the single units.

So much for preliminary clarification of the terms 'state,' 'government,' or the more general term introduced by Franz Oppenheimer, 'frame group,' [1] and its relation to the sub-groups which may be considered as 'society.'

There are innumerable ways of regulating intergroup relations within a frame group. In the Western world we may fruitfully distinguish four stages of development:

1. Absolutism [2] established the first frame group in modern history after the breakdown of the medieval system. Absolutism

tried to integrate many local units into a single jurisdictional
territory by superseding the limited powers of feudal lords and
independent corporate bodies such as city magistrates and ecclesiastic hierarchies. Usually one of the feudal lords or princes
became so powerful that he could subjugate the others. Thus he
not only created a unified territory, market, army, and bureaucracy, but also assigned a new specialization of functions to the
single units. The sub-units were combined in a new and more
comprehensive order. The absolutist state at this stage approached the totalitarian: it tried to regulate everything in tyran-
nical or paternalistic fashion, whether enlightened or not. The
failure of absolutism was not primarily attributable to the ruler's
shortsightedness in denying freedom and spontaneity to the societal sub-units. Rather the primitive state of technology restricted
his sway and efforts to govern. Modern means of transport and
communication were not available. The absence of modern industry and of an industrial bureaucracy especially prevented the
autocrat of old from becoming sole ruler of the whole system. The
prince engaged in production on his own account and at his
own risk in establishing state manufactures. Eventually he failed
and had to allow the rising *bourgeoisie* to carry through the industrial revolution. With the exception of a few military plants
and luxury establishments, the state-subsidized and princely
privileged plants of mercantilism proved to be abortive channels
of investment, a drain on funds that otherwise might have flowed
into capitalist enterprises producing not luxuries for the court
but goods for mass consumption.[3]

2. The growth in numbers and strength of the *bourgeoisie*
transformed the absolutist state into the liberal state. In the
liberal state two political classes essentially determined the social
structure: the *bourgeoisie* and the state bureaucracy. The tension between the two created and is reflected in the type of
political philosophy that to this day survives in many allegedly
modern theories.[4]

The liberal state arose with the advent of industry and free
enterprise, proclaiming the free market and the right of the individual to find his own economic niche as basic principles of
societal organization. The liberal believed in the voluntary co-
ordination of individual activities and intergroup relationships.

The state should not interfere; it should only provide the legal framework for the smooth functioning of the innumerable processes of voluntary association and free enterprise.

The free-enterprise theory, however, is adequate only so long as the contracting and competing social units are small and able to adjust swiftly to changing circumstances without overproduction, deadlocks, and bottlenecks, entailing special government agencies to iron out maladjustments.

3. A third stage is reached with the growth of the communal units and their rigid self-regulation. Scope for individual enterprise becomes rare and governmental intervention increases to forestall the catastrophic consequences of unco-ordinated business enterprise. The government is called in not merely to uphold the law but to prevent the ruin and victimization of smaller businesses.[5] When business asks for subsidies, when bankruptcy runs riot, in short, when the 'state' has to intervene in order to relieve symptoms of a maladjusted organism, the liberal state is finished.[6] At this stage, however, the symptoms are not yet recognized as a 'syndrome,' as a concurrent series of interrelated maladjustments; nor has talk begun of preventive action or foresight on the part of the government.

4. When state and government are called upon to prevent the growth of maladjustments instead of merely to relieve symptoms, the fourth stage is reached. Two alternatives are offered—the way of the old absolutist state leading straight to totalitarianism, or the way of planning for freedom. Under totalitarianism the state seeks to prevent the occurrence of symptoms by organizing the whole business of living efficiently, using all the social and material techniques which were beyond the grasp of the autocrat of old. The totalitarian solution follows the absolutist approach in developing a paternalistic attitude similar to that of the enlightened despot who claims to know what is good for his subjects.

This solution is intolerable in a democracy, as regimentation and paternalism curtail the opportunities of the citizen to make significant decisions. If the dangers of paternalism are to be avoided, the other way must be tried: we must invent methods to prevent maladjustments, setting careful limits to the scope of state intervention.

The modern state is a service state. It not only organizes pub-
lic-health services to combat existing disease but it seeks to prevent epidemics by numerous administrative and legal devices.
The state cares for the aged, the immature, and the unemployed. Public authorities may provide and manage 'public
utilities' such as gas, electricity, and transportation facilities.
Most European states own and manage the radio network as a
public service. Education may serve as one of the tools to make
the young and older generations understand the needs of a
changing society. In a word, the democratic state as a social service state is active in every sphere of social life.[7] But if the state
is everywhere, how does it differ in operation from the totalitarian state? How can we speak of democratic planning and of
planning for freedom if our state is to be all-pervasive? Despite
apparent similarities between the totalitarian state and the social
service democracy differences can be pointed out. In the following maxims we shall seek to define the extent to which our traditional governmental machinery will be affected by the type of
planning which we call preventive.

II. MAXIMS ON THE POLICY OF PREVENTIVE PLANNING

1. *Only strong central power can carry out planning.* Planning,
whether totalitarian or preventive, cannot become an efficient
tool in the hands of weak central authority. The British example
shows that democracy and freedom are not incompatible with
strong centralization; in fact, it has rightly been said that power
in Britain has been made responsible by centralization. Whenever the President of the United States assumes the role of
'people's tribune,' he has even greater authority than the British
Prime Minister, who is dependent upon the 'confidence' of the
House. In Great Britain neither the supremacy of Parliament
nor the responsibility of the Cabinet should be weakened as
focusing of authority is needed for planning. Freedom should
be guaranteed by democratic controls through established parliamentary channels and supplementary methods devised for this
purpose. We stress this point because many think the best way
to prevent totalitarianism is to deny authority to central government. The threat to freedom does not come from a government
which is 'ours,' which we have elected and which we can re-

move, but from oligarchies without public responsibility. Public accountability of administration and rotation in office are key provisions of democratic government to be guarded jealously.

2. *Centralization is necessary because co-ordination of different measures is essential to planning.* Agreement on certain basic objectives of long-range planning is indispensable. The nature and dignity of these basic issues are bound to differ from their ordinary legal aspect. Just as constitutional provisions can only be changed by qualified majorities, so basic planning laws should be guaranteed. The co-ordination of basic policies would call for standards of consistency only to be judged by experts. Just as the Supreme Court watches over the conformity of state legislation with Federal legislation, so a tribunal will need to be established to judge the intrinsic consistency of basic principles and the conformity of subsequent regulations and enactments. Of course, difficulties are bound to arise. Experts may disagree. They may belong to different schools of thought or they may be prompted by conscious or unconscious group interests. In this case they will have to explain their guiding principles to the educated layman, who acts as judge and catalyzer. Even so, erroneous ideas may occasionally influence policy, as has happened in the past, on a possibly larger scale. The experts were formerly less exposed to public criticism, since their theories usually served unofficially as inspirations for leading politicians. No idea of planning informed such comprehensive policies as the Reparations Policy of Versailles,[8] which contributed to the economic upheaval between the wars. Neither were the deflationist policies of the Brüning regime in republican Germany part of a consistent policy of planning. Yet Brüning's policy contributed measurably to the catastrophic unemployment that swelled the Nazi tide.[9]

The existence of a co-ordinating planning body to air the pros and cons of experts will not eliminate the experimental nature of human action, but may add valuable controls. The one-sidedness of an economic expert's argument may well be disclosed by others trained in perceiving bias and hidden motivation. Besides, the constant confronting of forecasts with actual events and their relentless analysis may lead to a method of learning from past experiences.

Thus far man has acquired the ability to learn from past experiences only in the limited context of personal life. Now is the time for groups to learn jointly from the past. In the atmosphere of planning a change of policy will be not merely a reflection of a changing mood but controlled by the process of social learning.

The New Deal is an interesting example, in which the old and the new approach were strangely mingled. On the one hand, some New Deal planning measures certainly stemmed the tide of advancing depression and raised the American economy to a level of moderate prosperity. On the other hand, one can learn from the New Deal that absence of a truly co-ordinated plan robs even otherwise well-conceived measures of full success, especially if at the same time rival pressure groups [10] must be appeased. Politicians will represent or be influenced by pressure groups; sensitivity to spontaneous and channeled currents of public opinion is part of the democratic process. But Democracy must have some mechanism for sifting ideas, for clarifying and defining truly common objectives, for recognizing special pleading of partisan interests and eliminating bias. This final policy-framing authority should aim at consistency in proposals rather than appeasement of pressure groups, and it should be empowered to revise policies that experience proves to be based upon false premises or expectations. In this connection we have to learn from those Russian statesmen who had the courage candidly to revoke erroneous policies and who educated their public to appreciate frank admission of past mistakes and the necessity for new beginnings.

Public education will need to emphasize the experimental nature of all living. It must devise techniques for interpreting fundamental issues to various levels of intelligence and educational background. In this connection, the Tennessee Valley experiment made an important contribution, for it combined economic planning with an educational campaign.[11]

3. *Centralization in a planned society is essential only in certain basic policy issues.* Just as the policy-co-ordinating body should insist on centralization where justified, so it should adamantly oppose the inherent tendency of centralized institutions to usurp all functions. The difference between devolution of power and self-government should be clearly under-

stood. Higher authorities practice devolution of power in delegating functions to lower authorities without surrendering final responsibility. Extension of local self-government [12] means allocating more policy-making decisions or responsibilities to local authorities. The choice of method expedient in each case depends on the nature of the function. Democracy, however, would seek to encourage self-help and popular initiative wherever compatible with planning. This would not only help to stimulate civic interest in public affairs and link it to common issues, but would also foster identification of the citizen with his government and its plan. Moreover, the people will be encouraged by such identification to bring their workaday experiences with the plan to the attention of central authorities and thereby benefit.

4. *In a planned society, government and the community are no longer separable entities.* Granted the ubiquity of government, the cause of freedom is not served by trying to limit legitimate governmental functions. More to the point is clear demarcation of the purpose, range, and machinery of governmental control as limitation of individual freedom. Analysis of governmental functions will show that controls in the direction of planning *serve* freedom. The true meaning of social control is to curb those tendencies of natural growth, which when left alone breed oppression or chaos, disturb the balance of forces, or injure public interest. It is a sad commentary on the misunderstanding of planning that controls *per se* should be interpreted as threats to freedom. The policeman in a democratic community is an agent of civic freedom, not of oppression, as law enforcement serves to prevent or suppress crime and the growth of destructive tendencies.

5. *Lawful state interference in economic life by its machinery and powers of regulation should serve to maintain full production and control arbitrary monopolies.*

Freedom of enterprise is compatible with control of industry, which guarantees full utilization of available resources for the benefit of the community. Later we shall discuss at greater length threats to economic stability and full production arising from the present organization of industry and the planning measures appropriate to democratic control. Here we confine ourselves to a few general observations.

Various business associations and combinations characteristic of the latest phase of capitalism frequently set up arbitrary policies of output restriction, capital investment, control of patents,[13] resources, and market outlets. Such power combinations lack public accountability and should be controlled in appropriate ways, according to their techniques of organization and management.[14]

Central authorities will have to define the scope of industrial democracy; that is, they must determine what share workers should have in the management of industry. Industrial democracy is the most powerful antidote to overcentralization in an industrial society. Its establishment is in many ways more vital to the community at large than is local government (which is not to deny the importance of the latter), as the individual's everyday interests in an industrial society are much closer to and more dependent upon his job than upon his local habitation.[15]

Clear enactments should define the manner in which industry can be controlled. The four possible forms of control are legislation, administration, representation,[16] and participation.[17] In applying controls the intervening authority must form a concept of 'public interest.' To ensure against arbitrary abuse the meaning of the term will have to be clearly defined. Undoubtedly 'public interest' allows of a great many interpretations in terms of underlying social philosophies. Despite these pitfalls a common definition must be reached as a basis for legislative enactments in the planning stage. It is generally agreed that manipulations in restraint of trade, undue restriction of output, or artificial raising of prices is against the public interest.

III. CONTROL OF THE SOCIAL STRUCTURE

In a world of ubiquitous 'rules and regulations' some are inclined to view all controls as purely negative in nature. Yet their function of safeguarding freedom must not be overlooked. Traffic regulations do not prevent, they facilitate the orderly flow of vehicles. Public control puts a stop to an endless flow of interferences which would work at cross purposes. This point of ours leads to reflection on how centers of social control can themselves be kept in check. Our concern here is less the vindication of state interferences *per se* than the preservation of democratic freedom.

In a system of planning for freedom the frame organization should not relieve the citizen of the responsibility of working out his own life or deprive him of self-reliance by providing for him from on high. The frame organization should merely prevent major maladjustments which in the absence of countermeasures tend to become cumulative.[18]

This form of intervention is new inasmuch as the prevention of chaos and tyranny in the past has been confined chiefly to planned distribution of power within the government, whereas the distribution of power in society, the class structure, as it were, remained intact. The *status quo* of society was considered as much a fact as the lay of the land. Both might be modified a little here and there but neither could be planned according to any fixed idea.

Modern controls are indeed moving toward a new form of manipulation of society. We not only deliberately create a balance of political powers, but enlist the help of power centers throughout society.[19]

Whereas the British political structure has developed gradually, the American and French constitutions were enacted and planned with an eye to organizing a balanced system of governmental authorities and institutions. The constitution-makers may be considered the fathers of considered planning for freedom. Their main concern was an equilibrium of powers to prevent the growth of forces leading to the tyranny of a single individual, of a small group, or of the masses. Yet even their planning stopped short of modifying the existing class structure, or of limiting industrial developments possibly leading to tyranny. There was no need for such controls in the agrarian economy of a predominantly rural society. Besides, the constitution-makers could hardly have done more, even had they wished to, for lack of techniques. Our new ways of planning the structure of society have to deal with the issue of high capitalism in an urban society. Techniques are at hand in modern methods of taxation, in new forms of regulating property and its uses, and like means.

These measures are necessary where control of the equilibrium of political machinery [20] is insufficient bulwark against the drift toward dictatorship in crises. In times of prosperity and peace one can watch the political game being played behind constitutional rules and ordinary enactments. In twentieth-century crises, when powerful nations may transfer to weaker ones the economic consequences of their own mistakes, no constitution-maker can prevent the emergence of secret armies, anti-democratic conspiracies of men in key positions, and the abuse of unequally distributed power. Catastrophic political landslides such as occurred in Europe between the world wars can only be prevented by addressing ourselves not to superficial symptoms but to the underlying structure of society.[21] The preservation of democracy in the face of modern crises demands that we look beyond the checks and balances of organized politics and focus on checks and balances in society.[22]

Societal balance can be achieved in two ways: by revolution or by reform. Social revolution may level a society, as was the case in Russia. In the Soviet Union almost all were made workers, whose differential pay allowed for some secondary social differentiation but no power differentiation.[23] The nonrevolutionary way of reform starts with the existing class structure as its point of departure, allowing voluntary movements to have their way until they lead to gross inequalities. Menacing inequality can be curbed by proper controls so as to achieve a fair degree of social homogeneity without which no consensus for planning can emerge. Whereas the Soviet aimed at such consensus by leveling all differences of wealth and power in the social structure, and whereas the Fascists sought to guarantee the power of a mighty oligarchy by violence and terror, the Third Way strives for peaceful reforms by consent of the majority.

True, only a fairly homogeneous society [24] can be expected to reach peaceful agreement on means and ends of planning. Such homogeneity does not imply uniformity as under proletarian dictatorship. Variety of occupation, status grouping, and ways of life not only adds color to Western civilization but makes for balance. This variety can be maintained so long as grave inequalities do not endanger the power equilibrium or create vested interests in opposition to planning for more equitable opportunities and stability.

Whenever concentration of power becomes excessive, it invites tyranny in critical situations. Power undergoes metamorphoses. Sometimes it shows itself naked, but usually it is disguised as economic or administrative power, as propaganda, or education. Hence in whatever form of manipulation power may appear, democratic vigilance demands that its ubiquitous presence and potential dangers be recognized by the people.

One of the most dangerous abuses of power is to manipulate fears, causing public panic deliberately in order to profit by the confusion. For instance, bankers and financial magnates who distrust a government they dislike sometimes instigate a general loss of confidence resulting in the flight of capital.[25] Regardless of the source and form of such influences undermining democratic freedom, they must be met by appropriate countermeasures. Objection may be raised that countermeasures would bring about undue regimentation and the end of a 'free' society. We can only reply that no limitation should be set on measures aimed at safeguarding the structural basis of freedom and democracy. Besides, democracy does not mean that friends and enemies of freedom are to be treated alike, nor does it mean inability to distinguish between controls against and in favor of tyranny. To speak of controls as always detrimental to freedom is to create confusion. We must distinguish between helpful and harmful controls and provide countermeasures in democratic ways. Often public exposure of intrigue suffices in a society where organs of public opinion are available to everybody. Sabotage through capital flight can be countered by an enlightened, alert public opinion. There is no limit to inventiveness in the field of democratic controls as opposed to the crude methods of police states.

IV. CONTROL OF THE ECONOMY

Let us begin with the strategic problems confronting the democratic planner today in the realm of economics. For a number of reasons the establishment of proper economic controls plays a preponderant role in contemporary discussion of planning. On the one hand, the impact of the economic order on man's existence is as fundamental as it is universal; no stability of society is conceivable without previous integration and stabilization of the economic process. On the other hand, and for the same reasons. problems of economic planning have for some time been submitted to searching investigation on the part of experts. The economists concerned have even reached considerable agreement in regard to the main defects of our Western economic system, though they still disagree about the basic causes of economic maladjustment and the most effective remedies.

At the same time the popularity of economic planning is not without dangers. Many economists and a wide section of the public have been led to believe that planning generally is identical with economic planning. Once the economic process is stabilized by a deliberate policy of co-ordination, the rest of society, the argument runs, may safely be surrendered to *laissez-faire*.[26] We have already taken occasion to dispel such complacency concerning maladjustments in the wider social process. We now hope to demonstrate that economic planning itself will be effective only if other phases of modern society are properly co-ordinated with economics.

The sociologist cannot enter into a technical discussion of the economic problems involved, or take sides in controversial questions.[27] His interest is confined to understanding the issues at stake, and to evaluating the sociological significance of the proposed solutions.

Most serious observers today would name as the most conspicuous defects of our inherited world economic order: excessive inequality both within national economies and among them; actual poverty of certain social groups and of large regions of the world; [28] maldistribution of resources; and dangerous instability of income and employment. Of these economic ills the periodic fluctuations of income and employment have created the greatest threat to political democracy, particularly in the more advanced nations. It seems that the working masses in an industrial society are prepared to put up with considerable inefficiency and inequality so long as they can look forward to steady work and to a gradually rising standard of living. But as the mass unemployment of the early 'thirties played a major role in destroying German democracy, most people agree that even the established democracies of the West would hardly survive a recurrence of the Great Depression. For this reason elimination of the traditional business cycle has become the key problem of democratic economic planning. All the more so since the assurance of a high and stable level of employment will go a long way toward eliminating the worst features of mass poverty and waste of resources.

The task of economic stabilization would certainly be easier had the experts succeeded in reaching agreement on the original causes of industrial fluctuations. Not that disagreement necessarily reduces the value of any one of the rival hypotheses, but rather that it reflects the multiplicity of influences at work. Thus it appears quite plausible, as the Keynes School [29] points out, that in rich societies the aggregate volume of savings tends periodically to outrun available investment opportunities, thereby reducing employment because the demand for new capital goods falls below the supply. Yet this hypothesis does not contradict the fact that even countries with a strong investment trend are not immune to periodic slumps. Characteristic dislocation may occur in such cases between the structure of production and the distribution of income and expenditure.

In either case the initial disproportion may be created by external factors, such as technological changes or crop variations. But what makes these and other sectional maladjustments a threat to the stability of the system as a whole is their tendency to spread. Such a cumulation of shocks, making depression nationwide and even world-wide, appears to be due to certain conditions inherent in industrial capitalism, particularly in the prevailing monetary system and in the growing immobility of capital and labor.

The detached observer can conclude only that the dangers periodically threatening economic stability in an industrial society are numerous indeed. It can hardly surprise us that the arsenal of stabilization measures is equally large.

For simple classification these measures may be subdivided into remedial and preventive policies; among the remedial policies a further distinction can be made between those intended to allay certain disturbing symptoms only and those attacking the causes of instability. We are again not attempting an exhaustive analysis of the available tools of stabilization, but shall select a few characteristic measures in each category in order to review them in the light of the principles underlying the Third Way.

1. The oldest tool of business-cycle policy is the *dole* in one

K

form or another. This is a typical symptomatic remedy, at least so long as its proponents accept the recurrence of depressions as inevitable and try only to alleviate the social fate of the unemployed.[30]

Since the dole does not interfere with the normal operation of private enterprise it has certain advantages, judged by the traditional conception of economic freedom. But these advantages are offset by the futility of the dole as a contribution to stabilization proper. Unemployment insurance and other forms of unemployment compensation will probably play a subsidiary role in any economic order. They tide the displaced workers over a temporary emergency until more effective measures can be brought to bear upon economic dislocation. But apart from serving as a stopgap, the dole contributes little to social amelioration. It has become general knowledge that depressions are manmade rather than acts of God. Therefore the workers demand offers of productive work at normal wages and are no longer satisfied with prolonged idleness made tolerable by public support.

2. For a long time *public works* were regarded as a second line of defense among measures designed to alleviate the symptom of unemployment. By offering the unemployed some form of at least semi-productive activity, it was hoped that the demoralizing effects of idleness could be combatted. However, during the last two decades it has been realized that the significance of public works, as of any other form of public spending during a depression, extends far beyond this specific function. As a form of compensatory investment public works may substitute for private investment whenever the latter does not keep pace with the public's savings. In this way they attack the deeper causes of certain depressions and can even, by a favorable effect on business expectations, initiate a new revival. If a public-works program is applied in time as a countercyclical measure it may prevent the spread of regional recessions into an economy-wide depression.[31]

Public works and public spending as a rule have gained popularity in proportion as more traditional measures of indirect interference with private investment have proved ineffectual. This is especially true of the manipulation of the *rate of interest*. In principle, timely increase of the rate of interest should prevent economic prosperity from degenerating into inflation. However, a world-wide policy of cheap money, based mainly on fiscal considerations, has during recent decades put this instrument out of commission. It is doubtful whether mere reduction of the rate of interest was ever effective in compensating for the business risks threatening private investment during a depression.

From the point of view of democratic planning, the manipulation of the interest rate and compensatory public works have important features in common. Both measures emanate from key positions, such as the central banking system [32] and the fiscal power of the government. These key positions are themselves above the struggle of forces in the market, and are therefore largely immune to business fluctuations. Neither of these key positions was originally created for the purpose of stabilizing employment. Here is another instance where, with the transformation of the social order, the function of an existing organ of public authority may be extended from the particular to the general.

At the same time, both measures keep direct interference with private initiative at a minimum, thereby safeguarding the interests of economic decentralization. This is certainly true of an interest policy that operates through the autonomous profit-and-loss calculations of borrowers and lenders. It is also valid for a public-works policy that is strictly compensatory and confines itself to fields of investment outside the range of private initiative.

3. The situation is different when public investment begins to compete with private investment. Then the ultimate effect on employment and income is difficult to forecast. On the one hand, public enterprise may well serve as a pioneer in technological progress, social welfare, and even managerial efficiency. In this respect public operation of transportation and coal mining in some European countries is enlightening: the most important, because most comprehensive, example is the Tennessee Valley Authority.[33]

On the other hand, it cannot be denied that the encroachment of public investment upon spheres traditionally reserved for private enterprise may discourage private investment and thus offset the governmental stimulation of employment. Much depends on prevailing economic ideologies, but in the long run such ideologies seem more flexible than defenders of the *status quo* are willing to admit. State and municipal enterprises, public utilities government-owned or under strict government control, have become familiar features even in the United States, the citadel of private-enterprise tradition. A 'Mixed System,' which reserves to private enterprise the spheres of pioneer adventure and initiative while subjecting to public ownership or control basic industries like power, transportation, mining, and distribution of the necessities of life, seems in process of development in most Western countries. This evolution, which has gradually taken place over the last few decades, points clearly in the direction of the Third Way.[34] If combined with the gradual redistribution of wealth and income through taxation, with the expansion of social services and with compensatory government spending, such a Mixed System should go quite a way in promoting economic stability, without prejudice to the dynamic forces making for progress and expansion.

4. None of these measures—compensatory public investment, manipulation of the rate of interest, gradual redistribution of wealth and income, or even the building up of a Mixed System —attacks the foundations of our inherited economy; namely, the price mechanism, free competition, and the prevalence of private ownership over the means of production. Apart from monopolistic interests, which will find little backing in a democratic society, none of the dominant social groups has any reason to feel threatened by the application of such measures. On the contrary, the strengthening of mass consumption (to which all these measures contribute) should actually stabilize the position of business, the farming community, and the professional and middle classes, thereby creating an economic basis for the political co-operation of the overwhelming majority.

Still there is the possibility that the measures so far discussed may not be sufficient to attain economic stability in all circumstances. We saw above that the success of compensatory public investment depends largely on the reaction of private investment to such a policy. No less important for the maintenance of full employment is the wage policy pursued by the trade unions or the price policy set up by business and farmers. In other words, in order to attain and maintain economic stability with that minimum of interference which leaves the market mechanism unimpaired, the large pressure groups will have to muster adequate rational understanding of the situation and self-restraint. Otherwise the overriding public interest of a stabilized economy may require interference with the mechanism of our traditional economic system.

In this connection *wage and price controls* may be only the first steps, to be followed by *investment control* over the whole range of the economy. Though such measures would still leave the form of private ownership intact, they would deprive it of one of the main functions traditionally associated with free enterprise. In the case of corporate business organization, where ownership and managerial function are already separated,[35] the latter would have to be subjected to government control. As capital risk would still lie with the private owner, however, all-round investment control could hardly be the last step. The logical outcome would be *nationalization of all large-scale industries,* which would reunite the functions of risk bearing and managerial responsibility in the hands of the community.

Such a development would definitely shift the emphasis in economic organization from decentralization to centralization, and might go beyond the point where economic stability is still compatible with democratic planning. It is not surprising that such a transformation is alluring to the minds of minorities on the left as well as on the right. It inspires the revolutionary activity of those who have lost faith in gradual reform and in the compatibility of planning with economic decentralization. It also arouses large groups in business, otherwise in favor of stabilization, against even moderate measures of state intervention. Both sides should realize that economic stability will require such an extreme step only if capital and labor fail to understand their common interest in a compromise solution. Or, to put it differently, by exercising sound judgment and self-restraint the contesting social groups can achieve stability and progress without radical economic transformation. By the same token these considerations should make it abundantly clear that the technical aspects of economic planning can be discussed properly only if we take into account group attitudes and group behavior. The latter require, obviously, readjustment to the new situation, and have therefore become, for economic if for no other reasons, an object of planning. It is in this sense that even democratic planning must be total if it is to be effective.

Redistributive taxation, investment control, and the extension of public enterprise all run counter to traditional concepts of private ownership in the means of production. Yet closer examination shows that only a very extreme interpretation of the concept of property, namely the one originally developed in Roman law, is violated by the economic reforms discussed above.

It is true, the Roman concept, which grants the owner unlimited use of his property including the right to destroy it, was adopted in legal reforms of the early capitalist era, and has dominated the Western economic system ever since.[36] Yet that concept could never blot out, at least in the minds of social reformers, the recollection of older forms of ownership that regarded property as a trust held in behalf of the community at large or of some higher authority. The same idea is now emerging again in the context of economic planning.

Thus taxation of income from property and of estates recognizes the right of the community to partake in the fruits of private ownership. Participation of business in the insurance of its employees against sickness, accident, and unemployment establishes the responsibility of the owner of the means of production for the social consequences of the use of these means. When during the last war it was decreed that previously unused farm land had to be brought under cultivation or that certain industrial plants had to shut down in favor of others, the priority of the community over the private owner was clearly established. Another expression of the new interpretation of ownership is the fight against private monopolies. It ostracizes what is regarded as an antisocial use of property and seeks to prevent the concentration of economic power in hands other than those of the politically organized community.

It has long been an article of faith of the capitalist creed that the desire for unlimited use of property springs from an immutable instinct of man. Rather, the study of history, the recent rise of new social systems, and a number of psychological experiments have established beyond doubt that the attitude toward property is a product of tradition, of education, and, above all, of the prevailing social order.[87] Even within the ranks of capitalism this attitude varies considerably. There is all the difference between the complete identification of a European peasant with his land and the abstract attitude of the owner of industrial securities toward his 'property,' the location of which he often does not even know. Experience in Soviet Russia, as well as capitalist experiments with profit sharing, prove that a feeling of 'this belongs to us in common' can be as inspiring a stimulus as the right of private ownership, and that we can educate men for such collectivist identification.[88]

Again the Third Way will refrain from extreme one-sidedness. To a large extent the nature of the work should decide whether individualistic or collectivistic identification is more adequate. It cannot be doubted that the need for collectivist identification grows in a large-scale society, if only to humanize work again for those who have to toil in huge factories and offices. On the other hand, the farmer and the small shopkeeper will fulfil their social function more effectively if their sense of private ownership remains unimpaired. Furthermore, the combination of managerial function with private ownership seems indispensable where pioneering initiative and imagination are required. Private property may well have a lasting educational significance for industrial leadership, and a planned society should deliberately foster small-scale enterprise as a training ground for such leadership, as well as another protection against overbureaucratization.

V. CONTROL OF THE ARMED FORCES

Among the most conspicuous organizations of concentrated power are the armed services, the Army, Navy, and Air Force. Their control obviously is a challenge to democracy, as precedents in European history have shown. Quite apart from the Spanish pattern of the pronunciamento, Bonapartism and Boulangism in France, Franco's ascent in Spain, Pilsudski's 'régime of the colonels,' and Hitler's generals offer good reasons for democrats to beware of war-lords. Despite these historical cases of Caesarism the fact remains that the regular armed forces have only rarely been the tool of unconditional tyranny. This may well be due to the fact that they are not products of natural growth but were planned from the beginning. They are among the first organizations in which power is distributed by well-conceived rank gradations and clearly defined authority. They incorporate habits and traditions that train people for a legitimate, well-defined, responsible use of power. Even top-ranking [39] commanders, who might be most tempted to reach for power, are restrained by the military code of ethics from reaching for it. It is true that armies are prone to use their power and political influence arbitrarily during crises of state authority and divided loyalties. Yet the army pattern of self-control conspicuously illustrates that even the 'practitioners of violence' and the arsenal of their weapons can be controlled by the democratic order under carefully devised safeguards.

Despotism by force of arms usually springs not from the regular army but from private armies,[40] and like industrial overlords it may threaten democracy as an uncontrolled center of power. The swift dissolution of defeated armies and the turning of an officer corps into a quasi-military Bohemia puts skilled groups at the disposal of demagogues for organizing private armies and countering argument by violence. The role of veteran officers and 'perennial soldiers' in Fascist and Nazi terror organizations is well-known.[41] The toleration of conspiratorial groups as independent sources of power is a grave menace to democracy. Here complacency is singularly out of place.

The establishment of standing armies in naval democracies,[42] the increasing influence of the armed forces in view of the new weapons, demand ever alert attention and control of future developments. Democratic theory of the place of armed forces in democratic society has shown little development, especially in view of the new weapons.

The social composition of the armed forces,[43] of naval and army officer corps, has to be watched. One of the well-established reasons for the collapse of the Weimar Republic, for instance, was that during the fights against the Communists, reactionary elements were brought back into the army. Once back, they gradually managed to gain control.[44] In passing we may recall the role of the republican President, Field Marshal von Hindenburg, and his advisers in crises.[45]

Which method of procuring the army for democracy is preferable, the French or the British? The French considered universal military service—that is, the establishment of a 'people's army'—a safeguard of democracy, unlikely to submit to tyranny. Given the cleavage of loyalties among the French people and their drift to the left and right, it is difficult to isolate the variables well enough to prove or disprove the French thesis.[46]

Formerly the British way of neutralizing the danger of the army in politics depended on professional soldiers whose turnover prevented the army from developing a caste mentality or overweening prestige. No militarist spirit could develop in conflict with civil allegiance. This pattern of army organization is characteristic of a naval democracy and an island state and can hardly serve as a model for land powers. Even Great Britain can no longer be considered an island state, militarily speaking, since the successful invasion of the Continent showed that trans-Channel attack is feasible, given the proper naval and air forces. Somewhat reluctantly Great Britain has followed the French model in her postwar conscripted army, and great emphasis is laid on the equation 'soldier citizen.' [47]

The new weapons such as the atomic bomb and rocket missiles with their global range have raised new problems for defense and security.[48] Their solutions will decide on the whole whether there will be democracy and freedom or servitude on earth. The issue of free enterprise *versus* state guidance in industry is much less relevant. This issue is likely to be decided to a greater degree by anticipated conditions of future warfare than by purely economic, legal, or ideological considerations, since the military strength of a country depends more and more on its scientific and industrial potential. Only against this background does it make sense to discuss the control of armed forces, and whether or not they are a safeguard for democracy.

Two antagonistic sets of facts deserve special attention:

1. Since the appearance of long-range missiles and atomic warfare the decisive importance of mass armies, great navies, and even mighty air forces, has decreased.[49] The marked mechanization of the future fighting forces puts a premium on small cadres of skilled specialists. Like the managers in industry these will control greater power and hence may turn into an usurping oligarchy.

2. On the other hand, survival in total warfare demands the participation of every civilian. For European nations World War II eliminated the distinction between combatants and noncombatants forever. Not only were civilians drafted for war work and civilian defense services in Great Britain, they often were exposed to greater risks than were the armed forces. The future co-ordination of soldiers and civilians is sure to be even further extended and emphasized.[50] The slogan 'soldier-worker' of the totalitarians anticipated between the wars social ramifications and demands of total warfare that naval democracies were slow to realize.

All this is bound to foster equalitarian tendencies [51] and is likely to make the armed forces more democratic in tone than ever before. It has been asserted that during the war paradoxically the Nazi army was more 'democratic' and freer of caste elements in the officer corps than the United States Army. Democratic societies may turn grim necessity into a virtue, the more so as new realities meet the need of democratic society for the dissolution of social inequalities and the demand for more than 'equality before the law.'

Standing armies may be viewed as survivals of times when wars were waged by the military only. The people's wars offer a last opportunity to the 'militia' idea, taking advantage of social democratization as the means of efficient defense and security. A national militia of civilian soldiers may prevent the growth of an officer caste selected from an exclusive set of families transmitting a caste spirit estranging them from the common people. No wonder political thinkers concerned with a heightened sense of civic participation in public affairs favor the militia system.[52]

British army education developed promisingly during the war and proved that discussion of public affairs by servicemen in no way weakens morale. This educational program should continue. Mosca's forecast that democratization of armies would import into them conflicting values of society holds true only in societies rent by class conflict and weak bonds of coherence. In a redistributive society class conflict is unlikely and consensus will be strengthened. Modern warfare and technology have brought home to nations and possibly to mankind the lesson that they share a common fate for better or worse. If army education cleaves to the idea that its spirit is an essential safeguard of freedom and equality, education for democracy will not be a sham but a living reality.

VI. THE CIVIL SERVICE [58]

Planning in a complex industrial society presupposes a technically competent, administratively centralized, and politically sound civil service, subject to democratic controls. What has been said about the Army in regard to societal equilibrium applies even more to the bureaucracy. From its beginning in the Italian city republics the dissemination of bureaucracy through the European continental states has been a planning operation. This spread of bureaucracy [54] went hand in hand with the spread of Roman law, establishment of more homogeneously administered political territories, and concentration of the prerogatives of feudal estates and medieval communes in the hands of absolutist princes and their machines. Politico-military competition among the majority of continental states fostered the development of more rational, extensive, and regular tax collections to support the newly established standing armies in place of the sporadic services of mercenaries under *condottieri* leadership. Official tax administration replaced the irrational, wasteful systems of tax farming characteristic of the *ancien régime* in France and the various tax exemptions under feudal estate privileges.

The university reforms of the eighteenth and nineteenth centuries served essentially to train bodies of officials by combining in varying degrees the legal and social sciences, if *Kameralwissenschaft*, the German version of mercantilism, may be included. During the 1740's examinations (the 'merit system') were introduced in Prussia; in 1770 a 'civil service commission' was established; Austria made similar moves during the second half of the eighteenth century. By and large the concept of a permanent, salaried, classified body of qualified and certified public servants, recruited by open competitive examination, has been accepted by all industrialized countries.

To be sure, there are differences in the conception of office depending on cultural tradition. Prussian officialdom,[55] abetted by Lutheran orthodoxy, managed to attach a peculiar religious sanction or *Weihe* to public office which is unknown in the naval democracies. The latter could afford to go slowly for reasons of greater military security, 'unlimited opportunities,' and different legal traditions. In Great Britain, for example, barristers were men of private income trained in interpreting the law under their elders on the King's Bench rather than at the University —English law is not based on Roman law, as is the Napoleonic Code. Nevertheless, Great Britain since the 1850's and the United States since the Civil Service Reform in the 1880's have followed much the same general pattern. In the United States the 'spoils system' championed by Andrew Jackson in 1829 has been increasingly displaced by the 'merit system.' However, many issues of patronage politics, lingering local traditions, inadequate training, overlapping jurisdictions, or deficient controls remain to be ironed out in the interests of efficiency, economy, better personnel, and morale.

Despite their tremendous growth during recent decades, bureaucracies are no real threat to democracy. To be sure, in situations of crisis and in countries of divided loyalties, such as Germany under the Weimar Republic, the Civil Service, though not the center of revolution and not necessarily hostile to democracy, may readily submit to dictatorial usurpation of power; just so the Civil Service submits to the occupation authorities of invading conquerors, as Max Weber rightly emphasized before World War I,[56] a point that has been borne out with minor variations in several countries of continental Europe under shifting political and military destinies. The upper tiers of policy-making officials usually are purged and replaced, but the machine remains essentially intact. Its methodical legalist mode of operation, jurisdictional integration, and the impersonal character of the machine greatly facilitate the reorientation of political ends and objectives from the outside without disruption of disciplined routines. Prussian bureaucracy was an amalgamation of heterogeneous social types, army-trained *Junker*, university-trained commoners, and French émigrés entrepreneurs. The amalgamation resulted in a special type of disinterested public servant with his own ethics and tradition; so modern, possibly class-recruited bureaucracies can under proper legal controls train the officeholder for greater detachment from class bias than he might attain as an individual. The integrated functions of the Civil Service foster an *esprit de corps* that supersedes individual bias.

Once this *esprit de corps* is crystallized and elaborated symbolically into an ethical code and outlook, it affects newcomers and remolds their earlier attitudes. Sociological and psychological investigations can contribute knowledge of the best ways of amalgamating recruits from different social levels in the public service and of adapting them to changing needs.[57] Groups could be planned with the idea of implanting special *esprit de corps* and developing mechanism for the settlement of internal friction and conflicts. Recent studies have contributed greatly to the understanding of informal processes within the formal services: all sorts of discretionary likes and dislikes of officials have been subjected to close scrutiny. (Officials after all are only human.) Cliques and neurotic personalities are realities which should not be overlooked, but rather brought out in the open for discussion and remedy. Field work in these areas of life will become increasingly important and at least as relevant as field work in slums. H. D. Lasswell [58] has made especially valuable contributions by developing methods of analyzing different types of officials and their behavior.

Besides these internal controls, new external controls have been devised. It is a rule of thumb, significantly verified not long ago, that one way of controlling a bureaucratic body is to establish a rival machine. Competition frequently sublimates antagonism into constructive criticism. Officeholders in rival departments may be one another's best critics. They know the tricks of the trade and are likely to penetrate behind the curtain of the 'official secret.' [59] Besides, provision can be made for regular, complete reports of administrative agencies of interest not only to parliamentary bodies and policy-making chiefs but to the public at large.

In industrial nations numerous and varied adult education services, a national health service, local and central housing authorities, elaborate insurance systems, and the like have greatly increased the functions and scope of public authorities. Some states, moreover, not only have become owners of a large part of the national resources including coal, electricity, and national transport, but also undertake to organize and apply research for industrial, agricultural, and defense purposes in addition to planning and supervising new regional and urban developments.

Obviously this changed situation is bound to modify to some extent the training and qualifications demanded of an efficient civil servant. As H. R. C. Greaves has pointed out, for instance, the principles of the British Civil Service laid down by the reformers about a hundred years ago, imputed to the properly qualified higher civil servant intellectual caliber and upperclass descent which would place him on an easy footing with the aristocracy. On the other hand, 'the qualities most urgently in demand for the public servant of the twentieth century state' are 'initiative and enterprise, originality and constructiveness of mind, of human understanding and democratic contact, of scientific training and acquaintance with social studies.' [60]

Before World War I the function of the State was largely limited to the passing of laws, which, in turn, were more or less an expression of the commonly accepted principles governing property rights and the relations between citizens. Then 'the power to make a logical analysis and to give a dispassionate judgment was the chief quality required of the higher civil servant.' In administering the law, he had 'to apply a general principle to a particular instance.' But with the new economic functions resulting from state controls the situation has changed indeed. 'A greater flexibility of mind,' as G. Williams has observed, 'is needed, an ability to relate cause and effect, the power to foresee a chain of developments so that future events may be discounted by present action, quickness of decision and readiness to take action.' [61]

VII. DEMOCRATIC CONTROL OF PRESS AND RADIO [62]

Next we shall deal with the Press and Radio and their great power to produce and disseminate information, opinion, and propaganda. Democratic control of these new power institutions is vital as their influence is bound to increase with the growth of society. Agencies reaching the masses could be left alone as long as their power was dispersed. Small competing newspapers and small propaganda organizations vying with each other could cause no great damage. But their increasing radius of influence and central management from key positions focuses attention on their public responsibility and frequent failure to live up to it. To this extent the growth and use of their power cannot remain outside public control.

1. *Freedom of the Press*

Frequently the issue is confused by discussing the long established corporate structure of news agencies and newspapers in terms of individuals whose liberty must be protected. C. J. Friedrich rightly remarks that the corporate structure of the press makes it imperative and legitimate for the state to find ways and means of restraining effectively the exercise of this institutional power.[63]

The original meaning and function of the press is to provide information and to help clarify opinion by free discussion. The first aim is not fulfilled unless reliable news presentation is guaranteed,[64] and the second is unwarranted if big business owns the papers and monopolizes opinion or, by indirect advertising influence, allocates undue space and radio time for the propagation of partisan interests. The balance of society cannot be maintained if privileged groups can use the most powerful apparatus for dissemination of their ideas while the less privileged are deprived of similar means of expression. It is not easy to find a remedy because the size of a newspaper concern often ensures the quality of its news service and the scope of its coverage. On the other hand the very size of the newspaper business would facilitate control by a body of public trustees comparable to the board of many universities, and this may well be the right approach. The London *Times,* the *Manchester Guardian,* and the *Observer* have thus been made independent in the public interest. Trusteeship need not interfere with the expression of political opinions on the part of different newspapers beyond guarding their conformity to democratic aims. Public trusteeship would free both press and radio from dependence on monopolistic interests.

It is characteristic of the growing awareness of responsible citizens, both of Great Britain and of the United States, that in both countries committees have recently carried on searching inquiries into the structure and current tendencies of the press.

In Great Britain the Prime Minister appointed a Royal Commission [65] at the request of a majority of members of Parliament in March 1947. The resulting reports constitute a mine of information obtained by painstaking cross-examination of editors, newspaper proprietors, and journalists; moreover they open up new possibilities for finding compromise between freedom of the press from all state control on the one hand and from the restrictions and pressures of newspaper chains on the other.[66]

While this enquiry throws much new light on the conditions, practices, and dangers of newspaper production in Great Britain, the report on American newspapers and other mass media by the Commission on Freedom of the Press clearly states both the dangers and the requirements of the present situation. There is an inverse ratio between the widespread influence of the press today and the size of the group that can use it as an instrument for expressing its views. Whereas the importance of the press to the people has greatly increased with its development as a means of mass communication, this development 'has greatly decreased the proportion of the people who can express their opinions and ideas through the Press.'

Through the clear exposure of this and other dangerous trends, emphasis is particularly laid on two of the five requirements indicating 'what our society is entitled to demand of its Press.' On the one hand 'all the important viewpoints and interests in the society should be represented in its agencies of mass communication.' On the other hand 'the projection of a representative picture of the constituent groups in the society is needed. . . The truth about any social group, though it should not exclude its weaknesses and vices, includes also recognition of its values, aspirations, its common humanity.' [67]

2. Responsibility of Radio Management

The problem of variety and balance of programs adapted to widely different opinions and tastes and appealing to different sections of the population is today no less vital in the field of radio. The structure and organization of the British Broadcasting Corporation (BBC) as a public corporation [68] is a very promising experiment in dealing with the problem of a centralized communication service in a democratic spirit. BBC regulations guarantee fair presentation of different views. Thus an instrument that lends itself eminently to totalitarian exploitation is brought under democratic control. It is democratic first because the BBC Board represents control not by business interests alone but shared by representatives of various sections of the public,[69] and the whole is put under parliamentary control. The pattern of the BBC shows that the will to organize an institution democratically is more important than the technical nature of the instrument. Radio by its very technique lends itself easily to over-centralization and dictation, but in Britain the democratic mind proved to be strong enough to invent an organizational pattern capable of stifling these tendencies.

The great problem was, of course, to agree on a fair method of allotting time to all representative opinions and tastes. In the past the equilibrium between tastes and opinions has been established largely through free competition. Now it must be planned in the spirit of fair play. Even if the result is not always so satisfactory as one would wish, it can always be improved, and what is more important, by open discussion rather than by unseen controls. Once more the growth of creative control did not diminish freedom but increased it.

In the emerging solution proportionate representation of opinion is not left to chance but is settled through voluntary agreement. The result may sometimes be unjust, partly because one can never overcome certain obstacles to the establishment of 'true proportion' of interests, and partly because such matters are never quite measurable in precise terms. But even so these inadequacies can continuously be revised as they happen on the plane of conscious agreement and are not due to decisions beyond public control.

Considering the power of radio propaganda from the point of view of a balanced structure of society, a clear stand should be taken against permitting anti-democratic propaganda. At the level of theoretical discussion, democracy should admit all views, if only for fully developing the democratic theory in continuous discussion with its opponents. But it would be suicidal to allow anti-democratic propaganda and, what is worse, incitement, to operate freely. One of the essentials of democracy is the belief in peaceful change. Democracy should defend this re-

L

quirement of its existence. The one thing it cannot tolerate is propaganda for violence as a method of settling disputes.[70]

For this reason it will be imperative to distinguish rational discussion from propaganda as a means of influencing public opinion. In small societies discussion and persuasion were intermingled. A speech in an assembly was partly based upon rational argument and partly on emotional contagion. With the growth of society the two functions often become dissociated. In a mass meeting, argument is only a façade, a sham. The main function of the mass meeting is to sway emotions and to focus attention on and reinforce creeds and aspirations. The contrary is true of committee meetings, where the emotional elements tend to be screened out of the argument so that sober discussion is feasible. The parliamentary system still allows for a good deal of genuine emotional discussion in the plenum, but one can hardly deny that the real working discussion is increasingly shifting to committee meetings.

3. The Nature of Propaganda [71]

We must begin our discussion of the control of propaganda by eliminating some prevailing misconceptions. Many people still conceive of propaganda as no more than the fine art of spreading lies and arousing dangerous emotions. Democratic society should firmly control any such dangerous maneuvers by plain censorship or by insisting upon strict accountability for untrue assertions.[72] Propaganda, however, can be fully appreciated only if one recognizes its most significant function, namely, the determination of the *reality level* on which people are going to discuss and act.

By 'reality level' we mean that every society develops a mental climate in which certain facts and their interrelations are considered basic and called 'real,' whereas other ideas fall below the level of 'reasonably acceptable' statements and are called fantastic, utopian, or unrealistic. In every society there is a generally accepted interpretation of reality. In this sense every society establishes a set of respectable ideas through its conventions, and ostracizes any others as 'diabolic,' 'subversive,' or 'unworthy.' Being 'real' or 'less real' is always an *a priori* reason for ascribing more or less worth to certain facts. Whatever different schools of philosophy may think about this, and however much instrumentalism and logical positivism may consider such ontology fallacious, it is a sociological fact that public thinking unconsciously establishes such reality-levels, and a society is only integrated if its members roughly agree on a certain ontological order.

Take, for instance, a country governed mainly by pacifist opinion and discussing the question of war, and contrast it with discussion of the same problem in a country where a militarist spirit prevails. The facts considered may be roughly the same. The main difference would lie in the fact that in the country with a militarist atmosphere pacifists are considered cranks who do not care to face the facts of life, people with a lower sense of reality. Contrariwise, in the country with a pacifist mentality the heroes of warring nations are regarded as sadists with perverted minds. In making the latter judgment, human nature would be defined as basically co-operative and peaceful, spoiled only by human institutions created in the interests of the few who produce the perverted mind, the dehumanized person.

The concept of a reality level also helps us to understand better the establishment of Marxism as dogma in the U.S.S.R., where it is not merely a whim of the ruling group but apparently is vital for stabilizing the popular sense of reality. This frame of reference ascribes supreme dignity to the economic dynamics of society, other factors being only incidental in character; class struggle is ultimate reality, tactics and strategy deduced from it are 'realistic'; any deviating approach is not only error in theory but partakes of subversive reality undermining the road to progress. One needs to be aware of the significance of the reality level in public thinking to understand why totalitarian states pursue philosophies different from our own. 'Those who differ in opinion need not be convinced, but simply suppressed.' A similarly inferior reality has been attributed to Jews, Liberals, Democrats, Marxists, Christians, and so on, in the Nazi system, and their persecution was spuriously justified by their falling below the 'truth' which was the inspiration of Nazism. In the totalitarian systems the main function of propaganda is to set up this platform, to establish what is practicable or utopian, true or subversive, as unshakable premises for further thought. The aim is to bring the integrative values of the society concerned into what H. D. Lasswell calls the 'focus of public attention,' and to charge these values and thought habits with emotion. By promoting unconscious acceptance in the people, fears of considering alternative approaches are inculcated. Before it can be argued pro and con, it is settled on the plane of propaganda what kind of world we live in, and the paramount value of the dominant doctrine in explaining reality.

4. The Democratic Realm of Discussion

The question arises whether Democracy has a reality level of its own and if so, whether it can exist without implanting its seeds in the unconscious mind of the citizenry.

Democratic society, I am convinced, develops a level below which no citizen should fall. The authoritarian mind, the dictator, the citizen as an automaton, the dogmatic mind, drop below the level of genuine humanity. But it is characteristic of Democracy to admit loose ends from the very outset and to appreciate greater variety in thinking. It is also part of democratic education to develop the type of mind that is not confused when it has to adjust to various fine shades of differences.

As we stated before, Democracy essentially admits competing reality levels to the realm of discussion and adjusts these reality levels through communication, living contacts, exchange of ideas, development of common rituals. Society is democratic as long as this mutual adjustment of reality levels is spontaneous. In a democratic society the pacifist and militarist, the anarchist and totalitarian points of view can be discussed so long as the synthesizing power of the public mind can see them as extremes of a series, the center of which is firm enough to balance both ends. The democratic spirit is experimental: it does not even fix the reality level as absolute, but considers life—the political process —as unceasingly dynamic.[73] Just so the parliamentary process continually adjusts the two extremes—Government and Opposition—to one another, not like a pendulum moving to and fro from a fixed center, but rather as the center itself moving in a given direction. Likewise, in the long run, the whole platform of democratic discussion shifts invisibly, but in keeping with shifts in public opinion. One has only to compare longer historical periods to become aware of how progress is made in a society allowing freedom of discussion. Take, for instance, the number of 'socialist' axioms tacitly taken for granted by conservatives today, which a few decades ago were considered utopian. This great ability to shift the ground of democratic discussion, changing the reality level invisibly, should not be exaggerated, however. If the free integration of a democratic society through public opinion is exposed to violent change, mental chaos ensues. Here lies the significance of a certain amount of direct propaganda for the democratic system and of education for Democracy. By deliberately creating an emotional atmosphere for the growth of loyalty sentiments a reality level is established—a set of beliefs and options with which the majority of the people identify themselves. It is often argued against Democracy that it can tolerate opposing views only so long as they represent dwindling minorities: that it can afford to treat the conscientious objectors leniently so long as their number does not grow beyond a modest percentage. But what would happen, the critics demand, if one of these divergent groups were to become too strong and tend to suppress the established reality level of democratic society? This argument raises a point we have to face squarely.

5. Loyalties and Consensus

In the balanced structure of society, power is not only vested in economic institutions, in the Civil Service or in the Armed Forces, but rests to a considerable degree with capricious public opinion. In this sphere the balance of Democracy is only maintained if divergent views are focused on a certain point of stability. Tolerance of deviations is only possible if all those who wish to be different accept the democratic method as the core of their moral code, as their own reality level. If this basic consensus is destroyed, the same kind of chaos ensues that we know in the economic sphere as 'crisis.' This would seem to justify allowing the majority to propagate with more insistence those views that are strong guarantees of democratic order.[74] Democracy likewise has the right to develop a core of democratic educational policy and to pave the way for its emotional acceptance by deliberate use of propaganda. In this way, loyalty to certain values and ways of life can be inculcated more thoroughly than would be feasible by merely theoretical discussion.

It is imperative for us to realize that public life is not based upon theoretical discussion only (in which total absence of emotion is indispensable for truth) but that it is rooted in habits and unconscious valuations. Democracy cannot survive without this: the mere intellectual interpretation of Democracy would shut its eyes to the most elementary preconditions of consensus. On the other hand, it shows lack of foresight to confuse a minimum of inculcated loyalty by education and propaganda with totalitarian indoctrination and the exclusive presentation of one point of view only. Admission of the need for basic integration of values in society is fundamentally different from the total attack of a one-party system on the citizen, leaving him no choice or independent thought.

The use made of inculcation in a democracy is, as in everything else, a question of degree. Doing nothing about it is as harmful as overdoing it: once more it becomes a matter of agreed policy defining the purpose, range, and technique of creating loyalty to the democratic system.

One of the reasons why inculcation of loyalties through propaganda should not go beyond certain limits is that it might endanger the smooth working of one of the most proper instruments of a dynamic Democracy—public opinion. Public opinion [75] is a genuine entity—it is more than the sum total of effects produced by the press, by propaganda, and other media. These are part of it, but do not make up the whole. Public opinion is an all-embracing fluid medium composed of moods, ethical valuations, attitudes, not produced by any agency by manipulation, but growing out of innumerable contacts existing in neighborhood units, in clubs, in pubs, in common rooms, and in the street. Where the tradition of Democracy is alive, it is cherished. Its power in Britain could best be seen when Chamberlain's appeasement policy was curbed by public opinion. In democracies common morality is believed to have its roots in public opinion, and the latter is in some ways the modern equivalent of taboos in tribal society and in those societies still rooted in tradition. Therefore the maintenance of public opinion as a spiritual power is essential to Democracy, and in planning the structure of society everything should be done to maintain free change of opinion without too much interference by artificial manipulation. Education and propaganda in the foregoing sense should indeed help to establish common attitudes and a definite sense of reality. But apart from these two influences, spontaneous sources of democratic agreement—the life of opinion in its genuine form —should be preserved. This is not an easy task in a mass society, as the real nuclei in forming opinion are the cells of society— the family, the neighborhood unit, and the workshop—and spontaneous interplay among them is the germinating power. Where conditions for such common living are destroyed, communication between men is blocked and spiritual life itself suffers. As we all know, the sudden growth of industrial civilization, especially the growth of the metropolis, destroyed the basic form of free integration in society, and therefore reconstruction will have to start with community and town planning, with the regulation of the physical structure of society. But opinion does not mean life in the basic cells only. From the primary cells a network of institutionalized and more artificial channels leads to the wider area where the nation's public mind absorbs views emanating from most diverse sources.

Among these centers above the primary cells, the factory will gain special significance, as it is bound to become an ever more important focus for forming opinion in a Democracy. The schools are bound to become another center. County councils, councils on higher levels, trade unions, chambers of commerce, and the endless numbers of other organized platforms for the formation of opinion should be linked with one another so as to make intercommunication easy. To maintain, in spite of mechanization, the fluidity of public opinion is all-important in a democratic society.

Free public opinion, apart from being the dynamic of Democracy, is also essential as a safety valve against the suppression that usually prevails in small groups and cliques. Very often only the fear that grievances may be ventilated prevents thousands of petty tyrants from suppressing the underdog. Those who are afraid of state tyranny should remember that the average man finds the dangerous tyrant near at hand in the form of his boss, and is less worried about a dictator who at least is out of reach. Therefore the sanctity and freedom of public opinion must be watched as carefully as any of the institutions previously considered.

In conclusion two things should be borne in mind: first, that at the present stage of development in social techniques, the growing power centers must be guided in such a manner that they interfere as little as possible with the people's freedom. Even though we claim that the structure of society has to be controlled, this does not imply that people should be controlled in their private and business life or in the sphere of public opinion. On the contrary, the inevitable interference of social techniques with private life and business should be controlled in order to prevent the complete subjection of society. To be against all control means to give free rein to the oppressive techniques of society. This is as stupid as to say that the freedom of a motorcar consists in having no brakes.

The second point to emerge is that external control becomes necessary only when adverse tendencies develop out of democratic freedom of action. The guiding principle should be that any regulation must be democratically agreed upon, carried out, and revised under public supervision, and that it interfere as little as possible with the spontaneous working of the institutions. The various agencies for public regulation may sooner or later be merged into an integrated Vigilance Committee to watch over the expansion of power centers as well as the preventive measures themselves, lest they become as autocratic as the institution they seek to check.

⑥

Democratic Control of Government in a
Planned Society

○

Clarification of the structure and equilibrium of society raises
the question of how to control government in the throes of moving toward democratic planning. Instead of describing the machinery of representative government in its various present
forms, we shall confine the discussion to those crucial situations
where parliamentary government is faced with the predicament
of the new age and its inherent institutional principles seem
imperfectly adjusted to the demands upon it. Although the representative system is not the only conceivable form of democratic control it may be fruitful to point out places where the
established system of representative government may have difficulty in adjusting to new functions.

I. HISTORICAL LIMITATIONS OF THE MODERN DEMOCRATIC IDEA

It is not always realized that the representative system as the
most widespread form of democratic government is often of
rather recent origin. In fact representative systems constituted
the first attempts of nations at conscious planning of their machinery of government. Though the idea of democratic control
by civic assemblies originated in ancient Greece and Rome, it
was more or less lost sight of in the Dark Ages or found but
shaky footing in medieval corporate bodies without claims to
sovereignty.[1] It was the rising modern middle class that brought
the democratic idea to the fore again. The middle class had the

will and power to control the affairs of the community which during the age of Absolutism had been placed in the hands of noblemen and/or bureaucracies.[2]

Ideas of puritan divines and philosophers regarding revolutionary natural law, notably of Rousseau and Montesquieu on the Continent, laid the foundation for a system that enabled the middle class to change from subjects into modern citizens and control society. Rousseau's philosophy justified the citizen in considering himself the final judge of his government in public affairs. Montesquieu taught us to control those who control and to develop a planned equilibrium, if not in society at large, at least among the groups in power. His famous theory demanded the 'division of the three main powers' of legislature, administration, and judiciary—a theory which he projected into the British parliamentary system. Montesquieu's theory is informed by a passion for constitution-making and foreshadows the planning mentality of our time.

The idea of equilibrium was elaborated in the rationalist manner of the eighteenth century and found its radical application in the American Constitution. The rational idea of balance, however, was refined to such a degree that this product of rationalism is badly in need of skilful reinterpretation. By picturing the organic balance of a historically developed system in clear-cut rational terminology Montesquieu and the eighteenth-century philosophers were the first to demonstrate the pitfalls of overrationalization held up to derision by Edmund Burke. Their overrationalization should be a reminder to keep all planned machinery flexible and adaptable to constant vicissitudes of change.[3]

The newly established or reconstituted modern systems of representative government with their usually bicameral legislature —the lower house representing the will of the people—served nineteenth-century society fairly well, although the vacillation of France between republican and Bonapartist regimes punctuated by revolutions and *coups d'état* possibly foreshadowed difficulties characteristic of European nations in twentieth-century crises.

The actual or potential breakdown of representative systems in contemporary crises may best be understood by realizing their original sociological purpose in its historical social setting as contrasted with the challenging conditions of today.

At the time of their origin the main purpose of representative systems in Europe was to balance the absolutist bureaucracy. As a newly risen power organ the bureaucracy appeared to be in a key position enabling it to repress the uprising and aspirations of other classes. Apart from the Army the bureaucracy was the first integrated large organization that could have curtailed the liberties of the *bourgeoisie* who considered their way of life the essence of human freedom. Hence the middle classes made every effort to limit this new bureaucratic power and attitude which was so different from that of the marketplace and free associations. It bore the imprint of hierarchy with its emphasis on legalist punctilio, predictable promotion, seniority claims, merit ratings, tenure, security, routine, and precedent.

The modern ethos of parliamentary control thus is rooted in a world of two distinct compartments, society and bureaucracy. The whole fervor of liberalism derives from this antithesis.[4] Liberalism fears that the bureaucratic mentality will invade non-bureaucratic areas of life, and that the new power positions will outweigh the dispersed power of competing small units. As shown above, this alternative and its setting no longer exist. Power is no longer concentrated exclusively in the Civil Service. Aside from the Army, social freedom can be impaired by big business, organized labor, or the centralized agencies of mass propaganda. All of these, we repeat, have to be brought under public control, since none of them represents the independent small units of spontaneous self-adjustment.

Furthermore, the clear-cut distinction between two types of mentality, that of the 'bureaucrat' and that of 'free enterprise,' no longer exists. Bureaucracy today implements big business. It is possible to blend the tradition and routine of the civil servant with the virtues and traits characteristic of free enterprise. Modern bureaucracy no longer represents what John Stuart Mill once called 'pedantocracy.' The distinction between 'real life' and 'blue print administration' loses in significance. So many key positions are connected with centralized bodies demanding control that the Civil Service would seem to be the least harmful and most restrained type of management—although, of course, it requires strict supervision.

A new situation has arisen with the tremendous increase of affairs calling for governmental attention and legislative control. This raises the question whether the machinery of parliamentary control is sufficiently strong and efficient to cope with the multitudinous issues raised by the various new key positions and their dynamic operations.

II. TWO OBSOLETE SAFEGUARDS OF DEMOCRACY

Balance in the structure of society is prerequisite to the maintenance of democracy. In the first place it denies one or several power groups the opportunity to apply pressure to harness the government to their special interests. Adopting a constitution is no substitute for such balance. Once it has been attained, safeguards should be built into the government machinery to preserve it, especially as the citizenry and their representatives have lost two once-powerful means of controlling the administration: control of the budget and the threat of armed uprising.

The latter threat was particularly effective so long as the rifle was still the chief weapon. The mere threat of armed popular resistance guaranteed popular democratic government. Thomas Jefferson in his often cited statements gave classical expression to this sentiment.[5]

In an age of machine warfare the practically unarmed citizenry cannot offer effective resistance in a critical situation. Barricades and small arms offer no serious obstacles to howitzers, as Viennese social democracy learned in 1934.[6]

As to budgetary control, John MacMurray [7] rightly says: 'In a country where the government has direct control of the country's economic resources, it simply reserves for its own purpose what it thinks necessary before distributing the remainder to its citizens for their use.' So long as wealth was dispersed and government could not collect without the taxpayer's consent, the acceptance or rejection of the budget served to check governmental activities. Today acceptance of the budget still is the strongest expression and symbol of consent. In a crisis situation, however, a powerful administration might refuse to submit to the will of the representatives and their refusal to vote the budget would hardly mean much.[8]

From these reflections on the essential weakness of popular control of government in modern emergencies we may deduce the following formula: The more the older safeguards against tyranny are weakened, the more weight falls on efficient organization of the common will. Permanent vigilance is required against all attempts of sectional powers to establish tyranny. The organized majority, even unarmed, is still able to curb attempts of minorities to usurp power through timely exposure and isolation. General strikes and organized passive resistance may suffice to bring usurpers swiftly down before they have time to organize and establish a totalitarian dictatorship.[9] Once tyranny is in the saddle, however, civic resistance has meager means at its disposal. The strategic time for action is in the formative phase bf dictatorship. It must be fought in the making. This requires a new and heretofore unknown level of public alertness to dangers in society from the personnel, techniques, and stratagems of usurpist groups.[10] Democracy in a machine civilization demands political mass education of the citizenry to heighten understanding of anti-democratic threats, their sources and techniques. Socialists, Conservatives, Liberals, or any other democratic party, regardless of differences, should recognize as their common enemy not the enlightened masses, but the demagogically exploited, and enraged mob.[11] The dangerous enemies of Democracy are not those conservatives eager to retain as much power as possible, but the *condottieri* out to overthrow democratic government as a means of lawful change, in order to set up a tyranny with the help of the mob. While progressives must learn to recognize conservatism as part of the democratic process, conservatives will have to learn that mass ignorance and low educational levels no longer are in their interest. They must learn no longer to look askance at representative assemblies and their work.

III. NINE VIRTUES OF REPRESENTATIVE GOVERNMENT

Whatever criticism may be leveled against representative government its outstanding virtues are bound to make it the point of departure for any social organization safeguarding freedom. The lasting virtues of representative government as the best instrument of democratic control may be summarized as follows:

1. *The Integration of All Social Forces.* Representative government integrates the whole people and all vital currents in society. It is to Mosca's credit that he has shown representative government to be the only political organization that utilizes all 'social forces,' i.e. the vital and politically significant currents of society.[12] The weakness of all other forms of government, however efficient, is that they can rely on only a few social groups to oppose all the rest whom they have to repress. This sociological definition does not base the art of government spuriously on the individual, but on actual basic tendencies and forces of society at large. This should not be taken to imply any lack of respect for the dignity of the individual: the full development of individual capacity is and will remain the main educational aim of a truly democratic society. The sociological approach to politics, however, represents a departure from individualist theory which overlooks the fact that the art of government consists in utilizing and co-ordinating basically antagonistic tendencies in society. Statesmanlike leadership takes account of these dynamic trends and would fall short were it aiming merely to satisfy individual demands or average wants. Only aspirations and trends of sufficient strength to integrate group demands can be politically relevant.

2. *Competition in Ideas and Bargaining.* The representative system achieves a dual purpose: It provides a platform for voicing sectional interests, at the same time amalgamating them into a dynamically balanced pattern of agreements by bargain. The democratic pattern of struggle and discussion trains the contestants to seek and reach maximum agreement. Democratic agreement does not mean uniformity, but co-ordination of plural strivings limiting each other and producing a co-operative scheme. Such co-operation springs from day-to-day struggles aiming at a negotiated constructive compromise.[13] Not all forms of converging sectional interests lead to constructive compromise. Their selection may be faulty in principle, the social pattern and spirit of their meeting may be such as to intensify rather than mitigate antagonism. It is one of the basic tenets of political sociology that varying responses can be elicited from the very same persons according to their social field of action, the pat-

tern of their interrelationships, and the nature of the challenging ideas. From this point of view the representative system has lasting merits. By defining constituencies according to the territorial principle, it sees to it that no sectional interest predominates at the polls. The voter is called out as a citizen, not as a member of a sect, profession, or class. Democracy provides maximum opportunities for integrating the citizenry along status, class, religious, and vocational lines. It allows for appeals to their special interests, for their organization into pressure groups. But when it comes to presidential and parliamentary elections of democratically organized nations the factors making for solidarity and the definition of the common good are given an opportunity to integrate the nation.

Elected representatives in Parliament dramatize conflicting ideas and they may plead special interests. Their cross fire and tested negotiating powers, however, usually make for the crystallization of an integral point of view and produces a constructive compromise by bargaining.

People do not become high-minded and capable of seeing the common good because they are told to do so. But under pressure from rival forces and cross currents, all parties are compelled to plead in the name of the common good, which may be defined as the end product of the parallelogram of forces bargaining for power.[14]

Parliamentary discussion and committee work make for the refinement of group egotism and eventually produce the 'common will,' the *volonté générale* as contrasted with the *volonté de tous* in Rousseau's terms. There is nothing mystical about this *volonté générale*. It is no metaphysical entity such as a 'group mind' or 'eternal justice and truth.' It is the simple result of a social technique which motivates political leaders to co-operate here and now in overcoming their sectional interests and rival definitions of situations and objectives.

3. *The Superiority of Parliamentary over Corporate Representation.* Parliamentary representation has been criticized both from the Left and the Right in the name of allegedly superior schemes of corporate or syndicalist representation able to express existing social forces more articulately.[15] For this very reason corporate representation cannot achieve the integrative

function of parliamentary representation based on territorially rather than functionally defined constituencies. The issue certainly is a grave one, as modern society cannot carry on without large functional organizations representing business, labor, farmer interests, and so on, which need to be controlled and on occasion forced into negotiated agreements.[16] But it is a fallacy to deduce from this the advisability of a new type of corporate representation to replace or supplement parliamentary bodies.[17]

Functional representation of sectional interests in a special chamber alongside a territorially elected assembly leads to dual government, which can have either of two results. If the chamber acts in unison it may overpower the assembly, paralyze and sooner or later suppress it, disintegrating the nation into scattered and conflicting interest groups. A superior force would then have to enter the scene, and this might well lead to a fascist development of the party system implemented by semimilitary organizations to curb the chamber of corporate interest groups and their machines. Both in the structure of society and its representational system the ascendancy of sectional integration would threaten democracy. Great tensions are bound to be generated in a sectionally organized and divided society, which can only be overcome by a repressive one-party system with fighting forces drawn from the various strata of society. The apparent 'unity' under Fascism, however, does not result from discussion but from propaganda, terror, and the dictatorial imposition of 'solutions.' Once in power the dictator and his band of followers turn their forces against the syndicalist organizations and infiltrate, capture, and turn them into tools of mass regimentation for the benefit of the regime—not their members.[18] A chamber of syndicates by itself cannot evolve a balanced approach because its very principle of election serves to play up rather than down the dividing elements of the community.

The integrative function of a system based on territorial representation according to constitutional allotment counteracts the splitting of the community along sectional lines. Corporate syndicates may serve as pressure groups; they may lobby; they may give advice without basically disturbing democratic balance and integration; but they cannot be built into the constitutional organism either as a second chamber or as an independent body.

As an element of sovereignty they are likely to represent 'dual government' leading to imbalance, disintegration, and totalitarian repression.

4. *Emotional Identification and Sense of Responsibility.* The representative system offers optimal satisfaction to the citizenry by driving home the lesson of self-determination. As the electorate ultimately gets the government it 'deserves,' the system deeply engages the sense of civic responsibility and promotes maximum identification of the citizen with the community. The strength of this sentiment is revealed when democratic institutions collapse and people suddenly realize what it means to live in servitude. In a smoothly functioning democracy of long standing, the delights of freedom usually are taken for granted, and many fail to appreciate their heritage. That is one of the reasons why identification with the community and its freedom is and should be nurtured continuously by acts of symbolic reaffirmation in the nature of elections and election campaigns.

5. *Public Accountability.* Public accountability is one of the most important principles of democratic control.[19] Modern society often produces social techniques that would seem to be similar in totalitarian and democratic systems. In such cases public accountability points to the essential difference. A society may be said to be democratic if its relevant institutions are publicly accountable.[20] To be sure, forms of accountability may vary. There may be accountability to public trustees, boards of regents, administrative, and finally parliamentary authorities, depending on the nature of issues, institutions, and their setting.

6. *Assignment of Responsibility.* The institution of periodic election of parliaments and chief executives establishes true responsibility of government to the governed. If things go wrong, the electorate know whom to remove. Responsibilities ascribed to leaders are kept very much in evidence, a fact that matters in a rather obscure mass society more than in a socially transparent parochial world. The artificially high-lighted presence of modern tyrants may in part account for the appeal of 'leadership states' among the masses. The 'changing of the guards' —that is, rotation in office—is a virtue of the representative system and allows it to dispense with the 'purges' familiar from ancient city-states and modern totalitarianism.[21]

M

7. *Flexible Policies.* Rotation in office gives opportunities to new men and new policies. This admirably suits the experimental character of the modern age, which has gradually taught man to assume an experimental attitude toward social reality [22] and to learn by trial and error in experimental policies. Such social experimentation differs from scientific experiments in that (a) political wisdom does not mean applying the hard and fast rules of controlled experiments but rather applying reasonable expectations to a highly complex and plastic reality, thus making flexibility one of the inherent principles in democracy; (b) too sudden changes of policies for the sake of experiment would destroy people's belief in stability and undermine the confidence necessary for co-operation; (c) planning requires constancy of basic enactments and objectives over predictable planning periods, allowing for flexibility of means within a stable framework.

8. *The Constructive Use of the Opposition.* A genuinely representative system, parliamentary or presidential, alone can make constructive use of opposition and criticism. It is the climax of societal integration founded on open legitimate competition in ideas.[23]

9. *The Resolution to Act.* The democratic vote settles discussion and enforces the decision to act here and now. Even those who doubt the sound judgment of the multitude [24] have to recognize this fact. Rational discussion may lead to endless debate, yet action imperatively demands decision. The absolutist monarch of old settled it by following the ancient maxim of despots: *Sic volo, sic jubeo!* Since belief in the divine origin and right of kings or rulers—not to mention the totalitarian propaganda of the Führer's infallibility—has been shaken, the majority has been made the irrational power to cut the Gordian knot of inconclusive discussion by its vote and resolve. Rational and convincing briefs can be made for indispensable and preferential means to given ends. Rational analysis may also help clarify what values we prefer, their implications, and likely consequences. In conflicts of values where rational analysis falls short of offering a decision, the majority vote settles the endless debate. We do not condemn its possibly irrational nature, but accept it as an oracular decision: *vox populi vox dei.*

IV. THE DEMOCRATIC PROCESS

The comparatively great assets of the representative system should not blind us to some of its weak spots which have been a great liability in the past and may well become greater liabilities under the changing conditions of an expanding society.

Enemies of democracy and representative government, and even some of its supporters, have long worried about the judiciousness of the multitude in matters of statecraft. In a small community such as the polity of Athens, one might reasonably expect the citizenry to understand and judge public affairs. But in a society as complex as ours—so the argument goes—it is superstitious to trust the judgment of the masses in complicated matters of supreme importance. In Athens, after all, the slaves were not active citizens, and its 'democracy' was actually the minority rule of what we would call a middle class.

The anomalies of modern mass democracy became quite evident when the German people under trying circumstances could be so manipulated by mass techniques that they helped their own tyrant into the saddle. The malfunctioning of mass democracy alone should suffice to discredit the tradition of Rousseau and his followers, i.e. the belief in the sovereignty of the people in the Age of the Masses, in all circumstances.

We must face the fact that the institutions of the representative system work only under certain conditions. Hence an adequate theory of representative government would have to give account of necessary and sufficient causes for both the success and the failure of the system. The crucial issue is the suffrage, the gradual extension of the vote to all adult citizens of the community regardless of property, education, race, or other qualifications except those of medical and criminal deviations from the normal.

1. *The Function of Suffrage*

Is there a theory that can account for and justify the 'control by the many' as rational and not absurd—a theory that can establish the indispensable formula for the successful functioning of the universal franchise? Neither the extremely individualist nor the collectivist approach can avail us in answering whether the multitude can judge what is right or wrong, prudent or imprudent in politics. It would be equally futile to ask individuals, one by one, in order to settle whether John or Bill can intelligently understand this or that political issue. Obviously none, not even the best of us, could know all the answers to the hosts of questions daily pressing upon us. Nor can we accept the doctrine of some mystical entity, *la volonté générale,* which allegedly guides the mass of the people and, like the Roman genius, helps them to find presumably better solutions to problems of the community than any individual or small elite could ever find. A satisfactory explanation must lie elsewhere.

First, we must realize that to understand the suffrage properly it must not be taken out of context but interpreted as part of the democratic process as a whole. If mass decisions were immediately put into effect and if the masses had to judge all issues directly, or even if their representatives were the only ones to shape policies, they would hardly stand the test. But neither the masses nor their parliamentary representatives are the only ones who govern. The electorate only approve or reject the proposals and declared intentions of their candidates. The elected representatives in turn support or check the policies proposed by a very small group—in Britain, e.g. the Cabinet. Thus, suffrage is but one phase in the whole democratic process of crystallizing public opinion and arriving at policy decisions for legislative and administrative action. Sociologically speaking suffrage is only a phase in a sociopolitical process of continually adjusting society to changing conditions and events. The general election is just the first ripple in a stream, and much depends on the subsequent course of the political process. The participation of the electorate, the molding power of the parties, the formation of a government, its co-operation with advisory bodies, committees, and the Civil Service, together produce what is to be judged on its merits. In this broader view the political process as a whole appears as a catalyst of raw impulses, and its function is to transform general indications of policy, the 'mandate' of the people, into workable policies.

The question whether the masses are capable of governing is, as it stands, sociologically misleading. It is more reasonable to ask whether they are able to express those underlying trends of the community which they experience in workaday life.

The theoretical question is whether we may reasonably expect the simmering of a multitude of attitudes eventually to lead to the automatic solution of minor deviations and to throw into relief the motivating mood which is most prevalent and profound in the multitude.

In this connection it is important to notice that the suffrage is not only based upon the cross section of opinions at a given moment in a society as expressed through polls or plebiscites and referenda.[25] The suffrage elicits choices on issues and personalities, which may or may not correspond to the more deeply rooted interests of the electorate. The electorate is not asked to react to superficial questions of the moment: voters are asked to side with men and policies that can be related to their own experience, inclinations, and bias. During the campaign candidates and their policies become symbols of major public tendencies. The electorate is not a mass of distinct individuals, choosing between isolated and unrelated alternatives, presented at a given moment. This would only lead to fortuitous casting of votes but hardly to a policy. The choice is confined to the alternatives that the historical parties present to the historically integrated community and its different organic sections at a historical moment. What emerges from election campaigns is therefore a set of choices on issues, which have a history and have been amalgamated into policies with which one roughly does, or does not, agree. Election results are poor only in the eyes of the extreme individualist who expects an election to express fully the individual personality and all his complex aspirations. Voting behavior, however, does not mean full self-expression, but the crystallization of basic leanings on which we agree or disagree with our fellow citizens. Hence an election is meant to voice only those demands that unite us, if not with the whole community, at least with one basic element. Thus suffrage does not express the individual but those forces that have to be adjusted through the process of government. Government does not simply rule millions of individuals, but masters and co-ordinates the underlying elements that constitute the life of the whole community. Now, the political parties may fail to organize and express these common desires and interests of the people. Then sooner or later the party system will change—as happened in

Great Britain with the virtual elimination of the Liberal party —in the direction of an organization more representative of the really dominant elements of the community.

These observations allow us to restate with slightly different emphasis the frequently voiced criticism of modern mass parties for their allegedly oligarchical tendencies. To be sure, party policies, party platforms, and nominations of candidates are drawn up and determined by leading minorities. However cliquish such minorities may be and however great their wish to manipulate public opinion from key positions, under conditions of free trade in ideas their maneuvers can have only limited success. Party leadership, after all, is out to get the vote: hence the nomination of candidates for election and the party platform for the election campaign will be adapted to the anticipated response of the electorate. By anticipating popular reactions party leaders explore the electorate's attitudes and under pressure of popular expectations they must voice such attitudes as the mouthpiece of the electorate.

Names of candidates and slogans are bound to be symbols of fundamental interests of the people. This shows that the really beneficent influence of public control works most strongly where the observer of institutions would not even realize its existence. The very fact that the dictator has to anticipate consent only to a very limited degree, makes his policy entirely different and ultimately self-centered. Just because of their appeal and acceptability, democratic policies in a sound community are concerned primarily with issues such as taxation, property, and family, i.e. not with bogus problems but with the essentials of civic life. In consequence, as Mosca, a keen observer of this process of transformation, pointed out correctly, the representative system leads actually not to majority rule, but to 'the participation of a certain number of social values in the guidance of the state.' [26]

This holds true, of course, only roughly, as all devices of political theory are bound to present rules of thumb with only approximate validity; yet for practical purposes they are quite satisfactory. The social and political system is no clockwork of fixed cogs and wheels. The political process of government is a co-ordination of dynamic forces, an approximate manipulation of broad tendencies leaving a great deal of detail to self-adjust-ment. But even this approximative theory and the indicated rough adjustment materialize only under certain favorable con-ditions. A multitude will always react as a crowd, that is to say, it may be swayed by momentary stimuli, follow impulses of superficial and short-lived integration, or react to stirred-up senti-ments of historical tradition, bound up with family, neighbor-hood, occupation and religion. Crowd characteristics may be pro-voked by agitation and manipulation and may lead to momen-tarily relevant integration, whereas the political process at its best operates to elicit reactions that represent people as histori-cal groups.

In the Central European democracies between the two wars there was not sufficient time to develop historical groups under democratic conditions, to play the roles of a democratic elec-torate. This is another way of saying that they had not yet as-similated the democratic tradition as a way of life. Besides, they had to employ this means of political self-expression when un-fortunately a number of economic and social catastrophes had weakened their deeper solidarity, and thus surface reactions and crowd responses were elicited.

Study of these abortive experiments shows that the basic social elements of a society can come into play only if the masses are prevented from reverting to crowd behavior. To modern psy-chology it is only too evident that the millions are not just mil-lions, but have a complex structure and articulation according to their molecular composition.[27] These millions can be made to revert to mass reactions by demagoguery, and deeper-seated mo-tivations can be elicited by propaganda techniques such as the totalitarian states use. The art of the demagogue consists in ap-pealing to those layers of the human mind that become domi-nant in crisis situations. The propagandist skilfully plays on fears and ecstasies which block or sweep away rational thought and judiciousness. The demagogue seeks to elicit from his audi-ence only mass approval or mass rejection, not public clarifica-tion of issues or policies expressing basic community trends.

With this description of the pitfalls awaiting the historical intercourse of a mass society, the threat to every democracy be-comes obvious: it is the danger of reversion to crowd behavior.

Just as the civilized individual potentially can be made to revert to blind impulse, so organized society is faced with the danger of reverting to the potential mass state. This danger of mass regression justifies our constant emphasis on the one means of resistance, that is, continuous education toward a sound social structure based on well-knit organic and local bonds and well-built large-scale organizations. The electorate is judicious only so long as it does not consist of an indifferent or chaotic mass, but lives according to well-defined group patterns in which the individual is firmly rooted.

In emphasizing basic social trends and stating that the individual *per se* can hardly find expression at the polls, we do not mean to belittle the importance of the electorate's composition and quality. We merely wish to emphasize the precedence of integration of wills in its historical social setting. The electoral will is more than a statistical mean of existing attitudes isolated from their dynamic element by the assumption of *ceteris paribus*.

Once this is realized we can appraise the nature of the electorate, its intelligence and experience, the upsurge of restless groups without a stable place in society, and so on. Equally important are the age, sex, occupational, regional, and religious composition of the vote; the number and availability of astute leaders, the relation between factors making for stability and conservatism or for change and landslides under the pressure of disturbing events and propaganda campaigns. As the quality of the electorate may improve or deteriorate, all effort should be made for improvement. The voter will obviously be burdened with growing responsibilities the more the social structure compares to a highly rational and co-ordinated mechanism. Modern social organization cannot readily absorb the shocks of irrational eruptions of crowd behavior and crowd thinking.

This task of enabling the electorate to give better expression to prevailing and inherent intellectual trends is no hopeless undertaking. Valuable empirical studies have been made: for instance, in Republican Germany a negative correlation was shown to exist between reading habits and voting behavior. Many readers of radical party papers did not vote the radical tickets. This reaction may be interpreted as indicative of the cathartic function of their newspaper reading. Many a voter in his reading found a vicarious outlet for emotions springing from frustrating conditions of life. At the polls, however, where it mattered, he may have doubted the judiciousness of demands for changes in which, as a reader, he enjoyed vicariously indulging.

Naturally, there is no universal and constant relation between voting and reading behavior. The picture may well differ in different political circumstances. Roughly speaking, however, under fairly stable conditions there is less inclination to revolutionary upsurge in modern industrialized society than existed during the nineteenth century, as upheavals entail greater risks today than, let us say, in 1848. Abortive experiments may lead to counterrevolutionary regimes to be removed only with great difficulty. For this and other reasons people in relatively secure places are fearful, less experimental-minded, and more concerned with maintaining than risking what they have gained. Under relatively stable conditions the tendency of regression to crowd behavior is not too great. It is more apt to happen if society is shaken by some sweeping disaster. In modern society this occurs whenever mass unemployment displaces millions of workers or brings about sudden shifts in power, ruining entire strata while raising others to menacing heights. In the long run such upheavals are bound to lead to repercussions in the working of the democratic system. Those who care to preserve democracy should therefore study the vote in its sociopsychological significance and historical social setting. The very meaning of suffrage changes in accordance with changes in the social structure. Better political education of the electorate can do much; but for effective prevention of deterioration the social structure must constantly be watched.

2. The Role of the Parties

In the democratic process the suffrage is followed by the integration of the political will through political parties. This phase leads to the elaboration of the raw material of diverse interests, wishes, desires, into reasoned directives ensuing eventually in policy decisions. It is a striking fact that neither Rousseau nor the founders of American democracy ever thought of parties or assigned them a place in the democratic system, although we know today that the Federal Constitution could not have worked without the integrative function of parties. This omission proves that the idea of democracy was conceived and developed over a long period as applied to small communities only, and that great effort is required to apply the same ideas to conditions in a large society.

The great paradox to be resolved by the elaboration and refinement of opinion and impulse through the party system may be stated as follows: The wider the application of the democratic principle, the greater the variety of tendencies and aims represented; whereas a larger and more highly integrated industrial society demands simple devices and answers—a 'yes' or 'no' to complex questions. If one sees but one side of the paradox one is driven either into the chaos of innumerable rival claims or into rigid regimentation under one principle. Again, the art of democracy consists in the technique of balancing contradictory claims.

In the old democracies a very important canalization of diverse views and interests occurs by virtue of the historical nature of the parties, which rely upon strong historical loyalties of groups, political families, and individuals. Such political traditions primarily help to intensify motivations, to call forth reactions rooted in the community, and to push surface reactions into the background. The party itself, however shrewd its manipulation of interests may be, represents a storehouse of memories, ideas, and images of leaders. The party reinvigorates these elements during campaigns. The strength of party allegiance in America may be illustrated by an anecdote. A Georgia judge said: 'I shall die a penitent Christian, but meet my Maker as an impenitent Democrat.' Agar, commenting on this anecdote, rightly explains that 'the devotion stems from an amalgam of history, tradition, regionalism, family bonds, civic pride, the feeling of "our side" and "our team." ' [28]

Another factor in the transformation of opinion through the party system could be fully appreciated only in terms of our theory of social integration, which cannot be fully developed here for reasons of space and balance. Instead of expounding the theory, therefore, we shall seek to convey the basic idea by means of a few illustrations. Simply to state that opinion and will are integrated through political parties is not enough, as different techniques of integration produce different amalgams out of identical human material and attitudes. As mentioned before, we may elicit a different mentality from the electorate according to the opportunity voters have to integrate their interests along sectional vocational lines or as local constituencies. Sectional emphasis tends to express and stimulate irreconcilable cleavages, whereas regional emphasis evokes the citizen's point of view. Another integrative rule is that single-member constituencies with plurality elections tend to favor rigid party lines and dogmatism.[29] Thus the respective election system and party structure not only determine the nature of likely electoral responses, but also exert different educative influences. The first type fosters a mind trained for reasonable compromise; the latter, a mind fond of doctrine. To give one more such observation: the opportunity to select and develop qualified political leaders is greater when seats are personally contested than under the list system used in Germany under the Weimar Republic. The list system combined with proportional representation gives more opportunities to men willing to bow to the discipline of the party machine than to men able and willing to fight.[30]

In all these cases the choice of method depends on our preference for faithful representation and expression of the voters' shades of opinions or for the crystallization of clear-cut decisions. The latter undoubtedly deserves priority as long as people preserve political sense and understand that politics means group action and not debate for its own sake. On the other hand, it would be a mistake unduly to suppress self-expression and real participation for the sake of the alternative. The solution seems to lie in stating clear-cut alternatives to be decided in a hot contest. The electorate should indeed reach a decision, but not at the cost of breaking or neutralizing its spontaneity. Popular interest in politics should be encouraged by all means. People should receive maximum opportunities for self-expression. Manipulation at a later stage should serve to reduce diversity of opinions to simple alternatives.

The two-party system is the ideal solution for a properly functioning democracy. It has a tremendous moderating effect, and clearly decides who should govern and who should be in opposition with a chance for a come-back. The price of the two-party system is well known: it promises great stability without consistency. This holds especially for the United States, where the two parties are not divided on fundamental principles or basic philosophies.[31] The reason is that overemphasis of a sectional, economic, or regional interest by one party in such a big country would always call forth violent opposition. Hence the basic principles of the system serve to smooth out differences and facilitate compromise. As the two parties represent overlapping interests there is always the possibility of reaching agreement on major issues. Hence no real upheaval ever threatens from the change-over from one party to the other. Despite the clamor of election campaigns, in the end radical change is unlikely. This creates an atmosphere of stability which is important for continuous and orderly progress. It is left to small third-party movements to be dogmatic and dramatize new ideas, which emerge residually in the life of the community. When these ideas become sufficiently mature and popular in appeal, one or both of the older parties sooner or later incorporate them in their platforms. Thus, the salient demands of the Populist Movement were taken over either by the Republicans or the Democrats.[32] The same happened in Great Britain to the Chartist Movement. After their defeat the demands of the Chartists were fulfilled by others.[33]

The question we must ask ourselves is whether such a two-party system, which tends to gloss over differences on principle, can serve as a democratic basis for planning. At first sight one might deny the possibility, especially judged in terms of continental European ideas likely to exaggerate differences and emphasize principles. For planning demands clear-cut issues, a choice between two different over-all systems. Now, despite our emphasis on consistency as a prerequisite to planning, despite our impatience with isolated measures and our advocacy of logically coherent policies, we think that the two-party system can well serve democratic planning. To be sure, this can happen only if we do not aim at total planning, but clearly separate essential planning issues from others allowing for variety. Total planning seems to demand a unified policy, hence logically a one-party system. A two-party system, however, is feasible and desirable for partial planning, once both parties are agreed on the need for preventive planning, in order to remove the most striking evils of a technological society. Though the parties must be agreed that this can be achieved by controlling some of the key factors, they could still differ on the issues to be left free and/or the best methods for making preventive planning effective. Under such a system if the party in power should prove a failure, the electorate could put the other party in power with a mandate to solve the experiment in its own way.

Although the parties of the United States may well be expected in the future to divide on the issue of planning, a new critical stage probably will be reached when another depression convinces the electorate of the need for preventive planning. Then agreement can probably be reached on essential minimum issues of planning, such as planning for full employment, and a bipartisan policy may crystallize in the emergency.

A multiple-party system based upon proportional representation and requiring coalition governments may, of course, have greater difficulties on the road to planning. Still, partial planning is possible. It would require a broad coalition government representing a 'national government,' and a basic agreement for the planning period to abide by a few essential planning measures, whereas other issues could be met as time and occasion might demand.

During the war the British Prime Minister and the American President could make Cabinet changes in response to public opinion and demands of the hour without changing their objective of winning the war. In the same way, in a policy of transition toward planning, means and men might be changed in the pursuit of a fixed goal. To be sure, war is a most compelling issue for basic agreement. But is it justifiable to assume that democratic nations cannot understand that a clash on issues of planning in an irreconcilable spirit might lead to civil war and dictatorship ultimately more destructive than war? Is it unjustifiable to argue that democratic nations in the face of havoc such as mass unemployment and/or the loss of democracy can rally to efforts comparable to those in wartime?

Excited masses cannot learn from history, but a nation moving along in the historical mold of democratic institutions without major displacement in its basic structure can be expected to manage the necessary transformation peacefully. Characteristically the expectations of those who predicted toward the end of the war a prompt return to 'normalcy' or 'business as usual' did not come true, at least not in England. The British people were ready and willing to consider the postwar period a national emergency similar to that of the threatening Nazi invasion after Dunkirk. The United States could agree on a continued bipartisan policy in foreign affairs and renounce isolationism for good. It is simply not true that nations do not learn from history. The question is, which social historical conditions facilitate and which block such learning? We all learned, for instance, that reparations like those after World War I are self-defeating, that large-scale inflation or mass unemployment undermines the social structure and harms everyone.[34] Such lessons are retained so long as the basic social structure and the psychological make-up of the community remain balanced and the democratic process continues to operate smoothly.

At this juncture we may ask whether democracies in the Age of Planning will not have to establish a new institution outside the general machinery of the representative system though forming an integral part of the political process. We may call it an Order. We would define it as a voluntary organization, recruited from the most prominent representatives of various strata and elements of the community. This body should serve to maintain democracy and freedom by mediating in cases where democratic pluralism might lead to a stalemate and to indecision in planning operations. This agency should be a kind of supreme tribunal to guarantee consistency and continuity in planning.[35] Whereas in dictatorial countries the paramountcy of the party guarantees such consistency and continuity in a democratic state the process of integration might be fostered by a nonpartisan body of highly esteemed and disinterested men. Just because it remains outside the contest for power, this body might gain great moral prestige and become the 'conscience of the country.'[36] The members should represent the diverse social and intellectual currents of the community, so that their agreement and joint resolve would represent a high-level mediation of tensions at large. As in a religious order, admission should require such rigorous commitments from members that the high-

est devotion and disinterestedness would be secured. The system
of election should combine co-optation and delegation. In critical situations, when mediation is unsuccessful, a committee might
be nominated by the body to arbitrate the issues.

This proposal is advanced less in the belief that it would materialize exactly as outlined, than for the sake of dramatizing
the need for top-level integration in an age of planning. Democracy must be on guard against situations where the margin of
permissible disagreement is shrinking and speedy consensus is of
the essence. In the past, democracies could do without such special provision for integration because unconscious traditions represented the integrating bond and unified even scattered parliamentary acts. With the weakening of tradition, substitutes of
similar dignity and authority must be found. Common conscience, which has ceased to function through tacit invisible integration as it did in small communities, should create new organs
equally plastic and subtle yet adapted to the potentialities of a
new age.

3. Transformation of Popular Will into Policy Decisions

The next stage in the democratic process consists in transformation of the popular will into workable policy. The voters express
their will at the polls in response to more or less vague programs,
party platforms, and the roll of candidates. They elect a number of representatives, or a President, who will deliberate, constitute a government, and control the administration. Representation, deliberation, and control are the next phases in the
transformation of the originally crude impulses of the electorate.

The act of representation is a complex phenomenon. The
ancient city-states knew only direct democracy and had no need
to go beyond it. If the city-state grew beyond a certain size a new
town or colony was created rather than the old one expanded.
Rousseau, who always focused on ancient models, believed representation incompatible with sovereignty. The idea of representation was a contribution of medieval politics. But representation
of corporate groups differs greatly from representation of the
people, which is a specifically modern product and developed
with the establishment and extension of the franchise. There is

all the difference between a medieval emissary representing a corporate group by following precise instructions, and a modern deputy who represents his constituency. The main difference is that the emissary of medieval corporations had to convey views previously crystallized in the catalyzer of the corporate body, whereas the modern deputy has to play his role within the catalyzing process. He operates in that phase of the political process which begins with the raw impulses and leads to a refined policy. Once he has been elected and appears in Parliament or in executive office he can be said to represent only an amalgam of social tendencies of his electorate. His 'popular mandate' contains a loosely defined general line which is not indefinite, yet is extremely vague. Personally he may of course stand for fully developed principles and practical proposals, but what he *represents* is not so articulate. It is for him to articulate these impulses for which he stands by blending them with his own personality and responsibility. Thus, a personal element enters into the process of transforming vaguely defined tendencies and raw interests into policy decisions which are more than a mass compound. This personal element—the individual ratio—lends flexibility and adaptability to otherwise vague emotional currents. By this process the inarticulate will of the many may be elaborated into what is no mere summation of many wills but their refinement, humanization, and individualization. All this develops in the phase of professional deliberation, debate, and bargaining. Often the deputy has no explicit philosophy and is much the same type of man as those whom he represents—a person with varying bits of experience and knowledge, some philosophical maxims, and certain emotional attitudes. These fragments and tendencies are not articulated primarily in writings and theoretical treatises but in policy issues, in discussion by administrative and legislative bodies. The critics of Democracy usually harp on the allegedly low level of parliamentary debate, the cheap and boring rhetoric, or they even deprecate all public speech. Undoubtedly, all these things should and could be improved, but the critics usually lack adequate perspective. They fail to realize the difference between a discussion and a parliamentary debate. The latter is no exercise in scientific clarification or semantics. The various pleas and briefs contribute rather to the aforementioned catalyzing process. Speeches and debates bring divergent issues and values to public attention, challenging and clarifying them by focusing on the legislation under consideration. The pressure for action and the need for agreement continuously produce interest and value adjustments. The parliamentary struggle serves to sublimate and transform hostile or antagonistic impulses into critical attitudes. Antagonisms of selfish interest and sheer impulse, as found in the life of the community, are subjected to adjustment; and constructive compromise may be reached in every phase of the debate. Whereas the antagonistic currents of workaday life may remain disturbing and unresolved, under the pressing need for a common policy policy-makers capitalize on them for constructively integrating will and thought. Whereas the individual citizen has only the limited experience and possibly shares the prejudices of his special region, community, profession, and class, the professional politician in Parliament or Congress acquires in the context of political pleading, interest clashes, and the like, broadened experience and political judgment.

At this stage in the political process it would be wrong to expect technically correct advice, expert knowledge of facts, and theoretically adequate formulae. The more these elements enter the debate, the better; but it would be wrong to expect them to result from the debate. The debate rather serves to state the contestant interests and values clearly and to reach necessary adjustment for a workable policy agreement. Everything is focused on policy decision and action. Legal, technical, and other detail is rightly delegated to committee work. It is no shortcoming of the parliamentary system to delegate to committees substantive discussion in contrast to plenary debate, since genuine discussion by its nature demands small groups. The fact that one can separate the policy-making level of will and interest integration from its more theoretical part belongs of course intimately to the democratic philosophy which asserts the possibility of separating clearly facts from valuations [37] and of distinguishing sharply between mere experts and real policy-makers.

N

PART III

New Man—New Values

7

From Custom to Social Science

○

The institutional reforms so far proposed would be inadequate without a remaking of Man and reconditioning of human behavior. Aristotle's wise observation that political stability depends on the adaptation of education to the form of government has been brought home to us again during recent decades. Experience shows that Democracy cannot exist unless all its institutions are thoroughly oriented to democratic ends. This requires a constant awareness of the educational effects of all institutions. We may well generalize that in the long run no society can survive unless there is some co-ordination between the network of institutions, educational devices, and basic valuations.[1] Not the necessity but only the extent and nature of this co-ordination will be discussed in the following chapter.

I. THE IDEA OF SOCIAL EDUCATION

Institutions, after all, are nothing but fixed behavior patterns of interrelated individuals. Institutions, therefore, require training for 'institutional behavior.'[2] There can be no school without training in classroom behavior: for comradeship toward classmates and teachers, for marks and other rewards, without training in loyalty and appreciation of the values that underlie the life of the school, e.g. appreciation of knowledge, of communal activities, of the specific traditions or ideals for which the school stands.[3] Obviously valuations do not exist for their own sake and in the abstract, but are traffic lights [4] guiding and regulating action and human behavior in concrete social situations. They are frames of reference for group experiences.[5] It is a simple but central sociological truth that a behavior unit is no isolated act but a phase of the social system.[6] Each action is a link in a chain of more or less co-ordinated social activities and therefore somehow dependent on society as a going concern, which shapes and co-ordinates human behavior. The fact that our institutions, educational devices, and valuations are only different aspects of the same process has been overlooked by the theorists of *laissez-faire* and has been overemphasized and exaggerated in the practice of authoritarians.

The *laissez-faire* attitude holds that the best policy on economics, education, and elsewhere is to let the individual adjust freely on his own, without outside interference. It overlooks the fact that no individual ever existed who made his adjustments 'on his own.' The self-reliant and independent-minded man is the product of older behavior-forming agencies, the family, the local community, school, and church, not to mention other institutions. His spontaneous adjustments contribute to the development of previously conditioned and assimilated behavior patterns. The totalitarians and authoritarians misinterpret conditioning and co-ordinating of behavior as indoctrination or as blind acceptance of rigid patterns of thought and behavior. Obviously, the individual does not achieve his best if left alone, nor are social influence and the co-ordination of activities identical with regimentation and drill. The Art of Democratic Planning consists in elaborating the Third Pattern, i.e. it steers clear of doing nothing or of overdoing things.

But what made the Liberal believe that his society functioned without conscious effort of conditioning and co-ordinating behavior? What made the Totalitarian interfere with everything and even dictate the co-ordination between various institutions? Closer scrutiny shows that their different attitudes and mentalities are oriented to and reflect different historical phases of social development. In the age of Liberalism no State or planning authority conditioned human behavior and cared for its social co-ordination, because the family, the school, the neighborhood, the Church and other primary attitude-molding institutions quietly created the necessary behavior pattern. Co-ordination resulted from tradition and custom, which restricted differences to the point where they could not endanger the unity of society.

In recent times our primary attitude-forming institutions have been greatly weakened. The family is losing its hold over the individual; community spirit is fading; school and Church tend to become conventional and thus paralyzed; the tacit, unifying philosophy that co-ordinated them is disintegrating. Tradition and custom formerly co-ordinated and integrated the personality-forming institutions and valuations, but gradually they ceased to function. Only since this has been realized have the social sciences raised the central issues of co-ordinating social institutions for the sake of deliberately molding behavior.

One may call this the change from custom to social science. So long as custom and tradition worked, there was no need for social science. The science of society emerged when and where the automatic functioning of society ceased to find adjustment. Conscious analysis of the situation and conscious co-ordination of social processes then became necessary.

To be sure, custom and tradition will not be replaced everywhere by social science. In England especially a strong tissue of tradition has survived and is tacitly accepted. There one need not interfere unless customs and traditions are simply harmful, as in the case of poor nutrition habits or over-competitiveness which is out of place in a well-ordered society. Only where the tissue of tradition and custom has disintegrated, and the individual is unable to create a new behavior pattern or to recast his institutions may social science in the broadest sense of the term help.

Social science will furnish basic knowledge for social education, a frequently used but rarely well-defined concept. Social education does not seek to create a gregarious social animal, but aims at creating a balanced personality in the spirit of real Democracy; individuality should not develop at the expense of community sentiment.

Furthermore, the word 'social' in the term 'social education' emphasizes the means of influence, that is, the deliberate use of existing social forces in creating the democratic personality type.[7]

In contrast, our traditional pedagogy focused attention primarily on person-to-person influences, overlooking the various environmental influences. It took those for granted and left them unexplored, considering them as a sort of second nature external to man. In the modern approach the social environment no longer figures as a vaguely observed entity, but as a set of patterns to be explored for their educational significance. Moreover, the permanent question will be, how to use these environmental patterns for democratic education without the application of totalitarian methods.

Social science in the place of unworkable tradition will assist democratic planning in three directions: it will clarify (1) the democratic idea of co-ordination in contrast to totalitarian regimentation; (2) the making and remaking of human behavior, i.e. social and psychological means of conditioning of man; (3) the pattern of democratic behavior, conscience, and personality as ends of democratic planning.

II. THE NEW SCIENCE OF HUMAN BEHAVIOR

1. *The Meaning of Democratic Co-ordination*

In clarifying the idea of democratic co-ordination in contrast to totalitarian regimentation we have first to realize that classical Liberalism has no theory of co-ordination. It believes final co-ordination of human activities to be the work of unseen forces in society. Man has to care for everything except the harmony of the whole of society which takes care of itself. The liberal theory of social action may roughly be stated as follows:

There is no need for planning, no need for being told what is the right way of action, no need for special inculcation of aims or stimulation of motivation so long as there is (a) opportunity for everyone; (b) free choice; (c) scope for experimentation, for trial and error by the individual; (d) available information about the relevant facts; (e) last but not least, free competition, which in connection with the previous factors will create both the incentives and the necessary wisdom to adjustment. Rightly understood, liberal theory trusts in self-centered individual adjustments to produce the right order in society automatically. Sociologically speaking, individual and competitive adjustment

—only one of many forms of adjustment—is considered the only valid one without regard to its prerequisite conditions.

There is undeniable wisdom in the ideas of Liberalism, and our Third Way will incorporate some of its elements. As a system, however, Liberalism is no longer applicable. Both in the cultural sphere and in economics the pressures of large competing units confound the individual, and there is urgent need for organization. In the bewildering complexity of institutional pressures the individual no longer sees his way to meaningful contributions to the common end.

At first sight the remedy might seem to be totalitarian organization. In the midst of chaos, regimentation might appear to be the panacea; where disintegration of behavior, flight from responsibilities, doubt of values prevail, inculcation and indoctrination, ordering and forbidding seem the best means for restoring certainty and security.

It may take a painfully long time to realize that this superimposed order lacks vitality, and that a properly ordered life differs greatly from organized regimentation. From the thesis of *laissez-faire* and the antithesis of rigid regimentation, the synthesis of the Third Way, the ideal of Democratic Planning, gradually evolves in the cultural sphere. This requires further elucidation. It is helpful to start from the opposite, that is, the absence of integration.[8]

Modern mass unemployment, for instance, may condemn whole age classes of adolescents to years of idleness. So long as nothing is done about it, youth during this phase of maturation drops out of the pattern of society; it emancipates itself from family life without finding an alternate role and responsibility in the world of adults. This is a typical case of a group dropping out of the social structure in consequence of unguided technological developments. A *laissez-faire* policy would do nothing about it, or at best grant a dole and wait for the individual's self-adjustment. The totalitarian state, on the other hand, in such a situation introduces compulsory labor service; that is, it answers the problem by rigid regimentation, irrespective of the need for individual development. This is definitely better than doing nothing under the pretext that the individual ought to take care of himself; but it is far from a real solution. The latter is only possible if the displaced group is restored to the social fabric and reintegrated in an organic manner.

A survey of disintegrative processes in society would have to establish types of displacements, their magnitude and selective mechanisms: wayward youth, old age without security, spinsters, foreigners without work permits or means, revolutionaries devoid of loyalties, and so on, are so many cases of maladjusted individuals who to varying degrees drop out of the co-ordinated interplay of group functions. The quality of a social order, in our view, consists in its ability to bring these individuals back by preparing creative adjustments on both sides.[9] On the objective side, society should provide functions and opportunities for the reabsorption and education of those qualified to play a constructive part in society. If, for instance, in the case of unemployed youth, the age for leaving school were raised and outlets for the creative urge provided, then not only would an evil be removed, but a fresh opportunity would be given for self-development and social betterment. Where the regimenting mind would see only the need for restoring order, the planner, motivated by the idea of reintegration, could suggest something more constructive than just putting the bird into a cage.

Early capitalist society was able to use the contribution of the foreign immigrant to shake loose the static habits of the country, spreading the spirit of adventure and enterprise to counteract the inertia of the native population. Unconsciously, early Capitalism thus made an experiment in integrating a group that would otherwise have remained an unassimilated alien body. In the same way, when for the first time the parliamentary system succeeded in acknowledging the creative function of the Opposition in lawful change, it reintegrated rebellious, previously merely disruptive, elements and brought them back into the social structure. A democratically planned society will approximate its ideal only if it makes similarly creative use of all problem groups that, without reintegration, remain a cause of disturbance. It can be foreseen that a creative society might provide elderly people with suitable work and functions enabling them to use their qualities and wisdom so that they would no longer be simply a burden.[10] Democratic reintegration differs from regimentation and rigid organization by its ability to use the most varied types of people, by exploring and developing suitable functions for every social group. Integration thus does not simply mean conformity, as the conservative would have us believe, nor does it mean order at any price. It means orderly interdependence and continuity between human institutions: co-operation, common aims, and common understanding instead of isolation, frustration, and self-centered egotism.

We have concentrated on the nature of democratic reintegration, because from here a way opens to the understanding of the new techniques of influencing human behavior. Democratic sociology [11] recognizes most behavior disturbances as symptoms of social disintegration. Remaking institutions and remaking behavior are two aspects of the same process, and the deterioration of the social structure can only be corrected by a co-ordinated attack. Thus the remaking of behavior and character is ʾhe concern of the psychologist and the social planner alike.

2. The Making and Remaking of Human Behavior

The last twenty years have seen an immense advance in various branches of psychology, sociology, and history, whose integration might be called the *science of human behavior*. Experimental psychology, psychoanalysis, and the various schools of general psychology, as well as the specialized branches of applied psychology—such as child psychology, educational psychology, and criminology—all have contributed to an ever-widening knowledge of the variability of human behavior. If we add to this our anthropological knowledge of primitive man and what sociologically informed historians reveal of human nature and conduct in different ages; if we observe the behavior patterns of different classes of contemporary society—man's reactions to gradual and to sudden changes, such as crises, wars, and revolutions—then we can no longer speak of ignorance concerning human behavior.

What are the great innovations of this science of human behavior in theory and practice?

Theoretically, the basis for further sociological observations was laid when the old idea of unchangeable and innate instincts gave way to insight into the great plasticity of human nature. We no longer believe, for instance, in such 'instincts' as aggressiveness or acquisitiveness; we only acknowledge vague, unorganized drives in the newborn, which within certain limits can be adapted to, and are shaped by, environmental circumstances. We no longer ask the obsolete metaphysical question: can human nature be changed? The true question, 'can human *behavior* be changed?' is no longer answered by guesswork and speculation, but by social-science research. We want to know what range of variable behavior patterns can serve in the light of available evidence to satisfy and express the few basic urges and needs that characterize man. Here the best guide is a study of the methods that have hitherto served to condition and recondition the behavior of man.

In raising this problem we enter the realm of 'social education.' Society has always been a powerful educational agent, but only gradually do we learn to realize the extent to which educational influences arise from social dispositions. Such new knowledge holds the promise that we shall gradually succeed in constructing a social environment that will foster desirable personality traits and attitudes.

No doubt, our forebears were not quite blind to these effects, but they relied rather on traditional maxims and had no key to the social environment and its influences. Speaking of education, they thought mainly of the relation between father and son, pupil and teacher, et cetera. Speaking of 'moral education,' they thought of 'don'ts' which served to thwart self-expression [12] in everyday life, and of 'preaching' to which they resorted on more solemn occasions. Yet they succeeded in rearing decent men. That they did was due less to their primitive pedagogy than to the slow and harmonious functioning of informal influences, to traditional precepts of correct action transmitted by the organic groups. The family, the neighborhood, the community presented images and ideals of good conduct. They were taken to heart by youth and served to motivate man and mold his pattern of conduct. If today we bring their silent work to awareness and reflect on them, it is because these informal influences are weakening and deteriorating, and because new, more comprehensive social patterns are developing which cannot be controlled without systematic exploration of their nature.

In what follows we shall enumerate some of the social forces that contribute to the shaping of personality. We shall concentrate on those likely to be under discussion in the future.

III. PERSONAL RELATIONSHIPS, PRIMARY GROUPS, AND THEIR EDUCATIONAL SIGNIFICANCE

Whatever changes the New Age may bring, person-to-person relationships and primary groups will remain the basic character-forming agencies of society. An increasing literature is devoted to the study of personality formation in the family and other primary groups: the playground, the neighborhood, the small community.[18] These studies show how the family initiates social learning by building habits of feeding, sleep, elimination, and so on, and how in their context the basic patterns of dealing with pain, fear, and other emotions are established. They reveal subtle differences in the management of emotional tensions, the development of different forms of self-control which account for quite a few group differences in temperament and culture.

Child studies show how the playground and the neighborhood teach the child to carry over acquired behavior patterns from his narrow field of experience at home into other groups, proving that social maturation consists in the ability to learn by participation in ever larger groups. They show that not only the family and school but also the gang, the club, the community, have specific educative influence in developing traits of character and in implanting their different traditions, special standards, interest, repressive and releasing influences. The educational strength of these organic groups consists in their all-embracing quality compared with which the place of reading and sermonizing as educative influences is recognized to be limited indeed. In early childhood we live our whole life in organic groups, hence they operate on all levels of the self. Primary groups and person-to-person relations exert lasting influences, because they shape our deeper experiences and thus affect what we call the rootedness of a character reflected in a feeling of belonging and stability. The great character mutation that leads to the excitability of the mass-minded person is due mainly to the weakening of these primary attitude-forming agencies, and democratic society in planning for freedom will have to strengthen these agencies.

The *laissez-faire* tradition and the totalitarians are quite definite in their respective approaches. The former follows a very respectable tradition of clinging to the idea of not interfering with primary groups and personal relations, as this would infringe upon the freedom of the individual. On the other hand, totalitarian societies intensely suspect the family and any form of privacy as loopholes for individual evasions of totalitarian control.[14]

A democratic society which plans for freedom should respect its liberal heritage not only by leaving primary and personal relationships free from regimentation but by using its authority to ensure their freedom. Free choice of personal companionships in private life, the inviolability of family life and tradition, the right of free association should be protected against all interference, because they are the breeding ground of independent-minded and self-reliant personalities.

Yet in two instances this policy, if upheld dogmatically, may defeat itself, and in this case the principle of planning for freedom opens the door to action.

1. *Decline of the Birth Rate*

Innumerable forces of modern society tend to weaken or even to dissolve the primary groups, especially the family and the community. A conspicuous case in point is the falling birth rate in advanced nations.[15] The more civilized our communities become, the smaller the families. Is this indicative of a changed mentality of modern man, a decadence fostered by the mass production and diffusion of means of birth control, or do external and internal conditions diminish opportunities to plan and provide for large families and the rearing of children?

The *laissez-faire* attitude takes the changed desires of individuals as final and considers birth control an elementary right of the individual. Those who plan for freedom will think of measures to ensure the flourishing of the family and of other primary groups and to remove difficulties of urban life that interfere with the rearing of children, so long as the family is cherished as an irreplaceable character-building agency. The totalitarian systems, on the other hand, assume an attitude of 'state parental-ism' [16] by taking over many parental functions. They seek espe-cially to control the psychological maturation of youth in the hope of thus making youth unconsciously displace family feel-ing.[17]

On such paramount issues the democratic community may be expected to agree readily on a constructive policy and a legisla-tive program to secure social and psychological conditions for family and home, encouraging parents to have and rear children, strengthening neighborhood relations and community life. This policy, like that of the totalitarians, considers the state as the only institution in the modern world with the means to support and co-ordinate efficiently the different groups and organizations. Therefore it must become instrumental in bringing about major changes in which success will depend on co-ordinating a great many means. Democratic policy will demand democratic agree-ment for the enactment of these means and democratic controls of their administration. Decisions that ultimately must be made in privacy should neither be prescribed nor forbidden (for in-stance, the sale of contraceptives would be permitted). Educa-tional propaganda campaigns will be used to convince people of desirable action, yet nonconformists would be free to choose their own way of life.

The purpose of educational propaganda is also to broaden the outlook and awaken the conscience of every citizen. Once favor-able developments are no longer thwarted by objective condi-tions, the citizen should be challenged to view his narrow and self-centered interests in the light of those of the community at large. In other words, in such cases the community produces, on a higher level of consciousness than that of private concerns, en-vironmental influences that deteriorate without public support. This should help to establish simultaneously that moral atmos-phere which was formerly maintained by custom and tradition.

2. Harmful Practices of Primary Groups

More complicated is the case of family and other primary-group practices that in the light of modern knowledge are definitely harmful: poor diets, parental superstitions in rearing and edu-cating children regardless of harmful psychological effects on mental development. In such cases the progressive planner might be tempted to follow the totalitarian path either by asking the state to take over educational functions or by controlling family behavior.[18]

The case is simple as long as unambiguous criteria of right and wrong can be scientifically established. A wrong diet, a wrong method of education for cleanliness, et cetera, could be so classified and forbidden as harmful interference with life. The position is much more difficult when the expert trying to remedy a situation by psychological advice is befogged by a host of valuations affecting his observations. In such cases outside interference by authorities can only be harmful, as it only replaces the well-meaning ignorance of parents by the conceited one-sidedness of the expert. Such cases had better be left to private or state-guided enlightenment.

We reach a marginal case when we consider educational and psychological devices that endanger the existence of a Democratic Order. In the light of modern psychological observations certain educational practices that inculcate authoritarian behavior by ordering and forbidding create undemocratic personality types if overdeveloped in the family. Here democratic society must realize that the adult world reflects the world of childhood and adolescence, and that attitudes, habits, and aspirations not developed in childhood cannot develop later. In view of this, public discussion should clarify and establish basic democratic patterns of behavior and character formation. This discussion could lead to agreement upon a minimum of prohibitions (e.g. of practices creating the sado-masochist character and practices of fear-mongering). The community might adopt recommendation of advisory groups whose concern it is to explore the needs of democratic society. In this the policy would still be that too much regulation is contradictory and defeats its own ends.

IV. ORGANIZED GROUPS AND THEIR EDUCATIONAL IMPACT [19]

Personal relationships and primary groups should by their very nature grow spontaneously. To plan for them cannot mean to manipulate them directly, but rather to change the environment to facilitate and set free their spontaneous and latent forces. For a growing society they are what infancy is for the person—they need protection. As long as society consisted mainly of small groups, their spontaneous interplay produced the necessary inner and outer adjustments. But in a world of large-scale organization they might easily be crushed and swept aside by the pressures of large groups. Labor follows capital, working-class people have to live where factories are established; communication facilities and income decide whether one will or can afford to live in a congested city district, a quiet neighborhood, or isolation. In our prefabricated world the stage is set for us before we enter it, and the habitat of urban masses is not primarily arranged in order to make life more human, but to yield speculative profit. From the point of view of efficiency, the small units are very often unprofitable. A large hotel or tenement house is a more profitable arrangement than a host of small houses. The psychological and educational implications, however, deserve priority over profit motives in planning the neighborhood and the home.

Strong emphasis on the social educative value of small units should not mislead us—as so often happens—to condemn large organized units, such as the Army, factory, bureaucracy, et cetera. Those who neglect to explore the potentialities of these bodies renounce modern society altogether, as the really great 'social inventions' of the future will probably be made in these fields. So far they have been explored largely from the point of view of efficiency in terms of greatest returns. But modern industrial psychology and sociology explore them in the light of social education and ask how to remedy the personal drawbacks of a highly regimented factory life.[20]

The way to improvement is twofold. In the first place, close observation shows that large units can be broken down into smaller ones, which may have the socializing effects of other small groups or even of primary groups. Factory life actually leads to spontaneous formation of small work teams which in their give-and-take generate the same rules of mutuality that prevail among primary groups and their numbers. These little work teams develop their own traditions and emotionalize their procedures in characteristic fashion. According to Whitehead, the art of management consists in not breaking up these spon-

o

taneous cells of group formation, but in using them. Thus the factory can re-establish or foster the growth of the social living tissue in its organized texture.

The second way of mastering the problems of great organizations consists in using them deliberately as an educational instrument wherever they are capable of producing favorable effects. It is not without significance that large units, which from the very outset are the result of deliberate organization, present legitimate opportunity to the planning mind to set the stage and define the rules of the game. Whereas in the case of primary groups we can modify only external conditions for their development, here no harm is done if the original patterns are subjected to scrutiny. Great organizations are ideal educators for certain purposes, such as systematic discipline. If arbitrariness is to be eliminated, bureaucratization [21] is very useful. It may check tendencies toward personal tyranny. By proper procedures, assignment of responsibility and public accountability can be achieved in a bureaucracy.

Not every organization is bureaucratic; there is a progression from loose to rigid organizations, as Charles H. Cooley has observed.[22] The problem of large-scale organization will be solved only if sociology explains the progression of types in detail and systematically explores the respective educational effects. Those who lament large-scale organization as suppressing the freedom and spontaneity of simple and organic forms of life should not forget one thing: if a healthy principle is embodied in an organization, it produces good effects even despite possibly bad intentions of the participating individuals. Gunnar Myrdal has brought home to us in a very impressive way that despite suppression, intrigue, personal hatred, and the like, the Negroes in America have made great advances, as the American creed of Democracy and Social Justice, embodied in welfare and educational institutions, has provided opportunities in an otherwise hostile environment.[23] Thus, if good principles are embodied in institutions, people protect themselves through these institutions against their own base strivings, jealousies, and hatreds. The American citizen as a high-minded voter supports these institutions, keeps less respectable impulses in check, and compels himself to do the right thing.

V. SOME SOCIAL INSTITUTIONS AND THEIR EDUCATIONAL IMPACT

By getting rid of our former blindness to society, we are learning also to appraise the educational influence of institutions. In using this somewhat loose term 'institution,' we have in mind such things as pecuniary compensation for services and goods or the system of property.[24] If we take the former as an example, we now realize that a certain money-mindedness goes with a social environment in which monetary reward plays a central role. It entails a specific form of possessiveness which, once established, will permeate the whole social structure and color our mentality.[25]

By manipulating these institutions we indirectly modify human behavior. We need not go to Russia to see the effects of such manipulations. During the war, three fundamental changes through institutional manipulations came about: full employment, redistribution of income through high taxation, especially through the excess-profits tax, and equalization of basic consumption through rationing and price control. It is highly enlightening to consider the psychological effects of these changes in an otherwise capitalistic environment.[26] Full employment plus rationing to some extent diminished the incentive value of money for the employee. The social body immediately tried to compensate for this by introducing additional incentives and even compulsory measures such as direction of labor. At the same time work conditions were made more attractive, the workers were given a share in the responsibility of management—thus, the prestige and status of manual work were enhanced. In other words, numerous gratifications were held out to satisfy man's wish for recognition.

If money could no longer buy everything, it ceased to define status and position in wartime society as it had in prewar society. The yearning for recognition found more satisfaction than before in nonmaterial rewards. Such psychological rewards recall the pre-capitalist situation, when income and wealth were not enough to define status. All this shows that there is a tendency in the social body to make compensations. This process of psychological compensation worked automatically in simpler societies, especially when the substituted gratifications could be worked out gradually through cumulative effects of trial and error. In our modern society, where we are able to control monetary rewards, the level of employment, and the equity of distribution, we are increasingly called upon deliberately to manipulate the concomitant psychological compensations. Thus, psychological substitutes for vanishing gratifications would have to be foreseen by the decision-making groups of society and controlled in the same way as the purely material changes.

But the more we manipulate material and corresponding psychological factors, the clearer it becomes that our system of monetary rewards is linked to the 'money mores,' a set of attitudes and habits. For instance, we can see that the neurotic compulsion to incessant work, the fact that we suffer from guilt feeling if we do not work, goes with scarcity, both natural and artificially induced. The distrust of leisure in the Victorian Age was linked to the capitalist compulsion to save and accumulate without end.

The educational impact on the individual of monetary rewards and artificial scarcity is intensified by another mechanism, that of competition. Its power of personality formation is even more radical than that of pecuniary incentives. The competitive system creates a competitive ego that is more self-centered than that stimulated by co-operation.

This may suffice to show that no institutional transformation can be complete without the requisite psychological and educational changes to make the new system work. Social education should penetrate into ever-deeper levels of the Self.[27] The thrilling but disquieting problem is that so far we cannot gauge the limits of psychological reconstruction. We can see that monetary rewards can be replaced by nonmonetary rewards, that status and income are not necessarily interlocked once and for all. We realize that society can gratify the wish for recognition by other means. But it is an open question whether this wish is a final datum to be taken for granted. It is possible and even likely that the wish for social recognition, so prevalent in our society, is itself socially induced. We know that philosophy and life techniques sometimes have encouraged withdrawal from these spheres, that the Far East has known how to paralyze, or at least stifle, this wish for social recognition. Even in our society we have marginal cases where that seemingly basic urge may collapse. Persons in permanently unemployed communities,[28] for example, who are deprived of monetary rewards, often develop a state of apathy symptomatic of a gradual weakening of any desire for social recognition.

When we said that capitalist society uses the urge to possess as the framework for character-building, we did not mean to say that once the money reward or the system of private property is removed, a self-assertive or self-centered ego can no longer develop. Obviously, self-centeredness and self-assertion can find other outlets besides those of appropriation, exploitation, and domination. In warrior societies [29] the Self was fashioned by heroic aspiration; the scholar may strive for fame and eminence, and often a sublimated wish for adventure of the mind informs his work. Much research has been devoted to this central issue and we hope before long to know far more about the most important topic of our time: the making of the Self in different social systems.[30] Still, we already know enough to assert that different character profiles and personality types go with different social systems. Once material conditions are manipulated from key positions, the deepest layers of the Self will be influenced.

Manipulation of institutional devices presents a peculiar case in the framework of planning. It coincides neither with planning for the free development of primary groups nor with the deliberate construction and reconstruction of organizations such as the Army or bureaucracy. It is a sphere *sui generis*. The creation of full employment or the redistribution of income through taxation are the deliberate result of democratic legislation and administration. Hence, there is nothing new about them. The novelty in a planned society will be the co-ordination of the different devices and their integration into a coherent policy of mutually interdependent innovations. Besides, the predictable psychological consequences will have to be guided.

Again, democratic planning differs radically from totalitarian manipulation of 'psychological compensations.' The totalitarian ministry of propaganda in World War II served as a central agency to sound and explore psychological reactions to relevant change and to provide and impose mass suggestions. A few crude devices served to compensate for scarcity, bombing damage, or defeat. Suppression of rebellious moods, promotion of submissiveness, deflection of aggression through pogroms of scapegoats, and Führer-worship formed part of this mass technique. The diametrically opposite policy of the democracies before the war was to do nothing, i.e. let the psychological effects of mass unemployment lead to general panic and emotional chaos.

The alternative of the Third Way suggests democratic planning of the social and psychological consequences of any comprehensive measure. This requires, first of all, social-psychological studies and a comprehensive information service on spontaneous reactions and attitudes of the people.[31] Constructive psychological alternatives must be devised to substitute for and channel displaced psychic energies too often fed into the scapegoat mechanism. A free society will avoid general inculcation by presenting a choice of outlets to the individual. With this approach there is every reason to hope that methods of sublimation may become part of the social atmosphere and that these will spontaneously appeal to the individual.

So long as the individual is free to choose, there is nothing undemocratic or illiberal in such a solution. T. H. Green has seen already that it is compatible with an advanced liberal view to arrange the environmental influences so that our 'better self' is encouraged to find the right solution. He is right in saying that it is not against the spirit of freedom to influence both the psychological and material environment so as to induce people to choose desirable values. Green's idea [32] may well be applied on a higher level to manipulations that may change the money mores. In that case we would undoubtedly rearrange more than purely material conditions. We would act in the spirit of planning for freedom so long as we did not force individuals into passive submission,[33] but encouraged active self-determination, and so long as the institutional changes of the money mores were democratically enacted. At first sight it may appear irrelevant that we plan the environment in order to elicit desirable behavior, but leave the door open for individual deviation; yet this makes all the difference. First, such procedure enlists the active part of the Self which is the ontological foundation of freedom.[34] Secondly, it provides scope for free integration and public competition in ideas. Innovations come about mostly through a free integration of deviating types who remain as insignificant dissenters outside the established social structure, yet often contribute new ideas and possible solutions in crisis situations of social change.

VI. SOME SOCIAL MECHANISMS AND THEIR EDUCATIONAL IMPACT: COMPETITION AND CO-OPERATION

Competition and co-operation have a peculiar educational effect upon individuals and condition distinct behavior patterns. Such social mechanisms differ somewhat from social institutions, but also lend themselves to planned regulation.

1. *A Fundamental Distinction*

Competition and co-operation may be viewed in two different ways: as simple social mechanisms or as organizing principles of a social structure.

Competition or co-operation as mechanisms may exist and serve diverse ends in any society, preliterate, capitalist, and non-capitalist.[35] But in speaking of the capitalist phase of rugged individualism and competition, we think of an all-pervasive structural principle of social organization.

This distinction may help to clarify the question whether capitalist competition—allegedly basic to our social structure—need be maintained as a presumably indispensable motivating force. Now, one may well eliminate competition as the *organizing principle* of the social structure and replace it by planning without eliminating competition as a *social mechanism* to serve desirable ends. The Soviet Union, for example, has made planning the basic principle of her economic and social organization, yet has introduced 'socialist competition' in the sphere of work and education.

In the envisioned mixed society the planner will introduce competition or co-operation as social mechanisms in those areas where their educational effect seems to be desirable. We realize only gradually the great role of competitive mechanisms in our forms of courtship, games, vocational pursuits, prestige aspirations, and a host of other areas.[36] How much of this should be maintained in a society planning for freedom is open to question and should be discussed on the merits of the given case.

Not even a fully planned society is committed to place a premium on co-operation in all spheres of activity. Further investigations of successful co-operation and its setting will help the
planner and social educator in their endeavor.[37]

In considering the educational effect of competition and co-
operation as social mechanisms, it is important to recall the
findings of modern sociology and psychology. As the Latin words
indicate, both terms mean 'striving,' joint striving and striving
against one another.[38] A goal may be pursued by joint or individual efforts. Modern experimental studies prove that the difference is not so fundamental as was formerly assumed. Neither
of these mechanisms is more deeply rooted in human nature
than the other, and neither has genetic priority. Man acquires
co-operative and competitive attitudes by being trained to adjust to given social institutions.[39] The prevalence of the one or
the other depends on the educational efforts and institutional
arrangements of a given society.

Competition will encourage and give more outlets to aggression than co-operation. Of course, one may ask whether it is good
to use aggression as a dynamo for achievement by directing it
toward competition for constructive ends, thus sublimating it
instead of letting aggression pure and simple flow into the channels of human contacts and personal relations. Advocates of economic competition maintain that it is preferable to direct competitive aggression toward economic rather than political ends.
Both propositions would seem questionable in the light of recent
history. The growth of the competitive urge may work itself
out no less ruthlessly in economics than in politics. Both, unre-
strained economic and political struggles, may destroy the community.

Competition as a social mechanism in the abstract is neither
good nor bad—it all depends on the kind of competition and
its setting. Hence we have to focus somewhat more closely on
the various types of competition and their respective educational
effects.

2. Individual and Group Competition

First we have to distinguish between individual and group competition. The former definitely fosters antagonistic attitudes; it

creates a pattern in which one person strives for something in order to exclude a rival. The first person's continuous aim therefore is to keep the other down and to throw all possible obstacles in his way. Each has an interest in the inefficiency of his competitor.

Group competition creates out-group antagonism but in-group co-operation. If two football teams compete for victory, the best player of the team will be interested in improving the play of the weakest member, will help him and practice with him. Were they to compete individually the better player might try to dominate the weaker by inducing feelings of inferiority. Instead, he will encourage a weak teammate and call forth his highest potentialities. Thus even motives of love and hatred are controlled by the setting of the scene. A society that reduces the number of individual competitive efforts and replaces them by group competition undoubtedly stimulates sympathetic emotions and provides more opportunities for democratic agreement. Of course, this does not hold if greater group solidarity is bought at the price of greater out-group hostility. This effect might be overcome if smaller competing groups on some occasions had to co-operate in competition against larger units, thereby learning to expand group loyalty.

This scheme of social education would not only broaden limited group loyalties, but would curb out-group aggressions or, at least, sublimate them. Such integration of limited loyalties happened during the war when many soldiers and civilians of the United Nations broadened their national loyalties in pursuit of the common aim. If the transfer of broader loyalties to a world organization succeeds without being indefinitely directed against the defeated aggressor nations, new methods may be found to sublimate aggressive energies into high-minded aspirations for mankind.

The vision of common disaster in another world war may operate as a unifying force. To prevent pan-destruction ought to be universally appealing—a sublime and concrete task. Failure will affect you and everybody else in all phases of human existence.

3. *Competition between Equals and Unequals*

In discussing the effect of competition we should further distinguish between the competition of equals and unequals. Most arguments in favor of competition apply to competition among equals; it is fallacious to suggest that beneficial effects exist in present-day society governed by competition among unequals. Competition between equals makes the individual self-reliant, independent, freedom-loving; it establishes mutual controls, and evokes jealousy to ensure fair play. When competition between equals turns into competition between unequals, the mental atmosphere changes. Competition still compels the competitor to adjust, but his self-adjustment no longer fosters independence and self-reliance, as may be illustrated by economic competition under conditions of inequality.

A certain outlay may mean for one person the risk of his last penny, whereas to another it is only the risk of an insignificant part of his fortune, which he can easily spare. The man who can afford to spread his risks will be in quite a different position from the man who has to risk his last dollar. To pretend publicly that this is still competition and equal opportunity creates an atmosphere of hypocrisy and evokes resentment among the victims of the struggle. This resentment is deeper than that felt in a rigid caste system, where the subject classes resign themselves to their fate from the very beginning by hopes for compensation in another life.

Competition among unequals always has a demoralizing effect. Its psychological impact differs according to the type of rewards, especially if they form part of our money mores. The effects of competition when linked to the institution of private property depend on the presence or absence of risks.

Competition for private and unlimited profits made sense in a freely expanding capitalist society where pioneering individuals on all frontiers of human enterprise faced great risks and unpredictable markets. Corporate enterprise today, however, has great stability and transfers major risks to the government, which in case of need has to grant privileges, subsidies, and protection. The creation of artificial scarcity becomes a major source of profit; competition loses its genuine function in many fields, and private profit of corporations no longer represents reward for personal risks or a reliable incentive for investment. Those who praise capitalism and seek to perpetuate it unconsciously or deliberately disregard all such distinctions and plead for competition as if it were always the same and had always an invigorating effect.

Therefore, educational efforts from the beginning should foster competition only among equals and at the same time enhance the spirit of freedom which will not tolerate unfair practice. Competition in the spirit of fair play and redistributive justice should be upheld wherever the mechanism of competition seems to promise best results. Of course, jealousy among competing partners checking each other's growth should not be allowed to block excellence. This is the liability of misplaced equalitarianism. On the other hand, the striving for excellence should not lead to megalomanic yearnings for privilege and power. Although this balance in attitude formation may be too much to ask for, English experience at least shows that not only extremist but greatly differentiated attitudes can be imparted through home and school training. This holds at least so long as the vision of the right pattern of behavior and the image of the desired personality type are clear. These observations on competition in general apply to all its concrete forms, whether it is a question of competition in school, in sport, in social work, or in religious teaching. All of them can be organized on a competitive basis and some of the general effects of competition described above can be detected in all instances.

4. Competition and Co-operation in a Planned Society

A planned society would first explore the various forms of competition and examine their functional value and educational significance. Whereas a totalitarian society is inclined to superimpose its social mechanisms, Planning for Freedom should aim at experiment and test each of the mechanisms for its specific fitness, expediency, and ease of democratic control. Diverse social mechanisms can implement the mixed system of a multi-patterned society at key points. We should admit competition in all fields where, as in science, competitive stimulation has unlimited opportunities without leading to accumulation of power. But we should jealously watch unlimited growth of rewards in the economic and political spheres.

What we have said about competition is equally true of co-operation. The term applies to a great many processes in different spheres of social life, which need to be evaluated functionally and judged on their merits. A society that appreciates variety in social interaction would not treat competition and co-operation as mutually exclusive, but would rather teach individuals and groups the techniques of changing from one form of striving to another. Education for variety and elasticity might teach children's play groups how to reach the same aim through either competition or co-operation. Youngsters can be shown that scarcity favors competitive selection of the few who can get a bigger share for themselves by excluding the rest, whereas co-operation means equal distribution among all.[40]

A society that wants youth to understand the more complex problems of adult life will not only try to demonstrate the functional aspects of these mechanisms, but will also familiarize young people with their corresponding social attitudes. This type of education will show how individual competition enhances concentration on success, that it tends to put the supreme value on achievement for the individual's own sake and exclusive benefit; how it thus creates an unfriendly society of men seeking fulfilment like robots in megalomaniac achievement, and that such ways can lead to the Nazi type of destructive efficiency. The same method of social interpretation will demonstrate that co-operation tends to bring out fellow-feeling and the desire for social recognition by one's fellows. Whereas in an excessively competitive society the mania for individual success which cannot be shared by others may develop into a neurotic trait, the normal person in a balanced society will be able to change from one type of gratification to another, a flexibility that may be acquired by proper childhood training.

This necessarily brief discussion of co-operation and competition may suffice to show how naive people are who fear that all the advantages of a competitive society would vanish if it were replaced by a more co-operative one, or who can conceive of a planned society only as a single routine of social mechanisms. A society planning for freedom will decide on secondary mechanisms such as competition or co-operation in terms of objective criteria, i.e. their functional adequacy as means to given ends and their educational impact.

Some plead for a competitive society on the ground that it offers greater powers of individualization and differentiation than a planned society. They see in competition the only mechanism for producing strong individuality and freedom. It is, of course, correct to say that both individualization and the will to freedom develop in competition among equals, but competition is far from being their exclusive social source. Any successful personal adjustment and mastery of difficulties will enhance individual initiative and self-reliance; it is not necessary that these should be provided by the economic system. Whenever opportunities for self-advancement are replaced by co-operative activities, a planned society by its educational policy may provide outlets for initiative and individual responsibility.

The balance should be restored by making education, social work, self-government at least as exciting as profit-making used to be. There are many fields for pioneering where everyone has the opportunity to contribute to social betterment.

Of course social inventiveness is alive in a society only if the public-spirited citizen feels that this society is 'his,' not 'theirs.' In such a society the choice of mechanisms is not primarily in terms of abstract profit calculations and private budgeting but in terms of the common good. A community that pursues an educational end is likely to give due weight to the educational implications of any change it may introduce.

5. Definition of Social Education

The primary forms of integration and the corresponding behavior patterns define the basic character of a society. The great alternative is authoritarian organization based upon dominating behavior or democratic co-ordination based upon integrative behavior.[41] Secondary mechanisms may implement both systems in different degrees, but do not determine the fundamental nature of society. The criterion is whether in crucial situations basic cohesion is achieved by dominating or integrative behavior. The secondary mechanisms are relevant only as permanent training grounds for behavior. On the field of action character is formed. If one mechanism fosters excessively dominating tendencies, the prevailing pattern of cohesion may be undermined.

Social education then has to take stock of the educational impact of social patterns and arrangements and modify them to serve desired ends. In this description, we have deliberately neglected the educational influence of ideals—ideals of good conduct and character. There has been a tendency of late to disregard ideals and emphasize realistic investigation of social situations and their educational significance. This is a healthy reaction to abstract Idealism, which expected to improve character by propagating ideas without reference to their social context. It is indeed irritating to listen to one who suggests in the midst of war that everybody become a pacifist, or who tells the butcher or baker in a competitive society that he should stop being selfish and renounce profits.

The new possibilities of improving the social order—of controlling social groups, institutions, and mechanisms—create the danger of shifting emphasis to their manipulation, thus disregarding the ideal or ethical side of social education. Those who go too far along this path and expect the new social order automatically to change human conduct and character should realize that competition, as recent research has proved, differs not only according to the combination it undergoes with other factors but according to the ideals with which it is associated. The idea of 'fair play' is a modifying ideal, which does not result automatically from the mechanism of competition, but is derived from the larger culture. Different social situations exert their educative influence; people exposed to them understand their educative meaning. The constant 'definition of the situation,' the continuous valuation of events makes values an educative power. This re-discovery of their significance in the social context will be welcomed by all who dislike abstract ideas, but are receptive to concrete idealism.

8

The Pattern of Democratic Behavior

o

I. THE CONCEPT OF INTEGRATIVE BEHAVIOR

We have seen that a new society demands new controls, and
that these in their turn require new patterns of behavior and
new personality types. If this is true, we must now substantiate
our expectation by a full discussion of what constitutes this new
behavior of a democratic type of personality. Exploration of the
ideal pattern of democratic behavior and character will thus
complete our previous discussion, which attempted first to clarify
the democratic idea of co-ordination and then the psychological
and technical possibilities of remaking human behavior. Having
dealt with the *means* of creating the new man, our present approach would establish the *idea*,[1] the *vision* of the type of behavior and the type of man that should guide all our educational and social efforts. A clear vision of the aims and content
of education is all the more desirable as there is a tendency in
democracies to discuss problems of organization rather than
ideas, techniques rather than aims. There is no doubt that Democracy has lost the clear conception of the type of citizen it
wants to create.

Obviously, elaboration of an ideal pattern does not mean that
henceforth everyone in a democratic society will act accordingly,
or that only the type of person whom we shall call democratic
can exist or be desirable. The ideal only indicates the direction
in which every educational effort in a democratic society ought

to move. It is obvious that all people will not achieve the ideal and that every sphere of action is not likely to conform in the same way to the democratic pattern. In spite of these modifications, there is no doubt that every social system has 'operative ideas'—as A. D. Lindsay called them—that is to say, patterns of thought and action that establish a mode of life, regardless of variations. Nobody can doubt that the totalitarian societies established such a *modus vivendi,* however much it may be rejected by our better judgment.

As a matter of fact, the easiest way to express the democratic pattern of life, action, and personality is to contrast it with the authoritarian or domineering pattern.

On a simple plane, what it is has always been obvious. As everybody will agree, it is part of our democratic creed to call 'democratic' behavior that implies the person's readiness for co-operation, especially with his equals. Everyone also realizes that this equality means readiness to respect our neighbor's personality, never using him as a tool or as a means to our own ends. Kant recognized this; recently it has been formulated as the principle of mutual deference,[2] undoubtedly implying the idea of co-operation between equals. Similarly, an essential feature of democratic as contrasted with dominative behavior is minimal use of violence, pressure, or power; and if we have recourse to the latter, it will be under the control of peers with equal controlling influence.

Although people have long been more or less aware of these main features of democratic behavior, a recent development to my way of thinking has greatly strengthened the concept of that basic pattern which ought to serve as a measuring rod for understanding human behavior. The psychologist, H. H. Anderson,[3] in another context Piaget,[4] and recently Herbert Read [5] have contributed a great deal to the better understanding of the fundamental quality of social relations in a democratic society. Whereas Piaget emphasized the idea of reciprocity in the democratic social process, H. H. Anderson and D. W. Harding [6] called 'integrative behavior' what I would term the archetype of democratic behavior. I think there are good reasons for adopting this term because it refers to something more fundamental than simple co-operation and contains the key to various facets characteristic of democratic behavior.

The important element in this conception of integrative behavior is that the person who acts in its spirit is not only unwilling to superimpose his own view and will upon the other fellow—the essence of the domineering attitude—but he is tolerant of disagreement. He is tolerant not for the sake of compromise, but in the expectation of enlarging his own personality by absorbing some features of a human being essentially different from himself. Practically, this means that the democratic personality welcomes disagreement because it has the courage to expose itself to change. Going to the root of the matter, we find that openness to change is only within reach of the person who really feels secure, and therefore is unafraid of losing either status or individuality by having his probity exposed to the testing powers of co-operation and exchange of ideas.

The most important point in this observation is realization of the link between authoritarian superimposition of one's view and fear of losing status. In an authoritarian relationship it stands to reason that one of the parties has a higher status than the other and in his activities is concerned with maintaining that status, whereas in the ideal case of democratic partnership the question of status is ruled out by acknowledgment of essential equality: in other words, the desire for prestige stands less in the way of willingness to learn from another person than under an authoritarian system. Indeed, there is no greater obstacle to real learning (by which I do not mean passive assimilation of established knowledge but the power of experiencing something new) than the fear of losing one's status. A status-ridden person cannot really learn. This was observed by an eighteenth-century German thinker who is unfortunately not well known in the Anglo-Saxon countries.[7] What G. Ch. Lichtenberg said was roughly that the longer he observed elderly people, the more he became convinced that apparent senility is in most cases not the result of physiological senescence, but is rooted in wrong psychological attitudes. Old people are often unwilling to learn because revising their views seems incompatible with their prestige and respectability.

Once this close interconnection between the pattern of be-

P

havior and the pattern of personality structure is recognized, all differences in modes of conduct and personality types become more intelligible. The pattern of action is, then, part and parcel of the personality structure. A society that creates the status-ridden type, incessantly afraid of losing face, is bound to express this concern for social esteem in an endless number of rituals [8] in which the 'superior' person can continually reassure himself of the submissiveness of his subordinates. Moreover, in such societies social approval, the most fundamental weapon of conditioning behavior, is always given to self-assertive behavior, especially on the part of those who are expected to rule. In contrast, in a really democratic society, public approbation tends to discourage the would-be domineering person who refuses to treat his fellow men as equals or even tries to humiliate them.

From the very beginning of this discussion we left no doubt about considering integrative behavior not as an already established reality, but as an *ideal* of Democracy. Setting up an ideal does not mean we shall ever attain it completely, but rather lends direction to education and to mutual controls. It is obvious that integrative behavior has greater chances of realization in personal relations than in large-scale organizations. The more social needs grow and organization becomes a necessity, the more elements of domination are bound to creep in. But as long as the ideal of integrative behavior is alive and is the real motive power, there will be a tendency to restrict blind obedience and to preserve or even introduce situations that support democratic behavior. In a society based upon domination, the opposite will hold true. Even in the realm of personal relations the self-assertive and vindictive character will be praised as courageous, and people will indulge in organization or rather over-organization, because they will feel that this alone gives them strength: the Self feels safe only if supported by regulations of a dominative character. Punishment and penalties built into the institutional pattern express the same self-assertive, aggressive tendencies so strongly prevalent in totalitarian society.

To the democratic mind integrative behavior is an ideal only, to be experienced in terms of approximation. To the anarchist, only behavior abstaining from the use of power and domination altogether is admissible. He wants a society based upon anarchy and maintains that even with growing organization no elements of domination may be introduced. The anarchist, in a sense, is a democrat in a marginal situation. The democratic mind differs from that of the anarchist in that it is closer to reality. While it acknowledges the need for authority in certain situations and on certain levels of social organization, yet the aim is still to minimize domination by new social inventions, to replace forms of organization based on domination by more humanized ones, and to bring power under the control of the community.

Once this is clear, we can follow more closely the implications and consequences of ideal integrative behavior.

We saw that co-operation, properly understood, means continuous integration of different purposes. One who has never been trained in integrating purposes has never experienced true democratic co-operation, since the essence of democracy is the integration of purposes and not mere compromise. Even dominative people may achieve a compromise. They try to suppress each other, to impose their will upon each other, and only when this fails will they try to reach a compromise.

It has rightly been said that compromise is rational adjustment between two or more opposing views and wills, and it is only a matter of expediency that the parties sacrifice some of their original claims. No dynamic progress, no truly creative power is expressed by compromise.[9]

Integrative behavior is more than compromise. It means that people, though fully aware of the fact that differences of constitution and social position, of drives and interests, shape their experience and attitude to life in different ways, yet transmute their different approaches for the purpose of co-operating in a common way of life. Such transmutation is a creative form of integration: out of the process of common living and co-operative pursuits, a new purpose emerges which the partners come to cherish even more than their original aims. From the very outset this kind of integration offers scope for the dissenter or the man of initiative whose contribution, which may differ from ours, is to be absorbed, not excluded. Only the Anglo-Saxon countries, where the dissenters have contributed importantly to the new idea of creative compromise, could develop this conception.

1. *Democratic Tolerance* versus *Fanaticism*

The real idea of tolerance, as A. D. Lindsay has strongly emphasized, is not passive acquiescence. It is rooted in the faith
that the voice of God may speak through even the humblest
member of the community. Thus, we must listen to him, for in
his peculiar life experience the humblest might have seen what
has even escaped the notice of the most sophisticated.

The term 'integrative behavior' is only a scientific definition
of latent tendencies that have always been present in the ideas
of democracy and tolerance. Apart from making these tendencies
more conscious and explicit, it adapts the idea of democratic
co-operation to a more advanced stage in history. When not only
members of the same clan or community, but essentially different individuals and groups have tô co-operate, readiness for assimilation becomes imperative. Integrative behavior transcends
the idea of simple co-operation also in so far as it applies the
latter principle to a dynamic changing world where new purposes are continually evolving.

Two further aspects of integrative behavior can best be explained by developing what has been said so far.

Democratic tolerance is incompatible with fanaticism, which
relinquishes the zealous search for truth and deprives one's fellow men of the opportunity to make creative contributions.[10]
No idea of a *Herrenvolk* can develop along these lines, nor a
conception of elites (at least in a fascist sense) claiming the monopoly of knowing what is best for others. This does not necessarily mean that there should be no experts in the community
whose knowledge of certain things is more exact than that of
others and whose information can be used; nor that there should
be no people who have a deeper concern for essential matters
than the rest. In a democratic society the existence of these bet-
ter-informed and more alert types of men is exceedingly important; however, their place in the community should not be
one of seclusion from or domination over others, but one in
which the community shares their higher qualities through mutual exchange. A truly democratic society will integrate those
with higher gifts and achievements, not by isolating them, but

by establishing lines of communication between them and the rest of the community.[11]

The other implication of the *ideal of creative tolerance* is the task of establishing a common purpose and real co-operation with dissenters who are forever in ferment.

The doctrine of the need for co-operation, even with those who disagree, has often deteriorated into the practice of neutralizing the really important issues. In a decadent phase of democracy this leads to the theory that there can be no agreement on fundamental ideas. Therefore, the best democracy can do to maintain co-operation is to agree on partial issues only. Needless to say, this is only another version of the 'need for compromise' theory. Compromise will, of course, be unavoidable in many instances. We cannot afford to wait for basic integration, i.e. till the community out of its own resources finds a new creative solution. Yet the more often we accept compromise as a satisfactory substitute for real and progressive integration, the more likely creative tolerance is to degenerate into a policy of neutrality with gradual elimination of discussion of fundamentals.[12] Thus less and less attention is given to essentials within the democracies. A type of emasculated mentality has become preponderant that cares neither for principles nor a deeper understanding of life, but only for working compromises.

In this atmosphere of general indifference, philosophy, religion, the sense of history are vanishing, and even in matters of the spirit the bargaining attitude of the businessman becomes the principal virtue. The scientist for whom only the measurable is exact typifies this attitude of regarding only the surface of things in terms of limited operations to which everyone can subscribe. In the sphere of morality and religion, it is considered enough to come to an agreement on externals only, and essentials are no longer considered.

This is why democracy has become so unattractive for people who yearn for a purpose to which they can be devoted. Spinoza was right in saying that we can supersede one emotion only by means of another. Enthusiasm untainted by fanaticism—this is what we need.[13]

On the other hand, we cannot hope for common understanding of essentials so long as we regard them as fixed and immutable. The only adequate form of democratic progress is a kind of co-operation that implies constant reinterpretation and reintegration of essentials in the light of progressive experience.[14] Only this attitude, rightly understood, is in keeping with a changing world: the other attitude forfeits the main source of change for the sake of agreement on the external issue of the present only.

2. *The Pattern of Democratic Responsibility*

It is but one step further to the democratic concept of responsibility. If the accent is on common living and integrative behavior, joy in the discovery of new truth will prevail over pride and self-righteousness. In this case one should be trained for responsibility not by blind obedience but through awareness of a new world with new situations which may be defined and regulated in the course of common experience.

As democratic truth is truth as it emerges in the process of common living, no sabotage of common agreement is permissible. As we have enacted our own law, there is no sense in resisting it or undermining its working. If alteration is needed, provision is made for changing the law by common consent. Loyalty to the law therefore consists chiefly in loyalty to the accepted procedure, and there is no greater offense against the spirit of democracy than that of denouncing its methods.

Now we come to the problems of responsibility in its subjective and objective aspects. Abstract Liberalism is concerned only with the former, whereas institutions, organization, and finally the State are overemphasized by objectivist theories. We seek to overcome the one-sidedness of both approaches by a method that strikes the balance between subjective and objective factors.

Abstract Liberalism, which considers the individual the only reality, seeks the roots of responsibility exclusively in him as a matter of course. Though obviously there can be no responsibility without the individual, since the seat of responsibility is his own heart, it is conceded to be something purely internal. Extreme liberalist individualism tends to view responsibility as a question of personal *intent* (*Gesinnung*) and to restrict the social and educational problem exclusively to creating the right attitudes within the individual. We can undoubtedly learn something from the liberal's appreciation of the psychological and educational factors, but we shall not neglect the social context and its influence as stressed by his opponents, the objectivists.

In the objectivist view, obligation and authority arise from objective needs. Intersocial regulation and the individual's conscience are but internalized commands which have their real origins in the social fabric, whether they are developed through traditions, embodied in custom, or enacted by some ruler or official decree.

The inclination to interpret obligations as part of the objective setting and to impute the phenomenon of conscience to it prevails in a dictatorship as well as in various types of conservatism. The 'objectivists' even go so far sometimes as to deplore the fact that conscience can become so subjective as to lose touch with the objective needs of the community or of the social order. However dangerous exaggerations of this approach may be, especially when the dictator's 'fiat' takes the place of the individual's decision, they contain an element of insight, i.e. that responsibility always works in an objective historical context and has not much meaning without it. This teaches us further that we cannot educate or re-educate a person by improving him alone, but only by endeavoring at the same time to reform the social context. Apart from working directly on the individual, we have to manipulate the environment so as to foster growth of the desired personality type.

II. SUBJECTIVE ASPECTS OF RESPONSIBILITY

As in many other cases, we must first realize that there is no innate form of responsibility. Every society consistently trains for or at least carefully prepares the individual for the assumption of responsibilities.

It is equally true that no society can survive unless its members are willing to take the consequences of their acts. Society would have to maintain devices for making people responsible for their deeds, even were psychology to prove that there is no such thing as free will.[15] Sanctions and punishment are therefore common to all societies.

In spite of this, great differences develop as soon as we relate certain sanctions to a particular social organization and correlate the social structure with the structure of mentality it requires.

If the basic structure of a society rests upon domination, not only dominative behavior but also a dominative type of responsibility will evolve. The same applies to democracy. Democratic patterns of integrative behavior are rooted in a democratic conception of conscience and a corresponding sense of responsibility. We must admit that no society carries principles to their logical conclusion. Every authoritarian society will set apart certain enclaves for democratic self-regulation, and in every democratic society certain patterns of domination will survive. Thus qualified, our generalization remains valid, for the proportion of behavior ingredients in the different types of society is fundamentally different. In an authoritarian society dominative attitudes prevail, and in a democratic society integrative behavior is preponderant. Apart from the preponderance of one or the other type of behavior, the distinction between the two social orders rests on whether important decisions are made and carried out in a spirit of domination or of integration, and whether the dominative or integrative behavior pattern meets with public approval.

The more closely we consider the different forms of behavior and responsibility, the more it becomes apparent that they correspond to the stages of human maturation. Dominative forms are closer to childhood; behavior patterns that make for trained participation in democratic co-operation and shared responsibility can develop only at a higher level of maturity.

1. *Identification of 'Führer' with Father*

One of the earliest forms of responsibility results from the child's identification with his parents.[16] For them the child does what is wanted, and his developing superego is somehow linked to his dependence on the parent. In an authoritarian society, this early stage of responsibility is preserved, when loyalty is directly focused on the *Führer* whose image replaces that of the father. Here obedience is demanded only for the sake of the *Führer,* all responsibility rests on him and none is really conceivable beyond this personal allegiance and dependence. With this type of responsibility scope for rationality is ultimately determined in the same way: as the 'father' or *Führer* alone knows the deeper reasons of your action, rational argument is needless. Blind obedience is considered not only an expedient but a virtue. If rational argument were admitted as an integral element, such uncertainty would result that the whole system would break down.

Another primitive method of creating consistent behavior with a corresponding form of responsibility is external conditioning that applies rewards and punishments as the most conspicuous mechanisms.[17] Any behavior that is determined either by identification or conditioned by reward and punishment implies a degree of consistency that demands a great deal of self-control on the part of the individual and therewith some elements of responsibility. Yet neither of these 'lower' forms of consistent behavior is based upon the individual's conscious decision, nor does it demand an intelligent appraisal of the situation and one's own contribution to communal living.

Man still moves at a level of unconscious habituation and drill, and the patterns of behavior that we want to make part of our personality and conduct are not yet acquired by intelligent selection. As long as responses and habits are mainly mechanical, responsibility, too, remains mechanical. Its principal virtue is a certain consistency and very often the ability to forego pleasure.

At this level improvement in behavior is possible only if the habits to be established are valued for their own sake: in other words, if the hero instead of the gangster is emulated, or if rewards are bestowed for co-operative and amicable social activities instead of destructive ones governed by the spirit of rivalry.

Totalitarian societies are skilful in exploiting the latent potentialities of lower forms of behavior and responsibility. Their limitation, however, lies in not wanting to put them at the service of nobler aims, or to encourage higher forms of behavior with corresponding types of responsibility.

In dealing with these lower forms of behavior modern democracy should realize that they are to some extent necessary. Plato's ideas about education may serve to illustrate the desirable attitude. He pointed out that we cannot educate a child without instilling blind obedience and useful automatic habits. If the first stage of education is devoted to implanting desirable habits, the next should aim at developing in the individual critical sense to discriminate consciously between the reasonable and the unreasonable.

2. *Recent Theories of the Super-Ego*

The problem of responsibility is closely related to the 'Super-Ego' of Freudian psychoanalysis, which seeks scientifically to explain what is commonly called conscience. Recently this concept of the Super-Ego has been revised more in agreement with democratic trends. Freud spent most of his life in a dominative and prohibitive society and keenly realized the negative aspects of the Super-Ego. To him it represented only the remnants of parental and cultural taboos, i.e. the inhibiting aspects of social education. H. A. Murray,[18] however, can claim the merit of having shown that the Super-Ego contains the element of creation as well as that of negation. Lewis Mumford [19] followed his lead by proving that the Super-Ego, far from being only an inhibitive force repressing asocial tendencies, is also a constructive power that sets up positive ideals. Thus the Super-Ego is capable of creating a whole system of values in elaboration of the Ego-Ideal. Works of art, ethics, religion, and science are objectivations of this Super-Ego system. It is true that the Freudians made allowance for this by recognizing the phenomenon and by coining the term 'sublimation'; yet on the whole they overemphasized the conception of education as a sum of frustrating techniques and were rather vague about the constructive and creative possibilities in socialization of the individual.

Socialization of human beings, as we understand it, is achieved not only negatively by 'don't's,' but also by positive images and creative ideals. Far from resting on the principle of pain, implying constant struggle against one's inclination, acceptance of ideals is linked to the experience of positive joy. It is part of the rebirth of democracy that we have got rid of those somber aspects of the Victorian Age when attention was focused on inhibitions only.[20] In our more hopeful constructive start, we are sufficiently critical to realize that we cannot completely do away with repression, yet we believe in a series of inventions that teach us to achieve by joint striving what formerly, in a world of domination, was done under the motive of fear. The key to this change in attitude lies in realization that most objectives that are painful to the individual, if externally imposed, can be joyfully accepted if their achievement is recognized as a common purpose, emotionalized as a positive goal, and shouldered as a common burden.

Work presents the best illustration of this point. As long as we are compelled to work because external authority demands it, the idea of work is associated with drudgery, pain, and displeasure. As soon as we perform the same task as a self-chosen contribution to the community, we very often try to excel in the job and would not give it up on any account. Of course, we react in this way only if trained for it, and if our Super-Ego is influenced in such a manner that its prohibitive formula can be gradually replaced by creative imagery and constructive vision. It is therefore no exaggeration to say that social reorganization will only become rooted in people's minds if we can remold the Super-Ego for this purpose. Supplementary to simple training in new types of behavior and habits will be the stimulation of creative drives and the urge for self-perfection. Thus ultimately we lay the foundations for the development of a new type of conscience and responsibility.

If we regard our problem in its historical perspective, we see that ever since Rousseau this optimistic approach to man—the shaking loose of taboos and relaxation of inhibiting elements in the Super-Ego, and the new emphasis on creative potentialities —has made itself felt repeatedly. It accompanied the democratic transformation of man and society and is one of the outstanding aspects of this development. Modern educational theory in many ways only substantiates in more scientific terms the insight underlying Rousseau's *Émile*. Our proposed substitution of direct experience for authoritarian punishment and the idea that education should start from human needs was anticipated by Rousseau:

Keep the child solely dependent on things (as opposed to other men); you will have followed the order of nature in the process of his education. Never oppose to his unreasonable wishes any but physical obstacles or punishments resulting from the actions themselves—he will remember these punishments in similar situations. It is enough to prevent him from doing evil without forbidding him to do it. Ex-

perience and impotency alone must take the place of laws for him. . .
I have already said that your child must not get anything because he
demands it, but because he needs it, nor do anything by obedience
but only by necessity; thus the words 'obey' and 'command' will be
excluded from his vocabulary still more rigorously than those of duty
and obligation; but those of force, necessity, impotency and coercion
will have an important place in it.[21]

The new educational drive between the two wars, led mainly
by Dewey's ideas, had its origin in Rousseau.

The optimistic view that one day we may be able to do without authoritarian methods has spread to other fields. The main
changes in the field of social education are merely attempts at
applying the same idea to new ways of living and thinking.

The tendency to relax the restrictive elements within the
Super-Ego, thus releasing a flood of sentiment and imagination,
as in the case of Rousseau himself, seems to be a recurrent phase
in the pattern of democratic development. Periods of expansion
and contraction alternate: a sudden outburst and general release of previously repressed emotions inaugurate a period of expansion, until a sense of fear develops within the Self, that 'fear
of freedom' which has recently been so ably described by Erich
Fromm.[22] This fear calls a halt to expansion and abundance and
leads to a new phase of contraction. The dynamic struggle between social classes is partially reflected in this development.
Whereas rising classes tend to favor expansion and would overthrow the established emotional equilibrium, the conservative
classes unconsciously cling to an emotional *status quo*. Within
this rhythm, the phases of expansion are the creative ones,
whereas the phase of contraction represents the effort to establish a new balance in the dynamic process.

3. *Training for Spontaneity*

The great achievements in the development of the democratic
spirit are the relaxing of the Super-Ego, the movement toward
the release of forces, the training for spontaneity and the removal of inhibitions to intelligence. In the light of modern educational studies, we realize that spontaneity or the ability to take
initiative is partly innate: thus the processes of releasing it are
crucial. But in part it also results from training.[22] This training

consists in placing the individual in unexpected unconventional situations in which he cannot draw upon his store of habitual reactions. This not only leads to greater mobility and adaptability, but also to a more satisfying way of life than one based on routine or confined to the closed circle of past experience.

While Romanticism in many of its variations is a further development of the potentialities shown by Rousseau, in advocating individualism drawing directly upon the resources of the imagination, it has also another implication. This is fully expressed in Bergson, who likewise made it the aim of life to set free the creative potentialities and pierce the shell of conventionality. Democratic education is triumphant not only in the exhortation to be constructive or spontaneous, but in planning the life of the individual so that it presents a constant challenge to initiative, to making one's own choices, to finding new combinations, to remaining self-possessed and swimming against the current for a while, if necessary. But the person who is 'against it' should not be so from neurotic negativism. Courage to oppose should emanate rather from the healthy, constructive personality. A totalitarian society could not bear such deviation; it pushes any opponent willy-nilly into the position of a social misfit unable to adjust himself to the established order. In contrast, it is part of the democratic vision that there should be some people swimming against the current and part of democratic education that there be good swimmers among them.[24]

The same idea of encouraging the use of intelligence is at work in modern educational philosophy, which conceives of the intellect, the *ratio* itself, as a dynamic entity. To the 'stabilizing outlook' the intellect is a rigid system of static categories in which otherwise elusive sensations are stored once they have been freed from transitory elements. To the 'romantic' who conceives of creative evolution as the basic experience, such a dehydrated intellect is a fictitious entity, an expedient for dealing somehow with the ever-changeable. The real process of thinking is in itself dynamic and part of the larger life process that continually invents new categories and methods in order to overcome the stereotypes of a merely assimilating intellect. New discoveries largely give names to facts, situations, and processes that have existed for centuries without names, because group fears and taboos compelled man to shut his eyes to what was under his nose.

The existence of infant sexuality is a case in point. It could be observed by every mother and nurse, yet none dared to admit it. Again, the discovery of the 'unconscious' produced a shock because it was one of the mind's defenses to deny it. New knowledge in these fields is therefore not only based upon more consistent thinking, but on prior removal of collective inhibitions.

Every society produces inhibited mental areas; therefore the act of freeing intelligence is a preliminary condition for further discovery. An individual who joins in the collective process of clearing away inhibitions that have lost their function and are preventing the growth of intellectual discoveries partakes, even if he himself is not a genius, in the work of genius. He, as well as the extremely gifted person, turns life into a voyage of discovery. Together with his fellow beings, he discovers novel aspects of the world because he succeeds in tearing aside the veil of conventionality. In this new approach, not only can fresh significance of things become the object of discovery, but human relations, too, reveal other potentialities since different types of experience are molded by new forms of common living.

One of the present-day discoveries is that of the dynamic conscience, the idea of a dynamic integrating responsibility—a responsibility for the venture of exploring the possibilities of living together in a world community with people who are different, in situations that cannot be foreseen, and under norms that have yet to be found by common effort.

Conscience has been considered for a long time as highly personal. Yet few sayings are truer than that of T. H. Green: 'No individual can make a conscience for himself. He always needs a society to make it for him. A conscientious heresy, religious or political, always represents some gradually maturing conviction as to the social good, already implicitly involved in the ideas on which the accepted rules of conduct rest.' [25]

To abstract idealism, the development of conscience is indeed a purely personal affair. In this view the growth of moral personality consists in purely individual development, in improving the powers of the Self, in sharpening the capacity to reason, in removing prejudice, et cetera. For the new integrative theory of personality the development of conscience cannot be purely an individual matter. It is bound up with a continual give-and-take, a joining with others for the purpose of common discovery of fresh fields of activity for which new norms must be found by common effort. Thus the conscience of the individual is rooted in the growing conscience of the community. This does not mean that the growth of conscience always leads to sudden and unexpected departure from what has been customary. As T. H. Green has shown, even a heresy represents a gradual maturing, a collective deviation related to the traditional set of ideas in so far as it implies opposition to it. The terminus *a quo* forms a common experience, and the terminus *ad quem*, the aim at which we tend to arrive, is also embedded in a common field of expectations and possibilities. A changing community is not determined by a set of unshakable commands, but is engaged in a permanent search for new norms to express changing experiences. The content of conscience is accordingly not determined by explicit and final rules but is continually shaping itself anew.

An education based on the vision of independent atoms living in worlds of their own, in which the individual is the maker of himself and his own conscience, as it were, must differ from one aimed at preparing individuals for the co-operative enterprise of creating a new world together for which they have yet to find the norms. The person who is educated in this sense acquires capacity for keeping his ear to the ground, and being acutely aware of the new creative tendencies and potentialities in common life. We cannot be expected to develop this capacity without special training, but innumerable experiments in group living show that it can be cultivated.

III. OBJECTIVE ASPECTS OF RESPONSIBILITY

We have been attempting to work out some features of responsibility as these appear in subjective experience. But from the beginning it has been clear that a realist democracy cannot conceive responsibility in terms of subjective experience only. Rather it must be realized that responsibility grows out of an environment from which alone it derives meaning and real validity. The philosophy and sociology of responsibility must therefore pay at least as much attention to the environmental

factors determining its shape and potentialities, as to the experience of the individual. The author's philosophy has always been
guided by the idea of *Seinsverbundenheit,* i.e. by the idea that
mental phenomena are related to the environment, the situation,
and the field, and do not exist in an abstract heaven.[26] Only a
philosophy able to give due regard to both sides of the problem
—the *subjective* meaning, emergence, and development of conscience as it affects the individual and the *objective* setting that
gives it content and purpose—can be considered adequate. Expressed in terms of education, training for morality that concen-
trates solely on subjective psychological devices for awakening
and developing individual conscience loses touch with real life.
The teacher as well as the pupil must have his eyes open to
awareness of the milieu in which conscience can actually emerge
and achieve power over the individual and others.

Therefore, it is an essential part of social education to refine
the sense of reality by training for understanding of the objective conditions in which action takes place, response can be expected, tasks solved, and rules of co-operation established.[27] We
usually feel responsible for certain people only, for members of
our family, our clan, our community. With growing contacts,
the sense of responsibility may embrace our fellow citizens, or
even mankind at large. This expanding sense of responsibility
depends not only on the individual's personal life history,
though this provides fertile soil for its growth; it is equally the
fruit of the expanding world of social groups in which we live.
This accounts for the fact that so many people feel responsible
for their fellow citizens, whereas they might remain untouched
by the fate of those belonging to a different race or nation. Their
sense of responsibility has never developed beyond the orbit of
their country. In the same way, some people who feel keenly
responsible for their own kin may yet fail to develop an active
interest in the affairs of the community. Their sense of responsibility has become arrested at the level of the family or tribe.

These examples show that the range of responsibility to which
the individual feels committed depends to a great extent on the
radius of communications and other forms of contact and methods of group unification immediately affecting him. A person
with far-reaching contacts may choose members of other nations

whom he is willing to draw into the orbit of his sympathy and thus accept responsibilities transcending the boundaries of the community; but the majority will hardly go beyond the confines of their own community. Thus, our personal conscience is, at least to some extent, a by-product of the historical process. It follows that the broadening of responsibility cannot be achieved solely by individual education but is primarily a task for social education. In consequence, it could and should be handled strategically. If a community is in a phase of expansion or fusion, the individual's range of responsibility is more likely to expand: at a time when the armies of the United Nations were fighting together, a new sense of communion could more easily be roused than in a period when they never met in common action. Racial and other forms of group prejudice break down more easily if people who formerly felt no responsibility toward each other begin to work together. In a common cause people will attach less and less importance to racial and other differences, finally forgetting them altogether. This, of course, does not happen if they are allowed to compete with one another, as rivalry automatically reinforces the attitude of 'being against.'

Our strategy in widening the range of responsibility should be based not so much on proclaiming abstract principles as on co-ordinating them with measures to bring about co-operation among groups. Ideas, in this sense, should not be taken merely at face value, but should be evaluated with regard to their fitness to implement group living and in the direction of co-operation or integration. Ideas fit to serve this process strengthen it greatly, and their power in turn is multiplied a hundredfold.

In the process of education for a world community and for international co-operation, strategic situations ought to be carefully chosen; any approach to the individual should be so timed as to form part of the general pattern of social change so as not to remain confined to the field of pure education.

1. Norms and Their Group Content

Various patterns of responsibility are determined by the nature and density of the group processes from which they arise. This aspect of our approach to the problem can best be demonstrated by means of a few observations from the new discipline of Sociol-

Q

ogy of Law, which in turn has its roots in Proudhon's social philosophy. The main thesis is that law, far from being an abstract social entity, in fact evolves out of the social process, the life of small and large groups. There are, accordingly, as many forms of control (norms) as there are forms of sociality, or, as we would say, of group integration. One of the foremost contemporary representatives of this line of thought is Georges Gurvitch,[28] who has put forward a competent classification of the forms of sociality; these in our view do not only generate different kinds of law but different types of conscience as well. Indeed, the quality of the social bonds uniting members of various groups and the corresponding fusion of their minds determine, I think, not only the character of the emerging norms but also the kind of conscience that corresponds to them.

Gurvitch bases his definition of three main types of law on three corresponding types of sociality, which in their turn are distinguished by the degrees of integration. The three types of sociality are: (a) Masses, (b) Community, and (c) Communion. This allows us to build a scale leading from mere interdependence to interpenetration of minds. *The masses* are held together by a very superficial fusion that can be communicated to innumerable individuals; but this form of sociality lacks coherence, as the bonds between the members are not strong enough to prevent the group from easily falling apart. *The communion,* as experienced, for instance, in religious sects, is based upon an integration of minds at their deepest level, affecting the most intimate spheres. In consequence of this intimacy, communion should be confined to small groups, as growth in numbers leads to increasing differentiation, ultimately so marked that schisms become inevitable. *The community* is the form of sociality that has achieved the best balance, as it rests upon interpenetration founded on stability. 'In it, claims and duties of the whole, on the one hand, and of the members, on the other, appear more or less equivalent.' [29]

It is not necessary for us to follow up this approach in detail; in Gurvitch's account of the theme it appears rather complicated and over-sophisticated. Yet his fundamental thesis is certainly sound, and I should like to supplement it by the following observations. Every society that is more or less complex contains these sociality types, but it makes all the difference which of them prevails. A *totalitarian mass society* is built upon the two extreme types of fusion, getting its driving force from the party *nucleus,* a sectlike center, and spreading outward to the masses. Although propagandists of totalitarian societies talk a great deal about the community, they have failed to establish the community spirit, the organic bonds of self-regulation and mutual control, and rely instead on organization and superimposed laws which have the character of commands. *Democracy* seeks stability by making mass and sectarian integration peripheral and promoting the community type of integration. In view of the growing size of society, however, it becomes increasingly difficult to maintain this specific kind of solidarity. Real community units will have to form the basis of future integration. Yet this must be supplemented by functional organization which follows other laws than those of communal life. Still there is hope for a combination of functional and communal integration taking place in such a manner that community spirit, while gradually broadened, may still be preserved. Thus deterioration into a state of mass organization pure and simple can be prevented.

There is another important point to it. It is obvious that living, acting, and feeling within the settings of these forms of sociality require training in corresponding forms of behavior. The educational practice of the Nazis concentrated on training for both sectlike and mass behavior. Youth camps and *Führer* schools for the elite tried to foster the communion spirit and corresponding forms of responsibility, while mass training attempted to condition young people for mass behavior, in which the sense of responsibility was replaced by susceptibility to manipulated slogans. Here the main tool of influence was large-scale propaganda for swaying groups after the fashion of mass psychology. As pointed out before, the Nazis claimed to develop community spirit, but allowed it to function only in subordinate fields of action. Wherever really responsible decisions concerning the conduct of major affairs had to be made, it was by command emanating from the top and gradually reaching the bottom through a hierarchical organization.

In our democracies, behavior training for all kinds of sociality is desirable, for a Great Society is not homogeneous and flexibility in the individual is imperative. But neither of the two extremes described should be allowed to become the main paradigm of socialization, as this would inevitably lead to totalitarianism. Communal behavior must remain the archetype of democratic behavior, and its integration pattern and law must accordingly prevail.

Last but not least, the type of conscience corresponding to the democratic pattern is bound to be the communal one. This implies a personality type neither oversusceptible to mass pressures, nor willing to merge completely with the multitude, nor craving sectarian ecstasy and fanaticism. A conscience nurtured on sectarian experiences is continually striving for the self-effacing sacrifice, but its loyalty is confined to the selected few to whom alone it acknowledges obligation. This type of person is hardly capable of leading in a democratic process, which depends essentially upon participation of all fellow citizens in the rights and duties of an ever-expanding community rather than the exclusion of all but the elect. A conscience that develops in the course of real community living is more sober than the sectarian type. It contains an element of equanimity which gives to each member of the community a sense of security and prevents reversion of the individual and the group to archaic states of mind—a process that easily occurs in connection with both sectarian and mass ecstasy.

Community integration and the corresponding type of conscience are still alive in England mainly because continuity of development allowed there for the small community to expand its spirit gradually; the transition to a national community on a large scale has never become cataclysmic. In the course of this process genuine forms of communal conscience could be preserved so that each member still feels acutely responsible for the other person and the whole of society.

2. *The Problem of Consistency of Responsibility*

In investigating the objective conditions of responsibility, we need to consider what has been called the greater or lesser consistency of responsibility in various spheres of social life.[30] In our society, for instance, responsibility in business life and administration is much more consistent than it is, let us say, in politics. Business insists on strict definition of obligations, which in most cases are strongly enforced, not only by legal sanctions but at the level of mutual control; whereas in the sphere of politics various degrees of unreliability are habitually tolerated or even taken for granted. This again shows quite clearly that responsibility is not simply a subjective phenomenon; it is reinforced and maintained by the fabric of society, particularly of the sphere in which people act. The very same person, for instance, who is most conscientious in business affairs or toward members of his family may be irresponsible in his love affairs. This also shows that behavior is not entirely determined by character, as some philosophers would have it. Certain areas of conduct may not be integrated into a man's character, or may have become severed from it in the course of development. In such cases he may respond more directly to a part of social reality, where established standards of behavior may not yet have been developed. Here we have to build the sense of responsibility at both ends simultaneously. In these Cinderella areas of social relations a new climate of opinion must be created that is unrelated to conventional morality and at the same time appeals to the individual's conscience by pointing out the immorality of limited responsibility.

Politics, the sphere of illicit love, and personal relations with group outsiders are the three areas left in a primitive state by our so-called civilized societies. In those areas consistency of responsibility is at a low level. To a large extent behavior toward the enemy during war belongs in a similar category. Morality in the field of international relations is still in the embryonic stage of development; but it may be useful to bear in mind that the remedies we shall gradually work out for the transformation of the above-mentioned three areas of lawlessness can to some extent be applied in this sphere as well.

IV. COLLAPSE OF OLDER INSTITUTIONS

Training for responsibility is not only a subjective affair, but depends also on the control of objective institutions. We shall now show the truth of this sociological contention by an analysis of some older institutions that in the past acted as educative agents promoting responsibility, but whose diminishing influence or collapse largely accounts for the declining sense of responsibility in the masses.

1. *The Weakened Role of Ownership*

In our changing capitalist system the institution of ownership loses more and more the educative value it wielded as long as it was fundamentally based upon the property of the small landholder, craftsman, or shopkeeper. The function of ownership as an educational factor making for responsibility is best illustrated by the example of the peasant.[31] Here the idea of *'this is mine'* determines the whole organization of the peasant's life. It stimulates him to work, urges him to use foresight and calculation, and drives him to take risks. The peasant's personal attachment to his property has been emphasized as often as the fact that ownership of mobile goods constitutes a less personal link and is felt to be more abstract. Yet the small entrepreneur's attachment to his factory, the small shopkeeper's affection for his business, function in the same way as social educators, creating in him that sense of responsibility which the individual needs if he is to meet the demands of his work.

During the era of the small owner, contemporaneous education at home and at school did all it could to foster a well-developed sense of property together with a keen awareness of the obligations that property implies.[32] The children received pocket money to teach them responsibility, and they were given pets so that emotional attachment to an animal of 'their very own' could be awakened. Such devices helped to create a particular frame of mind and particular virtues which later were developed in the daily life of business. Today, however, we can no longer rely upon this impact of social education to the same extent, mainly because the majority of people must resign themselves to dependent positions as employees of large firms in consequence of diminishing scope for small ownership. Along with the small owner, that particular type of responsibility is disappearing. Unless we can promptly find new methods of inculcating a sense of responsibility in keeping with the demands of the new spheres of action, our society is faced with the danger of degenerating into a shiftless crowd, taking things as they come, without aim or purpose in life. Indeed, those who can only imagine a world in a setting familiar to them from childhood may be inclined to regard our world as doomed. Only a broadened sociological outlook helps us to understand that social responsibility can express itself in other forms and can be created in new ways.

One of the major alternatives to the responsibility typical of the businessman and small farmer has been developed within the functional pattern of the Civil Service. Here pride in one's profession and status [33] has become the basis of a new type of responsibility. The Civil Service has shown that a framework for responsibility other than that of private ownership is possible, and it can teach us a good deal in that respect. Of course, we should not copy its methods slavishly, but adapt them to the new conditions: identification with one's job and status may be as good a source of responsibility as the profit motive, and we should combine it with training for adventure, supplementing dictation at the desk with field work.

Another type of responsibility—that of the craftsman—is closely akin to that created by ownership. The craftsman's pride in his work engenders a special sense of responsibility, which is kept alive by the perpetual realization that every piece of work produced is the result of personal effort. In consequence of the diminishing scope for craftsmanship, caused by mechanization of work, this type of responsibility is also declining; and here again we are faced with the danger that unless we can find substitutes for it adapted to the new conditions of work, the general sense of responsibility will decline.

2. Family Training for Responsibility

A great many forms of responsibility have been developed on the training ground of the *family unit*. Just as there are specific family sentiments,[34] so there are specific forms of responsibility whose quality and very existence is bound up with the family. It would lead us far afield to discuss their fate under present conditions of transformation—enough to point out one or two of them which are changing with the changing family structure.

The great changes affecting the family as a whole and the relations within the family are not so much symptoms of decay in this time-honored institution as indications of transformation of the family structure, displacement of the old rural by a new urban family pattern.[35] The changes in our society are in many ways similar to those in the family structure in Russia. The most fundamental of these changes has been due, of course, to a technical invention, birth control. This not only upsets the balance of population and causes progressive decline in the size of the population, which in turn affects economics and all other spheres of social life; [36] it also transforms basic relations between men and women and their sense of responsibility. 'Birth control has loosened the absolute relationship between sex and procreation, and thereby destroyed one of the natural constraints to continuity in sex relations.' [37] Genuine moral obligations cannot be explained in mere terms of expediency and must be stabilized by reinforcing natural or social constraints. If these constraining sanctions change or relax, it is likely that the moral definition of the situation also changes.

Russia and Sweden, two countries which in many ways seem to reflect most clearly the new approach to these problems, have one feature in common: they do not allow the institution of the family to disappear. But society is creating two ways of life and accordingly two codes of morality for women. If they marry and become housewives in the traditional sense, the State will do everything to improve conditions of family life and to encourage the desire for children. But even if women do not marry, the respectability of their position and that of their children is ensured by all possible means in both countries.[38] Thus, the State strengthens the institution of the family wherever possible; at the same time it not only tolerates but supports women who are prepared to rear several children, even by different fathers. Fully aware of the value of these children to the community, the State accepts responsibility for their upbringing and is willing to pay their educational allowances without suing the fathers. Such a change in policy, of course, is bound to increase the scope for irresponsibility, at least in its early stages. The male has always been the less responsible partner in sex relationships, and as his present responsibilities are removed, the door would seem to be left open for complete irresponsibility. This, however, will be so only if we fail to connect the new forms of freedom with a higher type of responsibility. Its expression would lie in a general readiness of the community at large to provide by generous social measures for all children rather than to provide for one's own offspring only.

The same weakening of the sense of responsibility may be observed as education in its widest sense is transferred from the family to nursery, kindergarten, primary, and secondary schools, and so on. Here the care for the welfare and mental development of the child is left mainly to outsiders. In this sphere, too, irresponsibility will increase in the absence of obligations, unless new demands can be made upon the parents. The remedy in this case lies in creating ever more effective forms of co-operation between parent and teacher, in the establishment of better nursery schools and community centers. In the course of these improvements, the parental sense of responsibility will be widened. It will be put on a communal basis instead of a purely personal one. Parents will love their children and accept responsibility for them by feeling responsible for all the children of the community. We see this new and broadened sense of responsibility at work when modern parents try, for instance, to discover the best ways of dealing with their children by reading books or attending a new type of Adult Education Courses, or when they devote a great deal of time to the study of educational methods in order to select the best schools for their children.

Apart from procreation, one of the main *raisons d'être* of the family in the past was to afford refuge to its members. This sheltering function of the family is being weakened by increasing social services and by contributions to publicly guaranteed social security in the form of life insurance, health insurance, and old-age assistance. It must be admitted that training for responsibility in private life may disappear, if the care of one's parents, one's relatives, and oneself ceases to be the concern of the individual. But again, this is true only so long as we cannot find new outlets for responsible action, for the exercise of a new type of responsibility more public in character. Care of the aged, for example, once a private commitment of family members, may now take the form of providing colonies for old people, as has been done in Denmark.[39] A new field of responsible action will be to make these communities of the old as satisfactory and humane as possible. Public provisions are likely to replace gradually older private ways of caring for the aged, the sick, the unemployed.

The loosening of the family bond, if not replaced by some other tie, is the beginning of a process of uprooting which spreads out to neighborhood and community relations. This implies a loss of the feeling of 'belonging,' which in turn weakens specific forms of the sense of responsibility. Since this sense is first of all based upon a feeling of solidarity, the more that feeling within different groups is diminished, the slighter the emotional foundations for corresponding forms of responsibility. Again it cannot be doubted that the general lack of stability in modern man had its beginnings here or that social mobility, both vertical and horizontal, has weakened neighborhood and community bonds. Yet if we succeed in replacing the old forms of responsibility with new ones, versatility of mind may take the place of the mental and moral chaos we now know.

3. *Disappearance of the Man of Independent Means*

Moving from the home to public life in our attempt to evaluate institutional sources of the sense of responsibility, we shall observe that one of the most spectacular changes results from the gradual disappearance of the man of independent means. Formerly he was the one who could afford to resist domination and imposition of views, the man who could afford to establish a responsibility of his own. He could resign from a post if he felt that the public institution he served was inefficient or failed to serve the cause for which it had been designed. He was able to propagate new ideas and could undertake pioneering experiments, because he was sufficiently independent to continue his support, even though official sources of power or income were withdrawn. The further centralization proceeds in society, and the more the accumulation of wealth in a few hands precludes this kind of financial independence, the fewer the opportunities left to develop that sense of public spirit and civic responsibility which distinguished the aristocracy of less centralized and stratified societies. The Greeks and Romans were quite serious about this, making it plain that only a free man, i.e. a man of the privileged class, could have sufficient freedom of mind to shoulder public responsibilities and be active in politics. Unless we can find some new ways of guaranteeing independence, not necessarily based on private property or income, society will suppress those very dissenters on whose resistance to vested interests progress depends.

The same undermining of preconditions for the development of responsibility may be found in politics, where mass parties with their mass machinery prevent the development of a policy rooted in the independence of personal conscience. Where a program is mapped out in advance, the source of independent decisions in politics is quenched.

These examples show that analysis of objective conditions conducive to responsibility is as important as psychological study of its subjective emergence. If a society cannot replace the vanishing institutions that fostered a sense of responsibility, it cannot keep responsibility alive by mere inculcation and preaching. The creation of democratic behavior and democratic personality depends on what sort of institutions society can provide to guarantee the development of responsibility and efficient social control.

9

The Pattern of Democratic Personality

o

I. HISTORICAL PATTERNS OF CHARACTER DEVELOPMENT

From discussion of the ideal of democratic behavior, culminating in the study of democratic responsibility and the conditions fostering its development, let us proceed now to consider the ideal of democratic personality and the conditions for its emergence.

Modern studies in psychology, anthropology, and sociology [1] make it increasingly evident that certain aspects of behavior are conditioned by fields of action, methods of participation in social life, and prevailing notions of right conduct in a society. Besides, the pattern of integrated personality corresponds to the conditioning forces of that society and to the ideal personality to which the individual tries to conform. Environmental conditioning—material and ideal—determines the aspirations and motives of individuals, i.e. their personal reactions, and influences the guiding principles of conduct. At the same time, as we have seen, it shapes the type of evolving conscience, just as it ultimately affects the development of personality. Next we must realize that the patterns of personality development, because of their socially conditioned nature, vary in different historical periods. The dominant personality patterns of a feudal society, for instance, differ from those of the Renaissance; and the prevailing social types in present-day English society differ from those which have been molded by the Soviet system or by the Nazi system in Germany.

228

One of the early observers of the social formation of personality patterns was Max Weber. His analysis of Puritanism [2] as one of the great factors shaping early capitalist mentality will remain the great example of historical studies on the personality formation of modern man.[3]

Enriched by knowledge gleaned from these historical studies we no longer assume that the character patterns prevailing in our own society are the only expression of human potentialities. Those whose vision is sharpened by history and sociology perceive that the patterns of character integration are subject to a continual process of remaking, influenced by various trends of development and by competing tendencies in a differentiated society. We cannot create personality patterns at will, but by correctly estimating the various tendencies at work we may very well strengthen some traits and weaken others; we may even foster every opportunity for the evolution of the type preferred —in our case the democratic personality pattern.

This is not the place to discuss how society, besides forming certain traits of the Self, manages to influence the variety of patterns out of which a certain unity and consistency develops in human personality. Later we shall be able to demonstrate that the Self develops through forms of interaction and through the roles it is allowed to play in a given social order. By influencing the nature of these patterns of interaction, by reshaping the social roles the individual has to play, we may change people considerably. This education of individuals through assigning roles is nothing new, as the process of history has always worked by such methods. The only novelty consists in our becoming aware of these processes so that we can manipulate them more consciously.

A simple example will show essentially what we have in mind. If a social system is based largely upon patronage, rendering a specific kind of subservience expedient, it is very likely that a great number of 'yes-men' will be found in it.[4] Those who are too rebellious will be squeezed out—they will be considered misfits—and those who submit will gradually forget how to stand on their own feet. This applies not only to single behavior patterns but to emergent character patterns as well. On the one hand, there will be the benevolent patron with all his carefully co-ordinated attitudes of charm and pressure; and on the other, the humble but resentful official who can hardly wait for the moment when he will treat his subordinates just as he has been treated.

Single character traits are largely the results of the interaction patterns prevailing in a specific social system; the character masks are the results of the roles played in the context of patterned situations.[5] Thus interaction patterns and the accompanying roles are the keys to understanding social education. Our task then is to define the ideal of democratic personality as the educational goal of our society.

II. THE IDEAL OF DEMOCRATIC PERSONALITY AND BEHAVIOR

Behavior, as noted above, is rooted in a specific personality type. Democratic behavior is characterized by open-mindedness and readiness for co-operation, which not only enables the individual to face disagreement but prepares him to expect substantial enrichment of his own personality by absorbing differences in the process.[6] Thus integrative or basic democratic behavior means exposure to change and criticism. But, as we have seen, only the type of person who is himself secure, and does not fear loss of either status or individuality, is capable of such behavior.

Here the deep bond between simple behavior and personality type becomes apparent. In our earlier discussion integrated behavior appeared to have been achieved by external influences, by habit formation or by holding up appropriate models. However, the more deeply we probe the question, the more obvious it becomes that integrative behavior is not simply peripheral, or merely the sum of acquired habits, but is deeply rooted in a definite type of personality structure.

The latter statement seems to take us back to a psychology of individual variations, suggesting that democratic integration is not a problem of sociology, or social psychology, but rather of individual psychology. It would imply that democratic personality is a matter of luck or of individual achievement, not a generally attainable way of life that might be created. Any such conclusion, however, would be misleading. Though integrated behavior is rooted in personality structure, the patterns of personality integration can be socially induced and to a large extent are the products of cultural environment. It is from society that we derive even the patterns of personality integration. Although allowances must be made for individual deviations, the predominant personality types of any society are also its products. If this is true, we may say that a society is democratic only so long as its members, consciously or unconsciously, are motivated by the ideal of democratic personality and try to abide by this ideal.

The underlying principle, that there is a correlation between social organization and personality pattern, applies, of course, *mutatis mutandis* to the interrelation between authoritarian society and the authoritarian personality type as well. As we have briefly outlined above, authoritarian society is bound to produce the dominative type of character. The very existence of an authoritarian order is based upon the socially guaranteed and absolute control of a commanding individual and his retinue, all other authority being derived from them. Thus by its very structure this society produces the status-ridden personality who draws all his strength and confidence from this pre-established status and not from the continuous approval of his authority by his equals.[7] Inability to bear criticism or the strain of real discussion is an essential feature of the status-ridden personality, as sooner or later the validity of his alleged superiority will be questioned by both. For him discussion is just a form of propaganda and indirect domination, propaganda being nothing but a method of breaking a person's will through psychological coercion.

Hampered by this necessity for maintaining an artificially enhanced status, the status-ridden person cannot perform the function of integrating groups from within, nor can he, in his foreign policy, do anything but strive to subject greater territories to his rule. He may master material techniques, but cannot learn the art of evolving creative—not dominating—patterns of social integration, simply because his imagination is limited to concepts of suppression and exploitation.[8]

1. *The Role of Status in Democratic Society*

It would, however, be wrong to assume that no such authoritarian and status-ridden character-types exist in our democratic societies.[9] It cannot be pretended that the latter are thoroughly permeated by the democratic spirit. As they exist at present, they are only partly democratic and still contain remnants of the feudal order, an older elaboration of the dominative attitude. This does not, however, negate the fact that it was through the democratic way of life that we first moved away from the hierarchy of ranks and estates. Today, on many different levels, experiments are being carried out for meeting people on a more equalitarian footing. In a democratic atmosphere the person who formerly found security in his inherited status must emancipate himself from this crutch.

As is well known, the assault on status by the idea of equality used to be confined to the political field. The claim of equal political rights for all in a democracy does not alter the great inequalities in the economic sphere that prevail in every advanced capitalist system. While this is admitted, it would be a serious mistake to deny that the new type of hierarchy based on property, income, and other devices establishing differences in prestige is less rigid than that which prevailed in feudal society. Status based upon mobile property is less static and allows greater social mobility; the boundaries between the different income levels are more fluid; and as ascent and descent cannot be legally regulated, the significance of status is less relied upon than before. New techniques are emerging to enable the community to subject the sources of wealth to ever-increasing control. The idea of shared responsibility, shared controls, and accountability penetrates many more fields and exposes more and more spheres of life to public discussion. Once this stage has been reached, democratic society can hardly develop without introducing democratic methods into factories and ultimately into the management of the economy as a whole.

All this, of course, is bound to have its effects upon the personality structure. Those who were previously in a position to rule and to make their own decisions, developing authoritarian characteristics in consequence of the role they had to play, gradually learn through various pressures to accept controls, take shared responsibility for granted, and keep their ears to the ground in order to detect changing community needs and demands.

It is therefore our contention that just as the idea of Democracy is not strictly bound up with a phase of Capitalism or even with Capitalism at all, but will develop further out of its own dynamics, evolving new forms and entering new combinations, so the corresponding pattern of democratic personality can undergo considerable modification.

2. From Rugged Individualism to Democratic Personality

We have seen that the alternative to the authoritarian Self is the free individual who is not concerned with rank. There are, however, variations within this personality type corresponding to the latest changes in the social structure. Let us formulate these changes briefly as we see them:

In our democracies we are in the process of moving from a high degree of individualism toward development of democratic personality. Our democratic education is bound to miss the mark unless it realizes the difference between these two concepts and the fact that each of them implies a different ideal of personality.

What we know as 'rugged individualism' prevails as long as political democracy is allied with a competitive economy based upon private property and the profit motive. In the early years, as long as competition between equals prevailed, the effects on personality formation were invigorating, since a competitive economy mobilized all the forces of self-adjustment in the dominant types. Competition at this stage fostered initiative and self-reliance, and the presence of checks and balances produced from the outset the 'I-beat-you' spirit. But as society turns more and more from competition between equals to competition between unequals, the chances are enhanced that the powerful and wealthy will swallow up their weaker competitors in the life-and-death struggle of the marketplace. This has developed the archetype of 'rugged individualism.'

Although at this stage society is partly disrupted by the competitive emphasis on everyone fending for himself, a certain unison still prevails. This is due partly to the existing balance of power between the competing individuals and partly to the survival of traditional self-restraints in custom and folkways. People are thus still in sufficient agreement on basic issues, and the forces of solidarity are powerful enough to isolate the habits of the

R

marketplace from those that obtain in private affairs and community life. However, as the strong become ever stronger and competition between unequals gains ground, the moral atmosphere deteriorates.

Unbridled competition also has the effect of severing the individual from his primary associations, of taking him out of his racial and social milieu, breaking up family ties, and generally tending to isolate him to such an extent that he becomes nearly asocial.[10] This is when the competitive pattern gains such a hold on the minds of people that it undermines their whole character. No longer does it affect only part of a man's behavior, but it changes the whole personality pattern of participants in the social drama. So long as competitive behavior was limited to certain spheres of life, it could be combined with integrative behavior; but when it becomes the exclusive pattern of behavior the psychological foundations of the older forms of democracy disintegrate.

The ruthless few become so domineering that all hope of developing the will to mutual understanding and co-operation vanishes not only in the economic sphere but in nearly all others. Suddenly people begin to believe only in power and violence, and by anticipating aggressiveness and dominating behavior in others they themselves revert to it.

While this goes on in the higher social strata and tends to contaminate society at large (a tendency ultimately leading to Fascism), another tendency is silently at work among the masses excluded from the big hunt: with them the self-regulating forces of society prevail, creating the new pattern of social action that can rightly be called 'controlled competition.' This form of competition combines the advantages of competition and co-operative discipline, evolving a form of individualism entirely different from that of unbridled competition. It is a new social invention, though many of its beginnings may be traced to the past. In its modern application to changed techniques, it is a promising pattern for the future.

Controlled competition means that competition is first allowed to operate in order to develop the will to self-adjustment and spontaneity in the participants, setting free, in its turn, those forces which have an individualizing influence on personality.

But this process is checked as soon as it threatens the community and tends to undermine integrative behavior.

All the new promising measures of limited community interference in developments tending toward unhealthy growth, all the devices of a redistributive economy for more equitable apportionment of income or power, or limiting in advance the size of the rewards that can be won by competition, are moves in this direction. The idea of death duties and of the excess profits tax was born of the same spirit. If such limited controls are at work in all spheres of life—controls to allow spontaneous forces to operate and only see to it that they are co-ordinated into a pattern decided democratically by the community—there is a fair chance that character types will develop deserving the name 'democratic personality.' Both in shaping social conditions and envisioning the personality type, the idea at work is that individualization and personalization are both welcome so long as they are not based on alienation from the community or achieved by the 'powerful few' at the cost of disregarding obligations to society. In this social structure self-realization is found in competition for the solution of community problems. Social organization and education are guided by the idea of continually mobilizing living forces conducive to individualization, at the same time trying to curb them as soon as they become anti-social.[11]

Thus we gradually learn to modify social mechanisms, mixing ingredients and influences within them to the end of promoting definite personality types.

As new tendencies toward co-operation and controlled competition emerge from the struggle of the masses to protect themselves from the arbitrary behavior of powerful minorities, they present us with spontaneous forces that need only be strengthened to counteract the urge for authoritarian rule among certain sections of the upper stratum.

III. DEMOCRATIC PERSONALITY REFLECTED IN DEMOCRATIC PHILOSOPHY

We may approach the problem of democratic personality in another way: instead of investigating how the pattern of democratic action and personality has evolved in the changed social environment, we can focus attention on the social theory of the times. In our approach, social theory in many ways represents only a higher elaboration of the dynamic purposes behind an endless series of experiments designed to help man in his practical life toward new patterns of action.

From the numerous problems presented by contemporary social theory, we select only a few that may throw further light on points already discussed. We shall consider the serious attempts to tackle the question of the social conditioning of personality, and the even greater problem of reconciling free initiative and independence of personality with the penetrating power of social conditioning.

In the phase of rugged individualism, the social medium is, to the theorist, a kind of vacuum in which self-centered individuals move freely, motivated only by the stimulating force of competition. At this stage no real interest is taken in sociology, and the Self is conceived as an entity essentially unrelated to the social and historical context in which it develops.

Yet there is a fundamental interdependence between personality and environment, and we may choose Karl Marx and G. H. Mead as two typical representatives of this point of view. Living in different ages and different social atmospheres, both came to the same conclusion, each in his own way, that environmental conditioning is not accidental but forms a constituent part of the make-up and structure of personality.

1. Marx's Conception of the 'Character Mask' [12]

There are a great many environmentalists but most of them do not go beyond what we have called 'segmental' conditioning. They admit that parts of behavior are influenced by segments of reality, but they do not explain the whole character pattern in terms of social conditioning, or show how the fact that it is a social product is imprinted upon the Self. Here Marx had the right idea when he spoke of 'character masks' which cover up the true nature of man. Marx raised the problem of man's alienation from his real nature in consequence of deteriorating human relationships, since it is only by virtue of these relationships that he unfolds or represses his abilities. He undoubtedly anticipated a great many modern anthropological, sociological, and criminological insights by saying that social misfits develop as a result of environmental conditioning. His main concern, however, was not the individual delinquent or criminal; he held it possible that whole generations might become misfits if they were conditioned by enforced and unnatural human relationships.

Capitalism engenders a frame of mind that conceives of everything in terms of calculation, turns everything into a commodity, and thus estranges man from the object and the real person.

> Money, seemingly a mere means, is the true *power* and the sole *end*. The *means*—which makes me a subject, which appropriates for me the material qualities of others, is an end in itself. This is true indeed, as we can see in the recognition as the real political powers of life, of land ownership, where the soil is the mainspring of life and of the horse and the sword, where these are the true means of existence. In the Middle Ages, an estate is emancipated as soon as its members are privileged to carry a sword. Amongst nomad peoples, it is the horse that makes man free, a member of the commonwealth.[13]

This and the following passage show that Marx considered precapitalist situations as not engendering the phenomena of alienation:

> The savage in his cave—this element of nature, freely offering itself for enjoyment and protection—feels no stranger or rather feels as much at home as the fish in water.[14]

Once within the network of capitalism man is confined in a world that no longer cares for the thing itself but only for its value in terms of money. Capitalism no longer deals with men or women, but only with those fundamental relations in which they are involved and wear the character masks of the banker, the entrepreneur, the wage-earner, and the like. At an early stage, Marx very clearly recognized the artificiality of the social web, the power of the situation to generate character masks. His idea of the liberation of man was not one of casual liberties (this or that liberty of speech, of association, and so on), but aimed at the liquidation of a set of social relationships and a system of values called 'capitalist.' This was in his view the most malevolent cage mankind ever produced to its own detriment.

When we say nowadays that we want a purposeful life, that our economic production should satisfy real needs, that profit should not be the universal measuring rod, we only put in a simpler way what Marx called the removal of the self-alienating powers of capitalism in order to liberate man from this fundamental perversion.

> Whatever I can buy, what money can pay for, what becomes my own by means of money, that is my Self, myself as the owner of money. My power is just as great as the power of my money. The properties of money are *my* properties, my essential qualities, since I am the owner. Therefore it is by no means my individuality that determines what I am and what I achieve. As regards my individuality, I am halt, but money lends me 24 feet—so I am halt no longer. I am a sinful man, without honour, conscience or spirit; but money is honourable, and so its owner must be; money is the greatest good, so its owner is good likewise; money allows me to dispense with the efforts of dishonesty, and thus I pass as honest; I am lacking in spirit, but money is the real spirit of all things—how, then, should its owner be lacking in spirit? [15]

Marx considered capitalism with its money economy the only dehumanizing historical system.

> Since money, the extant and active essence of value, confuses and converts all things, it is the universal confusion and conversion of all things, of all natural and human qualities—topsy-turvydom. . . The inhuman power reigns.[16]

But in my opinion, there is no reason to assume that feudal society, for instance, produced less self-alienation or that in primitive societies man was more genuine. There are many other problems hidden in the idea of man besides masks and self-alienation. Even without embarking upon the intricate problem of man's real nature exclusive of his historical realization, we can safely say that primitive societies with their fixed mores and habits seem like a strait jacket compared with more pliant societies with developed economic and social techniques, which at least offer alternative ways of doing things. This greater pliability of modern organization is in itself an advance toward self-realization, even if the paralyzing effects of a social system based on what Carlyle called 'the cash-nexus' must be admitted.

2. G. H. Mead's Conception of Role-Taking

The mask-forming effect of the social setting on personality, which Marx saw only in the historical framework of Capitalism, was recognized by G. H. Mead at the level of a wider philosophical generalization. He saw the basic mechanism by means of which living in society always produces what Marx called the character mask. Society creates the personality pattern it desires by making the individual play certain roles. By playing the role of the father, son, hawker, worker, or teacher, and the like, the individual becomes socialized and adopts a complicated behavior pattern with specific induced motivations, aims, and responses which grow to pervade everything so that we rightly speak of a 'mask.' In this sense the ancient meaning of the word 'person' (persona = a mask) is amply justified. The historical differentiation of personality patterns arises because individuals have to play different roles in different social systems, and by playing various social games they become different players altogether.

It is G. H. Mead's great merit to have pointed out, like Marx and before him Hegel, that society with its network of relationships in logic and in fact precedes the individual and ego-formation.

What I want particularly to emphasize is the temporal and logical pre-existence of the social process to the self-conscious individual that arises in it.[17]

Mind is nothing but the social importation of this external process into the conduct of the individual so as to meet the problems that arise.[18]

Mead was among those social psychologists who regard the Self as deriving from the social process in which it is implicated, in contrast to the other school that derives the process from the selves of the individuals involved in it.[19] He was thus opposed to the substantive view of mind as an entity, as contrasted with the functional one, and to thinkers like Cooley to whom the Self is accessible by introspective acts only. For an objectivistic naturalistic approach like his pays due respect to the external field in which the Self arises.[20]

The hypothesis that the social Self emerges from the patterns of social interaction and the concept of role-taking are great advances in our knowledge. We are now enabled to bring together psychology and sociology, to unite the purely psychological view

—always dealing with an abstract personality—with the sociological view, which understands man in his social environment.

Granted these merits, we cannot avoid asking: What is beyond the mask? Is man nothing but the sum of the activities in which he engages and the roles he plays? Were this the whole truth, the result would be a variety of stereotypes exactly reproducing the imprint of social forces as these play upon the individual in his development. No theory of change can be deduced from this conception of the Self as a merely passive reflection of the influences to which it has been exposed. From this static point of view, the dynamic qualities of the Self and of society could never be understood. This question of the uniqueness and nonconformity of each personality has greatly puzzled our best philosophers; it is significant that this part of the liberal inheritance is preserved even in those democratic theories which acknowledge the personality-shaping power of circumstances. To them even more than to theorists who just took the spontaneity of personality for granted, the dynamic element of the Self has been the focal point of thinking.

The emphasis on spontaneity in liberal and democratic theory goes back to the fact that these two first realized that it is to the interest of society to encourage individuality. Neither tribal society nor medieval society, the latter in many ways continuing tribal traditions, respected individuality. They were mainly concerned with the creation of conformities that would guarantee the smooth functioning of society. In order to make social life predictable, it was necessary to establish fixed habits and customs, not to foster deviation.

When we praise liberal, modern society as individualistic we mean a society that found ways of providing for the dissenter. But appreciation of uniqueness and of personal deviation is only a part of this new mode of life. On a deeper level, independent personality means some independent source of unpredictable change and creativeness in the individual. On an empirical level freedom refers to freedom from slavery, suppression, tyranny, and so on. On the metaphysical level it means even more—the right of the individual to develop within himself those resources which are the origin of change and creativeness.

The conviction that all the roles we play, and all the masks together, do not exhaust personality but that there is a person beyond the social roles and masks is a common tenet in all philosophies of freedom. On the religious level, this spirit is conceived as a metaphysical entity innate in the individual when it begins life. It is a nucleus somehow unaffected by causation, which itself touches only the surface of human existence. In the more empirical philosophies of Positivism and Pragmatism this dynamic core of the Self is not pre-existent but evolves gradually out of the social process as an 'I.' This 'I' is contrasted with the 'Me' which is the social mask we spoke about and which we acquire through the social role we are called upon to play. The 'I' in the language of William James [21] and G. H. Mead is the dynamic part of the Self which in all its responses to the challenge of the social situation escapes predictability. Our different Me's are so to speak the passive imprints of all those influences to which we are exposed when we play our particular social roles, e.g. as father, as business man, we respond to the expectations of others. But there is always something beyond this. There are always some unforeseeable deviations from expectations and these deviations become the source of uniqueness and endless variation.[22]

According to this positivist approach the Ego is first determined by constitutional factors,[23] the glandular system, physique, et cetera, then by social conditioning through participation in interaction patterns and exposure to various social surroundings, finally through the impact of cultural patterns. These factors taken together are the stuff out of which personalities are made. But each individual develops his peculiar way of merging them, a process that is best reflected in his unique way of organizing his life. That this pattern of organizing life is always different is at least partly owing to the creative accumulation of heterogeneous facts and the creative integration of experience by the 'I.' The 'I' that emerges out of these activities can never be grasped directly but is always present in them and somehow incessantly transcends established expectations. It is the activation of this 'I' that forms the central problem of the liberal tradition, and for its sake the independence of personality and freedom has become the main concern of the liberals.[24]

3. *The Fallacy of Liberalism*

Those who favor free competition for the sake of its social educational impact ultimately do so because they regard it as the only source of free initiative. They value this free initiative because it helps to overcome rigid customs, but also because they feel vaguely that only competition can produce certain patterns that compel a person to move beyond the social roles and social masks and become an independent actor.

To them free competition is valuable because they hope it will compel the individual to look out for himself, and to coordinate means and ends with a sense of responsibility for himself. They hope that it will expose him to such a host of unforeseen situations and unconventional demands that the Self will be shaken out of its conventionalized mold and become an independent source of life and action. Yet the liberals at the level of Individualism did not see that there are many other devices to foster individualization; nor did they realize that individualization in itself does not create an integrated personality but rather destroys it as long as it remains the exclusive source of influence upon man. We have learned from the experiences of the last decades that unlimited unbridled competition destroys the roots and security of the Ego, which are indispensable for freedom.

Whereas it is true that a society establishing authoritarian codes without democratic responsibility ultimately creates the prestige-ridden personality incapable of venturing upon the unknown, a society in which competition destroys the foundations of cohesion runs the risk of breeding personalities in whom in the end ego-security has been completely undermined—everyone is haunted by fear.

Those who regard democratic personalism as their new ideal, aim in their education at creating ego-security and rootedness as well as at overcoming the limitations of parochialism in its various forms. Too great rigidity kills personality, but breaking all ties creates fear and leads to reversion to mass behavior.

IV. THE THREAT OF REVERSION TO BARBARISM

The possibility of regression confronts us with another problem that the democratic personality has to face, and in order to do so, it must go to the roots of the educational process. Broadly speaking, education is a process of socializing the individual. This means, among other things, that society puts numerous restraints on the individual and regards the deliberate organization of these restraints as civilization. These restraints should be neither too severe, lest the primary drives be ungratified, nor too lax, lest deep fears arise. Their aim is to control our drives or to guide them into approved channels.

Behind the pattern of cultivated behavior and personality lurks the possibility of reversion to barbarism. Just as the growing weed flourishing everywhere indicates that nature continuously tends to revert to the primeval forest, and that our culture with its cornfields, meadows, and gardens cannot be maintained without constant care and weeding, so the dynamics of the original drives exert a continuous pressure against the wall of educational restraints. If this wall is pierced or collapses in consequence of some catastrophe, we revert not to an earlier stage of culture, but all the way to barbarism. The upheavals of the last twelve years on the Continent taught us that fears and uncertainties on a mass scale may become sources of regression, that the arch-enemy of Democracy is chaos—the breeding ground for dictators.

But only those understand the lesson who can see that this sudden reversion to chaos and barbarism is by no means confined to a few countries. Although some may have advanced further on the road to disintegration than others, the evil is rooted in the nature of our whole industrial development. As soon as industrial society reaches the highest stage of individualism and slashes the bonds of custom and tradition through overcompetitiveness, urbanization, and other processes, it leaves the individual without shelter. If no reintegration occurs at this stage on the level of economic reorganization and social education, the mob mind develops—without any roots in primary groups, without a feeling of belonging, open only to stimuli that radiate from distant centers, such as the radio, the propaganda of the central party, and the like. Thus only an education aware of the needs of a mass society and consciously dealing with the problems of rootedness and ego-security can create personalities able to stop the growth of the mob mind.

The method consists in rediscovering the educational effects of primary groups, in creating such groups where they are lacking (community centers, communal health centers) and in stressing their continuity and purposefulness.

V. THE DUAL ASPECT OF DEMOCRATIC PERSONALISM

The new ideal of democratic personalism has always a dual direction in its educational efforts, whether in school or in life. The one fosters socialization, the other individualization. Socialization or role-playing should never go so far as to stifle individualization, the emancipation of the 'I.' Individualization, on the other hand, should never proceed so far as to induce social chaos, since this might arouse fear in the Self and ultimately lead to total collapse.

The interests of the individual, as these develop out of his individuality and specific place in the social system, should promote his understanding of the needs of the community. On the other hand the demands of the community should never become so powerful as to stifle all resistance, for a trend towards conformity is liable to suppress the call of the 'I,' that dynamic source of continuous creativeness.

Democratic personalism should thus in its educational efforts continually keep the balance between overconventionalization [25] and overindividualization. It should have the attitude of the pianist who must know the keyboard and all the rules of playing, but can never hope to present a work of art creatively merely by playing the piece correctly. Once the rules are grasped, they may be superseded; once the rules of good style are known, one may transcend them in one's own way.

Freudian psychology, rooted in the liberal democratic tradition and expressing this ideal on its own plane in another way, confronts us with a similar problem. Here the Super-Ego stands for socialization. It represents primarily parental wishes that convey the demands of the community and the social inheritance of the group to the individual. Without a Super-Ego no one could be socialized; but too rigid a Super-Ego results in a neurotic and uncreative personality. Therefore here, too, we face the same paradox. We want to build a socialized personality who obeys the demands of the Super-Ego, but does not follow them so blindly that the individual cannot enter the path of creative living or deal with unforeseen situations.

Recalling now that the new ideal of democratic integration calls for a person ready for co-operation and living with others in a dynamic world, it becomes clear that the pattern of democratic behavior presupposes the pattern of democratic personality. The authoritarian personality that too strongly emphasizes status and role as the source of psychological security could never embark upon the venture of integrating various groups. Only a society that deliberately sets out to create personalities who feel sufficiently secure to take the risk of losing themselves will be capable of regeneration in the process of socialization. The dynamic idea of socialization is therefore not based exclusively on strict conformity and rote, as was the case in tribal societies, but on a continuous search for an emergent new truth in the dynamic process of co-operation for the common good.

10

Education as Groundwork

o

I. A WIDER CONCEPT OF THE SCHOOL AND ITS TASKS

If everything in society is an educational factor, what is the new function of formal education? Modern definitions of education emphasize various functions of formal education and may serve as a point of departure. Lloyd Warner and his colleagues define the school as an 'intermediary society between the family and the state, which serves to train children in the ways of adult social life.' [1] This definition expresses the modern spirit by emphasizing the social structure of the school. Thus it regards *living* in that intermediary society from the educational point of view as more important than formal subject matter. Warner maintains that school attendance as a way of life serves an end, namely that of training children in the ways of adult social life.

But the nature of contemporary adult society might be more clearly defined. Here E. T. Hiller's definition is helpful in stressing 'the preparation of the individual for participation in secondary groups.' [2] Instead of vaguely referring to 'adult social life,' this definition indicates that the individual will have to face more complex situations in which secondary relations will matter, i.e. relations that are not personal but institutionalized. It further implies that participation in secondary relations calls for special training. Hiller explains the main techniques of such training by defining education as 'the process of developing attitudes through the selection of appropriate personal and in-

246

tellectual examples.' [3] Selecting personal and intellectual examples and impressing the significance of certain patterns upon the individual will help to make him judicious and inclined to favor experiences modeled after these patterns when exposed to adult experiences. Parallel statements can readily be found in other writings, most of them indicative of a common social and educational philosophy expressing the needs and orientation of a dynamic society.

To these characterizations of the school as a transitional society preparing youth for life in an adult world of secondary relations, we may add that formal education may prepare a groundwork for social life by providing a focus for otherwise unrelated educational activities. The school may thus perform its special task by intensifying and systematizing social experience—a function that the various compartments of social life can hardly perform. The school can do this only if it is no longer regarded as an institution in which we spend only our early years, but as servicing in one way or another the whole social system and adult life. In other words, we conceive of man as forever learning.

There are promising indications that this view is gaining acceptance. Educational facilities are now provided from the nursery through primary, secondary, vocational, and adult educational institutions, to enable people to satisfy a desire for continued learning. In the United States as elsewhere university and university extension courses provide broad opportunities for adult education, and the idea of refresher courses in graduate schools bring home even to the highly trained that in a changing age no one can take for granted that what he has learned in his youth will carry him through life. Continued education gratifies the universal wish for both information about new discoveries in one's special field and general reorientation in the world at large. Psychological studies in adult education explore the changing interests of adults, and new methods and approaches are developed to make learning enjoyable and overcome the widespread apathy toward education.

So much for new directions in modern education that offer food for thought. It may be useful next to deal briefly with the difference between the schools of the past and the present, between the old and the new concept of learning.

II. EDUCATION FOR CHANGE [4]

The schools of the past were in every respect the diametric opposite of what has been described as the modern school. They were rather separated from life, had their peculiarly bookish, scholastic atmosphere, and were for the most part resistant to social change. This did not matter so long as they did not have to assume educational functions that the family, the neighborhood, the community, and society at large could tacitly perform. Moreover, in the past the school was considered a training ground for imitative adjustment to an established society.

Today all this is gone. We can neither call a halt to social changes, which our children will have to meet, nor wall the schools off from the rest of the world. Not even the most conservative expects his children to live in the world as he has known it. He is compelled to choose education for change, not for imitative adjustment, an education based on the assumption that Junior will have to cope with new challenges of the future. Moreover, the school may be considered not only an introduction into an already dynamic society, but an agency of social change. This in turn intensifies its connection with other compartments of life.

In the United States the question has been ardently discussed whether the school dares take part in transforming the social order.[5] When this suggestion was first made, it was more or less regarded as a communist proposal to use the schools as a political tool in preparation for social revolution. Of course, the political struggle must not be brought into the school lest democratic tradition be lost in the course of transformation. But who would deny that the schools should participate in that process of social education which prepares a new type of man, able to cope with the responsibilities that new techniques of social organizations, changing technology, and skills put on mankind? Who would deny that were the school a static agency, an ivory tower looking down unperturbed upon the stream of life, it would soon be so outdated and fossilized as to be considered ready for discard? The modern school has no choice but to intensify and broaden its contacts with other areas of life and social institutions; it will have to give up its older, purely scholastic character, the more it takes over functions neglected by other social institutions. The school will have to become more homelike, more like a workshop, more like the community, as the family, workshop, and community shed their educational functions. Children have to find in school what the home has lost, perhaps because both parents work and eat out. The more fugitive the atmosphere of the two-or-three generation family, the more the school environment must embody and seek to impart the humanizing qualities that formerly characterized good homes. No doubt, the assumption of ever-more responsibility by any institution is not without dangers. It may lead to confusion, and there is much truth in the statement that the school can hardly replace the home, or the teacher substitute for the mother. As numerous educational functions of the mother have already been assumed by a new social order, however, the solution must be sought in the direction of a wise redistribution of functions, rather than in nostalgic yearning for bygone days.

For still another reason the modern school is becoming less bookish and no longer considers the transmission of accumulated knowledge as its only task: learning itself has changed in meaning.

When books were rare, writing and reading were the privilege of a sacred caste and learning was considered a sacred pursuit removed from workaday life. Books were handled with humility and bookish men received great deference. In Europe this has helped to develop and diffuse the bookish attitude that the common people still are prone to associate with the scholar and student. An essential element of this attitude is formalism, i.e. belief in the magical truth of a scholastic approach and presentation which is deemed superior to common sense. The old attitude still survives in schools that emphasize learning by heart, as if treatises and reference works were not readily available.

In the static society of old, memorizing even served to petrify knowledge, instilling veneration for knowledge of the past and inhibitions against discarding the old for the new. As this way of learning absorbed much time, memorizing also shut out unwelcome information. The idea was not to create an expanding

S

mind, but a narrow one confined to accepted and approved doctrine. With increasing social dynamics this restrictive aspect of
learning had to give way. The quest for ever-more facts and approaches broke all fetters; inventiveness and contributions to
new knowledge gained the ascendant over erudition and mere
memorizing.

Since books belong in the home and libraries are within easy
reach, people no longer regard learning with awe, as something
remote. The increasing skill, speed, and scope of popularizing
and disseminating knowledge enhances the prestige of the trial-
and-error process at the expense of the old-fashioned inculcation
of sacred or quasi-sacred texts.

The proverbial wisdom of the Romans, *Non scholae sed vitae
discimus,* has gained new meaning. Instead of preparing the
child carefully for the demands of a secluded school atmosphere
and its formalism, we consider formal education more as preparation for adult life and understanding of society. Or, as Delisle
Burns puts it: 'To modern man education is an opening into
the wider world.' The task of the school is to show how to learn
more efficiently from life, how to draw correct conclusions from
experience, how to become one's own educator.

As schools should serve as stepping-stones to intelligent orientation throughout life, it will be their special function in a democratically planned society to interpret all phases of life in terms
of democratic experience. This should not be confused with
totalitarian propaganda, as in totalitarian societies the various
facets of life serve only as pretexts for hammering in orthodoxy
by endless repetition.

III. THE DEMOCRATIC INTERPRETATION OF LIFE

The democratic interpretation of life is meant to show the different ways of starting a family, educating the young, transacting
business, spending leisure, et cetera. Such education should help
men of good will to live up to democratic ideals whereas un-
aided they might be at a loss for the right patterns. Today many
yearn for knowledge and advice and want to know which solution deserves to be called democratic. All societies need definitions of social situations and patterns of response. In a limited
but intensive fashion, custom and tradition used to answer this

need. Christianity did it in a systematic manner by interpreting all vital knowledge in the Christian spirit. No future society could do without similar interpretation. The *laissez-faire* attitude would leave clarification of self and situation to the individual; the totalitarian systems would indoctrinate orthodox interpretations from on high. The solution of the Third Way is to present democratic interpretations for open discussion: this means, to admit alternative ways of accomplishing things and voluntary modifications. The vain belief that everyone is sufficiently creative to master his own difficulties has lost ground. At last it is admitted that various types of schools should provide a running commentary on life, new information and interpretation for the man of the machine age. The view of the adult mind as a finished product was a result of the inability of teachers to find the right approach and language, or to realize changing needs and interests. The apathy of the average adult is not so much his own fault as the result of lack of stimulation, encouragement, and guidance. Democratic society, depending on the judiciousness of the citizenry, must break the spell of apathy, for it is only mental vacuum that affords the ideal breeding ground for fascist slogans.

IV. CONTINUITY IN THE EDUCATIONAL SCHEME

If education is to become a groundwork in society, continuity of organization should be provided. English education, for instance, was formerly proud of its casual versatile character, but it has recently made conspicuous strides toward filling in the old gaps and gradually developing into a kind of unified service. The important Education Act for England and Wales (1944) authorized the Minister to carry out a national policy. The three main stages of education cover the whole ground: compulsory primary education from the age of five to twelve years; secondary education from twelve to nineteen; youth services and 'further' education—including county colleges, provision for university grants, technical and training courses, either full or part time—for persons above compulsory school age. Adolescence in particular is approached in an entirely new spirit, and there is hope that adult education will be invigorated in new forms.

A report of the British Youth Advisory Council develops bold principles which go far beyond casual palliatives. The report admits that before the war the government's youth campaign was intended to do hardly more than keep children off the streets; the new demand is for a constructive program instead of merely preventive measures.[6] One of the goals is to build youth organizations with wider community contacts, and it is pointed out that the Youth Service should be a training ground for community life. 'The point of all our suggestions is that young people may have in the narrower context of their own organizations experience which is in miniature that of the wider community in which they will in a fuller measure soon participate.' [7] Such policies should help to develop co-operation, tolerance, self-reliance, joint responsibility, and especially the feeling that every person counts. All this shows that the planners of the modern Youth Service were fully aware of the fact that they had to remedy social ailments. They knew that they had to cope with definite social and psychological maladjustments resulting from unhealthy urban environments and the influences of mass society. They also knew that it was not enough to protect youth against what we have called 'uprootedness,' but that opportunities had to be provided to stimulate the growth of social attitudes. This may serve to illustrate the meaning of 'Planning for Freedom' and its emphasis on voluntary participation.

Among deliberately planned opportunities for social integration Community Centers should be mentioned. In Britain they first emerged in connection with modern Housing Estates.[8] They can now be established and maintained by Local Educational Authorities in any area but especially in industrial centers.

One of the most interesting experiments in this field is the Peckham Health Centre.[9] It is a family club in South London which offers opportunities for both common living and health services in the spirit of preventive medicine. Urban families may join the Centre for a small fee and find there abundant opportunities for healthful and enjoyable leisure-time activities. A medical staff is available for periodical check-ups. The Centre occupies a functionally designed building flooded by sunlight. The authors of the project state that their idea of health is social, derived from epidemiology, which holds that animals living in colonies, unless previously injured, show unfailing resistance to disease. Thus resistance to disease may be said to depend upon healthy community living. This implies the necessity to study patterns of spontaneous sociability and good fellowship. Spontaneous attraction and repulsion [10]—the basic dynamics—should not be interfered with, least of all by building schemes that compel people to live in segregated little rooms. For this reason the center of the building is devoted to a large hall with many niches and corners where small groups can gather at ease. Permanent partitions would have interfered with that 'fluidity of constitution' essential to the functional day-to-day evolution of this society. Thus, the idea of planning for freedom is actually at work in many minds even though the principle is not fully recognized. To the founders of the Peckham Health Centre planning meant to establish a framework for free association, not a set pattern, and to foster spontaneous social groupings.

The question might rightly be raised whether this new trend will eliminate all privacy and seclusion and compel everyone to mingle freely, as happened in the Soviet Union; whether the period of segregation is coming to an end—a period when people, especially in northern countries, shut themselves up in their small houses and rooms, shunning the marketplace and public life. The answer depends on what we want. It is up to us to direct the development. We may encourage youth, as did the Germans, to become a segregated group in the community, or we may prefer 'insulation for them within the same whole but not isolation.' [11] Insulation is natural for youth groups banded together, but when youth aims at isolation, cutting off all healthy communication with other age groups, it is a symptom of social deterioration.

V. THE NEW TASKS OF ADULT EDUCATION

Adult education will have to perform for workaday life the same integrating function that the universities perform for the learned professions. Adult education will no longer remain a sort of substitute for higher education for the laborer and white-collar worker. Instead it will help all citizens to adjust intelligently to the changing demands of a new society.

Adult education is post-education and re-education for those who wish to keep abreast of scientific advances and swift social changes. We all learned many things at school by now obsolete; we have absorbed motivations and ends that today are outdated and out of place. Constant rejuvenation is essential in a pioneering age, and the demand for it surpasses the alternative demands of conservatism and progress. If conservatism means adjusting selected traditions to the demands of a new epoch rather than conserving prejudices of a bygone age, and if progressive-mindedness means emphasizing what is constructive and rejecting corrupting elements rather than blindly hailing whatever is new, then the old-fashioned alternative that puzzled previous generations need no longer be disquieting. Of the two slogans, 'education should transmit the heritage of the past to the young' and 'schools should help to build a new order,' neither is absolutely valid. If the new order is to be built with a bridge to the past, those alternatives need not be mutually exclusive.

Adult education can only form an organic part in the scheme of public education if it is planned as a smooth continuation of the newly integrated youth services.[12] Just as the youth services were designed with an eye to personality formation and training in civic virtues, adult education will have to be designed for a specific social structure requiring certain personality types.

Adult education in the spirit of *laissez-faire* was consistent in that it advocated offering the people what they wanted; but it went to extremes in not even trying to give access to deeper knowledge or to the creative forms of enjoying leisure. The prevailing low level of taste and ways of spending leisure were accepted as presumably the free choice of the people. If an institution, allegedly devoted to enlightenment, does not even try to enlighten, it merely sanctions the *status quo*. In the United States many are prone to take this line in interpreting Democracy—an approach that puts equal emphasis on the most diverse recreational hobbies and vocational pursuits. Courses of this type often are of equal rank on the curriculum with those serving the desire for reorientation in a changing world or for genuine self-education.

Although it would be snobbish to disregard the simpler needs of people, it cannot be the proper meaning of Democracy to give equal weight and standing to any and every popular demand. There must be institutions to serve vocational and recreational interests of all people, but they need not be identical with institutions that seek 'to satisfy the grown-up's desire when they have seen enough of life to formulate the questions to which they seek an answer, and to criticize the answers given them in the light of an experience which Youth cannot possess.' [13] If adult education truly seeks to help create judicious and public-spirited citizens in all walks of life, well-equipped to judge the current issues of Democracy, it will have to cease following the vagaries of the hour; if it is to become genuine groundwork it will have to discriminate and concentrate on the important issues and tasks.

To discriminate does not mean to dictate tastes or to impose the views of the high-brows upon the layman. The English Adult Education Movement, for instance, was sound in building its program first upon the wishes of the people. But this method is certainly compatible with the endeavor to avoid meaningless variety by organizing basic courses around the study of man, nature, or society. Although there should be alternative schemes of integration for the student to choose from, he cannot be expected to do the final integration of knowledge on his own. It has been one of the deceptive formulae of the age of *laissez-faire* that science can give only scattered segments of knowledge, not integration. This view is as detrimental as the opposite one held by the totalitarians who would indoctrinate their one spuriously integrated scheme as the official philosophy of the State. The *laissez-faire* attitude expects too much of the student: although untutored in methods of integrating knowledge, he is expected to achieve on his own what can hardly be expected even of eminent scholars. The totalitarian approach, on the other hand, presents a ready-made synthesis, thereby distorting the process of creative synthesis. It falsely proclaims a closed system of truth and imposes doctrines of the hour as political orthodoxies.

In view of all this, what is the solution of the Third Way? We assume that every sensible human being desires integrated knowledge and therefore we cannot put up with fragmentary learning. We further assume that tools are requisite for action and moral orientation. If science does not satisfy this demand, propaganda or dogmatic doctrine will. Responsiveness to these needs of the mature mind has been blocked especially by the prejudices of an

age of overspecialization, which asserts that science can only explore departmentalized fields of inquiry and that integration is
beyond its resources. Meanwhile we have learned that integration of knowledge is as important as analysis. Genuine science
surveys whole fields, explores borderline problems, and seeks to
visualize, even if only provisionally, the philosophical implications and ramifications of our ever-broadening outlook. The study
of *Weltanschauung* is as worth while as any other study. [14]

Scientific synthesis or integration of knowledge differs from
that of the layman or from dogmatic synthesis mainly in that
it is open-ended and ever ready for expansion. It emphasizes its
hypothetical nature and openly admits that the picture it draws
will have to be remodeled in the light of new knowledge. It
avoids pretension to finality also by honestly presenting alternative ways of philosophic integration. It shows plainly that in the
same age different trends of thought vie with one another. The
dogmatic approach falsifies this open-minded, provisional approach by suppressing inconvenient alternatives.

The educational significance of the Third Way approach rests
in its appeal to personal decision. It creates scope for individual
judgment by presenting knowledge as a dynamic entity with a
hypothetical framework. The work of integration is not simply
left to the student, but alternative ideas of his time are placed before him and he must choose between them.

Correctly understood, such an open-minded system leads not
to relativism, but to a deeper understanding of intellectual life
as advancing toward an ever-broadening outlook. In the process,
yesterday's knowledge and conceptual framework are revealed as
fragmentary, as something to be grasped completely only in
retrospect.

VI. THE TASKS OF A PEOPLE'S UNIVERSITY

Some may argue that such a deepening of knowledge is only possible at the university level—assuming that the universities incorporate supreme intellectual endeavor and attainments.

The universities certainly should and do present intellectual
life on a higher than workaday plane. One contention, however, is that in a healthy society sophistication may create differences in the level of achievement, though not in the quality of

intellectual interest and depth of insight. The latter is a product of maturity. A mature mind, which has been trained mainly by life experience, may understand the basic problems of the age as well as any scholar. The questions and answers of such a man will be less sophisticated; he will not be proficient in handling technical terms, but our problems should be substantially no less accessible to him than to the academic man. In a new way we shall have to aim at a goal reminiscent of the great asset of medieval culture—the presentation of a unified world view on all levels, for the educated in the language of theology and for the community in the language of symbols, legends, fables, and the like. Due to the increasing techniques of popularization, universal literacy, and education, our age can pursue this objective even better than medieval society was able to do under the primitive conditions of an agrarian economy.

Adult education should be considered one of the most important cornerstones in the educational groundwork, where integration of knowledge should be attempted because a democratic mass society needs to recruit leaders from all strata. Democracy can no longer afford a caste of pundits claiming a monopoly on knowing what knowledge is. The fundamental dilemma of our age and the predicament of man should come within reach of all levels of education. Our society can afford diversity of training and specialization only if we constantly seek to broaden and deepen our common educational groundwork.

Here it may be well to mention the recent British suggestion that technical colleges and other institutions of the same level should become 'nuclei of a new type of people's colleges, equipped both to train students for a wider range of vocations and to play an active part in the widening sphere of adult education.' [15] The grouping of the technical college and other suitable institutions upon a common 'campus to form a People's University with provision for the easy exchange of teaching staffs and for close common intercourse among all the students' should provide the man-in-the-street with an establishment parallel to the University which mainly serves the professional pursuit of learning.[16] Similarly the suggestion that there should be permanent refresher courses for managers, technicians, ultimately for all, and especially for people in their thirties, is in keeping with

our characterization of the need in a dynamic society for continuous adult education to keep everybody mentally alert and
enable them to meet the modern requirements of democratic
citizenship.

VII. THE NEED FOR UNIVERSITY REFORM

The present-day dilemma of the universities has been ably reviewed by Ortega y Gasset.[17] The universities serve mainly three
ends: they train students for various professions; they teach and
do research; and they provide what is vaguely called a general
education.

As these three approaches have been disconnected for the most
part, research has become overspecialized and remains without
focus, particularly in the humanities and social sciences.

Liberal education has gradually lost all substance and tended
to become an ornament and badge of the privileged. Today
hardly anybody is satisfied with the state of affairs, as the old idea
of *universitas,* i.e. universality of knowledge which aspires to be
more than a mere tool for earning one's living, is no longer
achieved. It has suddenly been realized that one of the reasons
for moral breakdown is the mentality of the specialist who has
remained a barbarian. Great advances in science and technology
have prepared for leading positions many specialists who from a
civic and political point of view often represent 'trained in-
capacities.' Their training has made them technically proficient
specialists, but failed to impart the philosophical spirit that
alone could have deepened their technical knowledge. They
lacked opportunity to acquire understanding of our human and
social situation.

Ortega y Gasset is right in saying that a renaissance of the
University requires that liberal education be made the core of
the curriculum. He proposes a faculty of culture as the heart of
university life, to develop what he calls 'the cultural synthesis.'
Neither research nor professional teaching can revive the Humanist tradition, which first educates man and then trains the
professional expert and the research worker. But what sort of
curriculum is fit to educate both the man and the citizen? Ortega
y Gasset has the right idea that the educated man is distinguished
by his knowledge of the vital philosophies that govern his Age.

In our view this basic orientation would need supplementing by factual knowledge to enable everybody to form sound ideas about man's place in nature and society. In this connection, the problems of our contemporary society, especially the challenge of democracy and its related educational problems, should be discussed. Once such a core curriculum has been established for all students, preparation for research and the professions can find their proper place. None of these would hang in mid-air, as so often happens now, but rather all could be related to this core.

It is, I trust, not a professional bias of the writer to maintain that the sociologist is best qualified for organizing such interdepartmental teaching. At any rate, sociology ought to be taught in such a way that its synthetic function in the field of the social sciences prevails.[18]

Last but not least, no university reform will be satisfactory unless it faces the problem of education on an international plane.[19] This applies to universities and other institutions of adult education. How far permanent contacts, the exchange of students and teachers, joint discussions, and agreements on curricula will suffice, whether and to what extent international universities ought to be established, is open to discussion. Possibly both methods can be combined in the endeavor to promote international integration through education. To be sure, education alone cannot solve the problem of social disorganization; yet without educational endeavor, no plan for integration can be of lasting significance.

VIII. SOME REDISTRIBUTIVE ASPECTS OF DEMOCRATIC EDUCATION

It may be held against us that we overestimate the intellectual capacities of the man in the street, that we have a naive trust in the power of education in assuming that everyone can be educated for judicious and intelligent participation in public affairs. This reproach is characteristic of the general mental climate of capitalism in the monopolistic stage. An all-pervasive pessimism and skepticism is unconsciously communicated and serves to frustrate every progressive move beyond the *status quo*. Those who fear for their vested interests look with suspicion on every genuine advance of Democracy. Any progress in the propagation of critical judgment calls forth Caesar's reaction: 'He thinks too much, such men are dangerous.' Wilful men concerned for their oligarchic rule do right to recognize that their regime cannot be perpetuated once it is brought before the bar of democratic public opinion. But they do wrong to close their eyes to the possibility of peaceful adjustment which would maintain social stability during change and eliminate irresponsible ways of power.

The idea that adequate knowledge belongs only to the privileged few is part and parcel of a restrictive system of production which thrives in an atmosphere of man-made scarcity. In the field of education the restrictive attitude is rationalized by claims that the masses can make no good use of educational opportunities because of their innate incapacity.[20] Medieval society accepted the inequality of rank and station as God-ordained. Non-theological justification of class distinctions seeks to interpret differences of nurture as natural by projecting inequalities determined by social environment into the human mind and assuming that the higher strata inherit superior endowment. Defenders of this dogma have turned to biology for support, as modern man is inclined to submit to 'scientific' authority. They set out to prove the dogma of the fixed average intelligence quotient of various social strata by pointing to superior average school performance and mean intelligence quotients among the children of the well-to-do.

Sociological criticism of unwarranted claims for the theory of testing and improved experimental studies have made us more careful in ascribing tested differences in symbolic skills to innate personality traits and immutable nature. We are no longer so sure when measuring differences whether they are due to nature or nurture. Certainly, man's height would seem to be determined by heredity. Yet Sir John Boyd Orr's investigations have established that differences in the mean stature of upper- and lower-class school children in England are largely due to nutritional differences depending on income.[21] The increased height of school populations and of soldiers in various countries, as measured during recent decades, points in the same direction.

Test results have shown that in the United States Negro children in Northern schools are 'more intelligent' than underprivileged white children in Southern schools, i.e. that such measured differences reflect cultural, not ethnic differences. A careful study of cultural differences in intelligence among children of Italian, German, Irish background in Chicago has established related variations of numerous mental and social factors. Sex ratios, age-grouping differentials, types and vacancies of dwellings, delinquency rates, registered voters and infant mortality, length of residence, size of family, schooling completed, illiteracy, median rentals, home ownership, radios owned, and families on relief were examined. All were found to vary concomitantly in greater or lesser degree with the test data variations. The author concludes that the 'home background which involves differences in books, radios, magazines and so on varies with the intelligence of the children. That is to say, assuming the adequacy of the tests, the child can adjust socially in a variety of situations at a variety of intelligence levels, but he needs the equipment of learning that an optimum economic background provides to reach the level of intelligence of such a group.' [22]

1. Democratization not Leveling of Education

Reluctance to provide adequate and equal educational opportunities is even less justifiable and convincing than reluctance to go along with proposals for greater equality of income. Broader educational opportunities yield returns to the community incomparably greater than their cost. Their value consists essentially in deepening and refining the transmission of our cultural heritage. Broad participation of the people in cultural life is bound to result in encouragement, in removal of the inferiority complex which is carefully nurtured in the condescendingly so-called 'little' or 'common' man in authoritarian and plutocratic societies.

The removal of frustration through the opening of new opportunities, the possibility of testing one's own ability, often stimulates creative imagination, and expanding opportunities call forth intellectual endeavor and broaden intelligence. As J. L. Gray rightly says:

It may be that intelligent behavior is stimulated to a high pitch of performance in occupational groups engaged in the rapid ascent of the social ladder. Where the conditions of mobility are present, individuals selected for other qualities as well as intelligence will often make exceptional efforts to promote the social advancement not only of themselves but also of their children. On the other hand, when people have achieved a comparatively high economic status and have ceased to feel precarious, these efforts may slacken. It is clear that lack of opportunity to rise out of their class must deaden the response of the unskilled worker's children to intellectual stimuli. Environmental differences may be more potent in producing differences in test-intelligence in intermediate groups than in those at the top or the bottom of the social scale.[23]

Such raised self-esteem and efficiency is feared by vested interest groups.[24] If no other arguments are left the phrase, 'we cannot afford it,' i.e. to expand and improve educational opportunities, is on tap. This method of frustration never states criteria for limiting opportunities. The last war—one would assume—should have shattered the magical spell of the phrase by teaching the public what industrial nations *can* afford and achieve, given the will. The phrase 'we cannot afford it' always implies reference to 'under the given circumstances,' i.e. those of income distribution, taxation, deliberately tolerated scarcity, the production of luxury goods, plus an attitude of complacency. Redistribution of income and public control of resources and their use may well serve considerably to broaden educational opportunities.

Such educational policies are not merely matters of finance; they are questions of how to exploit existing resources to the best advantage. It is not enough just to open the doors of a museum; [25] the visitors should be attracted by proper methods of teaching art appreciation. It is not enough to draft favorable rules of admission to a library; instruction should be provided in the best ways of using its facilities. We must link suggested readings to life situations and bring books to the mother to help her educate her child well, to young people to help them choose a career, and so on. During the war citizen's advice bureaus sprang up in Great Britain as an organized method of applying knowledge to life. The columns of 'advice for the lovelorn' in the daily press and the size of radio audiences mustered by the voices of Mr. Anthony and Dorothy Dix in the United States are indicative and should offer food for thought.

The democratic process has fostered the art of plain thinking and speaking among writers in quest of wider publics and audiences. Books are now written to suit the various mental levels of the population. The presuppositions under which the different classes and groups start their reading, their hidden expectations, their intellectual premises and their preferences are increasingly taken into consideration.[26] We observe a secular trend away from the scholastic seclusion and monopolization of knowledge of sacred Scriptures and classic texts to the opposite attitude, which wants to make knowledge accessible even to the humblest. This development is accompanied by advances in the psychology and sociology of literary taste and of education at large. A simple, lucid style serves to emphasize the essentials. Snobbery and artificial segregation are discarded in the spreading of knowledge.

All this is healthy and contributes to the expansion of democracy. It is creative as long as it seeks to eliminate gradually inequalities of educational opportunities and to break down barriers between two or even more nations within a nation. Yet the principle of putting 'knowledge into circulation' (Dewey)[27] may easily miscarry. In an age of mass-produced education, advertising ideas and 'circulation building' may swamp all sense of quality, which matures slowly in society. Mass production and standardization of goods to satisfy routine demands is one thing. In education, however, this principle can only make the lowest common denominator the universal norm. Reluctance to accept the principle of leveling as a tendency to 'level down' is far from being snobbish disdain for the lower strata as of inferior innate human quality; on the contrary it is based upon realization that as the culture and education of the less privileged have been neglected down the centuries, they can now assimilate and appreciate only things of inferior quality.

Many point to the presumably high and intrinsic value of folklore. Even in the past folklore was for the most part the slow-moving plebeian adaptation of cultural patterns that the upper classes had created in previous centuries. The substance and form of upper-class culture slowly sifted to the lower strata and represented *gesunkenes Kulturgut*, as Hans Naumann put it.[28] As long as folklore and folk culture retained their vitality, this process did not necessarily imply deterioration in quality. It was a process of acculturation, in which the lower strata assimilated the substance and forms of experience of the top stratum. Today, however, so-called 'folklore' is artificially diffused by the machinery of the amusement industry. Under the impact of the industrial revolution, of urbanization and mass migrations, the lower strata have largely become an inarticulate mass of consumers whose taste and discrimination are questionable.

The sudden recognition of 'popular culture' and the propagation of its false standards are often justified by the advertising slogan 'the customer is always right.' This motivates commercial recreation and its mass outlets. It pays only lip service to human dignity and aims rather to perpetuate and popularize all the sins society has committed in the past by failing to educate the citizenry for the real thing. Education, however, will not accept any given level as final, but sets out to improve it. Of course, this approach cannot disregard the existence of actual illiteracy and mental inertia in our midst.

2. *Toward Successful Democratization of Culture*

What is requisite for the successful democratization of genuine cultural values in contrast with the leveling-down process that degrades them into commodities for commercialized amusement? All expansion of education on both the social and intellectual level should be a matter of strategy. In both respects improvement can be effected by degrees. In the social field educational and social opportunities can be broadened systematically and scientifically by better over-all planning of the educational system in connection with vocational guidance. On the intellectual level advancement should proceed gradually to progressively higher intellectual and moral levels. The common fund of knowledge could be presented in different forms to different social groups, taking their background, mentality, and varying educational levels into consideration. Democratization does not necessarily mean to level down in order to eliminate differences, but rather to allow for variety in cultural life and to appreciate cultural differences as valuable points of departure in man's quest for knowledge.

One particular social group that should be preserved as a check against monotony and leveling tendencies in a planned culture is an independent intelligentsia.[29] A society composed only of professional groups, bureaucracies, and sectional-interest groups is in danger of developing a rigid mentality mainly concerned with institutional improvement and expediencies of the here and now. It will lack dynamic ideas and social imagination capable of transcending the existing structure of social institutions. In the past, groups of independent intellectuals have produced a dynamic mentality that reached beyond the boundaries of what happened to exist. Their function would be hard to replace. Rather a democratic society should deliberately plan for careers outside the regular social and educational ladders.

The intelligentsia will form a parallel in the intellectual field to pioneering minds in the economic sphere, preferring untrodden paths to routine ways of conduct and thought. In the same manner scope should be allowed for competing cultural and intellectual groupings. Their antagonisms are not mere whims with which society can well dispense. These groups are the social mainsprings of productive cultural life, which is threatened today by the mechanical reproduction and mass consumption of the old, the 'classical,' the safe. To support and protect such creative groups from the impact of bureaucratization and over-organization not only sets up a bulwark against leveling downward, but ensures the opposite, upgrading process. Such groups may be dangerous if isolated or segregated. Stationed in the main stream of public opinion, they are strongholds of gradual growth, shelters for the development of sensitivity, strong sentiments, and imaginative ideas.

New ideas always have originated in small groups with enduring personal contacts. Ideas circulate in the marketplace by the medium of mass publicity, but they are not produced there. It is still the dissenting small group that favors inspired adventures of the mind and intellectual enthusiasm. Such groups nurture and test new ideas before they assume form fit for dissemination among broader circles of the public. Thus intellectual oases protect society in an Age of the Masses from great danger lest the patterns of propaganda and advertising become models for cultural planning.

T

11

Work and Leisure

○

I. WORK INCENTIVES AND GRATIFICATIONS

The silent transformation—the move from the frustrating tendencies of monopolistic capitalism toward planning for freedom—is evident in the new views of work and leisure. The early phase of capitalism and industrialization considered work painful and money the most important incentive. Modern thought has emphatically revised these prejudices.[1] No doubt, certain types of labor, slave labor or overmechanized factory work, are unpleasant.[2] But skilled and responsible work is gratifying and enjoyable.[3] For this reason handicraft work is often considered pleasant.[4] Besides, the experience of growing proficiency at one's job seems to be stimulating. The urge to know oneself and one's potentialities, and the satisfaction found in progressive achievement are inexhaustible stimuli.

Although it is wrong to speak of an innate 'instinct of workmanship,' which would have to comprise many complex, culturally acquired habits and attitudes, Western man does generally crave opportunities for self-expression and activity. (We may by-pass the techniques and values of Far Eastern, especially Indian, religious aristocracies pursuing a contemplative way of life.[5]) Once work habits and skills have been acquired and implement a way of life in which workmanlike contributions are socially esteemed, pursuit of workmanship becomes an urge. Enforced discontinuation of work creates feelings of frustration and unhappiness, as we know from studies in unemployment. Once a person is trained for significant and self-expressive work, working means joy and the withdrawal or denial of work is not only painful but disorganizing to the personality. Hence utilitarian psychology, based upon the concept of *homo economicus,* is only partly correct in asserting that the unpleasantness of work can be overcome by pecuniary compensation alone. This theory applies only to monotonous machine operations in an industrial society with money mores.[6]

Besides money, other gratifications—joy in co-operation, the sense of team membership, response to discipline, pride in skilful mastery of tasks are all relevant components of work experience. To be sure, we should not fall into the opposite extreme and derogate the money incentive altogether. By and large, man has to work in order to live—not for the sake of 'gratification' by more or less symbolic 'rewards.' Money should be looked upon not merely as one type of reward among others, but as a symbol of the fact that goods (means of subsistence) can be had only by work.

The Third Way will follow neither those who believe in complete abolition of pecuniary incentives nor those who consider money the only permanent and reliable work incentive. The manifold and simultaneous motives entering into artistic and scientific experimentation and invention have hardly been explored with regard to their relative significance, although such study might help considerably to define the true problem. We may find the artist, scholar, or doctor engaged in his work for the sake of fame, service to humanity, the intrinsic value of the task at hand, as well as for money, although the mores and codes of professional men repress the overt pursuit of profit openly acknowledged among businessmen.[7]

Again a different array of motives holds for the civil servant. Personal fame and unlimited profit matter less to him than security of tenure and retirement, the satisfaction of public service, opportunities to organize and, last but not least, to wield administrative authority.[8]

Adequate job analysis should take multiple factors into account. It should observe (a) the nature of the work; (b) the position accorded by a given society to different occupational pursuits; and (c) the degree of gratification resulting from many historical factors. Hierarchies of prestige, once established and lived in, are apt to survive changing conditions and often escape functional or rational explanation. (d) All this must be seen in the context of the social process that consciously or unconsciously shifts prestige from one type of work to another. In the future shifts in prestige may well play a far greater role than in the past.[9]

The crucial point is that expectations should not be raised above the level of gratification provided by society. The level of expectation should be adjusted to the nature and amount of available gratification. Disproportion between the level of aspiration and available gratification causes mass frustration and anxieties.

In an unplanned society expectation levels follow erratic and unpredictable trends. Today, however, expectation levels can be manipulated through many official and semiofficial, overt and covert channels. Before the war manual workers felt less respected. During the war even democracies without publicly defined policies on this matter managed to make manual labor respectable by revaluation. (In Britain, for example, the status of the motor-lorry driver rose to that of a gentleman's pursuit.)

Democratic planning should question how far to go in such matters as manipulating prestige. The policy of the Third Way might be left to a policy-forming body responsible (a) for defining issues calling for direct intervention sanctioned by public opinion; (b) for officially recommending changes in policy without using administrative compulsion; (c) for favoring certain aspirations without narrowing the scope for individual decisions.

Intellectual work and its problems in a Third Way society deserve some attention along this line. Walter Kotschnig has shown in an interesting book, *Unemployment in the Learned Professions*,[10] how the planless overproduction of a jobless intelligentsia in Europe between World Wars I and II contributed in a major way to social unrest. He indicates how an unplanned society provides incentives for higher education without providing the corresponding job opportunities. Unemployed professional men without a stake in the social order turn against it.

In such an unbalanced situation two remedies are conceivable: One would be artificially to discourage the pursuit of higher education and of intellectual careers; the other, to greatly expand opportunities for intellectual leadership,[11] promote self-government and voluntary associations. The first method was carried so far by the Nazis that for some time they were short of professional men.[12] The second method appears to be the American way, where university education has been greatly expanded and subsidized. The cost is not forbidding in industrial societies. The widespread aversion to such a policy in the monopolist phase of Capitalism may be ascribed to fear of devaluating central authorities and of reducing the distance between executives and office workers or the governed. The covert objection to democratizing and broadening educational opportunity rests on the fear of the educated classes lest such policies threaten their intellectual and cultural monopoly.[13] Moreover, the narrowing of chances to rise through business success heightens the significance of educational prerequisites such as academic degrees and fosters tendencies to fence off competitive jobs by educational prerequisites and barriers. The vested interest of the educated classes in limiting higher education is at least as powerful as the vested interest of capital.

II. THE PURSUIT OF LEISURE

The attitudes toward leisure in many ways complement the prevailing attitudes toward work. The same holds for methods of dealing with work and leisure respectively.[14] The mechanization of industry and its schematized routines deny creative outlets and personal initiative to the many, and demand compensation in leisure-time pursuits. Leisure, besides being the natural balance to man's work, becomes increasingly the place for personality development and self-expression. While pre-industrial societies shaped individuals at their work, impersonal work in a machine age has lost this function, which is now confined to leisure-time pursuits. These had never before served such ends. For the majority leisure instead of work has become the road to civilization.

Leisure became a problem only recently as *laissez-faire* Liberalism maintained that leisure was the 'private' sphere of man and that everyone should follow his own inspiration in spending his after-work hours. On a philosophical plane that argument has merit. It is bad enough if in the machine age we have to manage, organize, and manipulate human relationships under factory discipline. Why also meddle with the free time and energy left after work? But this theory of abstention from interference with leisure takes on a different aspect in the light of its actual operation and setting in a highly developed but unplanned industrial society.

In his village or small-town life, the old-world peasant or pre-industrial artisan followed a natural rhythm of work and leisure without any special problems.[15] The situation was simple; there were traditionally established ways of spending one's leisure time. Everybody knew them, nobody had to search out and invent any for himself. Free energies flowed in socially provided channels. Besides, no conflict existed between work and leisure attitudes. Work in the artisan's shop and household involves personal contacts in which work and chatter are interwoven; relaxation follows exertion in a natural rhythm. There is no monotony as in mechanized work, where relaxation is stored up for the end of the day.[16] An element of play permeates all activities, and Huizinga in his *Homo Ludens* correctly points out that any society is doomed that eliminates the element of play altogether from the organization of public life.[17]

Metropolitan urbanization and its ramifications have disrupted traditional patterns of leisure. Never before was the individual left to his own devices in his quest for recreation. Leisure-time activities always resulted from trial and error and found their place in tradition. Now that patterns of crowd enjoyment can be produced on short notice, they become what skilful managers make them. Commercial leisure characterizes our age. Hollywood and other profit interests dictate the taste of the masses. This also is planning, even large-scale planning, and as long as this is done by business for business and not by public authorities for the good of the community, Liberalism does not object. Here as elsewhere the *laissez-faire* policy has failed. Far from fostering liberal attitudes, Liberalism has allowed the few to influence the many for self-seeking advantage. Little concerned with educational and spiritual consequences, business tends to appeal to the lowest appetites [18] if it is profitable to do so.

In the organization of leisure the totalitarians took the path of planning in a one-sided and dangerous fashion. They realized, to be sure, that in the machine age the use of leisure time cannot be left undirected. Some agencies with greater knowledge, circumspection, and organizing ability provide guidance for unorganized individuals. Nations traditionally given to worship of state power took naturally to the idea that the State should fulfil this function. The State exploited this additional opportunity to promote the mental docility of its subjects. The facilities of commercial leisure and all types of skills were regimented for promoting the same blind subservience to the State that the meshes of education, propaganda, and economic organization already imposed upon the individual.[19]

The totalitarian solution, however perverted, raised two problems that the Third Way must solve on a higher plane. Democratic planning of leisure-time activities must beware of dictating patterns of leisure. It must avoid compulsory regimentation; regulatory measures should merely aim at providing conditions for spontaneous and creative leisure-time pursuits. This is contrary to the idealist fallacy which assumes that leisure-time activities result from mere inspiration and personal intuition. Appreciation of music and other arts—not to speak of musicianship and active pursuit of the arts—results from education and training, and the so-called musical and artistic sense is, despite inspiration, largely a matter of tradition and education. Interest in such pursuits has to be stimulated, and appreciation results from education and self-educational effort. The excellent broadcasts of the London BBC for school children or the demonstrations and lectures in music appreciation that Sir Walford Davis inaugurated in England show what can be done. In the United States one may refer to the cultural and educational programs of many a college radio station such as, for instance, that of the oldest U.S. broadcasting station, WHA of the University of Wisconsin, and its regular programs 'School of the Air' and 'University College of the Air.' Democratic planning might greatly expand subsidized and noncommercial opportunities for valuable leisure-time activities and cultural pursuits, acquaint broader audiences and publics with higher forms of enjoyment and relaxation.

Democratic planning need go no further, since democratic citizens are likely to make good use of available opportunities and appreciate worth-while offerings. What planning should not destroy or disregard is the individual's right to develop his own preferences. The democratic idea maintains that despite conditioning and adjustment to social expectation, there is a spontaneous nucleus of the human personality, in George H. Mead's term the 'I,' which should be activated on every occasion. The fact that the poorly educated, weary masses of the cities should have low standards of taste in reading matter—often providing daydreams for rush-hour traffic—should not blind and discourage us. In fact, it is difficult to decide whether the city crowds learn to like what they can get or whether they get what they want.

III. THE REDISTRIBUTIVE ASPECTS OF LEISURE

The recent revaluation of work and leisure provides a further key for understanding the great change both have undergone. As long as work was primarily interpreted as punishment for sin, leisure was suspect. While work meant punishment for sin, leisure meant the opportunity to commit sin. A new concept of work and leisure developed during the industrialization of society, at the same time an epoch of rational revision of traditional ideas. Sociology has clarified the older valuations and greatly contributed to their explanation in the light of social history.

The rigorous attitudes of pre-technological ages can readily be explained in terms of the hardships and drudgery of workaday life. During the industrial revolution, the phase of 'original accumulation,' investment capital was scarce. Society for its capitalist development needed great savings; the psychological equivalent seemed to be the repression of consumer demands and subjection of the worker to harsh workshop discipline. The more society moves from an age of natural scarcity to one of artificial scarcity, the more questionable is this taboo on self-expression and expanding consumer demand. The stronger man's realization of the potentials of available resources and production, the stronger grow popular craving for equitable distribution of incomes, for release from discipline and enjoyment of man's products.

These mass desires are more and more recognized as irrepressible forces. It would seem that the same restrictive mentality that fails to provide opportunities for self-expression for millions or allows the 'housing problem' to remain perennially unsolved is at work when production capacities are not fully exploited and 'full employment' is deemed impracticable. The worker can hardly be expected to put up with the ugliness of an outmoded factory and unsatisfactory work conditions if during his leisure he learns to appreciate beauty and the art of self-expression.

These popular cravings are bound to spread. Man, unafraid to pursue happiness during his leisure time—a process bound up with far-reaching changes in sexual mores [20]—becomes self-assertive likewise in other respects. In the past, ruling groups sensed such tendencies and countered them by linking the idea of leisure-time activities with guilt feelings.[21] A democratic society views the issue in a more constructive way. As every unchanneled release of energy is destructive, the problem is how to make this force creative. Psychoanalysis teaches that freely available energy after the removal of repressions or perversions is an asset only upon immediate sublimation.[22] Social education in a period of expanding leisure should foresee the danger and provide outlets for mass sublimation. Artistic pursuits and more general appreciation of works of art seem to provide the most promising outlets.

In this connection Herbert Read's broadened concept of art becomes significant.[23] Art as a way of life, not a mere compartment, can serve to convert otherwise destructive energies into constructive ones. The ascendancy of new classes in history offers an example of creative energies channeled into ostentatious luxury or devotion to higher ideals. It should be possible to establish models worthy of aspiration and to stimulate creative leisure-time activities leading to the democratic and social expansion of cultural pursuits without lowering general standards. The emotional transformation of the people and popular optimism should sweep away the fog of frustration emanating from fear of widespread change as a threat to those in high positions. In comparable periods of the past creative individuals of the ruling group were isolated and powerless; often they deserted the old order to join forces gladly with new movements and trust to the rising tide. Scorned as 'deserters and renegades' by their former associates and hailed as 'converts' by the social new-comers, they gained greater satisfaction by sharing their culture than by withholding it. Such spirits today will enjoy expanding social contacts more than seclusion or segregation.[24]

To be sure, the exuberance likely to accompany popular op-timism, the messianic expectation of paradise near at hand or of 'plenty round the corner,' is as demoralizing as the pessimism that cherishes scarcity for the sake of repressing mass aspiration. Planning for social change means overcoming the shocks of rev-olution and counterrevolution, both bloody and destructive. Po-litical planning, as the art of the possible, should enable us to reach out with intelligence for the new patterns and values that formerly, as, for example, in the French Revolution, crystallized only in political and social upheaval. Today, techniques of eco-nomic management available enable us to predict changes in the direction of production and realize possible increases pre-dicted on redistribution of incomes. Today, we can predict and determine the socially desirable optimum of such redistribution. Moreover, thanks to heightened awareness of social statistics and their recent development, we now have means to time planned changes with greater wisdom and foresight.

Planning the transition can only succeed in an atmosphere of moderation free both of restrictive egotism and overexpansive fervor. The attitude we need to cultivate is neither asceticism nor hedonism. Education should aim at making the pursuit of lei-sure-time activities a welcome opportunity for developing demo-cratic personality not by rules and regulations but by example and the encouragement of a well-balanced attitude. Thus, lei-sure may be integrated into the democratic plan like work and education. A type of mind should mature that is eager to expand yet ready and willing to curb itself in the face of demands of the community.[25]

12

The Discipline of Freedom [1]

◗

There is neither freedom nor discipline in the abstract, but only in concrete forms that depend on the cultural context. Among the determining factors we intend to deal with are the impact of group organization and aims. [2]

C. H. Cooley, in comparing the structure of the play group and the Army, made some suggestive remarks. These social organizations demonstrate that freedom and discipline are functions of group organization and have no meaning apart from it. Robinson Crusoe was not free, as there was no social discipline or organization that could shape his freedom. Nature poses obstacles, but no one would be called unfree because illness hampered his activities. The football team and the Army not only pursue different aims, but they differ in organizational means. As the movements of the ball can hardly be foreseen and the variety of situations is considerable, the organization of a football team must be extremely flexible. A great many choices and decisions have to be left to individual players. More important than the few rules of the game is the unwritten law of team spirit which forbids the individual to dominate at the expense of the team.

Army organization, on the other hand, requires the main decisions to be made at the top; therefore real choices and decisions are beyond the scope of the lower ranks; their choices derive from systematic delegation of initiative, responsibility, and freedom. If freedom means the power of making over-all decisions and choices, there is little scope for it in the lower echelons of the Army. Still on every level down to the individual soldier in the platoon relevant decisions have to be made from time to time. Thus every private has certain freedom compatible with army organization, or, more precisely, with a given type of army organization.

Similar considerations apply, of course, to discipline, the reverse of freedom. Discipline means to establish social restrictions on initiative and choices for the sake of organizational routines.[3] Just as the football team allows for greater individual initiative, its discipline evolves only during the game by constant redefining of rules. In contrast army discipline is rigid, most of its conduct patterns are preconceived, standardized, and thoroughly inculcated, enabling army personnel to operate predictably under long chains of commands. Similar is the discipline of a centralized bureaucracy, and it might be said that the Army is a bureaucratized fighting unit.

The Army and the football team may be seen as two extreme types in a series of social organizations. The most rigid organization would seek to extend the army pattern to all spheres of life, whereas the most elastic organization might conceive of society and its sub-groups more or less as a team. Needless to say, the Third Way will try to combine the two techniques by allowing for rigid organization where efficiency demands it, and by pleading for the flexible pattern wherever feasible. Progress toward freedom consists in a steady advance toward flexibility.

II. CONTEMPORARY CONCEPTS OF FREEDOM

This measuring rod can help us to place the different concepts of freedom in present-day discussion. Disagreement springs mainly from different and unclarified meanings of the same word. As in our discussion of power, the prevailing currents of thought can best be classified under the headings 'anarchist,' 'totalitarian,' 'liberal,' and 'plutocratic.'[4]

1. *The anarchist view*[5] holds that there is something in human nature, a kind of self-regulating power, which, if allowed complete freedom, will lead to spontaneous self-discipline. One

of the basic convictions of this school of thought is that the more we use repressive devices for enforcing discipline, the more we foster what is called 'negativism' in the individual. We pay for repression by blocking human spontaneity and readiness to cooperate under good working self-restraint. Anarchists are not simply individualists against any and all forms of discipline, but they believe 'real freedom' to result from spontaneous submission to the rules of group life. Statements like 'Der Gegenpol von Zwang ist nicht Freiheit sondern Verbundenheit' ('The opposite to coercion is not freedom, but fellowship') [6] and 'Certain forms of freedom can only be realized in group life' may serve to make the point.

The anarchist idea of freedom contains a great deal of truth but lacks sociological qualification. Certainly, such self-regulating powers exist, but only in small groups. The larger an organization becomes, the less one can expect or wait for the self-imposed discipline of the whole to emerge out of a lengthy process of minor adjustments. The Greeks realized this and established new social units when the old ones reached the prescribed limits. Today this is impracticable, for modern economic and social techniques are efficiently geared to large-scale operations.

The anarchist idea suggests, however, to the Third Way—the mobilization of self-regulating powers of small groups whenever possible. Vital social interaction is generated primarily in small groups; real understanding of life, new ideas, originate in them; when they lose vital energy, society is apt to become anemic.[7]

2. *The totalitarian approach to discipline and freedom* [8] realizes that the idea of a spontaneously emerging discipline is inapplicable in a large-scale society. Accordingly, a discipline of command and obedience is hailed under the *Führer* principle, which represents a universal scheme of strictly militarized central organization. The Army and bureaucracy serve as models. Two factors foster this spirit of over-organization.[9] On the one hand, herdlike masses, which have never known or cherished real civic freedom, accept the dictatorial structure readily after a panic that makes them crave order. On the other hand, minorities, skilled in mass management, may grow power-drunk in expanding their military organizations. They no longer offer free-

dom, but tyranny and mass regimentation, drilling the community by shouted slogans: 'Leader, command—we follow.'

3. *The liberal view of freedom and discipline* [10] is in many ways the rash application of the anarchist idea of emerging freedom and spontaneous self-discipline to mass society. It also presupposes that out of individual freedom of choice will result mysterious harmony by self-regulating powers of society. What the anarchists observe only in small groups, the liberals apply to an ever-growing society. There was some reason in their expectations under a prevailing handicraft and peasant economy before the days of big enterprise and organized pressure groups. Liberalism worked fairly well in the former setting, but has lost its validity and applicability under modern conditions. By insisting on their idea of freedom and discipline in disregard of the changed social structure, the liberals deliberately block the invention of adequate controls. To them, any freedom differing from their own will seem to be the opposite of freedom.

4. *The plutocratic concept of freedom and discipline* [11] emerges at a stage in society when a limited class of wealthy people apply the liberal ideology in disregard of social change. The plutocratic concept of freedom and discipline upholds basically the investor's right to invest and speculate freely, and the owner's right to use his property without restraints. Whenever these freedoms are endangered, the plutocrats bewail the loss of all freedom, complaining of regimentation and bureaucracy. This narrow idea of freedom overlooks the fact that private property, free enterprise, competition, occupational and consumer choice have new meaning in an age of corporate big business. As Tawney rightly has pointed out, freedom of property originally meant ensuring the legitimate use of his tools to the craftsman or farmer in a society antedating large-scale industrial techniques. Needless to say, 'free' private investment and enterprise even if intrinsically desirable, would mean freedom only for the few.

The liberals likewise disregard the number of those who can actually use certain freedoms. They emphasize freedom in the political sphere, freedom of expression, freedom of occupation and consumer choice—all freedoms that primarily concern educated people in fairly secure positions. These freedoms mean less on lower economic levels, and are frequently not available to low-income groups.[12] Money, being the one indispensable means for acquiring goods and skills, limits freedom of choice for many who legally and politically enjoy these nominal choices. Consumer and occupational free choice are illusory for men who cannot afford to buy certain goods or acquire the prerequisite skills for higher occupations. This objection has rightly been raised by the socialists against the liberals, and applies even more in a plutocratic society with its disproportionate accumulation of wealth.

On the other hand, it is equally short-sighted to say that freedom prevails if a society produces goods and services on a sufficiently large scale and distributes them more or less fairly, but leaves the regulation of discipline and freedom in the political and cultural spheres to a bureaucratic or political elite. A society that sacrifices cultural and political freedom for greater equality of income and education demonstrates its low appreciation of the former values. The issue is not that political and cultural freedoms are less relevant than material welfare, but how to extend self-determination to all spheres of life for the full development of personality, which requires both material and cultural opportunities.[13]

III. FREEDOM AND DISCIPLINE UNDER DEMOCRATIC PLANNING

These reflections on the social setting of the various concepts of freedom and discipline may reveal their one-sidedness and serve to combine their desirable features in a system of democratic planning. Freedom and discipline under democratic planning will be defined by the nature of groups, sub-groups, and their purposes.

A democratically planned society will have a personal concept of freedom in social relationships, i.e. it will foster flexibility, afford maximum opportunities for choice, and favor self-expression in small groups and private relationships.

In large groups and mass organizations, the Third Way will make use of the insight and wisdom of both the syndicalist movement and certain tendencies in corporatism. These movements emphasized that in mass society the liberty of small and large corporate associations is more important than that of the individual to pursue his advantage regardless. In an age of mass action, the individual can often be protected only by his group organization.

Liberalism, by juxtaposing the individual to society or the State, disregards the significance of intermediary and functional groups.[14] The sacred claim, 'Rights of Man,' needs to be translated into the Age of Planning. A planned Democracy has to look after the individual's right to personal development. Sociologically speaking, the man who prefers free-lancing to work in professional and other organizations should not go unprotected, but should have opportunities to follow his bent. But in an age of mass organization it is not enough to guarantee rights to individuals, it is equally important to protect the liberties of groups and associations.

The right of groups to propagate their ideas, to defend their way of life is no less sacrosanct than that of the individual. Thus, freedom and self-discipline apply also to groups. Group self-discipline demands the same self-restraint in intergroup relations as we expect in personal relations. If the State's main function is to control intergroup relations, it will have to control group egoism, which is more dangerous than individual egoism, as discussed in another chapter.[15] Attempts of groups to usurp a monopoly position must be checked; many forms of discipline and freedom derive not from life in small, self-adjusting units, but from the regulated interplay of organized groups. Such rules of intergroup life differ from primary group disciplines as the anarchist conceives of it. They affect the individual only segmentally and are experienced as 'organized' rather than 'spontaneous' relations, as you might compare behavior toward an official or toward a friend.

The State will partly guarantee existing intergroup relations and their freedoms, and partly initiate change, if existing patterns prove to be unsatisfactory. As in all other cases, such external control of group discipline by the State must, of course, be exercised in constitutional forms. The support of an existing group equilibrium and/or its gradual transformation has to be agreed upon and sanctioned by the electorate and carried out by publicly accountable officials.[16] These examples should make clear that it is folly to accuse all manipulation from a center of being despotism. Manipulation is democratic as long as it is based upon consent and carried out in a spirit that guarantees freedom among groups, even if the planning controls concern themselves with all activities of the group. If a group is as large and powerful as in the case of economic corporations, for instance, we must control not only their external relationships, but also their internal organization, in favor of industrial democracy.[17]

IV. FREEDOM OF CHOICE IN AN AGE OF PLANNING [18]

Behind the ambiguous use of words such as 'freedom' and 'discipline' and the failure to relate them to different societies, a fundamental transformation is silently in the making. This has not yet been recognized and clarified sufficiently.

One of the striking changes in modern society is the increase in the number of deliberate choices. The chief reason for this is that, in the past, natural scarcity and poverty automatically limited opportunities for choice; these now increase automatically with the increasing capacity to produce. Another factor, which works in the same direction, is the rising volume and efficiency of means of communication, distribution, and of advertising, which spreads knowledge about desirable things far and wide. A third factor formerly restricting choice resulted from habits and customs of self-restraint. These often prevented wishes and desires from coming to the fore, whereas they are now allowed much wider scope. Fourth, even where wealth was present and luxury goods existed, the tacit or open exclusion of certain social classes from their use reduced the number of relevant choices in society.

This striking change has come about because the choice-restricting factors have largely been reduced to price-income relationships. Therefore the generally raised level of aspirations and wants fosters intense and widespread desire to rise in the social scale. If not accompanied by a general rise in mass income, the new aspirations must result in a resentful yearning to equalize wealth and income opportunities. An unplanned, unlimited expansion of aspirations, continuously outdistancing available means, readily produces dissatisfaction in the midst of plenty. We must realize that scarcity is only one source of dissatisfaction.

U

The disparity between wants and their possible satisfaction is no less powerful a source.[19] Formerly people accepted the impersonal mechanism of supply, prices, and income differentials that ruled the distribution of purchasing power as natural processes, not amenable to conscious regulation. Now we realize that the creation of such equilibrium lies more or less in our own hands. New methods of distributing goods at differential prices [20] —cheap milk for school children, reduced movie tickets for the unemployed or for soldiers, reduced railroad fares, and so on—or the wartime experience of combining price controls with rationing in order to give low-income groups a better diet for efficiency's sake, have raised the problems of free consumers' choices and of planned intervention in the price mechanism to a new level of social awareness.

In a planned society the freedom of the individual will operate on two planes: The individual will still have maximum opportunities for free choice compatible with the organization of society; but he will also have to decide whether by planning and central co-ordination consumers' choices should be stimulated and in which direction. Whereas formerly profit-motivated advertising, price policies, and income distribution determined what should be consumed in what quantities by whom, central planning allows for the guidance of consumers' choices under dietary and social welfare considerations by means of price privileges, consumer credit, subsidized consumption, low-cost public housing, educational campaigns and—if need be—rationing and price controls. The yardstick for freedom and discipline cannot be the freedom of the well-to-do to monopolize high-priced goods, but the common good.

We are at the beginning of a process in which a dualism of attitudes that formerly occurred only occasionally will become permanent. Owing to this dualism, the individual in one context is compelled to follow his self-interest, and in another he will curb his egoism by institutions in the interest of the community. He will, e.g. accept heavy taxation if he feels it necessary for the maintenance of Society, yet make every legitimate effort to keep his own contribution as low as possible. Egotistic and communal attitudes formerly fluctuated; there was a kind of confusion, the situations alternatively provoking self-assertive and altruistic reactions. Now, such a dualism is built into the structure of the Self. In a planned society a citizen can only behave adequately if he clearly distinguishes between the field where planning—and, therefore, collective discipline and collective freedom—must prevail, and the other areas in which self-centered reactions are evoked by the circumstances.

With these formulae in mind, we can see that many of the old demands for freedom cannot be realized in the old way in the new planned society. In an unplanned society freedom of occupational choice was largely theoretical for those without money, educational opportunities, and information. Many young people chose a job because it was the only one within their reach. People still believed in freedom of occupational choice, because the limitations seemed to be caused by unseen natural forces and were not recognized as by-products of the social order, which was accorded tacit support.

If a man living in a planned society were sent back to such conditions of freedom, he would feel unhappy and restricted to an intolerable degree: unhappy if he should realize that in an unplanned society his occupational choice might be determined primarily by chance factors; that many young people may find themselves in blind-alley jobs, and that in a world of free competition it may take years to find a satisfactory place in society. As compared with this old unregulated freedom, he may praise his new type of freedom, which, in spite of the increase of bureaucracy and, if necessary, of State guidance, leads him to a job required by society that, fitting into the pattern of future development, is promising and no blind alley. He can find his job by consulting agencies for occupational guidance, which may cooperate with the schools; by turning to the respective services of vocational associations and public agencies devoted to the management of the labor market. Provided these agencies pay sufficient attention to his specific aptitudes and preferences, their broad scope of operation and central co-ordination of information may offer the individual actually wider and sounder occupational choices and career opportunities than he could find on his own. Disparities between planning goals, available opportunities, and possibly irrational vocational aspirations—as often found today under the influence of mass fiction and screen images of heroes [21]—could be reduced, if not gradually eliminated, by educational effort. Although writers on social and political affairs make highly individualized choices, most people, however, have no strictly formulated occupational preferences to begin with and thus may be amenable to and even grateful for expert advice and tactful suggestions shifting them from less promising to more promising occupational pursuits in line with economic plans and predictable developments. Furthermore, labor turnover in the Soviet Union as well as in the United States shows that millions of modern men acquire with relative ease the ability to adjust to a great variety of occupational demands. By placing special premiums, pecuniary and/or honorific, upon possibly less desirable pursuits one can attract the required number of job applicants.

Thus, freedom in a planned society should not be judged in terms of the absence or presence of bureaucracy and regulation, but in terms of the common good and the best use of individual potentialities. Intelligence tests, interviews, expert observation of physical and mental development and dispositions, and expert guidance of vocational choices in agreement with planned and predictable developments—and at the same time provision of unplanned sectors which give scope to people of specific gifts or aspirations—may serve man's quest for freedom in a planned world.

13

Thought, Philosophy, Religion, and the Integration of the Social Order

○

I. RELIGIOUS INTEGRATION IN A DYNAMIC SOCIETY

The ultimate integration of the social order has always been an important problem. What holds society together—whether it is power, the division of labor, or a spiritual bond—is one of the most profound questions the sociologist has to answer. Of course, social integration occurs at all levels of thought and action. We rarely do anything that does not have integrating or disintegrating effects. Still there is no doubt that the proportionate relevance of spiritual ferment or naked power is a differentiating characteristic of social systems, and even more so of great societies. The ancient empires, such as the Sumerian or the Egyptian, were built upon the integrating influence and predominance of the priestly and warrior castes. Today we can see much better how the one relied upon the other and how neither could have held society together without the other's contribution.

Moderns gradually have lost the sense of need for spiritual integration, so obvious to medieval society. Characteristically, most modern sociologists have had little understanding of the need and methods of integration. Perhaps this was because they were mostly the products of protest against the existing social order, as was the case with Liberalism, Marxism, Anarchism, and Syndicalism. They saw only an obstacle in their way and rebelled against compulsion and austerity which seemed to them outmoded. With a few important exceptions, such as Comte (who recognized the problem of social integration), it seems to have been a part of the critical and revolutionary temper out of which sociology arose that the sociologists were either blind to the question of integration or took it too much for granted. They thought as, for instance, the liberals, anarchists and syndicalists did, that integration would occur spontaneously.

The problem presents itself quite differently for the Third Way, which would seek to transform society without endangering its fundamental integration. It would have to pay equal attention to the factors conducive to dynamic and creative change on the one hand and to fundamental integration on the other. The old-fashioned *laissez-faire* thinker or the radical would disregard the significance of tradition and religion and the forces making for stability and continuity, because in his time these matters took care of themselves. In the new situation, the strategist of reform will have to maintain integration in the midst of rapid change. He will have to concentrate on stability and continuity at the same time that he seeks to change society. This is when he realizes the need for religion and quasi-religious integrating powers in society. But with him religion is not allowed to become, as in the case of the reactionary, a bulwark of vested interests, but rather a force to help to bring about change and, in the process, regenerate man and society.[1]

In another context we have tried to show that the age of Liberalism was rather exceptional in thinking that change could be accomplished without bothering about religious and other forms of basic integration. John Stuart Mill even went so far as to say that it was to the interest of society that the fundamental issues of creed be continually revised and that, therefore, there should be no basic agreement on them. Otherwise they were bound to be a groundwork for hierarchy and arbitrary institutions so incompatible with a dynamic society. There is, no doubt, penetrating insight in Mill's statement as far as one aspect of the story is concerned. He points very clearly to the difficulty which every planned society meets when it sets out to develop a totalitarian philosophy for the whole system, whether it happens to be a racial dogma or the Marxist theory of economic determination and class struggle. Once such philosophies become the sacred source of interpretation for all events—a form of basic theology—they lead to a new sort of clericalism.

Today, of course, we have greater understanding than ever of the achievement of a medieval basic theology and even of the need for an organized spiritual power. We now realize that a social order can only maintain itself satisfactorily on the basis of a sound statement of belief that performs in a new way the role of the old dogma. We have learned from the chaos through which we have passed that certain things must remain exempt from doubt, even if only for a while. Wiser in this respect, we who plead for a Third Way, are nevertheless still reluctant to achieve this basic integration of society through any form of superimposed system of thought. We are now sober enough to know that the ultimate integration in a disturbed mass society is unlikely to come about spontaneously as the *laissez-faire* thinker was prone to believe. On the other hand, we are unable to accept the idea that the only alternative is inculcation and indoctrination.

While it is difficult to find a satisfactory answer in the alternatives of abstract theory, a third solution seems to be developing in England. In the course of historical development, this country gradually worked out a solution that accepted the Christian foundations of society. In most cases this approach sets up religion as supreme judge on moral issues, allowing it to criticize even the State, especially on questions of conscience. Yet the very same historical tradition does not allow the primacy of religion to be turned into a kind of intolerant clericalism. The idea of a religious society with a fundamental belief in tolerance is the paradoxical pattern that has emerged from the history of the Anglo-Saxon countries. After stressing this fact, it is necessary to add that this astonishing equilibrium between conformity and heterodoxy, between established creed and relativism, is not only due to exuberance of vitality and genuine tolerance, but too often results from indifference and neutrality.

The Established Church and the nonconformists, the fundamentalists and the atheists, tolerate one another not only because the idea of toleration is so strong, but also because in many groups the religious and nonreligious impulses have gradually become neutralized. Very often they get on nicely with each other because neither has sufficient energy any longer to become excited about its own fundamental creed.

Even if we admit that something that was once genuine tolerance has deteriorated too often into indifference, there is still present in some countries of the Western world the residual experience from former struggles which in any important situation recalls the significance of creative tolerance and tends to offset the temptation of fanaticism. These countries have learned that the fact of there being only one Truth does not mean that any group believing itself to be in possession of that truth has the right or even the obligation to extirpate believers in some other creed. If there is indeed only one Truth, it is bound to be more comprehensive than any one human being or any one party could grasp. It is worth listening to everyone, because you can never tell through what individual or what group the voice of God may speak. This is the only way of religious unification and integration compatible with a dynamically planned society based on the ideal of planned freedom.

A planned society should make up its mind about ultimate issues. On the other hand it is saved from becoming totalitarian, rigid, and a strait jacket to the community by making the search for basic truth a dynamic issue, honestly putting a question mark after statements that require it. But even if the question mark were often to point to infinity, to the insoluble problematic nature of human knowledge, this would not mean that in the next five or ten years that same society need live in uncertainty. After having ironed out our differences we could agree on a certain plan, even if we know that all the social and philosophical implications have not finally been settled.

Democratically decided principles will be valid for practical purposes over a limited period, and fundamental revision will only be forthcoming when a new start seems necessary. Even so, certain circles in society will continue to discuss the fundamentals of life, religion, and society. Such discussions will have their place in a democratically planned social order. There will be provision for discussion, though no license will be granted for destructive action or sabotage of co-operation whenever it pleases the objector.

Certain unchanging aspects of the human mind seem to indi-

cate the need for a transcendental religious foundation in society; and several factors make this need even more urgent in
our present situation. There exist some archaic patterns in the
human mind and in the nature of human action that lead to the
quest for certainty and deeper foundations. The very fact that
in our practical procedures we always think in terms of means
and ends and have a purpose in mind when we perform something makes it difficult for us to conceive of a universe without
such an end. Although this may be a thought habit acquired
through the process of living and doing things, it is so deeply
rooted that a world without purpose would mean a kind of
homelessness hardly tolerable to a thoughtful being. It is one
of the great paradoxes of our age that the more our technical
skill permeates the details of everyday life, where we seek for
purposeful arrangements, the more our philosophy tends toward
the idea that purpose as a concept does not apply to Nature as
such: even those things that seem to be purposeful are the result
of selection, the chance product of endless variety and forms of
adaptation. Such an idea can be conceived, but it can hardly be
lived. It is like admitting in theory that the earth moves round
the sun while still experiencing the sun as a rising disc that radi-
ates light day by day. In the same way, calm assurance that the
highest thing in life is communion with One to whom we can
speak and who will respond with unfailing understanding and
forgiveness is so deeply ingrained that despondency would reign
if this religious belief were lost. Only through satisfaction of
these deep-rooted aspirations (that there is a Purpose in what
we are doing, and that there is a Personal Power to whom man
can appeal) can man develop the sense of belonging in a world
where he can find his place and where there is an order that supports him and dispels his anxieties.

These are some of the inalienable features in human nature
that in one way or another will always make for some form of
religion. They will not be satisfied with 'scientific' interpretations that fail to answer the basic needs of the inquiring mind.

In what follows, I should like to discuss certain trends in
present-day society that, apart from these needs of all time, make
integration on a religious level even more important. First of all,
a number of factors at work produce a specific intellectual pre-

dicament in modern society, while others are causing a special predicament of human existence in our society.

II. THE PREDICAMENT OF THOUGHT IN MODERN SOCIETY

1. *The Segmentation of Intellectual Functions*

Man is a being in whose life thought has different functions to fulfil, or, to put it more concretely, in many ways it is difficult for the human being that the same organ, the mind, with its ability to think, has such entirely different functions to fulfil. These different functions were not quite apparent in the past but have of late years become a problem. Thought has always been not only a fact-finding tool but also an instrument of persuasion, propaganda, education, a pathfinder and pacemaker for action. In their inner nature these are fundamentally different processes; the fact that the abyss separating them was not realized earlier was owing to lack of differentiation in functions in a relatively simple society.

Modern psychology was responsible for isolating thought as a fact-finding instrument from its other functions. Man began using his fact-finding function in relation to Nature; but now it is extended to the realm of inner experience and social relations. To free concepts from emotional undertones and statements of fact from evaluations—in other words, to remove ambiguity—was a necessary development. Exactness of fact finding, factual observation, and fact reporting was impossible without breaking up the units of observation in our common-sense experience. The method of theoretical analysis, when applied to social life, focused our attention on particles of social and psychological reality that had passed unobserved on the level of everyday practical life. Although this breaking up of units of observation as they evolved from common-sense experience is essential from the point of view of science, it is bound to be calamitous when we realize that we must use the same apparatus of thought for both purposes, everyday orientation and scientific research. Frequently what is a gain for scientific knowledge is a loss for integration of personality and social cohesion. For this reason conservative minds more concerned about social cohesion and co-operation than about new discoveries were inclined to deplore the disintegrating effect of analytical knowledge.[2] They were wrong in wanting to turn the clock back and have us believe in all the Biblical myths and other ancient lore as literal truth. Yet they instinctively felt that folklore had an integrating function in society and if it were removed without being replaced by another vision of life and the world order, a void in our outlook would be inevitable.

Pre-scientific thought is persuasive and educative at the same time. Scientific thought should be neutral, not concerned either with persuasion or with the question whether it is good for a person to know just this or that at a given stage in his development.

Of course, scientific thought is all right in its own sphere. It has to aim at an exact statement of fact and nothing but fact. But society cannot live without persuasion and due appreciation of the need for the educative process.

Today at last we are able to formulate the dilemma that unconsciously has puzzled man for centuries. Should we state scientific facts at all levels of human growth and in all manner of social situations irrespective of their educative and psychological effects? Should we always formulate facts in the language of instrumental thinking, irrespective of the circumstance that man is used to thinking in terms of images, and that destruction of this imagery destroys the appeal value of our ideas and the human element in them? Or else, should we tell stories that have educative value and humanizing power, but do not correspond with what our fact finders present as tested truth?

Here it is no longer the obscurant who protests because he fears the dissemination of knowledge; it is the educator seeing the dissolution of those basic images of our fantasy—the core of our everyday experience and the light in which we move and co-operate. Take the following example:

On the plane of scientific thinking there is neither tragedy nor comedy. There are facts and processes, neutral in themselves. But is it possible to experience human events in an atmosphere devoid of the tragic sense, where there is no climax, no one responsible, no hero but a lot of atoms that just behave in a certain way?

The dilemma in its most acute form applies to the political

scene. As a fact finder every human being comes upon unpleasant data which may correspond neither with his personal desires nor with ideas he shares with a sect or party. As a fact finder he must also admit that there are tremendous gaps in our knowledge, and that things are in a state of flux. There is no clear-cut, finally established knowledge; all that we think in the spirit of responsible science can be stated only in terms of probabilities. But, in order to move the multitude, to unite huge parties, our aims should be clear-cut, and history presented as if it were supporting our cause alone. In a word, it is essential for group action that planners should pretend to certainty and eliminate skepticism and ambiguity.

This shift in the presentation of facts and ideas, as I see it, is not due simply to the dishonesty of the demagogue or of the politician, but is in the nature of human action, especially of collective action. As long as everyday language was used both in politics and fact finding, ambiguity allowed identical terms to be utilized either as tools of observation or as goal setters. But as social and psychological science increasingly insists upon the removal of ambiguities and the stating of probabilities as just that and not certainties, the politician and the actor are left, so to speak, without a language.

2. *Organized Thought*

Through this differentiation of functions, which separates the language of fact finding from that used in the educative process and in influencing collective action, a kind of split consciousness arises. It causes a feeling of uncertainty, an ambivalence of attitudes, all the more disturbing as it is deep-seated and hardly realized in the subject's mind. This gulf becomes even deeper as we follow the further consequences of social growth in its bearing on human thinking.

The life in organized political parties produces not only the need for clear-cut statements but the phenomenon of 'organized thought'—a rigidly defined system of ideas with a catechism of ready-made answers for any possible question, a system of statements enabling the propagandist to settle any doubts and bring into line any deviation from socially accepted dogma. This means that any person who tries to think honestly, to face all the facts and changes that do not fit into the prearranged system of thought, is bound to be ousted from the field, the acknowledged universe of discourse, from the start. This method of having a ready-made answer at hand was first developed in the modern age by the Jesuits, though it was first used systematically on a large scale by the Marxists.[3]

However, the Marxists only began where other parties follow and will increasingly follow, unwilling to leave their partisans gaping before the tricks of the thought-juggler on the opposite side. Organized thought produces ever more organized thought, and the original nature of thinking, which was so magnificently demonstrated by Socrates in his relentless dynamic search for truth, completely collapses. One of the nightmares of mass existence is the danger of petrification in systems of organized thought from which the spirit of inquiry has been squeezed out.[4] Our predicament is even more tragic when we realize that at the same time, in the same epoch and in the same human mind, entirely different yet equally absorbing patterns of thinking have developed. The further science proceeds, the more we realize that there is nothing definite in our thought mechanism, that all we can hope for are hypotheses subject to reorganization when factual evidence changes. As our concepts have no reality in themselves and therefore must be abandoned as soon as others explain more facts more adequately, the idea of an open system with changing concepts becomes more and more dominant in the sphere of research.

In the times of classical philosophy, one assumed the existence of fundamental reality, the validity of certain ideas on a high plane of generality. For us today this ontology is hardly secure; at best its concepts can be considered parts that must continually give way when facts do not support the framework. Thus, whereas we develop rigid systems of political thinking with preconceived answers for every contingency, modern intellectuals renounce any enduring frame of reference and tend toward a kind of fathomless existence. In this tendency, modern thought is a fair counterpart to the rigidity of organized ideologies.

There is no doubt that the two extremes are the products of the same age and, even though rarely confronted with both at once, the human being living in their atmosphere is torn between them. To him the artificial certainties of dogma are often the only refuge from the challenge of eternal uncertainties.

3. The Delocalization of the Mind

The dualism between endless search for the truth and artificial stabilization of outlook did not exist in simple societies. The split begins when the mind is gradually severed from the locality and the concrete context in which it originated. The beginnings of this process, for which we suggest the sociological term 'delocalization of the mind,' are rather ancient but the final results are just becoming visible.

Originally the thought habits and the content of the mind were part and parcel of the tribal or local unit in which they developed. Thought was at first a part of folkways, traditions, and habits, an untranslatable idiom referring everything to a concrete setting in which the world was experienced in a primitive community. So long as we live at the level of customs and folkways we do not accept statements and prescriptions because they are true and have been tested by experiment, but because they have authority. They are authoritative, and if one lives and acts according to them, one is right. If not, one breaks a taboo and is wrong.[5]

It is not chance that scientific thinking begins by inviting the individual to doubt whatever comes to him as part of tradition, and to test anew for himself what part of it is true in the light of his own experience. By this process we 'delocalize' thought, tear it out of the context in which it was valid through the authority of tradition and at the same time relate it to a 'supercommunal subject—the mind as such,' out of which the idea of pure (i.e. delocalized) reason developed.

Thought then becomes an abstract instrument for statement of facts by every human being and not only for those members of a community who are held together by common conventions and traditions. This development from the tribal to the cosmopolitan mind (the beginnings of which in our own civilization are connected with Descartes) results in a painful process of uprooting which involves continuously upsetting the mental balance of those exposed to it.

One result of this delocalization is that we tend to overrate experiences that can easily be translated from one mental idiom into another. The formal statements of mathematics are trusted more, because they seem self-evident. Concrete experiences are reduced to abstract symbols, squeezed dry of their essence, and appreciated infinitely more than flashes of insight that involve the whole person and his community background. In this process our universe of discourse is split in two: one-half is associated with the process of delocalization, the other with the untranslatable qualitative elements in our communal experience.

As the first type of knowledge emancipates itself from the second, a countermovement develops to save the values of qualitative experience from depreciation. Those who argue in favor of qualitative experience sooner or later contend that there is nothing to be said against the development of abstract thought in an expanding society moving toward a cosmopolitan attitude, but that it is going too far to insist that man distrust and give up all the experiences he owes to his rootedness in a concrete community.

It is perhaps not chance that in fulfilling the demands of a cosmopolitan consciousness we become at the same time more aware of the community background, which heretofore we have taken for granted. The process of delocalization of mind adds value to the locality from which we are about to be severed. Although obviously in perspective the processes of being uprooted and becoming more aware of our roots are both aspects of the same historical development, to those undergoing both processes, it only contributes to the fundamental uncertainty. In the process of delocalization of mind we witness something that perhaps has its only parallel in the growth of the child who is suddenly removed from the shelter of the family to a world in which all emotional signs and meanings that had previously lent direction to his wishes and activities become meaningless.

4. *The Process of Debunking*

Another characteristic of our modern age is the prevalence of the 'debunking' attitude. It was present among others in Marxism and in the Freudian approach. But here, too, as in so many instances, these two schools of thought only developed more fully a mental attitude that was in effect a product of the historical process and part and parcel of the modern mind. Both invalidate a pattern of thought by revealing hidden reasons or unconscious motives that cause a person or a group to produce the thought or to believe in it. The Marxist, for instance, says that when the bourgeois speaks of 'freedom' he really has in mind the freedom of the capitalist to invest and make profits; while the Freudian asserts that prudery is very often a 'reaction formation' against too strong a sex urge in ourselves; or our feeling of being persecuted by somebody is a projection of our unconscious tendencies to hate; or passion in scientific research is nothing but transformed sexual curiosity. Both believe that the real meaning of individual or group behavior and accompanying thought is to be found behind the cloak of immediate justification given them. In both cases the method of looking beneath the surface of thought and action led to scientific revelation of obscure social and psychological mechanisms, which might not have been detected at all without the pressure of the debunking attitude.

This debunking attitude in which mistrust is directed not so much against a given person or group as against the ability of the mind to detach itself from hidden motivations is typically modern. There has always been mistrust and suspicion, but it was a concrete affair rather than a method of understanding better the working of the mind itself both in the individual and in the group. But under the impact of social change this fundamental mistrust has been developed as an instrument of sociological and psychological understanding. For it is social change in its various forms that loosens the bonds linking us to the content and habits of our minds.

If a person never leaves his home town to go to other countries, never leaves one stratum for another through rise or fall in the social scale, or if, in his group, no violent psychological changes occur for a lifetime, that person is so strongly identified with established habits of thought and interpretation that he can hardly conceive of their ability to change. Even less would he attempt to discover the hidden rational or irrational motivations behind this outlook.

Great change occurs when we realize not only that different

groups think differently about certain issues, but that the whole frame of reference may be different. When change not only is external but affects our mental concepts, it becomes possible to look beneath the surface and to detect the mental dynamic. The tendency to deprecate the validity of certain statements by un-veiling their hidden motivations is intensified when—through so-cial differentiation—different social groups explain the same things in different ways. In a highly stratified society it is likely that segregated groups will develop different approaches, valua-tions, and interpretations of the same things. If the interests of these groups are antagonistic there will be a tendency to realize that, even in our own society, different ways of thinking exist, a tendency that weakens, through the attitude of debunking, the public prestige of the opponents. But what we do to our enemy he will try to do to us. Debunking gets to be a general mental habit; what was originally one group's weapon is now a popular approach—and one that essentially belongs to our age.[6] Thus, however much we may owe to this process that has freed our minds from habits, we cannot fail to recognize that debunking in general only adds to the fundamental uncertainty of our time.

5. The Manipulative Approach to Thought

Along with a characteristic tendency to regard man's thoughts as ideologies and rationalizations, another technique is develop-ing in modern mass society that bears especially on our relation to the mind. Once we are used to regarding man's emotions and ideas as products of certain environmental or psychological mechanisms, it is obvious that we are going to try to produce these mental states or ideas through manipulative procedures.

Again, there is nothing new in trying to persuade or impress a person or group. This was always the method of demagogues and groups skilful enough to serve as models, i.e. silently to impose their manners and ideals on the rest of the population. But they all have done this more or less intuitively, either through per-sonal appeal or unconscious suggestion. A new phase begins when technicians of propaganda use their skill to produce certain ideologies or emotional trends through rationally conceived methods. It is no longer transference through intuition but the skilful exploitation of certain rules of psychology that teach us

X

how to condition responses and how to plan ideologies. The new feature is that leading people acquire the manipulative attitude, and gradually that attitude becomes general.

By implication person-to-person appeal is forced into the background. It does not, of course, disappear completely. It will still exist in family life, neighborliness, and friendship; but if we were to make a time budget in the life of a typical inhabitant of a modern metropolis, we would see how this rubric shrinks, compared with activities in which he is the manipulator or in which he is manipulated. Needless to say the time budget only indicates the disappearance of person-to-person experiences in terms of time spent. The real loss could only be ascertained if we realized how the inner quality of personal experience is bound to be weakened by being shunted to the margin of life.

As usually happens with a type of experience that is about to be ruled out by social development, we have suddenly become aware of the significance of the person-to-person experience or, in Martin Buber's terms, the 'Thou experience.' We speak a great deal about community because community experience is becoming increasingly rare. We speak about the meaning of person-to-person relations because they, too, are becoming increasingly scarce. We romanticize them, embellishing their memory, because we dread their disappearance. Formerly we had little to say about them because we took them for granted. Now we still have them but with that flavor of ideological beatification, which in itself indicates a certain loss of reality. Community experience on the level of reflection, 'Thou experience' on the level of romantic elevation, is a compensating move of the mind in mass society and develops in strict correlation with the growth of the manipulative approach.

The real paradox of this process is only fully realized when we see the primary experiences—community feelings and person-to-person appeals and what we call the human touch—produced by those in charge of manipulating the mind in human society. A radio voice is loved because it creates the illusion of a strong personality whom the listener imagines he knows better than his own friend. This yearning for the 'personal touch' is mechanically projected. We suddenly prefer a film star who is not starlike at all but just 'homey'; yet this very 'homeyness' is quite as much a product of conscious manipulation as the Hollywood reproduction of genuine Parisian atmosphere.

What we call inspiration is still another quality that goes astray with the growth of the manipulative approach. As long as primary contacts prevail, the monotony of life and the frequent repetition of customary behavior patterns are occasionally transcended by meeting persons who have the gift of vision and the dynamics of real inspiration. Sometimes at least we enjoy being carried away by them and, in crucial situations, such individuals may become centers of regeneration, reform, or revolution either in political or religious life.

Room for the beneficent influence of such individuals shrinks in normal times or whenever the organization and bureaucratization of human affairs grows in modern society. Man, however, in the desire to overcome the dehumanizing effects of being a mere cog in the social machine, still yearns for inspiration and vision. Thus again in response to manipulation, a romantic enhancement of vision and inspiration as human values has developed. It is sometimes grotesque to see how, in the wilderness of manipulative approaches, the cry is strongest for the man who has the powers of inspiration and vision. It is even more grotesque to observe the premium put upon the services of such individuals by the vast social machines which have developed manipulation into a gigantic technique. This may be observed, for instance, in the American party system, where often the party machinery is admittedly a 'racket' with division of spoils the only integrating factor. However, the party's chances are dependent upon the people of integrity who stand as its candidates—not the racketeers who may be uncovered in the cross fire of the campaign. In addition, the candidate must not be predominantly calculating but rather a man of inspiration and vision; at any rate the latter type has had good chances on the political scene. Of course, all of this applies equally to democracies and totalitarian systems. It is perhaps even more important in the case of the totalitarians where the leaders, the visible personalities, are those who can inspire (whatever the content of their inspiration) and who have a vision (whatever it may be).

The same applies to films and radio, both of which are subject to the manipulating mind whose calculation of emotional effects and profit returns often has to include the person of vision and inspiration in a top position. The outstanding effect of such moves is the development of a new type of personality: the specialist in vision and inspiration, who projects into the ether or on a gigantic screen those human qualities which are genuine only so long as they spring directly from the unconscious and are not manipulated.

Thus, the extension of the manipulative approach, without which no mass society could exist, again augments that hidden insecurity, whose growth we have observed in other modern trends. Never seeing quite clearly which experience is genuine and which the result of artificial manipulation makes for insecurity for everyone, even for the simplest members of the community. Repercussions of the film, of faked oratory, of planned propaganda, of deliberately concocted fashions of the mind are found in our secret distrust of the mind itself. There are, of course, a few exceptional people among the poets and critics who are rarely deceived, and who can still judge whether one artist simply imitates a pattern common to the age or to an intellectual circle, while the work of another is the original result of personal struggle and genuine creative experience. The average person, brought up on the superficial journalese of the daily press, on the standardized broadcast language and patter, on films that must be conventional since the industry cannot risk capital on experiments, gets trapped in that jungle without knowing which of his feelings is genuine and which is merely borrowed. When is privacy really privacy? When is friendship true friendship? And when is the homely touch reality and not just pretense?

This uncertainty about what is genuine and what is manipulated or even faked leads to a peculiar form of skepticism. It is the skepticism of the person who has seen too many new literary fashions or new common ideas come and go, who has heard too many new words that once touched off a spark in him become common coin.

This kind of skepticism is not the creative skepticism of the inquiring scientific mind which rejects a hypothesis because it is not yet fully tested. It is not the skepticism of the real art critic who has the vision of what is genuine and knows the deepest sources of inspiration and will not put up with anything that is a fake. It is the skepticism of the common mind reflecting that basic uncertainty which has become general in an age in which large-scale manipulation of mental states is behind most of the experiences we share. Even if the common man cannot give reasons for his skepticism and uncertainty, these have become as much part of his character as for those who realize the philosophical, psychological, or historical bases of their skepticism.

So far we have described uncertainties that are closely linked to the social development of thought in an expanding society. At first sight, some may be inclined to regard these observations as too subtle and some may take the line: 'Give the people social security, food, shelter, and jobs, and all these problems will disappear.' Those who say this do not realize that economic and social insecurity are only part of the general insecurity. They overlook the fact that psychological and spiritual insecurity are sometimes even more disturbing than the former. It is simply practical politics to know all the main sources of psychic insecurity in our time.

III. THE PREDICAMENT OF HUMAN EXISTENCE IN MODERN SOCIETY

1. *Irrationalism in Mass Society*

Apart from the insecurities caused by the present predicament of thought, there are other sources of human insecurity that characterize man's existence in modern mass society. The latent drive toward irrationalism or, to put it more crudely, the tendency toward mass hysteria is the first of these broader and more fundamental disturbances to be noticed.

Life in a mass society seems to accumulate a latent psychological explosive power which, in situations of general insecurity, spreads like wildfire and tends to become a permanent part of the popular mental attitude, as was shown by the Nazi experiment in Germany. Undoubtedly a great many special causes—economic, historical, and psychological—contributed to making the German a typical example of this attitude. Still, very few of us will deny that this mental state is latent in modern mass society as such, and we should do our best both to understand

the causes of these conflagrations and to find methods for preventing them.

Perhaps the simplest formula for mass irrationalism such as
occasionally breaks out is that normally human emotions are
fixed on concrete objects. What the psychoanalyst calls the
'cathexis'—the fixation of emotional energy on certain objects:
love of one's home, garden, children, work, job, or emotional
satisfaction gained from status, success, et cetera—normally binds
the emotional energy. When these fixations are loosened through
sudden shock, when, for example, a man's self-respect is shaken
by loss of his job so that the satisfactions of ordinary life are
upset, then he and the thousands or millions like him are pos-
sessed of unattached emotional energies that await direction
and fixation on certain goals—to be dictated by the new manipu-
lators of mass society. When disintegration of the social texture
breaks down social allegiances and deprives us of the usual satisfactions, it is obvious that this unattached energy is like electric
power, which, as long as it is guided into proper channels, is creative but, once set free, becomes destructive.

Usually this unattached energy in man regresses to more primitive forms of expression. It will become open aggression if the
social controls are weakened. Since possible relapse into mass
hysteria is always latent in great societies and since that irrationalism, itself partly caused by insecurity, creates more insecurity, it is up to those responsible for dealing with man's mental and spiritual problems to provide deliberate restraints and
curbs for it in their institutions. The power that can overcome
irrationalism is not mere rationalism, but, as John Dewey rightly
has said, 'refined passions.' [7]

The short-sightedness of the Enlightenment lies in the conception that irrational elements in human nature and their disturbing effects upon human relations could be mastered by mere
intellectual analysis. Certainly, intellect as a means of intelligent
control has a great role in our social life; but this does not alter
the stuff of irrationality. The humanization of the latter comes
only with its sublimation—the 'refinement of passion.' Passion remains what it is, but is devoted to the service of a good cause
and wrought into shape through artistic or religious spiritualization. For this reason there is no protection against mass irration-

ality in turning away from passion; it should be treated in its own realm. Latent insecurity in mass society—for irrationality has not disappeared even in civilized man—can only be counterbalanced by spiritualization or refinement of passion at all levels of human action and co-operation. If strongly developed, spiritualization can be a bulwark against regression, but it will be swept away unless modern art and religion become again a significant part of the fabric of human life.

2. *Dual Morality as a Source of Insecurity*

By dual morality I refer to the peculiar fact that man has gradually developed two types of responses to right and wrong simultaneously. On the plane of general argument and insight, he will plead for the right thing, not in his particular interest but in the interest of his community. Acting in a given context, however, he will very often disavow what he proclaimed on the level of generality. In its simpler forms this is a well-known phenomenon which we refer to in the saying that a person 'preaches water and drinks wine.'

The problem becomes more acute when it is not merely the expression of weakness resulting from an instinctive urge, as in the above-mentioned case, but when we realize that this dual morality is frequently the consequence of the fact that we live in society on two different levels and develop two moralities accordingly: one which we may call 'general morality' and the other what might be called 'contextual morality.'

As we have already pointed out, people in their intellectual approach to social affairs acknowledge that taxes should be paid and agree to being heavily taxed, if necessary. In the personal situation, however, many still try within the legal limit to reduce their share to the minimum. This egoistic or self-centered manipulation is acknowledged even by the State, which frankly admits everybody's right to consult experts in order to minimize his contribution. It would seem to be contradictory to bargain over one's share of the taxes while presumably acting in the interest of the common weal. Yet we recognize the dual attitude and acknowledge living and thinking on two different levels: thinking for the whole, yet being on guard and reacting as a self-centered unit. The existence of these two levels is even more marked if we vote for laws that will compel us to act on the contextual level in terms of our higher abstract morality. I, as an individual, will not raise my taxes, but I want the State which compels me to raise taxes.

This shows quite clearly that there are, so to speak, two selves within us. With certain modifications, they correspond to what psychoanalysis calls the superego and the ego—the one sets up the idea of higher morality; the other wants to be practical in the real situation.[8]

The same dualism predominates when somebody in the field of political theory pleads strongly for co-operation *versus* competition and for social justice *versus* profit making. In concrete action, in spite of these ideals, he will still go on being competitive as long as society is organized on competitive lines, as he knows that he is bound to fall in line under penalty of failure. In the same way he will try to make profits as long as profit making is the basis of enterprise. Yet inwardly he may still want a social order in which the actual circumstances allow him to be community-minded instead of reaping bigger profits for himself. All of this suggests that dual morality is not solely the outcome of personal frailty but often the expression of the fact that society, which after all defines the conditions under which we have to play the game, is still organized differently from what our social consciousness tells us is just and right.

The progress of social education therefore consists in strengthening our abstract morality more and more—that is to say, the morality that can abstract itself for a while from our egocentric horizon and see what is good for the community. We are then in a position to proceed to policies with the help of which the whole community will alter the concrete situation. Then we should be able to act in greater conformity with the principles our abstract intelligence dictates to us.

The great mistake of the old-fashioned preacher was that he appealed merely to our abstract conscience, suggesting that we should be altruistic instead of selfish; he failed to criticize the social structure in which action had to take place and the rules of which compelled the individual to play the self-centered game. There is much wisdom in developing our social sense and our responsibility on the abstract level, but only if simultaneously we find methods for transferring those ideals to the pattern of our social order. To put it briefly, to improve social responsibility in the individual can only be effective if at the same time, through social reform, we are able to alter the rules of the game in our social structure.

One of the great uncertainties of our age follows from this dual development: the individual belongs to two worlds, his mind reacts to the demands of society on two levels. There has always been tension between abstract high ideals and concrete practical morality, but this duality has usually been taken for granted. One simply admits that man is a sinner and the world of itself corrupt, and that unless one is a saint, one cannot live up to high ideals. The most one can do is to mitigate things here and there, with a bad conscience over one's ineptitude and imperfections.

The disquieting but perhaps promising thing today is that our sensitivity to our own responsibility for the prevailing social order is becoming increasingly acute; we feel that our responsibility goes further than an occasional bad conscience; that we are jointly responsible for the social environment that compels us to act in the wrong way.

As in the case of tax paying, we recognize the existence of a tendency in us to want to alter and create laws compelling us to act altruistically in real situations. The same abstract morality is forcing us to create a social order that will cease to compel us to act egocentrically or even asocially.

Although all this is very promising, as long as the relation between practical morality and abstract morality is not clearly understood, the increasing social sensitivity and the increasing pressure to act egocentrically despite it is very disquieting and only adds to the same basic uncertainty we have diagnosed from so many angles. Without some higher moral or religious authority to interpret to the individual these trends in the transformation of his conscience, it can hardly be expected that people will understand what is going on in them and in the world.

3. The Crisis in Valuation

This transformation of our moral sensitivity is only one aspect of a more comprehensive crisis in valuation, which is a part of our changing age. While to the sociologist it is a matter of course that men's values are bound to change in an age of transformation, it greatly bewilders the man in the street, and is a mental burden to many thinkers who have not yet related their findings to the social context.

Changes in social organization bring about changes in patterns of action and social preferences. Therefore it is only natural that a change in valuations should be part of a dynamic society. It is secondary whether the change is caused by technological inventions provoking a new division of labor which, in turn, calls for new work habits and a revaluation of achievement, and so on; or whether change results from greater social mobility, many people rising in the social scale, others falling, and thereby coming into contact with the different standards of a different social status. Social change again may be the result of the necessity for migration, labor following capital, relocation of industry, enforced transfer of population, in order to solve problems of political or racial discord; or, finally, change is brought about by the fusion of regions or the collaboration of nations who through trade, communication, and travel learn about each other. In all these cases, the basic process is the same. Through some sort of change, individuals and groups learn different ways of acting, of forming human relationships, of consuming goods or enjoying leisure, of making contacts and building up friendship, of shaping their political organization and choosing their leaders, or of worshiping God.

Social change makes us live in a multipatterned society with various ways of doing the same thing and achieving the same end. Where simple society has but one or two ways of doing the thing, and it is more or less pre-established which is the right choice, we are constantly faced with a surfeit of choices. To a person conditioned and educated for a static society, there is something bewildering in that very increase of choices and of valuations. Very soon an awareness of the variety of valuations develops and with it consciousness of the crisis this engenders. In the approach of the sociologist, valuations are traffic lights set up by society to inform the individual in which direction he should move, how he should behave or react, of what he should approve or disapprove. Without such valuations, no co-ordination of action and no organization of a consistent character is possible. It is no wonder, therefore, that the most disturbing effect of changing society is experienced in the uncertainty of valuations.

Innumerable disturbances and conflicts are caused if people who are expected to co-operate have different preferences or cling to different patterns of behavior. When one wants an authoritarian organization of work where there is strict command and obedience and everyone knows his place and task, while the other wants an informal organization where more initiative is left to individual members of the group, then it is difficult to see how the two can co-operate.

Similarly, it is difficult to foresee how groups will get on with one another if some adhere to the ascetic way of life and praise self-denial while others seek self-expression. Very often this difference in our society parallels the conflict between rural or small-town tradition and cosmopolitan tendencies—the former still maintaining the discipline of family influence and primary-group habits, whereas the latter affords opportunities and inducements to self-indulgence natural to cosmopolitan living on imports and exports, both material and mental.

The first effect of the clash between different valuations, as we have said, is confusion—a fundamental bewilderment—producing the same type of basic anxiety we have discussed repeatedly. This anxiety is different from concrete fear. When we are afraid of something, we know what it is and the concreteness of the object provokes a concrete type of fear with which we are familiar; but anxiety partakes of that uncertainty implied when we say that the bottom has fallen out of our world. The reaction to anxiety is a philosophy of relativism, which may readily lead to nihilism. In the recent past this appeared first in the form of 'historism' teaching the relativity of all values as products of their culture only: hence nothing is absolutely right or wrong. As a defense against this relativism, two methods are feasible. One is that of denial: we may deny that such relativity exists or that the problem exists at all. Thus we deal with it identically as we dealt with the problem of prostitution and venereal disease —by not talking about them. And by ignoring them it was hoped that they would somehow disappear or that fewer people would be affected by them. But as the number of conflicting situations increase, conflict has to be admitted. We reach a higher stage when we admit the conflict and try to find methods of coping with it.

The method of denial will, of course, be in the spirit of orthodoxy. The person who has to admit that there is something wrong in the world which cannot easily be denied, and that this new thing threatens his previous beliefs, tends first of all to reassure himself by emphasizing even more the significance of the orthodox attitudes and values which he harbors. Orthodoxy is not simply conservatism—not a primary, direct attitude of the mind—but a form of reaction. The conservative lives in his traditions unconsciously, taking them for granted and handling them lightly because he is not afraid of losing them. The reactionary, however, is rigid because he is afraid of losing a kind of certainty that is an integral part of his life. Endless uncertainty leading to relativism and nihilism on the one hand and to orthodoxy on the other are just two sides of the same coin, different reactions to the same disturbing process which we call the crisis in valuation. From another angle they both reveal the same fundamental uncertainty, and a remedy for them can only be found if their significance is acknowledged and brought within the scope of conscious planning.

There can be a solution to uncertainty and anxieties only if we learn how to live in a changing society, how to think in terms of an open system, and how to balance ourselves when everything is 'on the move.' A moving bicycle, to use the nearest analogy in the physical world, cannot be made safe by static support but only by a technique that copes with change through the rider's adapting himself to the ever-changing equilibrium. This new technique of balancing is not relativism but rather the formula of changing equilibrium—stability during change.

4. The Self and Its Anxieties

Different sources of uncertainty do not exist separately but converge, reaching a climax when they affect the core of personality. We feel that not only certain segments of life are unstable, but that the source of our inner unity, the experience of the Self, is also exposed to the jarring effect of a changing world.

What we have discussed so far has referred primarily to partial influences. Behavior and conduct have been shaken out of their traditional settings and have become uncertain. But the continued collapse of behavior patterns and the fact that criteria of conduct are changing are sooner or later bound to lead to changes in our whole personality structure. Such mutation of personality is a phenomenon well known to the historian of civilization. In the traditional religious language, one would speak of 'conversion.' Indeed, it is a great asset to a culture if it has given a name to such sudden changes, because the existence of such accepted patterns of personality transformation helps greatly in transforming ourselves. The sociological meaning of the idea of conversion is that it sanctions the total change of personality, it admits that such a thing may happen and is even necessary as long as it leads to the realization of a new vision of life and personality. The concept of conversion implies that the small shocks we suffer are gradually integrated into a powerful urge to head ourselves in a different direction in the realization that these changes are bound to affect the core of personality. Through the idea of conversion we can consciously cling to the new way of life and liquidate old forms of conduct along with their criteria of right or wrong. In a society in which the pattern of conversion has not been admitted or fully developed, change will be more difficult and much of it will have to take place under cover. If social change is slow and protracted, one can hide the gradual change from oneself. But if great changes occur within one's lifetime one can scarcely fail to take cognizance of them. In such cases conversion—the admitted changing of one's mind and personality—is the fundamental pattern of successful adjustment.

The idea of conversion in religious experience focuses our attention not on the transformation of behavior and conduct, but directly on something that the person too much inclined to externalize social observation will hardly notice. The fact is that the greatest anxiety occurs in a person not on the level of his outward behavior but in the inward revaluation of himself. Everybody lives by established forms of self-esteem.

The ultimate source of self-esteem is society, and it is a situation peculiar to highly differentiated societies that this self-esteem may emancipate itself from social controls. Normally, the source of self-esteem or self-evaluation is society, because the pride we take in ourselves is instilled very carefully through our whole education. Society keeps its hold on us by developing strongly this pride and self-esteem. A person bereft of self-respect and no longer caring, tends toward personality disintegration. Now this carefully build-up self-esteem is normally, as we have pointed out, the molding factor of our conduct. It tells us, 'You are not a gentleman unless you play the game according to the rules.' We appeal to the pride of the person, in this case pride linked to social status, in order to elicit a well-defined type of response. This is quite different from conditioning and habit-forming, where through a hidden mechanism, we merely condition automatic responses. Here, every stimulus to act in a given way works through an appeal to the core of our personality, that is to say, our self-assurance.

The source of this pride and self-esteem may vary with societies. But no society can survive in the long run without building up in its members such a focus of self-assurance from certain clearly visible sources. One of the great upheavals, accompanied by deep anxiety, develops when the sources of self-esteem change. In our rural and urban societies one of the deepest sources of self-confidence was the family. The family as a center of social pride and social esteem is strongly developed in the world of rural and urban property. Man derivés his most obvious social prestige from his family background. You are born into a status and you find your place in the world, your duties and privileges defined according to this status. Now this source of status is shifting in our society. At present our rural and urban family-and-property complex still matters as the ultimate source of social and self-esteem. We still play social roles developed in connection with these older institutions. But with the rise of the new organized social units and metropolitan life, the primary definition of status as family extraction gradually recedes.

One of the more recent sources of self-assurance based upon organized group life was the Army, which, of course, also relied upon feudal and even older sources of the idea of honor; but its way of regulating and distributing status and rank according to objective functions was quite different. The same applies to business and its power to define status and self-esteem, and to what we call public life with its free-lance career patterns and the pride and self-confidence that go with success. Whereas military prestige belongs to the Army, in the life of the artist and scientist fame is the criterion of self-esteem borrowed from society. Add to this in totalitarian societies membership in the hierarchy of the one-party system, which cuts across and overshadows earlier forms of self-assurance. All of these shifts from one source of self-esteem to another, from one mainspring of pride to another, are frightening; the more so since conventional roles accompanying one or the other form of self-confidence are also changing.

The earthquake is felt more strongly when it reaches the level of the Self and causes mutation in it. The Self is the deepest point to which social transformation can penetrate, and if there is no external support, no social provision for overcoming the fear of losing one's niche in society from which self-assurance originates, basic insecurity will be recognized as one's greatest bedevilment. It is from this standpoint that the fear of freedom, described in such a masterly way by Erich Fromm,[9] appears as one typical fear concerning the Self. Fear of freedom comes from mobility from one society to another or from one age into another, in which the patterns of coercion and freedom are different. There are people who are accustomed to rigid discipline regulating many things. If they are set free suddenly their first reaction is fear—just as an Englishman will first react with anxieties in French surroundings where there is greater or at any rate very different scope for self-indulgence.

In the same way, if we move from a society with a well-established ritual to one in which enlightenment and social mobility create more and more liberty or even license, the first reaction will again be one of anxiety leading, for some people at least, to orthodoxy—a kind of enforced reversion to the previous rigidity and the certainty that seemed to accompany it.

Anxieties of the Self cause the deepest insecurity. They are the culmination of uncertainties arising from various sources. If there is nothing to aid us in overcoming these fears, only destruction and chaos can ensue.

5. The Need for Diagnosis, Guidance, and Integration

On the intellectual level, insight into the main sources of anxiety, which develop from the uncertainties of life in a changing society, points in the same direction. As such changes as we are expected to meet cannot be mastered by the average person as an individual, some collective guidance is wanted. A new type of thought is necessary to cope with the magnitude of the problems.

To the minds of men in the past the changes in external conditions might have seemed even greater. But these men lived in an age when adjustment was unconscious, and not yet conceived as a process about which something could be done in the way of guiding human affairs. In our age we are passing from the stage of tacit adjustment and tacit integration to deliberate reconstruction; we believe in the purposeful guidance of human affairs. This does not mean that we can hope to master the whole turmoil of facts and the onslaught of an entirely changing world system. But social intelligence has reached a stage where we can be satisfied only if we have done our best to disentangle the causes and to master the course of events from the strategic points available to us.

Even though we know that we may ultimately be driven by forces stronger than ourselves, we should lose our moorings altogether were we to give up at least trying to interpret the situation in which we live. Responsibility for social matters has increased since we have learned to disentangle causes and effects on the social scene.

In periods of change in the past it was the function of religions and of the Church to interpret the transition: to let the members of the community know man's fate, his place in the world, and what man should live by. Today, such collective guidance will have to embody the sociological approach, in order that we may understand social change and its causes.

It is obviously equally wrong to think that the formidable transformation through which we are passing can be endured without spiritual guidance, or to think that religious guidance with its traditional means of interpreting the world situation is sufficient. If the sociologist realizes that for many reasons there is need of spiritual power to integrate people, this does not mean that he endorses clericalism or any superimposed creed. He merely recognizes that religion fulfils certain indispensable functions in this age of transition. Without such guidance there may be many more or less successful individual and group adjustments. But if these have no focus and no direction, and if there is no authority and no consistency in what they do, disorganization is bound to continue. The personality pattern is disrupted because it gradually becomes meaningless. There remains only a split personality: no consistent conduct can develop. On the level of group adjustment we have shifting policies but no central policy derived from understanding of the whole.

In the past religion fulfilled these functions of interpretation and integration. In the old days religion was a stabilizer; today we turn to it again for assistance in the transition. That means that our religious leaders must keep up with the changing order, building their world outlook and policy upon deeper insight and intellectual comprehension. In view of our need for balance, their interpretation must not be so extremist as to destroy the psychological equilibrium and feeling of security during the transition.

Thus, apart from its internal significance, in the period ahead dynamic religion has three major functions in the social order: (1) diagnosing society in transition; (2) focusing attention on important issues; and (3) integrating human conduct on the various levels of social life.*

* Here the MS. breaks off, not, however, without an indication that the author intended to elaborate this integrating function of a progressive religion. Ed.

Notes

○

CHAPTER 1. MAIN SYMPTOMS OF THE CRISIS

1. This development can be traced from the following table, taken from J. R. Hicks and A. R. Hart, *The Social Framework of the American Economy* (New York, 1945), p. 39.

Population (in millions)

	1650	1800	1850	1900	1940
Great Britain	6	10	21	37	46
France	16	27	35	41	42
Germany	14	20	35	54	70
Italy	13	17	24	32	44
U.S.A.	..	5	23	75	131
Ireland	1	5	6½	4½	4¼

2. Cf. Gilfillan, S. C., *The Sociology of Invention* (Chicago, 1935). Ogburn, W. F., *Social Change* (New York, 1929).

3. Sir George Cornewall Lewis, in 1841, summed up 'the advantages derived by the dominant country from its supremacy over a dependency under the following heads:

   1. Tribute or revenue paid by the dependency.
   2. Assistance for military or naval purposes furnished by the dependency.
   3. Advantages to the dominant country from its trade with a dependency.
   4. Facilities afforded by dependencies to the dominant country for the emigration of its surplus population, and for an advantageous employment of its capital.
   5. Transportation of convicts to a dependency.
   6. Glory of possessing dependencies.'

From *An Essay on the Government of Dependencies*, ed. with an Introduction by C. P. Lucas (Oxford, 1891), p. xlv.

4. Mumford, Lewis, *Faith for Living* (New York, 1940), p. 149.

5. 'It is argued that the economic opportunities for investment available in the 19th century were the consequence of there being vast uncultivated or semi-cultivated areas and great demand for goods by an increasing population. More recently, it is argued, the basic capital installations—mines, railways, factories, tele-communications, etc.—have been provided and required, not total replacement, but only maintenance, repair and improvement. Even such improvement, it is argued, gives more productive results with less capital

outlay than before. Hence, economic expansion is to be sought by more intensive cultivation, industrial or otherwise, of the opportunities still remaining. Even then it is thought difficult to discover ways of using all the natural savings and feared that in default of a comprehensive fiscal policy some of the savings may be simply sterilised by hoarding.' H. Finer, *The T.V.A.* (Montreal, 1944), p. 218, note 2.

Hansen, A. H., *Fiscal Policy and Business Cycles* (New York, 1941), ch. xvi.

Temporary National Economic Committee Hearings, Part 9.

Ibid. Currie, pp. 352off.

6. Easum, Chester V., *Karl Schurz* (Weimar, 1937).

7. Arendt, Hannah, 'The Concentration Camps,' *Partisan Review,* vol. xv, no. 7, pp. 762f.

(Balticus), 'The Two "G"s: Gestapo and GPU, Phenomena of Modern Revolution,' *Foreign Affairs* (1939), vol. 17, pp. 489-507.

Baron, Salo W., *A Social Religious History of the Jews* (New York, 1937).

Bettelheim, Bruno, 'Concentration Camps, German,' *Ten Eventful Years* (Chicago, 1947), vol. 2.

—— 'Individual and Mass Behavior in Extreme Situations,' *Journal of Abnormal and Social Psychology,* vol. 38, no. 4.

Bloch, Herbert A., 'The Personality of Inmates of Concentration Camps,' *American Journal of Sociology* (Jan. 1947), vol. 52.

Bondy, Curt, 'Problems of Internment Camps,' *Journal of Abnormal and Social Psychology,* vol. 38, no. 4.

Bramsted, Ernest K., *Dictatorship and Political Police* (London, 1945).

Kautsky, Benedict, *Teufel und Verdammte* (Zurich, 1946).

Kogon, Eugen, *Der SS-Staat* (Berlin, 1947).

Rousset, David, *The Other Kingdom* (New York, 1947).

8. Coulton, G. G., *The Medieval Village* (Cambridge, 1925).

9. For sociological definitions see Max Weber, *The Theory of Social and Economic Organization,* tr. by A. M. Henderson and Talcott Parsons, ed. with an Introduction by Talcott Parsons (New York, 1947), pp. 140, 238-45.

Cahn, Edmond N. (ed.), *Social Meaning of Legal Concepts* (New York, 1948), no. 1, 'Inheritance of Property and the Power of Testamentary Disposition.' (An annual conference conducted by the New York University School of Law.)

10. See note 53, ch. 5.

11. Cf. Brady, R. A., *Business as a System of Power* (New York, 1943).

Schumpeter, Joseph A., *Business Cycles* (New York, 1939).

12. See, for instance, the observations made in the recent social development in Central Asia by G. and M. Wilson, *The Analysis of Social Change* (Cambridge, 1945).

13. It is characteristic that in England after the war Field Marshal Montgomery laid down the rule that the patterns and standards of life in the Army should be similar to those of civil society.

14. Cf. Cooley's idea of over-formalization, 'Formalism and Disorganization,' *Social Organization* (New York, 1924), ch. xvi.

15. For a case study of a radio-manipulated public scare and the confusion of the public, cf. Cantril, Hadley, *The Invasion from Mars* (Princeton, 1940).

16. 'Freedom of Inquiry and Expression, a Collection of Facts and Judgments concerning Freedom and Suppression of Freedom of All Forms of Intellectual Life,' *The Annals of the American Academy of Political and Social Science* (Nov. 1938), vol. 200.

Lippmann, Walter, *Public Opinion* (New York, 1922; Pelican, 1946).

Lovejoy, A. D., 'Professional Ethics and Social Progress,' *The North American Review*, vol. 219, pp. 398-407.

MacIver, Robert, 'The Social Significance of Professional Ethics,' *The Annals* (Amer. Acad. Soc. Pol. Science), vol. 101, pp. 5-11.

Parsons, Talcott, 'The Professions and Social Structure,' *Social Forces* (May, 1939), vol. 17, pp. 457-87.

Steed, Wickham, *The Press* (London, 1938, Penguin ed.).

Whitehead, Alfred North, 'Aspects of Freedom,' *Freedom Its Meaning*, planned and edited by Ruth Nanda Anshen (New York, 1940).

17. Durkheim, Emile, *Le Suicide, étude de sociologie* (Paris, 1897), pp. 272-88. (Translated by William C. Bradbury, Jr., with an Introduction by Sebastian de Grazia. *University Observer*, Chicago, Winter 1947.)

CHAPTER 2. ALTERNATIVE RESPONSES TO THE SITUATION

1. Stern, Bernard J., 'Soviet Policy on National Minorities,' *American Sociological Review* (June 1944), vol. 9, no. 3, pp. 229-39.

Kohn, Hans, *Der Nationalismus in der Soviet Union* (Frankfurt, 1932).

2. *Soviet Russia: A Selected List of Recent References*, Library of Congress, Division of Bibliography (Washington, D.C., 1943), pp. 56-65.

Juergens, Adolf (ed.), *Ergebnisse deutscher Wissenschaft: Eine bibliographische Auswahl aus der deutschen wissenschaftlichen Literatur der Jahre 1933-1938* (New York, 1939), esp. pp. 301-440.

Sington, Derrick, and Weidenfeld, Arthur, *The Goebbels Experiment: A Study of the Nazi Propaganda Machine* (New Haven, 1943).

3. Linden, Franz, 'Sozialismus und Religion: "Konfessionssoziologische Untersuchung der Labor Party 1929-31,"' *Koelner Anglistische Arbeiten* (Leipzig, 1932), vol. 17.

Laun, Justus F., *Soziales Christentum in England, Geschichte und Gedankenwelt der Copec-Bewegung* (Berlin, 1926).

Wearmouth, Robert F., *Methodism and the Working-Class Movement of England* (London, 1937).

4. Lenin, V., 'Karl Marx,' *Collected Works* (New York, 1930), vol. 18, pp. 13-58. (Bibliography on Marxism, pp. 47-58.)

Venable, Vernon, *Human Nature: The Marxian View* (New York, 1945). (Reviewed by Oscar Lange in *The New York Times*, 15 July 1945.)

5. Rosenberg, Arthur, *Democracy and Socialism* (New York, 1937).

6. For a comparison of Marx's, Bakunin's, and Sorel's concepts of 'rich and poor,' of 'proletariat and Lumpenproletariat,' 'mass and class,' see Michael Freund, *Georges Sorel: Der Revolutionaere Konservativismus* (Frankfurt, 1932), pp. 41ff., 286ff.

7. Cf. Harding, T. Swann, 'Strikes are Anachronistic in Industrial Conflict,' 1939. *Yearbook of the Society for the Psychological Study of Social Issues* (New York, 1939).

8. Rudolf Hilferding before World War I observed the emergence of the ' "new middle class" the growth of which surpasses even that of the proletariat.' He predicted that 'the development will drive these strata, indispensable for production, to the side of the proletariat, especially when the power relations will have been shaken,' in his *Finanzkapital: eine Studie ueber die juengste Entwicklung des Kapitalismus* (Berlin, 1910; reprinted 1947), pp. 482, 483. This prediction was not realized. With the exception of the Viennese Social Democratic party, Marxist parties on the Continent, whether revisionist or revolutionary, failed to win the support of anticapitalist-minded middle classes. Nationalism and imperialist militarism won out. The Leninist alliance of the proletariat with the peasantry could not be repeated in Central Europe.

9. Leninist theory worked out the revolutionary 'strategy of defeat' in an age of imperialist war and linked the problems of revolution and war. The Spanish and the Chinese civil wars, the agrarian revolution of Eastern Europe under Soviet occupation, have demonstrated the interrelation between war and revolution.

10. Cf. note 5, ch. 6.

11. As Georg Lukacs advocated: 'Freedom can represent a value *per se* as little as socialization. *Freedom has to serve the rule of the Proletariat, not vice versa.*' Lukacs, Georg, *Geschichte und Klassenbewusstsein* (Berlin, 1923), p. 296; see also pp. 317ff., 322, 324.

12. The enumeration of principles that should guide our interference with a changing environment is a first step in the application of scientific thinking to social affairs. When we act, we usually act for the sake of one or more guiding values, although we usually fail to make those values explicit. Practical action therefore resembles quite often the behavior of an infant who, even while acting, changes his purpose. If we act reasonably, however, we choose between competing values and act accordingly. But in political action, we usually proceed once more in an infantile manner. The accepted hierarchy of values is adumbrated, but our preferences oscillate. Even if we agree on a value to guide our decisions, we fail to examine the alternative desiderata on the basis of a careful deliberation. In an unplanned society, this is, so to speak, the natural state of affairs; but the more we move toward a planned society—in which non-interference in most spheres is an accepted principle—the gradual elaboration and conscious awareness of our agreed value-hierarchy tends to become normal. This will be followed by a thorough evaluation of the means at our disposal. In no other way is it possible to establish agreement on long-range policy. It is for this reason that we try to supplement the previous haphazard enumeration of purposes and aims in democratic planning in a more systematic manner. It will help to make our choice more consistent.

13. Dicey, A. V., *Lectures on the Relation between Law and Public Opinion in England during the Nineteenth Century* (London, 1905).

CHAPTER 3. ON POWER—A CHAPTER IN POLITICAL SOCIOLOGY

1. The bibliography on 'Power' in Mannheim, Karl, *Man and Society in an Age of Reconstruction* (New York, 1940) may be supplemented by:

Anderson, H. D., and Davidson, P. F., *Ballots and the Democratic Class Struggle* (Palo Alto, 1943).

Bryce, James, 'Obedience' in his *Studies in History and Jurisprudence* (New York, 1901), pp. 463-502.

Bryson, Lyman, *et al.* (eds.), *Conflicts of Power in Modern Culture* (New York, London, 1947).

Burckhardt, Jakob, *Weltgeschichtliche Betrachtungen* (Berlin, Stuttgart, 1905). (Ed. by James Nichols as *Force and Freedom: Reflections on History*, New York, 1943.)

Heller, H., 'Power, Political,' *Encyc. Soc. Sciences* (New York, 1937), vol. XII, pp. 300-305.

Laski, H. J., *A Grammar of Politics* (2nd ed., London, 1929).

Lasswell, H. D., *Politics: Who Gets What, When, How* (New York, 1936).

—— *Psychopathology and Politics* (Chicago, 1934).

—— *World Politics and Personal Insecurity* (New York, 1935).

—— *The Analysis of Political Behaviour: An Empirical Approach* (New York, 1948).

—— *Power and Personality* (New York, 1948).

MacIver, R., *The Web of Government* (New York, 1947).

Schmitt, Carl, *Verfassungslehre* (Munich, Leipzig, 1928).

Willoughby, W. W., *The Ethical Basis of Political Authority* (New York, 1930).

2. Burckhardt, Jakob, *The Civilization of the Renaissance* (London, New York, 1944), p. 2.

3. Mosca, Gaetano, *The Ruling Class* (Elementi di Scienza Politica), tr. by Hannah D. Kahn, ed. and rev., with an Introduction by Arthur Livingston (New York, 1939), ch. II, 'The Ruling Class,' ch. IV, 'Ruling Class and Social Type.'

4. Ibid.; see also Cox, Oliver Cromwell, *Caste, Class, and Race: A Study in Social Dynamics* (New York, 1948), ch. X, 'The Political Class.' Cox's work contains 14 pages of bibliography on social stratification.

5. Barnard, Chester I., *The Functions of the Executive* (Cambridge, 1938).

Dimock, Marshall E., and Hyde, Howard K., 'Bureaucracy and Trusteeship in Large Corporations,' *T.N.E.C.: Investigation of Concentration of Economic Power*, Monograph no. 11 (Washington, D.C., 1940).

Gablentz, O. H. von der, 'Industriebürokratie,' *Schmollers Jahrbuch* (1926), vol. 50, pp. 539-72.

Moore, Wilbert E., 'Industrial Organization: Management,' in his *Industrial Relations and the Social Order* (New York, 1946). (Extensive bibliography.)

'The 30,000 Managers,' *Fortune* (Feb. 1940), vol. 21, pp. 58-63, 106, 108, 111.

6. Cf. Max Weber's comments on collegiate bodies of notables and the advisory function of interest groups as supplementary to bureaucratic man-

agement. *From Max Weber: Essays in Sociology*, tr., ed., and with an Introduction by H. H. Gerth and C. Wright Mills (New York, 1946), pp. 238f. (Hereafter cited as Max Weber, *Essays in Sociology*.)

7. Lederer, Emil, and Marschak, Jakob, 'Die Klassen auf dem Arbeitsmarkt und ihre Organisationen,' *Grundriss der Sozialökonomik*, Abt. IX. Part II (Tuebingen, 1927), ch. IV, pp. 106-320.

Mills, C. Wright, *The New Men of Power, America's Labor Leaders* (New York, 1948).

Perlman, Selig, and Taft, Philip, *History of Labor in the United States* (New York, 1935), vol. IV, *Labor Movements* (1896-1932).

'Trade Unions,' *Encyc. Soc. Sciences*, vol. XV, pp. 3-57.

Webb, Sidney and Beatrice, *The History of Trade Unionism* (rev. ed. London, 1920).

8. Childs, Marquis W., *Sweden, the Middle Way* (New Haven, 1936; Pelican ed. 1948).

9. Merton, Robert King, 'Bureaucratic Structure and Personality,' *Social Forces* (May 1940), vol. 18, pp. 560-68

10. Mosca, op. cit. p. 159.

11. Thompson, D., *et al.*, *Patterns of Peacemaking* (London, 1945).

12. Hacseert, J., *Essai de sociologie* (Ghent, 1946), pp. 176ff.

13. Goldhamer, H., and Shils, Edward A., 'Types of Power and Status,' *The American Journal of Sociology* (Sept. 1939), vol. 45, no. 2, pp. 171-82. Cf. also Mannheim, *Man and Society*, p. 167.

Weber, Max, 'Herrschaft,' in his *Wirtschaft und Gesellschaft*, Abt. III, *Grundriss der Sozialoekonomik* (Tuebingen, 1925), pp. 603-12.

14. Weber, Max, 'Hinduismus und Buddhismus,' *Gesammelte Aufsaetze zur Religionssoziologie* (Tuebingen, 1921), vol. II, p. 72. Cf. Mannheim, op. cit. p. 276.

15. Colm, Gerhart, 'Masse,' *Handwörterbuch der Soziologie* (Stuttgart, 1931).

Davenport, F. M., *Primitive Traits in Religious Revivals* (New York, 1905), ch. III.

Dollard, John, *Caste and Class in a Southern Town* (New Haven, 1937).

DuBois, Weis E., *Dusk of Dawn* (New York, 1940).

Freud, Sigmund, *Massenpsychologie und Ich-Analyse* (2nd ed. Wien, 1923). (Tr. by James Strachey, London, 1922.)

Geiger, T., *Die Masse und ihre Aktion* (Stuttgart, 1926).

Hardman, J. B. S., 'Masses,' *Encyc. Soc. Sciences*, vol. X; see also the articles on 'Mob' (L. L. Bernard), 'Lynching' (F. W. Coker), 'Violence' (Sidney Hook), 'Riot' (K. Smellie), 'Crowd' (L. L. Bernard), 'Massacre' (H. H. Brailsford).

Hecker, J. F. C., *The Black Death and the Dancing Mania of the Middle Ages* (New York, 1885). (Tr. by B. G. Babington.)

Ichheiser, Gustav, 'Fear of Violence and Fear of Fraud with Some Remarks on the Social Psychology of Antisemitism,' *Sociometry* (Nov. 1944), vol. VII, no. 4, pp. 376-83.

LeBon, Gustave, *The Crowd* (London, 1920).

—— *The Psychology of Revolution* (New York, 1913).

Lederer, Emil, *The State of the Masses* (New York, 1940).

Mackay, Charles, *Extraordinary Popular Delusions and the Madness of Crowds* (Boston, 1932).

Martin, Everett Dean, *The Behavior of Crowds* (New York, 1920).

Moll, A., *Hypnotism* (London, 1891).

Myrdal, Gunnar, *An American Dilemma* (New York, 1944), ch. 27, pp. 558-69.

Wiese, Leopold von, and Becker, Howard, *Systematic Sociology on the Basis of the Beziehungslehre and Gebildelehre* (New York, London, 1932), ch. XXXIV-XXXVI, pp. 445-73.

16. Cf. Jaspers, Karl, 'Die enthusiastische Einstellung,' in his *Psychologie der Weltanschauungen* (Berlin, 1921), p. 125.

17. Elias, Norbert, *Ueber den Prozess der Zivilisation, Soziogenetische Untersuchungen* (Basel, 1937-8), vol. I: *Wandlungen des Verhaltens in den weltlichen Oberschichten des Abendlandes;* vol. II: *Wandlungen der Gesellschaft. Entwurf zu einer Theorie der Zivilisation.*

18. Sumner, William G., *Folkways* (Boston, 1906), p. 57.

19. Hughes, E. C., 'Institutions,' *An Outline of the Principles of Sociology*, ed. by Robert E. Park (New York, 1939), p. 332. Cf. also Lumley, Frederick Elmore, *Means of Social Control* (New York, 1925) and 'Power, Political' (Hermann Heller), and 'Sanction, Social' (Radcliff Brown) in *Encyc. Soc. Sciences*, vols. XII and XIII.

20. Gaus, John M., *Great Britain, A Study in Civil Loyalty* (Chicago, 1929). Ziegfeld, A. Hillen, *England in der Entscheidung: Eine freimütige Deutung der englischen Wirklichkeit* (Leipzig, 1938).

21. Kosok, Paul, *Modern Germany, a Study of Conflicting Loyalties* (Chicago, 1933). Becker, Howard, *German Youth: Bond or Free* (New York, 1946).

22. See examples in Ogburn, William F., and Nimkoff, M. F., *Sociology* (New York, 1940).

23. 'Des Grossen Macht zeigt sich darin, dass man innehaelt,' Z-King (*Buch der Wandlungen*), vol. III, 34, Chinese, 1000 B.C. Cf. also Jakob Burckhardt's discussion of Historical Greatness in *Force and Freedom*, op. cit.

24. Weber, Max, *Essays in Sociology*, op. cit. pp. 162f.

25. MacIver, R. M., *Community* (New York, 1921). Toennies, Ferdinand, *Fundamental Concepts of Sociology: Gemeinschaft und Gesellschaft*, tr. and supplemented by Charles P. Loomis (New York, 1940; first ed. 1887, 8th ed. 1935).

26. The fact that the various immigrant stocks have a varied prestige in the U.S.A.—the Italians, Negroes, e.g. as contrasted with British, Norwegian, and Dutch settlers—is the case in point.

27. Weber, Max, *Gesammelte Aufsaetze zur Wissenschaftlehre* (Tuebingen, 1922), pp. 64f. 132f.

28. It is hardly necessary to point out that in our view, too, one of the driving forces of Imperialism is to be found in economic interests. Their man

agement is a task in itself. What we are discussing here are the purely emotional roots which are equally significant determinants and deserve a structural analysis of their own. A thorough discussion ought to envisage the explosive force that ensues from the combination of economic and emotional expansionism.

On Nationalism see:

Bauer, Otto, *Die Nationalitaetenfrage und die Sozialdemokratie* (Wien, 1924).

Bishoff, Ralph Frederic, *Nazi Conquest through German Culture* (Cambridge, 1942).

Hayes, Carlton J. H., *Essays on Nationalism* (New York, 1926).

―― *France, a Nation of Patriots* (New York, 1930).

―― *The Historical Evolution of Modern Nationalism* (New York, 1931).

―― 'Nationalism,' *Encyc. Soc. Sciences*, vol. XI, pp. 231-48.

Hertz, F., *The Historical Evolution of Modern Nationalism* (New York, 1931).

―― *Nationality in History and Politics* (London, 1944).

―― 'Zur Soziologie der Nation und des Nationalbewusstseins,' *Archiv fuer Sozialwissenschaft und Sozialpolitik* (1931), vol. LXV, pp. 1-60.

Klineberg, Otto, 'A Science of National Character,' *The Journal of Social Psychology*, S.P.S.S.I. Bulletin (1944), pp. 147-62.

Kohn, Hans, *Geschichte der nationalen Bewegungen im Orient* (Berlin, 1928). (Tr. by M. M. Green, London, 1929.)

―― *The Idea of Nationalism, a Study in Its Origins and Background* (New York, 1944).

―― *Nationalismus und Imperialismus in Vorderen Orient* (Frankfurt, 1931). (Tr. by M. M. Green, London, 1932.)

Lenin, N., *Ueber die nationale Frage* (Berlin, 1930-31), 2 vols.

Marr, Heinz, *Die Massenwelt im Kampf um ihre Form* (Hamburg, 1934).

Meinecke, F., *Weltbuergertum und Nationalstaat* (5th ed. Munich, 1922).

Nationalism (London, New York, 1939), A Report by a Study Group of Members of the Royal Institute of International Affairs.

Nicolson, Harold. *The Meaning of Prestige* (lecture) (Cambridge, 1937).

Riemer, Svend, 'Individual and National Psychology: A Problem in the Army Area Study,' *Social Forces* (March 1944), vol. 22, no. 3, pp. 256-61.

Sulzbach, Werner, *Nationales Gemeinschaftsgefuehl und wirtschaftliches Interesse* (Leipzig, 1929).

Stalin, J., *Marxism and the National and Colonial Question* (New York, 1936).

Weber, Max, *Essays in Sociology*, op. cit. ch. VI, 'Structures of Power,' pp. 159-79, esp. p. 162.

Weinberg, Albert K., *Manifest Destiny, A Study of Nationalist Expansionism in American History* (Baltimore, 1935).

Ziegler, Heinz O., *Die moderne Nation, Ein Beitrag zur Politischen Soziologie* (Tuebingen, 1931).

29. We may refer to the conflicts between the State and Catholic Church in Bismarck and Hitler Germany, in Mexico, in Italy before 1929, in France at the beginning of the century. Cf. also Barker, Ernest, *Church, State Study* (London, 1930), ch. V, 'Christianity and Nationality.'

Borkenau, Franz, *The Communist International* (London, 1938).

Commons, John R., 'Labor Movement,' *Encyc. Soc. Sciences*, vol. VIII, pp. 682-96.

Latourette, Kenneth Scott, *A History of the Expansion of Christianity* (New York, 1937).

Lorwin, Lewis L., *Labor and Internationalism* (New York, 1929).

Perlman, Selig, *A Theory of the Labor Movement* (New York, 1928).

Sombart, Werner, *Der proletarische Sozialismus* (Marxismus) (10th ed. Jena, 1924), 2 vols. (Tr. from the 6th ed. by M. Epstein as *Socialism and the Social Movement*, London, 1909.)

Wach, Joachim, *Sociology of Religion* (Chicago, 1944), ch. VII. (Extensive bibliography.)

Weber, Max, 'Staat und Hierokratie,' *Wirtschaft und Gesellschaft*, Abt. III, *Grundriss der Sozialoekonomik* (Tuebingen, 1925), pp. 779-817.

30. Liepmann, Kate, *The Journey to Work* (London, New York, 1944), ch. IV, pp. 67-84. Cf. 'Housing,' *Encyc. Soc. Sciences*, vol. VII.

Park, R. E., Burgess, E. W., *et al.*, *The City* (Chicago, 1925); also the appendix, Wirth, Louis, 'A Bibliography of the Urban Community.'

Simmel, Georg, 'Die Grosstädte und das Geistesleben,' *Jahrbuch der Gehestiftung* (Dresden, 1903), vol. IX, pp. 185-206. (Tr. by H. Gerth and C. Wright Mills as 'Metropolis and Mental Life,' in *The Sociology of Georg Simmel*, Kurt Wolff ed., Glencoe, Illinois, 1950.)

Sutherland, Edwin H., *Principles of Criminology* (Philadelphia, 1939).

Thrasher, Frederic M., *The Gang, A Study of 1,313 Gangs in Chicago* (Chicago, 1927).

31. See Harold D. Lasswell's 'The Rise of the Propagandist,' in his *The Analysis of Political Behaviour: An Empirical Approach* (New York, 1948), pp. 173-9; further references in Smith, Bruce L., Lasswell, H. D., and Casey, Ralph D., *Propaganda, Communication, and Public Opinion, A Comprehensive Reference Guide* (Princeton, 1946).

32. Bird, Charles (W.), 'Suggestion and Suggestibility: A Bibliography,' *Psychological Bulletin* (April 1939), vol. 36, pp. 264-83.

Brailsford, H. N., 'Atrocities,' *Encyc. Soc. Sciences*, vol. II.

Cantril, Hadley, Gaudet, Hazel, and Hertzog, Herto, *The Invasion from Mars*, with the broadcast script of 'War of the Worlds' (Princeton, 1940).

The Chicago Commission on Race Relations, *The Negro in Chicago* (Chicago, 1922).

Frank, Walter, *Nationalismus und Demokratie im Frankreich der Dritten Republik 1871-1918* (Hamburg, 1933).

Gumbel, E., *4 Jahre politischer Mord* (Berlin, 1923).

Lasswell, H. D., *Propaganda Technique in the World War* (London, 1927), pp. 81-9.

Schumann, F. L., *The Nazi Dictatorship* (2nd ed. New York, 1936).

Silone, Ignazio, *Der Fascismus, seine Entstehung und seine Entwicklung* (Zurich, 1934), pp. 108ff., 179ff.

Weber, Max, *Essays in Sociology*, op. cit. pp. 394f.

33. The bibliographies of Roberto Michels' article 'Intellectuals,' *Encyc. Soc. Sciences*, and of Mannheim's *Man and Society*, op. cit., may be supplemented by the following titles:

Farrell, James T., 'The Fate of Writing in America,' *New Directions* 9 (New York, 1946).

Kandel, I. L., 'Overproduction of Intellectuals,' *School and Society* (Dec. 1946), vol. 64, no. 1169, p. 438.

Kohn-Bramstedt, E., *Aristocracy and the Middle Classes in Germany. Social Types in German Literature* (London, 1937), Part II.

Lasswell, H. D., 'Policy and the Intelligence Function: Ideological Intelligence,' *Ethics* (Oct. 1942). (Reprinted in *The Analysis of Political Behaviour*, op. cit.)

Lukacs, Georg, *Fortschritt und Reaktion in der deutschen Literatur* (Berlin, 1947).

McLuhan, Herbert Marshall, 'The New York Wits,' *Kenyon Review* (Winter 1945).

Michels, Robert, 'Zur intellektuellen Oberschicht,' cf. his *Umschichtungen in den herrschenden Klassen nach dem Kriege* (Stuttgart, 1934), pp. 58ff.

Mills, C. Wright, 'The Powerless People: The Social Role of the Intellectual,' *American Association of University Professors Bulletin* (Summer 1945), vol. 31, no. 2, pp. 231-45.

Russell, Bertrand, 'The Role of the Intellectual in the Modern World,' *American Journal of Sociology* (Jan. 1939), vol. 44, no. 4, pp. 491-8.

Schumpeter, Joseph A., 'The Sociology of the Intellectual,' in his *Capitalism, Socialism, and Democracy* (2nd ed. New York, London, 1947), pp. 145-55.

Spigelman, Joseph H., 'The Role of Intellectuals,' *Harper's Magazine* (Aug. 1946), vol. 193, no. 1155, pp. 183-92.

Weschler, James, *Revolt on the Campus* (New York, 1935).

34. See 'Motivation,' *Encyclopedia of Educational Research*, ed. by W. S. Monroe (New York, 1941), pp. 740f.

35. See D. Mitrany's theory of functional integration in his *A Working Peace System. An Argument for the Functional Development of International Organization* (London, 1943).

Bauer, Otto, *Rationalisierung, Fehlrationalisierung* (Wien, 1931).

Berle, A. A., and Means, Gardiner, *The Modern Corporation and Private Property* (New York, 1933).

Hilferding, Rudolf, *Das Finanzkapital* (Berlin, 1910; reprinted 1947).

Kehr, Eckart, 'Munitions Industry,' *Encyc. Soc. Sciences*, vol. XI, pp. 128-34.

Liefman, Robert, 'Cartel,' ibid. vol. III, pp. 234-43.

—— *International Cartels, Combines and Trusts* (London, 1927).

On Economic Imperialism see:

Bucharin, N., *Imperialismus und Weltwirtschaft* (Berlin, 1929).

Friedjung, Heinrich, *Das Zeitalter des Imperialismus* (Berlin, 1919-22), 3 vols., vol. II, ch. XXVI.

Hobson, J. A., *Imperialism* (rev. ed. London, 1905).

Luxemburg, Rosa, *Die Akkumulation des Kapitals* (Berlin, 1923).

Neumann, Franz, *Behemoth: The Structure and Practice of National Socialism* (New York, London, 1944).

Schumpeter, Josef, *Zur Soziologie der Imperialismen* (Tuebingen, 1919).

Sering, Paul, *Jenseits des Kapitalismus* (Nest Verlag, Lauf bei Nürnberg, Dec. 1946).

Sternberg, Fritz, *Der Imperialismus* (Berlin, 1926).

36. Cf. Mannheim, Karl, *Man and Society*, op. cit. Part V, I and II.

37. Cf. Lorwin, Lewis, *Time for Planning, A Social Economic Theory and Program for the 20th Century* (New York, London, 1945), pp. 258-9.

38. Cf. Merriam, Charles E., and Gosnell, Harold F., 'Disgust with Politics and Other Disbeliefs in Voting,' and 'General Indifference and Inertia,' in their *Non-Voting. Causes and Methods of Control* (Chicago, 1924), ch. VI and VII.

Fromm, Erich, *Escape from Freedom* (New York, 1941).

Horney, Karen, *The Neurotic Personality of Our Time* (New York, 1937).

Mannheim, Karl, *Man and Society*, op. cit.

Mills, C. Wright, 'The Powerless People: The Social Role of the Intellectual,' loc. cit.

39. These observations, made by the author immediately after the end of the war, have meanwhile been confirmed by experts in this vital field. E. M. Friedwald, for instance, points to the fact that 'saturation weapons have taken away a good deal of the margin of safety given by a vast territory. . . Straits, mountains, and geographical barriers, in general, have lost much if not all of their strategic value.' E. M. Friedwald, *Man's Last Choice* (London, 1947), pp. 53, 65.

CHAPTER 4. THE RULING CLASS IN CAPITALIST AND COMMUNIST SOCIETY

1. The following select titles are pertinent:

Abshagen, Karl Heinz, *King, Lords, and Gentlemen: Influence and Power of the English Upper Classes* (London, Toronto, 1939).

Almond, G. A., *Wealth and Politics in New York City*, MS. (New York, 1944).

Bauer, C., Strieder, J., and Corey, L., 'Fortunes, Private,' *Encyc. Soc. Sciences*, vol. VI, pp. 389-99.

Beach, Moses Yale, 'The Wealth and Biography of the Wealthy Citizens of the City of New York' (New York, 1855).

Beard, Miriam, *A History of the Business Man* (New York, 1938).

Brady, R. A., *Business as a System of Power* (New York, 1943).

Bienenfeld, F. R., *The Germans and the Jews* (London, 1939).

Bromfield, Louis, *Weal vs. Wealth* (New York, 1946).

Buchanan, D. H., *The Development of Capitalist Enterprise in India* (New York, 1934).

Corey, L., *The Decline of American Capitalism* (New York, 1934).

Cox, O. C., 'Estates, Social Classes and Political Classes,' *American Sociological Review* (Aug. 1945), vol. X, pp. 464-9.

—— *Caste, Class and Race* (New York, 1947), bibliography, pp. 587-600.

Davenport, N. E. H., *Vested Interests or Common Pool* (London, 1942).

Davis, Jerome, *Capitalism and Its Culture* (New York, 1935).

Delaisi, F., 'Les Financiers et la democratie,' *Crapouilliot* (Paris, Nov. 1936).

Ehrenberg, Richard, *Grosse Vermoegen, ihre Entstehung und ihre Bedeutung* (3rd ed. Jena, 1925), 2 vols.

Emden, Paul H., *Money Powers of Europe in the Nineteenth and Twentieth Centuries* (New York, London, 1938), bibliography pp. 411-15.

Ferrat, André, *La République à refaire* (Paris, 1945).

Ferré, L., *Les Classes sociales dans la France contemporaine* (Paris, 1936).

Greenslet, Ferris, *The Lowells and Their Seven Worlds* (Boston, 1947).

Haebich, Theodor, *Deutsche Latifundien, Ein Beitrag zur unserer Vorstellung von der bestehenden Verteilung des laendlichen Grundeigentums* (2nd ed. Koenigsberg, 1930).

Hamon, A. F. A., and X.Y.Z., *Les Maîtres de la France* (Paris, 1936).

Haxey, Simon, *England's Money Lords* (New York, 1939).

Hiller, E. T., *Social Relations and Structures* (New York, 1947).

Hughes, E. C., *French Canada in Transition* (London, 1946).

Jones, A. W., *Life, Liberty, and Property* (New York, 1941), ch. VII.

Kolabinska, M., *La Circulation des élites en France* (1912).

Laski, H., 'Can Business Be Civilized?' *Harper's Magazine* (Jan. 1930), vol. CLVIII, pp. 170-79.

Lasswell, H. D., and Serene, R., 'The Changing Italian Elite,' in his *The Analysis of Political Behaviour* (New York, 1948), pp. 158-72.

Leopold, Lewis, *Prestige* (London, 1913).

Lewinson, R. (Morus), *Das Geld in der Politik* (Berlin, 1930).

Lundberg, Ferdinand, *Imperial Hearst: A Social Biography* (New York, 1936).

––– *America's Sixty Families* (New York, 1937).

Mannheim, Karl, *Man and Society in an Age of Reconstruction* (New York, 1940), bibliography, pp. 383-455.

McConaugh, John, *Who Rules America?* (New York, 1934).

Michels, Robert, *Umschichtungen in den herrschenden Klassen nach dem Kriege* (Stuttgart, Berlin, 1934).

Mosca, Gaetano, *The Ruling Class* (New York, 1939). (Tr. by H. D. Kahn.)

Muehlen, Heinrich von zur, *Entstehung und Sippengefuege der britischen Oligarchie* (Essen, 1941).

Muir, R., *How Britain Is Governed* (London, 1933).

Myers, Gustavus, *The Ending of Hereditary Wealth* (New York, 1939).

––– *History of the Great American Fortunes* (Chicago, 1907-9), 3 vols. (Modern Library, 1936.)

Neumann, Franz, *Behemoth: The Structure and Practice of National Socialism 1933-1944* (New York, London, 1944).

Nicolson, Harold, *The Meaning of Prestige* (Cambridge, 1937).

North, C. C., *Social Differentiation* (London, 1926).

Page, C. H., *Class and American Sociology* (New York, 1940).

Ponsonby, Arthur, *The Decline of Aristocracy* (London, 1912).

Prokopowicz, S. N., *Russlands Volkswirtschaft unter den Sowjets* (Zurich, 1944).

Rosten, Leo C., *Hollywood, the Movie Colony, the Movie Makers* (New York, 1941).

Sauermann, Heinz, *Die Gestalt des Unternehmers* (Berlin, 1937).

Sombart, Werner, *Der moderne Kapitalismus* (Munich, Leipzig, 1916-27), vols. 1-3.

Sorokin, P., 'American Millionaires and Multimillionaires,' *Social Forces* (May 1925), vol. III, pp. 627-40.

––– *Social Mobility* (New York, 1927).

––– 'War and Post War Changes in Social Stratification,' *American Sociological Review* (April 1945), vol. X, pp. 294ff.

Takizawa, M., *The Penetration of Money Economy in Japan* (New York, 1927).

Taussig, F. W., and Joslyn, C. S., *American Business Leaders* (New York, 1932).

Tawney, R. H., *The Acquisitive Society* (New York, 1920).

Thomme, J., *Les Problèmes des classes* (Paris, 1938).

Veblen, Thorstein, *The Theory of the Leisure Class* (London, 1924).

——— *The Vested Interests and the Common Man* (London, 1924).

Wector, Dixon, *The Saga of American Society* (New York, 1937).

Wedgwood, Josiah, *The Economics of Inheritance* (Penguin, 1939).

2. Davis, C. K., 'Classless Society,' *Spectator* (12 Sept. 1944), 179:330.

3. For the question 'reform or revolution' see:
Anderson, H. C., Davidsen, P. E., *Ballots and the Democratic Class Struggle* (Stanford, 1943).

Bernstein, E., *Die Voraussetzungen des Sozialismus und die Aufgaben der Sozialdemokratie* (Stuttgart, 1899). (Tr. by E. C. Harvey as *Evolutionary Socialism*, London, 1909.)

Davenport, N., 'Social Revolution: Conservative Style,' *New Statesman and Nation* (to Oct. 1942), vol. XXIV, 232-3.

Henderson, Kenneth T., 'Is Class War Still Necessary? An Australian View,' *Quarterly Review* (July 1944).

Lenin, V. I., 'Marxism and Revisionism,' *Karl Marx: Selected Works* (New York), vol. I, pp. 60-69.

Luxemburg, Rosa, *Reform or Revolution*, tr. by Integer (New York).

Sorel, G., *Reflections on Violence* (London, 1915), ch. I, II, III.

Wormuth, F. D., *Class Struggle* (Bloomington, Indiana, 1946).

4. For leftist theories see:
Cannon, J. P., *History of American Trotskyism* (New York, 1944).

Hilferding, R., 'State Capitalism or Totalitarian State Economy,' *Modern Review* (June 1947).

Kautsky, K., *Terrorism and Communism*, tr. by W. Kerridge (London, 1920).

Lukacs, Georg, *Karl Marx and Friedrich Engels als Literaturhistoriker* (Berlin, 1948), pp. 231ff.

Schachtman, M., *The Struggle for the New Course* (New York, 1933).

Souvarine, Boris, *Staline* (Paris, 1935).

Stalin, Josef, *et al.*, *Socialism Victorious* (1935).

Trotsky, Leon, *The Revolution Betrayed. What Is the Soviet Union and Where Is It Going?*, tr. by Max Eastman (New York, 1937).

5. Bingham, Alfred M., *Insurgent America: The Revolt of the Middle Classes* (New York, 1935).

Brauer, T., 'Mittelstandspolitik,' *Grundriss der Sozialoekonomik*, Abt. IX, II, pp. 368-411.

Corbin, John, *The Return of the Middle Classes* (New York, 1922).

Corey, Lewis, 'The Middle Class,' *The Antioch Review* (Spring 1945), vol. V, no. 1.

——— *The Crises of the Middle Class* (New York, 1935).

Duncan, Hugh D., *An Annotated Bibliography on the Sociology of Literature*, with an introductory essay on methodological problems in the field (Hectograph, University of Chicago, 1947).

Gretton, R. W., *The English Middle Class* (New York, 1933).

Karpovich, Michael, *Imperial Russia* (New York, 1944).

Kecskemeti, P., and Leites, N., *Some Psychological Hypotheses on Nazi Germany* (July 1945), Library of Congress, Document No. 60.

Kosok, Paul, *Modern Germany, A Study of Conflicting Loyalties* (Chicago, 1933), pp. 31-40.

Lasswell, H. D., 'The Psychology of Hitlerism as a Response of the Lower Middle Classes to Continuing Insecurity,' *The Analysis of Political Behaviour*, op. cit. ch. III.

Lederer, Emil, and Marschak, J., 'Der neue Mittelstand,' *Grundriss der Sozialoekonomik*, Abt. IX, I, pp. 70-120.

Lynd, Robert S. and Helen M., *Middletown in Transition* (New York, 1937).

—— *Middletown* (New York, 1929).

Marbach, Fritz, *Theorie des Mittelstandes* (Bern, 1942).

Masaryk, Thomas G., *Zur russischen Geschichts- und Religionsphilosophie* (Jena, 1913). (Tr. as *The Spirit of Russia*.)

Mavor, James, *An Economic History of Russia* (London, 1925).

Meusel, A., 'Middle Class,' *Encyc. Soc. Sciences*, vol. X, pp. 407-15.

Mills, C. Wright, 'Small Business and Civic Welfare,' *Report of Special Committee on Small Business* (Washington, D.C., 1946), U.S. Senate Document 135.

—— 'The Middle Classes in Middle Size Cities,' *American Sociological Review* (Oct. 1946), vol. XI, pp. 520-29.

Palm, Franklin Charles, *The Middle Classes Then and Now* (New York, 1936).

Pankratova, A. M. (ed.), *Istoriya SSSR* (History of USSR) (Moscow, 1946).

Pares, Bernard, *A History of Russia* (New York, 1947).

Pesl, L. D., 'Mittelstandsfragen: Der gewerbliche und kaufmaennische Mittelstand,' *Grundriss der Sozialoekonomik*, Abt. IX, I, pp. 70-120.

Speier, Hans, 'The Salaried Employee in Modern Society,' *Social Research* (Feb. 1934), vol. I, pp. 111-33.

Sumner, B. H., *A Short History of Russia* (New York, 1943).

Tugan-Baranowski, M., *Geschichte der Russischen Fabrik* (Weimar, 1900).

Wernicke, J., *Kapitalismus und Mittelstandspolitik* (2nd ed. Jena, 1922).

6. Schuecking, L. L., *Die Familie im Puritanismus. Studien ueber Familie und Literatur in England im XVI, XVII, und XVIII Jahrhundert* (Leipzig, 1929).

7. Carlton, F. T., 'Capitalism and Social Change,' *Sociology and Social Research* (July, 1944), vol. XXVIII, pp. 440-51.

8. Laidler, Harry W., *Social Economic Movements* (New York, 1944).

Gurvitch, Georges, *Sociology of Law* (New York, 1942), p. 211; (London, 1947) pp. 166ff.

Lasswell, H., 'On Social Balance and Public Opinion,' in his *Democracy through Public Opinion* (New York, 1941), pp. 132ff.

9. Kulischer, Eugene M., 'Recent Migration in the Soviet Union,' *American Sociological Review* (June 1944), vol. 9, no. 3, pp. 223-8.

10. Griffith, E. S., *The Modern Government in Action* (New York, 1942), pp. 22-3.

Reimann, G., *The Myth of the Total State* (New York, 1941).

11. Bergson, A., *The Structure of Soviet Wages: A Study in Socialist Economics* (Cambridge, Mass., 1944).

Bienstock, G., Schwartz, S. M., and Yugow, A., *Management in Russian Industry and Agriculture* (New York, 1944).

Brutzkus, B., *Economic Planning in the Soviet Union* (New York, 1946).

Chapmay, S., 'Profit Motive and Economic Incentive,' *Journal of Economics*, vol. LVI, pp. 51-6.

Court, A. T., 'Wages and Economic Efficiency,' *Academy of Political Science Proceedings*, vol. XXII, pp. 17-19.

Craukshaw, E., 'Privilege in Russia,' *New Statesman and Nation* (4 May 1946), 31:315.

Fairchild, M., 'Social-Economic Classes in Soviet Russia,' *American Sociological Review*, vol. IX, pp. 236-41.

Hubbard, L. E., *Soviet Labor and Industry* (New York, 1942).

———— *Soviet Trade and Distribution* (New York, 1938).

Hughes, F., 'Incentives and the Soviet Inventor,' *Discovery* (Jan. 1947), 8:10-12.

MacIntosh, A., 'Differential Effect of the Status of the Competing Group upon the Level of Aspiration,' *American Journal of Psychology*, vol. LV, pp. 546-54.

Markus, B. L., 'The Stakhanow Movement and the Increased Productivity of Labour in the USSR,' *International Labor Review* (Geneva, July 1936).

Mather, W. G., 'Income and Social Participation,' *American Sociological Review*, vol. VI, pp. 380-83.

May, M. A., and Doob, L. W., 'Competition and Cooperation,' *Social Science Research Council*, Bulletin 25 (New York, 1937).

Meyer, Peter, 'The Soviet Union: A New Class Society,' *Politics* (March and April 1944), pp. 48ff., 81ff.

Moore, W. E., *Industrial Relations and the Social Order* (New York, 1946), ch. XVI, 'The Question of Motives.' (Extensive bibliography.)

Pressey, S. L., and Hanna, D. C., 'Class as a Psycho-Sociological Unit,' *Journal of Psychology*, vol. XVI, pp. 13-19.

Tawney, R. H., *The Acquisitive Society* (New York, 1920), ch. IX, 'The Condition of Efficiency.'

12. References on degrading and depersonalizing effects of the division of labor in modern mechanical industry:

Engels, Friedrich, *The Condition of the Working Classes in England in 1849* (London, 1936), ch. V-X.

Marx, Karl, *Capital*, vol. I, ch. XIV, sections 4, 5; ch. XV, sections 3, 4, 5, 8, 9 (New York, The Modern Library).

'. . . the degradation of labor is greatest in those crafts where there is the least division of labor . . . the monotony of the machine system has helped to make labor more mobile and broadened its horizon,' Salz, Arthur, 'Specialization,' *Encyc. Soc. Sciences*, vol. XIV, p. 284.

Soule, George, 'Standardization,' ibid. pp. 319-22.

Venable, V., *Human Nature: The Marxian View* (New York, 1946), ch. IX.

13. Other treatments of relationship to the product of labor and of personality formation in 'traditional type' societies offer widely differing contrasts to Mannheim's views. For Marx, the worker in a society where the

z

social division of labor obtains is a 'craft-idiot' (Marx, K., *The Poverty of Philosophy*, Marxist Library, vol. XXVI, p. 121); in the guilds '. . . the labourer and his means of production remained closely united, like the snail with its shell . . .' (*Capital*, p. 394). For Engels the independent weaver-farmer displayed respectable servility to patriarchical domination (*The Conditions of the Working Class in England*, pp. 2-3).

W. E. Moore sees the guild craftsman in a manner similar to Marx—though not a 'machine slave' he was 'from the modern point of view . . . a "slave of tradition."' (*Industrial Relations and the Social Order*, New York, 1946, p. 292.) Cf. also Fromm, Erich, *Escape from Freedom* (New York, 1941), ch. I, II, III.

> Simmel, Georg, *Philosophie des Geldes* (Munich, 1922).
> Weber, Max, *General Economic History* (New York, n.d.), ch. IX, X, XI.

14. Simmel, Georg, *Ueber soziale Differenzierung: soziale und psychologische Untersuchungen* (Leipzig, 1890).

15. Cattell, R. B., 'Cultural Functions of Stratification: regarding the Genetic Bases of Society; Individual and Group Dynamics,' *Journal of Social Psychology*, vol. XXI, pp. 3-55.
> 'Distinction without Difference,' *Saturday Review*, vol. CLVIII, pp. 264-5.

16. Galsworthy, John, *The Island Pharisees* (New York, London, 1908).
> Renier, Gostaaf Johannes, *The English: Are They Human?* (New York, 1931).
> Thackeray, William Makepeace, *Vanity Fair*.

17. Ortega y Gasset, J., *Revolt of the Masses* (New York, 1932).

18. Weber, Max, 'Class, Status, Party,' *Essays in Sociology*, op. cit. pp. 180-94.
> Goldhamer, H., and Shils, E., 'Types of Power and Status,' *American Journal of Sociology* (Sept. 1939), pp. 171-82.

19. Day, G. M., 'Folkways versus Stateways: with Special Reference to the Social Institutions of Family, School and Church in Soviet Russia,' *Sociology and Social Research*, vol. XXIII, pp. 334-44.
> Harmsworth, H. C., 'Pecuniary Group Relationships in Modern Society,' ibid. vol. XXXI, pp. 291-6.

20. Elliot, W. Y., *The Pragmatic Revolt in Politics, Syndicalism, Fascism, and the Constitutional State* (New York, 1928).
> Freund, Michael, *Georges Sorel, Der Revolutionäre Konservativismus* (Frankfurt, 1932).
> Herbert, S., and Rees, J. M., 'Syndicalism,' *Encyclopædia Britannica* (Chicago, 1947).
> Lorwin, L. L., 'Syndicalism,' *Encyc. Soc. Sciences*, vol. XIV.
> Perdrieux, N. P., 'Notes sur le corporatisme,' *Revue des Sciences Politiques*, vol. LI, pp. 606-28.
> Sorel, Georges, *Reflections on Violence* (London, 1915).

21. Weber, Max, 'The Meaning of Discipline,' *Essays in Sociology*, pp. 253-64.

22. Lenin's concept of a party of professional revolutionaries, 'What Is To Be Done? Burning Questions of Our Movement,' *Collected Works* (New York, 1929), vol. IV, Book II, pp. 89-258.

23. Gothein, Eberhard, *Ignatius Loyola und die Gegenreformation* (Halle, 1895).

24. Good observers of the transformation of Republican Germany recognized the growth of sectional mass organization as the paramount problem of German democracy. The German Parliament itself was composed mainly of rigid mass parties representing single interests or creeds. They therefore lacked the flexibility characteristic of Democracy in its oligarchic stage, when parties rest predominantly on local interests, personal connections, etc. Cf. Schlesinger, R., *Federalism in Central and Eastern Europe* (London, New York, 1945), pp. 122ff.

Bergstraesser, L., *Geschichte der politischen Parteien in Deutschland* (Berlin, 1932).

25. In order to reduce the preponderance of the managerial factor in the party, a large number of new members was admitted after 1938. The membership of the party grew from 2,477,666 (including candidates) in 1939 to 3,876,885 (including candidates) in 1941. The new members were won through mass recruiting in the Red Army, which at the same time meant greater control of the latter. (Cf. the article by B. Moore, Jr., 'The Communist Party of the Soviet Union 1928-1944. A Study in Elite Formation,' *American Sociological Review* (June 1944), vol. 9, no. 3. p. 269.

Williams, A. Rhys, *The Russians* (London, 1943), pp 88f.

Laidler, H., op. cit. pp. 429f.

Further literature on the topic:

Baykov, A., *The Development of the Soviet Economic System* (Cambridge, 1936).

Bienstock, G., Schwarz, A. M., and Yugow, A., op. cit.

Dobb, M. H., *Soviet Economy and the War* (London, New York, 1941).

——— *Soviet Development since 1917* (London, New York, 1948).

Prokopowicz, S. N., op. cit.

Schlesinger, R., *Soviet Legal Theory* (London, 1946).

Soltykoff, A., 'Le Parti communiste et l'économie soviétique,' *Revue Politique et Litteraire*, vol. LXXV, pp. 444-7.

26. Cf. Moore, B., op. cit. pp. 267-78.

27. Weber, Max, *The Theory of Social and Economic Organization*, tr. by A. M. Henderson and Talcott Parsons (New York, 1947), pp. 139-43, 245-50.

28. Pear, T. H., 'Psychological Aspects of English Social Stratification,' *John Rylands Library Bulletin*, vol. XXVI, pp. 342-68.

——— 'Social Stratification in British Society; Abstracts of Papers Read at the General Meeting of the British Psychological Society, Section of Social Psychology,' *Nature*, vol. CXLIX, pp. 487-9.

Sorokin, P., 'War and Postwar Changes in Social Stratification of the Euro-American Population,' *American Sociological Review*, vol. X, pp. 294-303.

29. Mannheim, Karl, *Ideology and Utopia* (New York, London, 1936), pp. 215ff.

'The condition for the emancipation of the working class is the abolition of every class, just as the condition for the liberation of the Third Estate, of the bourgeois order, was the abolition of all estates and all orders.'

'The working class, in the course of its development, will substitute for the old civil society an association which will exclude classes and their antagonism, and there will be no more political power properly so-called, since political power is precisely the official expression of antagonism in civil society.' Marx, Karl, *The Poverty of Philosophy*, op. cit. vol. XXVI, pp. 146f.

'The first action undertaken by the State as genuinely representative of society at large, the seizure of the means of production in the name of society at large, is simultaneously its last independent action as a State. In one domain after another, the intervention of a State authority in social relations becomes superfluous, and therefore spontaneously ceases to occur. The Government of persons is replaced by the administration of things and by the management of the processes of production. The State is not "abolished," it dies out.' Engels, Friedrich, *Anti-Dühring*, p. 102.

'When in the course of social evolution, class distinctions have disappeared, and when all the work of production has been concentrated into the hands of associated producers, public authority will lose its political character. Strictly speaking, political power is the organized use of force by one class in order to keep another class in subjection. . . The old bourgeois society, with its classes and class conflicts, will be replaced by an association in which the free development of each will lead to the free development of all.' Marx, Karl, and Engels, Friedrich, *The Communist Manifesto*, ed. by D. Ryazanoff (London, 1930), pp. 53-4.

30. Branch, E. Douglas, *The Hunting of the Buffalo* (New York, 1929).

Thurnwald, Richard, *Die menschliche Gesellschaft in ihren ethnosoziologischen Grundlagen* (Berlin, 1931-5).

31. Schlesinger, R., *Federalism in Central and Eastern Europe*, op. cit. pp. 122ff.

On the concepts of the organized ruling group and the historical ruling groups cf. Mosca, *The Ruling Class*, ch. II, sections 2-5, and ch. XII.

32. Somerville, John, *Soviet Philosophy, A Study of Theory and Practice* (New York, 1946).

33. Moore, B., 'The Communist Party of the Soviet Union,' loc. cit.; cf. Hook, Sidney, 'Liberalism and the Case of Leon Trotzky,' *Southern Review* (Autumn 1937), pp. 267-82.

Mosely, Philip E., 'Freedom of Artistic Expression and Scientific Inquiry in Russia,' *The Annals* (Amer. Acad. Pol. Soc. Science) (Nov. 1938), pp. 254-74.

Scheffer, Paul, 'From Lenin to Stalin,' *Foreign Affairs* (April 1938), vol. 16, no. 3, pp. 445-53.

34. See note 7, ch. I.

35. For a detailed discussion see ch. 6, 'Planned Control of Government in a Democratic Society.'

36. Since the days of the muckrakers, literary protests have been characteristic of the American scene. For the nineteen-twenties the names of Dreiser, Sinclair Lewis, Mencken come to mind. For a profound criticism of advertising culture see Horkheimer, Max, and Adorno, Theodor W., *Philosophische Fragmente* (New York, 1944).

37. Cf. Friedmann, Georges, 'Revolt against Formalism in the Soviet Union,' *Science and Society* (Summer 1938), vol. II, no. 3, pp. 300-321.

Lukacs, Georg, *Fortschritt und Reaktion in der deutschen Literatur* (Berlin, 1947).

38. Concerning the ladder of social ascent see Weber, Max, 'The Protestant Sects and the Spirit of Capitalism,' *Essays in Sociology*, pp. 308ff.

Ferguson, Charles Wright, *Fifty Million Brothers. A Panorama of American Lodges and Clubs* (New York, 1937).

39. Bavelas, A., and Lewin, K., 'Training in Democratic Leadership,' *Journal of Abnormal Psychology*, vol. XXXII, pp. 115-19.

Bell, D., 'Selection of Leaders in a Democracy,' *Commentary* (April, 1948).

Duprat, Gil, 'Les Elites et le prestige, formes élémentaires de la vie sociale,' *Revue Internationale de Sociologie* (Jan., Feb. 1935), pp. 1-52.

Eaton, J. A., 'Experiments in Testing for Leadership,' *American Journal of Sociology*, vol. LII, pp. 523-35.

Mills, C. Wright, 'American Business Elite: A Collective Portrait Based on the *Dictionary of American Biography*,' *Journal of Economic History*, vol. V, supplement, pp. 20-44.

Mosca, G., *The Ruling Class*, op. cit. ch. XV, esp. sections 4 and 5.

Murphy, A. J., 'A Study of the Leadership Process,' *American Sociological Review*, vol. VI, pp. 675-87.

Murray, H. A., *The Assessment of Men* (New York, 1947).

Neumann, S., 'Leadership: Institutional and Personal,' *Journal of Politics*, vol. III, pp. 33-53.

Riemer, S., 'Upward Mobility and Social Stratification' (Sozialer Aufstieg und Klassenschichtung), in *Archiv fuer Sozialwissenschaft und Sozialpolitik* (1932), vol. LXVII, pp. 531-60. (Tr. by A. Lissance, published by the (N.Y.) State department of social welfare and department of social science, Columbia University.)

Ward, N., 'Problem of Leadership,' *Sociology and Social Research*, vol. XXX, pp. 275-81.

Zeleny, L. D., 'Objective Selection of Group Leaders,' *Sociology and Social Research*, vol. XXIV, pp. 326-36.

40. Ichheiser, Gustav, *Kritik des Erfolges* (Leipzig, 1930).

41. Farago, L. (ed.), *German Psychological Warfare* (New York, 1941-2).

42. For references on personality see Murray, H. A., et al., *Explorations in Personality* (New York, 1938, 1947).

Spearman, C. E., *The Abilities of Man; Their Nature and Measurement* (London, 1927).

See. also: 'Scientific Recruitment. Modern Methods of Selecting Army Officers. Application in Civil Life,' *The Times* (London, 25 Feb. 1945).

Recruitment to Established Posts in the Civil Service during the Reconstruction Period, British Government White Paper (Cmd 6567).

'Personnel Selection in the Army,' *P.E.P.* (June 1943), no. 207.

43. Fleming, C. H., 'Cumulative Records, Notes on Their Content and Use,' *Educational Research Pamphlets* 1 (London, 1945).

44. Munroe, Ruth L., *Teaching the Individual* (New York, 1942), Sarah Lawrence College publications no. 3, p. 42.

45. Martindale, Don, *Morale of the Civilian Soldier*, doctoral thesis (University of Wisconsin, 1948).

46. Greaves, H. R. G., *Civil Service in the Changing State* (London, 1947), pp. 218ff. On Civil Service see ch. v.

47. Laski, H. J., 'The British Cabinet, A Study of Its Personnel,' *Fabian Tract No.* 223 (London, 1928).

48. Nightingale, R. T., 'The Personnel of the British Foreign Office and Diplomatic Service 1851-1929,' *Fabian Tract No.* 232 (London, 1930).

49. All quotations are from Jones, A. J., *The Education of Youth for Leadership* (New York, London, 1938), pp. 74, 77, 79.

50. Collingwood, Robin George, *The New Leviathan* (Oxford, 1942), p. 226.

51. Lindsay, A. D., *The Modern Democratic State* (London, New York, 1943).

52. We may recall the oft-quoted statement of Earl Baldwin: 'When the call came to me to form a Government, one of my first thoughts was that it should be a Government of which Harrow should not be ashamed. I remembered how in previous Governments there had been four or, perhaps, five Harrovians, and I determined to have six.' Baldwin, Stanley, *On England* (1926, Penguin), pp. 237-8.

53. This process of broadening the loyalties of the individual may be compared with G. H. Mead's formulation of 'expanding the generalized other.' Cf. Mead, G. H., *Mind, Self and Society*, ed. by C. W. Morris (6th ed. Chicago, 1947), pp. 90, 154-5, 161. Also his 'The Psychological Bases of Internationalism,' *Survey*, vol. XXXIII, pp. 604-7.

54. Lindsay, A. D., op. cit.

55. In this connection, the advanced position of the United States has been recently acknowledged by one of Britain's leading educationalists. Sir Ernest (now Lord) Simon, who revisited a number of leading American universities during the last war, 'was immensely impressed with the scale of American university life, the magnificence of their buildings, the amount of active discussion on all kinds of university problems.' He pressed, not without success, for an increase of scholarships and grants in Great Britain. For this purpose he published the following table which shows in millions of pounds the total university income in Great Britain and the U.S.A. for the year 1937-8:

	U.S.A.	Great Britain
Fees	34	2
Grants from all government authorities	32	3
Endowment, income, gifts and sundry	31	1.5
	97	6.5

Sir Ernest Simon adds: 'The total expenditure on American universities was fifteen times greater than ours. Allowing for the fact that their population is three times greater than ours, the ratio of expenditure was five to one.' Sir Ernest Simon, *The Development of British Universities* (London, 1941), p. 4.

Data on U.S. High School Enrollment

1934	5,669,156
1936	5,974,537
1938	6,226,934
1940	6,601,444
1942	6,387,805
1944	5,553,520

Data taken from 'Table 152, High School Enrollment 1934-1944,' *Statistical Abstract of the U.S.* (Washington, D.C., 1947). (Prepared by the U.S. Dept. of Commerce, Bureau of the Census.)

High School Graduates 1870-1944

1870	16,000
1880	23,634
1890	43,731
1900	94,883
1910	156,429
1920	311,266
1930	666,904
1940	1,221,475
1942	1,242,375
1944	1,019,233

Ibid. table 154.

56. On 'Secret Societies' see Simmel, Georg, *Soziologie* (3rd ed. Munich, Leipzig, 1923), ch. v, pp. 257-304.

57. Veblen, Thorstein, *The Theory of the Leisure Class: An Economic Study of Institutions* (New York, 1935).

58. Robinson, J. H., *The Mind in the Making* (New York, 1930).

CHAPTER 5. THE REFORMATION OF POLITICS

1. Oppenheimer, Franz, *System der Soziologie* (Jena, 1926), vol. I, p. 465, vol. II, p. 18.

2. Heckscher, Eli F., *Mercantilism*, tr. by M. Shapiro (London, 1935).

3. Weber, Max, *General Economic History* (New York, 1927), pp. 170f., 174f.

4. Ebenstein, William, *The Pure Theory of Law* (Madison, 1945).
   Hallowell, John H., *The Decline of Liberalism as an Ideology* (Berkeley, 1943).
   Hayeck, Friedrich A. von, *Individualism and Economic Order* (Chicago, 1948).
   ——— *Road to Serfdom* (London, 1944).
   Hobhouse, L. T., *Liberalism* (London, 1911).
   Laski, Harold J., 'The Rise of Liberalism,' *Encyc. Soc. Sciences*, vol. I.
   Lippmann, Walter, *An Inquiry into the Principles of the Good Society* (Boston, 1937).

Mannheim, Karl, *Ideology and Utopia* (New York, London, 1936), esp. pp. 197-206.

Mises, Ludwig, *Liberalismus* (Jena, 1927).

Ruggiero, Guido de, 'Liberalism,' *Encyc. Soc. Sciences*, vol. IX.

5. Gerth, Hans, 'The Nazi Party: Its Leadership and Composition,' *The American Journal of Sociology* (Jan. 1940), vol. XLV, no. 4, pp. 517-41.

Palyi, Melchior, 'Economic Foundations of the German Totalitarian State,' ibid. (Jan. 1941), vol. XLVI, no. 4, pp. 469-86.

Sering, Paul, *Jenseits des Kapitalismus* (Regensburg, 1946).

6. Smellie, K. B., *Our Two Democracies at Work* (London, 1944), pp. 58-60.

7. 'Increasing Government Control in Economic Life,' *The Annals* (Amer. Acad. Soc. Pol. Science) (March 1935).

'Government Expansion in the Economic Sphere,' ibid. (Nov. 1939).

8. Keynes, John Maynard, *The Economic Consequences of the Peace* (New York, 1920).

9. German unemployment figures rose to over 6 millions in 1932. Hourly wages fell from December 1930 to January 1932 for many categories of skilled labor from 15 to over 22 per cent. See Forsthoff, Ernst (ed.), *Deutsche Geschichte seit 1918 in Dokumenten* (Stuttgart, 1938), tables on pp. 240-41.

Cf. also Anderson, Evelyn, *Hammer or Anvil, the Story of the German Working Class Movement* (London, 1945), pp. 135ff. 'Those out of work among the total membership of the free trade unions were . . . in 1932 [February and March] 45 per cent.'

Neumann, Franz, *European Trade Unionism and Politics* (New York, 1936), p. 30. Published by the League for Industrial Democracy.

10. Cf. Chase, Stuart, *Democracy under Pressure; Special Interests vs. the Public Welfare. Guide Lines to America's Future as Reported by the Twentieth Century Fund* (New York, 1945).

Crawford, Kenneth G., *The Pressure Boys* (New York, 1939).

Herring, E. P., *Group Representation before Congress* (Baltimore, 1929).

MacIver, R. M., 'Pressures, Social,' *Encyc. Soc. Sciences*, vol. XII.

Perlman, Selig, *Labor in the New Deal Decade* (three lectures) (New York, 1945), Educational Department International Ladies' Garment Workers' Union.

T.N.E.C. Monograph No. 26 (Washington, D.C., 1941).

Waring, P. Alston, and Teller, Walter M., *Roots in the Earth* (New York, 1943) (on 'the farm bloc').

11. Cf. Finer, Herman, *The T.V.A. Lessons for International Application* (Montreal, 1944), esp. ch. 'Multi-Purpose Authority,' pp. 220ff., 'Clearly Defined Scope of Powers,' pp. 226ff., 'Application for World Scale.' 'There could be no supra-national agency endowed with unlimited powers and uncovenanted rights of intervention. On the contrary, as the T.V.A. has continually shown, it would be vital to convey the impression of disinterested helpfulness, advisory character, defined purposes and clearly stated procedures,' p. 228.

12. According to Mosca, Self-Government is the only remedy against democratic overcentralization. Democracy means belief in the power of spontaneous group-integration and its creative powers, and that dynamic change

is even in Great Society the product of organic growth the tendencies of which have to be interpreted by rulers or elites. Mosca, *The Ruling Class* (New York, 1939), p. 159.

Cf. Frantz, Constantin, *Der Föderalismus als das leitende Prinzip fuer die soziale, staatliche und internationale Organisation* (Mainz, 1879; abridged ed. Stuttgart, 1921).

―― *Die Naturlehre des Staates* (Leipzig, 1870).

Oppenheimer, Franz, *System der Soziologie*, op. cit. vol. II, *Der Staat,* 'Der Föderalismus,' pp. 774-84.

Proudhon, P. J., 'Du principe fédératif et de la nécessité de réconstituer le parti de la révolution,' *Oeuvres complètes* (Paris, 1875), vol. VIII.

13. Stern, Bernhard J., 'Restraints upon the Utilization of Inventions,' *The Annals* (Amer. Acad. Pol. Soc. Science) (Nov. 1938), pp. 13-31.

For an argument against exaggerating the importance of 'patent shelving' policies see Schumpeter, Joseph, *Capitalism, Socialism and Democracy* (2nd ed. New York, 1947), pp. 96ff.

14. An important report of the General Council of the British Trades Union Congress in its section 'Industrial and Commercial Monopoly' suggests setting up an official body to report to Parliament annually on the nature, extent, and development of monopoly, and the establishment of a permanent tribunal authorized to investigate the operations of any monopoly and to propose appropriate state intervention.

T.U.C. proposals: (1) public control or regulation over cash and credit facilities in connection with the use of land; (2) establishment of an economic advisory committee at the highest level of administration with (3) industrial boards including experts; (4) nationalized industries: establishment of public corporations with members appointed by the Minister and including workers' representatives. Cf. also *The Times* (London, 30 Aug. 1945) (leader).

Gordon, Lincoln, *The Public Corporation in Great Britain* (Oxford, 1938).

―― *Britain without Capitalism* (London, 1936).

Employment Policy and Organization of Industry after the War (Oxford, 1943), Nuffield College.

See also note 7 above.

15. Such planning can influence active citizenship, negative or positive, as Kate Liepmann showed in *The Journey to Work* (London, New York, 1944). A planned society, of course, will try to alter this by emphasizing the neighborhood unit anew through modern city planning.

16. Lord Nuffield, for instance, suggested a Public Industrial Board.

17. A good discussion of the pros and cons of the various forms of control is Schumacher's 'Essay on State Control of Business,' *Agenda* (Feb. 1944), vol. 3, no. 1. His suggestion that the control of industry by Government should be accomplished not so much by participation in the process of production as by becoming the most powerful buyer is as a technique very important. The powerful buyer always sets the standards of performance, can influence the methods of production, quantity, quality, prices, profits, and therefore, as he says, 'transforms private buying into state-buying' (pp. 152-7). This technique is of particular interest to the sociologist because it contains ele-

ments of interference and compulsion with strong effects which yet are not experienced as *compulsion* but as *freedom* by the industrialist because they give the illusion to the person controlled that he himself makes the adjustments to pressures and does not obey them, and because acceptance of these pressures is part of our 'Western culture.' Yet culture may be changed. In this connection the following observations seem to me to be extremely important: 'As Walton Hamilton has remarked, private business succeeds better than government in imposing its coercions because they are disguised as choices.' Lynd, Robert S., 'The Implications of Economic Planning for Sociology,' *American Sociological Review* (Feb. 1944), vol. IX, no. 1, p. 20.

18. The only exceptions to this are cases where the State socializes industries in order to run them as state enterprises. There one may say that planning means active participation in the process of production. But even here the justification is that the State does not want to become a producer, but that this position over the socialized sector alone gives it the regulating power which is necessary for prevention.

19. Here as nearly always the totalitarian states began to realize the new possibilities by transferring populations on a large scale, removing entire ruling classes, deliberately creating vested interests which served their ends. The democracies followed their example reluctantly after the war: insisting on certain types of governments, transferring populations wherever this promised to ease tensions. The new question has not yet been faced squarely: how far should democratic planning go in taking such measures, and what are the methods of group resettlement and the reconstruction of power in the spirit of a progressive democracy. For the transfer of populations by totalitarian states see J. Isaac, *Economics of Migration* (London, 1947).

Men without the Rights of Man, A Report on the Expulsion and Extermination of German-speaking Minority Groups in the Balkans and Prewar Poland (New York, n.d., later than May 1947). Committee against Mass Expulsions, Christopher Emmet, Chairman.

Kulischer, Eugene M., *Jewish Migrations, Past Experiences and Post-War Prospects* (New York, 1944). (Pamphlet Series, Jews and the Post-War World, no. 4.)

20. Vagts, Alfred, 'Die Chimaere des europäischen Gleichgewichts,' *Zeitschrift fuer Sozialforschung* (mimeographed ed. 1942).

21. The pattern of the deterioration of Democracy into Dictatorship ought to be studied in all its phases most carefully. There are some analogies, in spite of considerable differences, between the development toward Dictatorship in Germany in 1932-4 and that in Czechoslovakia in 1946-8.

22. The equilibrium of checks and balances is summed up in Lasswell's statement: 'We know that in harmony with the *principle of checks and balances* the Presidency is balanced by Congress and Court, the Congress by the Presidency and Court, and the Court by the Presidency and Congress.

'The principle applies to the relationship between the federal government and the states. A zone of authority is reserved to the states which the federal government is not authorized to enter. In harmony with the limited and specific delegation of powers under the Constitution, the federal government may exercise only the authority assigned to it by the Constitution. Whatever is not delegated to the federal government and specifically prohibited to the states, may be exercised by the states, not by the federal government.' Lasswell, H. D., *Democracy through Public Opinion* (New York, 1941), pp. 134f.

23. Relevant differences in power exist, however, in the party. Cf. ch. 3.

24. Cf. Schmitt, Carl, *Verfassungslehre* (Munich, Leipzig, 1928), pp. 226ff.

25. Cf. Rist, Charles, 'The Financial Situation of France,' *Foreign Affairs* (July, 1938), vol. 16, no. 4, pp. 601-11.

26. Wootton, Barbara, *Freedom under Planning* (Chapel Hill, 1945).

27. Lowe, Adolph, 'Wie ist Konjunkturtheorie ueberhaupt moeglich,' *Archiv fuer Weltwirtschaft und Seeverkehr* (1926), vol. 24, pp. 165-97.
   Kalecki, M., *Essays in the Theory of Economic Fluctuations* (London, 1939).
   Schumpeter, Joseph A., *Business Cycles* (New York, 1939).

28. Clark, Colin, *The Conditions of Economic Progress* (London, 1940). (An international and statistical survey.)
   Rostas, L., 'Industrial Production, Productivity and Distribution in Britain, Germany and the U.S.,' *Economic Journal* (Cambridge, 1943).

29. Keynes, John Maynard, *General Theory of Employment, Interest and Money* (London, 1936).
   Schumpeter, Joseph A., *Capitalism . . .* op. cit.

30. Bakke, E. W., *The Unemployed Worker* (New Haven, 1946).
   Abboth, Edith, *Public Assistance* (Chicago, 1941), 2 vols.
   Lane, M. S., and Steegmueller, Francis, *America on Relief* (New York, 1938).
   Lazarsfeld, Paul, and H. Zeist, *Die Arbeitslosen von Marienthal*, Psychol. Monographien (1933).
   ——— *Men without Work* (Cambridge, 1938).
   Eveline Burns, Director of Research of the National Resources Planning Board's report, *Security, Work, and Relief Policies* (1942), criticizes the relief measures of the prewar decade: 'Too little emphasis was placed upon preventive as against palliative measures. Public aid was not equally available to all needy people, regardless of their place of residence or the cause of their need. The level of living allowed to those dependent upon socially provided income was for the vast majority of programs extremely low and, for some groups or for all persons in some areas, was shocking in a country of such great potential wealth. Public work was available for only a fraction of the unemployed . . . the majority of the dependent group could receive aid only under conditions which certainly were not calculated to enhance self-respect and were often highly destructive of it.' *National Resources Development Report for* 1943, 78th Congress, House of Representatives, Document No. 128, part I, p. 75.

31. Schumpeter, Joseph A., *Capitalism . . .* op. cit. p. 397.
   For the Works Progress Administration of the United States cf. McMahon, Arthur, Millet, J. D., and Ogden, Gladys, *The Administration of Federal Work Relief* (Chicago, 1941).
   Burns, Eveline, *Security, Work and Relief Policies*, op. cit.
   Douglas, P. H., *Social Security in the United States* (New York, 1939).

Lorwin, Lewis, *Public Works and National Planning* (Washington, D.C., 1941).

—— *International Development—Public Works and Other Problems* (Washington, D.C., 1942).

32. For the United States cf. Whittlesey, Charles R., 'Federal Reserve Policy in Transition,' *The Quarterly Journal of Economics* (May 1946), vol. LX, no. 3, pp. 340-50.

33. Cf. Lilienthal, David E., *T.V.A.: Democracy on the March* (New York, London, 1944).

34. For the Scandinavian countries the following books may be mentioned:
Childs, M. W., *Sweden: The Middle Way* (New Haven, 1936; Pelican, 1948).
Cole, Margaret, and Smith, Charles (eds.), *Democratic Sweden* (New York, 1939).
Hacker, Louis, *American Problems of Today* (New York, 1938).
Howe, F. C., *Denmark: The Cooperative Way* (New York, 1937).
Strode, Hudson, *Finland Forever* (New York, 1940).

35. Berle, A. A., and Means, Gardiner C., *The Modern Corporation and Private Property* (New York, 1933).
'Distribution and Ownership in the 200 Largest Nonfinancial Corporations,' *T.N.E.C. Monograph No.* 9 (Washington, D.C., 1940).
Hilferding, Rudolf, *Das Finanzkapital* (Berlin, 1910).

36. Karl Mannheim would seem to agree with sociologists such as Ferdinand Toennies, who links the victory of the Roman concept of property to the ascendancy of the money economy and capitalist development. *Geist der Neuzeit* (Leipzig, 1935), p. 59.
Max Weber has emphasized against this view that Great Britain did not follow the continental tradition of borrowing Roman law, and that 'many specifically capitalist legal institutions are of medieval and not of Roman origin.' Cf. *Wirtschaft und Gesellschaft*, pp. 427, 448ff., 453f., 467, 471, 487f., 492ff. [Ed.]
Hallowell, A. Irving, 'The Nature and Function of Property as a Social Institution,' *Journal of Legal and Political Sociology* (April 1943), vol. I, pp. 115-38.

37. Moore, Wilbert E., 'The Emergence of New Property Conceptions in America,' ibid. pp. 34-58.
—— 'Sociology of Economic Organization,' *Twentieth Century Sociology*, ed. by George Gurvitch and Wilbert E. Moore (New York, 1945), pp. 438-65. (With bibliography.)
For further references see Karl Mannheim, *Man and Society*, op. cit. pp. 413-14.

38. See note 7 above.

39. Characteristic are the cases of Generals Boulanger and Gallifet, see Frank, Walter, *Nationalismus und Demokratie im Frankreich der dritten Republik*, 1871-1918 (Hamburg, 1933), pp. 223ff.
For Germany see Huber, Ernst Rudolf, *Heer und Staat in der deutschen Geschichte* (Hamburg, 1938).

Rosenberg, Arthur, *The Birth of the German Republic*, 1871-1918, tr. by J. F. D. Morrow (London, 1931).

On the relation between military and political leadership at the end of World War I, see Schwertfeger, Bernhard, 'Die politischen und militärischen Verantwortlichkeiten im Verlaufe der Offensive von 1918,' *Die Ursachen des Deutschen Zusammenbruches im Jahre* 1918, ed. by Philipp Albrecht (Berlin, 1928), vol. II. Cf. also vol. III.

Rogers, Lindsay, 'Civilian Control of Military Policy,' *Foreign Affairs* (Jan. 1940), vol. 18, no. 2.

Schwertfeger, Bernhard, *Das Weltkriegsende, Gedanken ueber die deutsche Kriegsfuehrung*, 1918 (Potsdam, 1937).

40. For a description of the ascendancy of the Italian Fascisti and the role of 'shock troops,' see Silone, Ignazio, *Der Fascismus seine Entstehung und seine Entwicklung* (Zurich, 1934).

For National Socialism it may suffice to mention that '48.6% of all political leaders of the National Socialist party took active part in warfare during the period 1914-1921. About 25% of all party members who took part in the fighting which marked the war and post-war periods are in the leadership, while of those party members who did not participate only 20.2% are leaders.' Gerth, Hans, 'The Nazi Party: Its Leadership and Composition,' *The American Journal of Sociology* (Jan. 1940), vol. XLV, no. 4, pp. 530-31.

'Even after the demobilization proper 20,000 officers had to be discharged who had hoped to continue their vocations chosen in accordance with century-old family tradition. From among the disillusioned often associations were recruited where the enemies of the new state met.' Friedensburg, Ferdinand, *Die Weimarer Republik* (Berlin, 1946), p. 239.

41. 'When army officers figure actively and ex-officers *ex officio* in political councils, they are certain eventually to dominate those councils and replace the civil authority—the seemingly incurable cancer of the Spanish world.' A. Livingstone in the Introduction to Mosca's *Ruling Class*, op. cit. p. xxv. Cf. also Chorley, Katharine, *Armies and the Art of Revolution* (London, 1943). Also Lauterbach, Albert T., 'Militarism in the Western World,' *Journal of the History of Ideas* (Oct. 1944), vol. 4, no. 4.

Earle, Edward Mead (ed.), *Makers of Modern Strategy* (Princeton, 1943). (Extensive bibliography.)

Lauterbach, A. T., *Economics in Uniform: Military Economy and Social Structure* (Princeton, 1943).

Wright, Quincy, *A Study of War* (Chicago, 1943), 2 vols.

42. Both Weber and Fueter have stressed the connection between Democratic Freedom and Naval Power. Cf. Weber, Max, *General Economic History*, tr. by Frank Knight (London, n.d.), p. 329.

Fueter, Eduard, *World History* 1815-1920, tr. by Sidney Bradshaw Fay (New York, 1922), pp. 37f., 84ff.

43. Vagts, Alfred, *History of Militarism* (New York, 1937).

Demeter, K., *Das deutsche Offizierskorps in seinen historischsoziologischen Grundlagen* (Berlin, 1930).

44. Schmidt, Major Ulrich, 'Die Reichswehr,' *Das deutsche Wehrwesen* (Stuttgart, 1935), pp. 239-343.

Fried, Hans Ernest, *The Guilt of the German Army* (New York, 1943).

45. Heiden, Konrad, *Der Fuehrer: Hitler's Rise to Power* (Boston, 1944).
—— *A History of National Socialism* (London, 1934).
Schwertfeger, Bernhard, *Raetsel um Deutschland* (Heidelberg, 1947).
Wheeler Bennett, John, *Wooden Titan: Hindenburg in Twenty Years of German History*, 1914-1934 (New York, 1936).

46. Mosca, who holds the view that the guarantor of an impartial Army in the Western development has been its corps of officers of aristocratic origin, would see in the French case only a confirmation of his forecast that a democratized army is bound to lead to military dictatorship. According to his hypothesis a corps of officers that comes from the ruling class reflects the balance of multiple and varied social forces which are recognized by and within these forces, whereas in democratization of the Army those would only make active in the Army social conflicts at variance in society at large. Cf. Livingstone, op. cit.

Cf. also Davis, S. C., *The French War Machine* (London, 1927).
Mayer, Colonel E., *La Guerre d'hier et l'armée de demain* (Paris, 1921).
Monteilhet, J., *Les Institutions militaires de la France* (Paris, 1934).
'Pertinax' (A. Géraud), *Les Fossoyeurs* (New York, 1943), 2 vols.

47. Cf. Chorley, Katharine, op. cit. pp. 248-9.

48. Cf. ch. 3, section XII.

49. Mass armies have to a large extent ceased to be a fighting instrument, though a modern army, as Friedwald remarks, 'may have to perform certain tasks, both military and administrative, and for these purposes smaller highly mechanized forces may be the most suitable,' Friedwald, E. M., op. cit. p. 88.

50. A memorandum sent to British Local Authorities by the Home Secretary and the Secretary of State for Scotland, at the end of 1947, devising plans for the rebuilding of the Civil Defence Services on a new basis, shows that it is intended to organize the community in case of war into three main elements:
    1. A highly mobile, disciplined, and well-trained full-time force available for service in any part of the United Kingdom.
    2. Local forces mainly part-time, but with some whole-time nucleus, sufficiently mobile to serve anywhere within a more restricted area.
    3. A well-prepared force of citizens, able in an emergency to care for themselves, their families, and neighbors.
The Manchester Guardian (11 Dec. 1947).

51. Cf. Speier, Hans, 'Ludendorff: The German Concept of Total War,' in *Makers of Modern Strategy*, ed. by E. M. Earle (Princeton, 1943), p. 319.

52. Ferrat, André, *La République à refaire* (Paris, 1945), pp. 87-108.

53. Allport, F. H., *Institutional Behavior* (Chapel Hill, 1933).
Appleby, P. H., *Big Bureaucracy* (New York, 1945).
Barnard, Chester I., *The Functions of the Executive* (Cambridge, 1938).
—— 'Functions and Pathology of Status Systems in Formal Organizations,' *Industry and Society*, ed. by W. F. Whyte (New York, 1946), ch. 4.
Beck, J. M., *Our Wonderland of Bureaucracy, A Study of the Growth of Bureaucracy in the Federal Government, and Its Destructive Effect upon the Constitution* (New York, 1933).

Belsley, G. Lyle, 'Why Bureaucracy Is Belittled,' *Personnel Journal* (Jan. 1947), pp. 19-23.

Bendix, Reinhard, 'Bureaucracy, the Problem and Its Setting,' *American Sociological Review* (Oct. 1947), vol. 12, pp. 493-507.

—— 'Bureaucracy, and the Problem of Power,' *Public Administration Review* (Summer 1945), vol. v, no. 3, pp. 194-209.

Bendiner, Robert, *The Riddle of the State Department* (New York, 1942).

Blachley, F. F., and Oatman, M., 'The Position of the Civil Service in Germany,' *South Western Political and Social Science Quarterly* (Sept. 1929), vol. x, pp. 171-89.

Boehm, Franz, 'Berufsbeamte oder Angestellte des oeffentlichen Dienstes?' *Die Wandlung* (March 1949), vol. IV, no. 3, pp. 195-208.

Brady, R. A., *The Rationalization Movement in German Industry* (Berkeley, 1933).

Burnham, J., *The Managerial Revolution* (New York, 1941).

Cochran, T. C., 'The Social History of the Corporation in the U.S.' *The Cultural Approach to History*, ed. by C. F. Ware (New York, 1940).

Cole, Taylor, 'Italy's Fascist Bureaucracy,' *American Political Science Review* (December 1938), vol. xxxii, pp. 194-209.

Demetviadi, Sir Stephen, *Inside a Government Office* (New York, 1930).

Finer, Herman, *The British Civil Service* (London, 1927).

—— 'The Civil Service in the Modern State,' *American Political Science Review* (1925), vol. 19.

—— 'Organization, Administrative,' *Encyc. Soc. Sciences*, vol. xi.

—— 'Personnel Problems in the Post-War World,' *Personnel Administration* (Sept. 1942), vol. 5, no. 1.

Friedrich, Carl J., *Constitutional Government and Democracy* (Boston, 1941).

—— 'The Continental Tradition of Training Administrators in Law and Jurisprudence,' *The Journal of Modern History* (June 1939), vol. xi, no. 2, pp. 129-48.

—— et al., *Problems of the American Public Service* (New York, London, 1935).

—— *Public Policy* (Cambridge, 1940).

—— and Cole, Taylor, *Responsible Bureaucracy, A Study of the Swiss Civil Service* (Cambridge, 1932).

Gaus, John M., and Wolcott, Leon O. (with a chapter by Verne B. Lewis), *Public Administration and the United States Department of Agriculture* (Chicago, 1940).

Hintze, Otto, *Der Beamtenstand* (Leipzig, Dresden, 1911).

Handman, Max, 'The Bureaucratic Culture Pattern and Political Revolutions,' *American Journal of Sociology* (Nov. 1933), vol. 39, pp. 301-13.

Hewart, Lord, *The New Despotism* (London, 1932).

Hughes, Everett C., 'Institutional Office and the Person,' *American Journal of Sociology* (Nov. 1937), vol. 43, pp. 404-13.

—— 'Personality Types and Division of Labor,' ibid. (March 1928), vol. 33, no. 3, pp. 754-68.

Hsu, Frances L. K., 'A Closer View of China's Problems,' *Far Eastern Quarterly* (Nov. 1946), pp. 50-64.

Kingsley, J. D., *Representative Bureaucracy* (Yellow Springs, Ohio, 1944).

Kosok, Paul, *Modern Germany, A Study in Conflicting Loyalties* (Chicago, 1933), ch. viii, 'The Administrative Bureaucracy,' pp. 100-123.

Laski, H. D., 'Bureaucracy,' *Encyc. Soc. Sciences*, vol. III.

MacMahon, Arthur W., and Dittmer, W. R., 'Autonomous Public Enterprise—the German Railways,' *Political Science Quarterly* (1939), vol. 54, pp. 481ff., and vol. 55 (1940), pp. 25ff., 176ff.

Mendelsohn-Bartholdy, A., 'Bureaucracy in Germany,' *The New Social Science* (Chicago, 1930), pp. 21ff.

Merton, Robert King, 'Bureaucratic Structure and Personality,' *Social Forces* (May 1940), vol. 18, pp. 560-68.

—— 'The Role of the Intellectuals in Public Bureaucracy,' ibid. (May 1945), vol. 23, pp. 405-15.

Mises, Ludwig von, *Bureaucracy* (New Haven, 1944).

Morstein Marx, Fritz, 'Bureaucracy and Dictatorship,'. *The Review of Politics* (Jan. 1941), vol. 3, no. 1, pp. 100-117.

—— 'Bureaucracy and Consultation,' ibid. (1939), vol. 1, pp. 84ff.

—— 'The Bureaucratic State,' ibid. pp. 457ff.

—— *Government in the Third Reich* (New York, London, 1936), ch. 4.

—— and Wood, Bryce, 'The Brazilian Civil Service,' *Inter-American Quarterly* (1940), vol. 2:4, pp. 42ff.

Mosca, G., op. cit.

Mosher, William E., and Kingsley, J. Donald, *Public Personnel Administration* (New York, London, 1936).

Muir, Ramsay, *Peers and Bureaucrats* (London, 1910).

Phelan, E. J., 'The New International Civil Service,' *Foreign Affairs* (Jan. 1933), vol. 11, no. 2, pp. 307-14.

Selznik, P., 'An Approach to a Theory of Bureaucracy,' *American Sociological Review* (1943), vol. 8, no. 1, pp. 47-54.

Sharp, W. D., 'The Evolution of the Civil Service,' *The University of Toronto Quarterly* (Jan. 1939), vol. VIII, no. 2, pp. 155-64.

Sharp, W. R., *The French Civil Service: Bureaucracy in Transition* (London, 1931).

Sullivan, Lawrence, *The Dead Hand of Bureaucracy* (Indianapolis, New York, 1940).

T.N.E.C. Monograph No. 11, 'Bureaucracy and Trusteeship in Modern Corporations.'

Weber, Alfred, 'Der Beamte,' *Ideen zur Staats- und Kultursoziologie* (Karlsruhe, 1927), pp. 81-102.

—— 'Bürokratie und Freiheit, *Die Wandlung* (Dec. 1945), vol. I, no. 12, pp. 1033-48.

—— 'Das Ende des modernen Staates,' ibid. (Aug. 1947), vol. II, no. 6, pp. 463-77.

—— 'Deutschland und Europa. Zugleich eine Betrachtung des Ruhrstatuts,' ibid. (Feb. 1949), vol. 4, no. 2, pp. 99-111, esp. the section 'Die Ruhrbehoerde—ein Manager-Koloss,' pp. 109ff.

—— 'Fluch und Segen des Buerokratie,' *Die Neue Zeitung* (8 Jan. 1940).

Weber, Max, *Essays in Sociology*, op. cit. 'Bureaucracy.'

—— *General Economic History*, op. cit. 'The Modern State.'

—— *Theory of Social and Economic Organization*, op. cit. ch. III, section II, 'Legal Authority with a Bureaucratic Administrative Staff,' pp. 329-41.

White, Leonard, *The Civil Service in the Modern State* (Chicago, 1930).

—— *Introduction to the Study of Public Administration* (New York, 1926).

—— *The Prestige Value of Public Employment* (Chicago, 1929).

White, Leonard, *Trends in Public Administration* (New York, 1933). (Recent Social Trends Monograph.)

—— Bland, C. H., Costberg, F., *et al.*, *The Civil Service in the Modern State* (Great Britain, Canada, France, Germany, Australia, Japan, etc.) (Chicago, 1930).

Woody, Carroll H., *The Growth of the Federal Government* 1915-1932 (New York, London, 1934). (Recent Social Trends Monograph.)

54. Cf. Mosher, W. E., and Kingsley, J. Donald, op. cit. ch. 1. Brief historical survey.

55. Carl J. Friedrich quotes the essential literature in 'The Continental Tradition of Training Administrators in Law and Jurisprudence,' loc. cit.

56. Weber, Max, *Essays in Sociology*, op. cit. p. 229.

57. At the same time Mannheim realized the importance of recruiting the bureaucracy on a broad basis, expressing his full agreement with this postwar statement of M. A. Ferrat: 'Today it is not enough to change a few heads. It is the general spirit of the administration which has to be modified. It is the sources of recruitment that have to be transformed; it is even the spirit of education given to its members that must be renewed. It is necessary to create a school of administration, the various specializing branches of which would be accessible to the large public bodies, the civil and military servants of the state. It is necessary to ensure access to this school, and through it to the more important public functions, to deserving children of the people, in particular of the working and peasant classes,' op. cit. p. 9. [Ed.]

58. Lasswell, H. D., 'The Participant Observer. Studies of Administrative Rules in Action,' in *The Analysis of Political Behaviour* (New York, 1948), pp. 261-78.

59. Simmel, Georg, on 'Secret Societies,' in *Soziologie,* op. cit.
Weber, Max, *Essays in Sociology*, op. cit. pp. 233f., 437.

60. Greaves, H. R. C., *The Civil Service in the Changing State* (London, 1947), pp. 218ff. See also the chapter 'Personnel' in *The Reform of the Higher Civil Service* (London, 1947), pp. 3-117. (A report by a special committee for the Fabian Society.)

61. Williams, G., *The Price of Social Security* (London, 1944), p. 189.

62. Cf. the annotated bibliography of Smith, Bruce L., Lasswell, H. D., and Casey, Ralph D., *Propaganda, Communication, and Public Opinion: A Comprehensive Reference Guide* (Princeton, 1946).
Albig, W., *Public Opinion* (New York, London, 1939). (Extensive bibliography.)
Doob, Leonard W., *Public Opinion and Propaganda* (New York, 1948).
Kris, Ernst, and Speier, Hans, *German Radio Propaganda* (New York, London, 1944).

63. Friedrich, C. J., *Constitutional Government and Politics*, op. cit. p. 448.

64. It has been suggested by Carl Joachim Friedrich that the dangers resulting from unreliable and distorted news could be combated by subject-

ing the process of news dissemination to judicial restraints. 'The most effective guardianship of individual liberty is achieved by entrusting a high court with the function of rendering an "interpreting" judgment concerning the meaning of constitutional clauses whenever a private party wishes to question the interpretation of another authority such as Congress or the President. May it not also be possible to "judicialise" press procedure by outlawing certain types of sensationalist disregard for the truth and then leaving it to aggrieved parties to bring their complaints before a court-like body which would consider the evidence?' Friedrich, op. cit. pp. 448-9.

65. ṭhe terms of reference of this Commission are: 'With the object of furthering the free expression of opinion through the Press and the greatest practical accuracy in the presentation of news, to inquire into the control, management and ownership of the newspaper and periodical Press, and the news agencies, including the financial structure and the monopolistic tendencies in control, and to make recommendations thereon.'

66. The Royal Commission on the Press has published minutes of evidence taken before it in 1947-9 (Royal Commission on the Press [1947-9] *Report*; H.M. Stationery Office, London, 1949).

For America see the report of the President's Committee on Civil Rights: *To Secure These Rights* (U.S. Government Printing Office, Washington, D.C., 1947). 'The Committee reaffirms our tradition that freedom of expression may be curbed by law only where the danger to the well-being of society is clear and present,' p. 9.

Cf. Ickes, Harold L. (ed.), *Freedom of the Press Today: A Clinical Examination* (New York, 1941).

Lasch, Robert, 'For a Free Press,' *The Atlantic* (July 1944).

67. *A Free and Responsible Press*, a general report on newspapers, radio, motion pictures, magazines, and books by the Commission on Freedom of the Press (Chicago, 1947).

An interesting experiment in the reorganization of the press, avoiding both state monopoly and commercial monopoly, was carried out in Czechoslovakia in the period between the end of the last war and the Communist coup in February 1948. In May 1945, the Czech Government issued a decree that made it illegal for any individual to own a newspaper. Papers and periodicals could be run only by political parties, trade unions, co-operative societies, and cultural bodies. A 'Board of Affairs of the Periodical Press,' drawn from the parties and other organizations and attached to the Ministry of Information, issued instructions on internal matters concerned with publication and finance. There was no censorship, but each group owning a paper put up securities and could be fined for infringing decisions of the Board. Cf. Martin, Kingsley, *The Press the Public Wants* (London, 1947), p. 107, and *The Manchester Guardian* (11 Nov. 1947).

68. Cf. Gordon, Lincoln, *The Public Corporation in Great Britain* (London, New York, 1938), pp. 156ff. Also Saerchinger, Cesar, 'Radio, Censorship and Neutrality,' *Foreign Affairs* (Jan. 1940), vol. 18, no. 2, pp. 337-49.

69. In this connection the composition of the Board of Governors of the Northwest German Radio (*Nordwestdeutscher Rundfunk*) in Hamburg is of interest. Based on the Charter of the NWDR issued at the end of 1947 by the British Military Government, the Board consists of 16 members repre-

senting various regional, political, occupational, and religious sections of the population. Besides the Prime Ministers of the three *Laender* of the Zone, the Mayor of Hamburg, the President of the Central Judiciary Office of the Zone, the Chairman of the German Trade Union League, the President of the Association of Chambers of Commerce, there are representatives of the churches, of the universities, of education, art, the theater, and journalism. *DENA Report* (17 Feb. 1948).

70. Lasswell, H. D., 'Free Speech? Yes; Free Incitement? No,' (Unfortunately the reference could not be located. [Ed.])

71. For guidance to pertinent and timely discussions, see *The Public Opinion Quarterly* (Princeton).

72. For the United States see *To Secure These Rights*, op. cit. pp. 52f. and 164f. See also Ernst, Morris L., and David, Lotte, *The People Know Best: The Ballots vs. the Polls* (Washington, D.C., 1949).

73. Cf. Dewey, John, 'What Is an Aim?' in his *Democracy and Education* (New York, 1916).

74. In the United States the President's Committee recommends 'a long-term campaign of public education to inform the people of the civil rights to which they are entitled and which they owe to one another.' *To Secure These Rights*, op. cit. p. 173.

75. Cf. Toennies, Ferdinand, *Kritik der oeffentlichen Meinung* (Berlin, 1922).
Mannheim, E., *Die Traeger der Oeffentlichen Meinung* (Bruenn, Prag, Leipzig, Wien, 1933). (Studien zur Soziologie der Oeffentlichkeit.)
A Free and Responsible Press, op. cit. pp. 9-1 \.

CHAPTER 6. DEMOCRATIC CONTROL OF GOVERNMENT IN A PLANNED SOCIETY

1. Weber, Max, *Wirtschaft und Gesellschaft*, Abt. III, *Grundriss der Sozial-oekonomik* ('Tuebingen, 1925), ch. 8, 'Die Stadt,' pp. 514-601, esp. § 5, 'Antike und Mittelalterliche Demokratie,' pp. 583-601.
——— *General Economic History* (London, n.d.), ch. 28 and 29, 'Citizen-ship,' 'The Rational State,' pp. 315-51.
Altheim, Franz, *Italien und Rom* (Amsterdam, Leipzig, n.d.).
Glotz, G., *The Greek City and Its Institutions* (London, 1929).

2. Mosca, G., *The Ruling Class* (New York, 1939), pp. 376-86.
Ducros, L., *La Société française au six-huitieme siècle* (Paris, 1920).
Hanotaux, Gabriel, *La France en 1614* (Paris, 1914), ch. 2 and 3, 'Les Institutions politiques,' 'L'Ordre Social—Les Classes,' pp. 105-392.
Cf. note 15, ch. 5, section VI, 'The Civil Service.'

3. Becker, Carl L., *The Heavenly City of the Eighteenth Century Philoso-phers* (New Haven, 1932).
Bolingbroke, H. St. J., *The Idea of a Patriot King* (1738).
——— *Dissertation on Parties* (1733-4).
Boucharin, N., *Historical Materialism* (New York, 1925).
Kaeber, Ernst, *Die Idee des europaeischen Gleichgewichts in der pub-*

lizistischen Literatur vom 16. Jahrhundert bis zur Mitte des 18. Jahrhunderts (n.p., 1907).

Montesquieu, Baron de, *Esprit des lois* (1748), Book 11, ch. 6.

Sichel, Walter, *Bolingbroke and His Times* (London, 1901-2), pp. 150ff.

Schmitt, Carl, *Verfassungslehre* (Munich, Leipzig, 1928), pp. 182-99.

Vagts, Alfred, 'Die Chimaere des europaeischen Gleichgewichts,' *Zeitschrift fuer Sozialforschung* (mimeographed ed. 1942).

4. Cf. ch. 3, section 1.

5. 'A little rebellion now and then is a good thing and as necessary in the political world as storms in the physical. . . It is a medicine necessary for the sound health of government.' (To Madison, 1787.)

'What country can preserve its liberties, if its rulers are not warned from time to time that this people preserve the spirit of resistance. Let them take arms.' (To Colonel Smith, 1787.) *Thomas Jefferson on Democracy*, ed. by Saul K. Padover (Pelican, 1946), p. 168.

6. Deutsch, Julius, *The Civil War in Austria*, tr. by D. P. Berenberg (1934).

Gulick, Charles A., *Austria from Hapsburg to Hitler* (Berkeley, Los Angeles, 1948), 2 vols.

7. MacMurray, John, *Constructive Democracy* (London, n.d.), p. 26.

Corwin, Edward S., *The President: Office and Powers* (New York, 1948), quotes Senator Borah from a debate on 20 April 1928: 'Congress might, by refusing to make an appropriation or by limiting it to a specific purpose, make it physically impossible for the President to discharge his duty in a particular instance. . . But, if the Army [or] the Navy is in existence, if it is subject to command, he may send it where he will in the discharge of his duty to protect the life and property of American citizens. Undoubtedly he could send it, although the money were not in the Treasury.' (Notes to ch. 4.) Arthur Krock adds: 'In executing the supreme law of the land, the President could obviously do as much and more.' *The New York Times* (9 June 1949).

8. For government by emergency decree in the Weimar Republic see Friedensburg, Ferdinand, *Die Weimarer Republik* (Berlin, 1946).

Henemann, H. J., *The Growth of Executive Power in Germany* (Minneapolis, 1934).

9. Cf. Bergstraesser, L., *Geschichte der politischen Parteien in Deutschland* (Mannheim, Berlin, 1932), p. 168.

Borkenau, Franz, *The Communist International* (London, 1938).

Gumbel, E. J., *Verschwörer* (Berlin, 1924).

Noske, Gustav, *Von Kiel bis Kapp* (Berlin, 1920).

Oertzen, F. W. v., *Die deutschen Freikorps 1918-1923* (Munich, 1939).

Posse, E. H., *Die politischen Kampfbuende Deutschlands* (Berlin, 1930).

Schemann, L., *Wolfgang Kapp und das Märzunternehmen vom Jahre 1920* (Munich, 1937).

Schmidt-Pauli, E. v., *Geschichte der Freikorps 1918-1924* (Stuttgart, 1936).

Schweyer, F., *Politische Geheimverbaende* (Freiburg, 1925).

10. Lowenthal, Leo, and Guterman, Norbert, 'Portrait of the American Agitator,' *The Public Opinion Quarterly* (Fall, 1948), vol. 12, no. 3, pp. 417-29; and the authors' *Prophets of Deceit* (New York, 1950).

11. Cf. Lederer, Emil, *The State of the Masses* (New York, 1940).

12. Mosca, G., op. cit. pp. 154-5, 158f., 474, 488.

13. In a somewhat simplified and therefore over-optimistic fashion Burke voiced this view in his famous statement: 'Parliament is not a *congress* of ambassadors from different and hostile interests; which interests each must maintain as an agent and advocate, against other agents and advocates, but Parliament is a *deliberative* assembly of *one* nation, with *one* interest, that of the whole; where not local purposes, not local prejudices ought to guide, but the general good. . .' Quoted by C. J. Friedrich, *Constitutional Government and Politics* (New York, 1937), p. 230.

14. The essence of organization is that it creates fixed configurations that elicit a type of response and integration. Another trait of good organization is that it incorporates an idea which is better than the person acting as an individual. 'Today the opposition of the part to the whole has a functional basis.' . . . 'A powerful labor union or, *a fortiori*, a league of labor unions can impose its will upon the state. . . In order to obviate this danger, it is necessary to prevent at all costs, the rise of new sovereignties intermediate between the individual and the state.' Mosca, op. cit. p. 481.

15. Beckerath, E., 'Der moderne Absolutismus,' *Archiv fuer Weltwirtschaft und Seeverkehr* (1927).
     Coker, F. W., 'Pluralistic Theories and the Attack upon State Sovereignty,' in *A History of Political Theories*, ed. by W. A. Dunning (New York, 1902-20), vol. IV, *Recent Times*, pp. 80-119. (Extensive bibliography.)
     Cole, G. D. H., *A Short History of the British Working Class Movement* 1900-1927 (New York, 1927), ch. IV, pp. 63-77.
     —— *World of Labour* (London, 1928).
     —— and Postgate, Raymond, *The British Common People* 1746-1938 (New York, 1939).
     Elliott, W. Y., *The Pragmatic Revolt in Politics, Syndicalism, Fascism, and the Constitutional State* (New York, 1928).
     Freund, Michael, *Georges Sorel, Der Revolutionäre Konservativismus* (Frankfurt, 1932), bibliography p. 351, note 33.
     Greer, Thomas H., *American Social Reform Movements, Their Pattern since 1865* (New York, 1949).
     Lorwin, L. L., *Syndicalism in France* (New York, 1916).
     —— 'Syndicalism,' *Encyc. Soc. Sciences*, vol. XIV.
     —— *Labor and Internationalism* (New York, 1929), pp. 559-77.
     Perlman, Selig, and Taft, Philip, *History of Labor in the United States, 1896-1932* (New York, 1935), vol. IV, *Labor Movements*.

16. Cf. note 10, ch. 5.

17. Cf. Forsthoff, Ernst, *Deutsche Geschichte seit 1918 in Dokumenten* (Stuttgart, 1938).
     Moellendorff, Richard von, *Konservativer Sozialismus* (Hamburg, 1932), esp. 'Dokumente zur Gemeinwirtschaft,' pp. 212ff.

18. Neumann, Franz, *Behemoth* (New York, 1944), part III.

19. Griffith, E. S., *The Modern Government in Action* (New York, 1942), p. 51.

20. *A Free and Responsible Press* (Chicago, 1947), p. 17.

21. Bergstraesser, L., op. cit., pp. 140ff. Cf. note 7, ch. 1.

22. Lorenz von Stein has thrown into relief the 'experimental' attitude to-ward life of Saint-Simon, who stated, 'I have used marriage as a means to study the scholars which seemed to me indispensable for the execution of my undertaking.' Lorenz von Stein cites Louis Reybaud's characterization of Saint-Simon as 'correct and beautiful': 'Tranquil in the midst of this turmoil, judging others without being judged himself, gourmant, man of the world, spendthrift more by system than inclination, Saint-Simon crowded fifty years of living into one; he plunged into life instead of taking to it in a measured way in order to prematurely attain the wisdom of old age; he used and abused everything in order to put everything into his calculations at a later time; he vaccinated himself with the diseases of his century in order to determine their physiology at a later time. His was a completely experimental way of life. It would have been foolish to judge it in terms of ordinary standards.' Karl Mannheim, in lectures at Frankfurt University in 1932, used to trace a specifically modern attitude of experimentalism to Saint-Simon as one of the source points of sociological thinking. [Ed.] Cf. Stein, Lorenz von, *Der Sozialismus und Communismus des heutigen Frank-reichs, Ein Beitrag zur Zeitgeschichte* (Leipzig, 1848), vol. II, part III, pp. 239f.

Pragmatism, especially in the form of George H. Mead's 'social behavorism' and Max Weber's emphasis on an 'ethic of responsibility' as opposed to ethical absolutism are equally indicative of this experimental attitude. Cf. G. H. Mead, *Mind, Self, Society* (Chicago, 1934), and Max Weber, 'Politics as a Vocation,' *Essays in Sociology* (New York, 1946), pp. 118ff.

23. Characteristic is the fact that in England the Leader of His Majesty's Opposition is salaried by the administration he is opposing.

24. One may think of Friedrich Schiller's proverb 'Verstand ist stets bei wen'gen nur gewesen' and contrast it with Lincoln's sentence, 'You can fool some of the people all of the time, and all of the people some of the time, but you can't fool all of the people all of the time.' For modern socialism and its attitude characteristic is the line of the song of the German Las-salean's 'Das ist der Unverstand der Massen den nur des Geistes Schwert durchdringt. . .

For Lenin we may refer to the oft-cited passage, 'The history of all countries shows that the working class, exclusively by its own effort, is able to develop only trade-union consciousness, i.e. it may itself realize the necessity for combining in unions, to fight against the employers and to strive to compel the government to pass necessary labour legislation, etc.

'The theory of Socialism, however, grew out of the philosophic historical and economic theories that were elaborated by the educated representatives of the propertied classes, the intellectuals. The founders of modern scientific Socialism, Marx and Engels, themselves belonged to the bourgeois intel-ligentsia. Similarly, in Russia, the theoretical doctrine of social democracy arose quite independently of the spontaneous growth of the labor move-ment. . .' Lenin, V. I., 'What Is To Be Done,' *Collected Works* (New York, 1929), vol. IV, Book II, pp. 114f.

25. See Gallup, G., and Rae, S. F., *The Pulse of Democracy* (New York, 1940). Lazarsfeld, P. S., Berelson, B., Gaudet, H., *The People's Choice, How the Voter Makes Up His Mind in a Presidential Campaign* (New York, 1944).

26. This discussion owes a great deal to Mosca's approach to the problem. I tried to embody certain points of his theory in my own approach as I feel they are sounder than most of his explanations which have not yet assimilated the most skeptical arguments against Democracy. (Cf. Mosca, op. cit. p. 155.)

27. Moreno and his associates made a good beginning in exploring the nuclear composition of small social groups. Cf. Moreno, J. L., *Who Shall Survive? A New Approach to the Problem of Human Interrelations* (Washington, D.C., 1934). Nervous and Mental Disease Monographs.

28. Cf. Agar, Herbert, *Political Parties in the U.S.A.* (1904), p. 6. (Only in private circulation.)

29. Friedrich, C. J., *Constitutional Government* (New York, 1937), p. 283.

30. Ibid. pp. 283f.

31. Cf. Carpenter, W. S., *The Development of American Political Thought* (Princeton, 1930).
   Carter, Edward W., and Rohlfing, Charles C., 'The Constitution of the United States—A Bibliography,' *The Annals* (Amer. Acad. Soc. Pol. Science) (May 1936), pp. 190-200. (314 titles.)
   Gosnell, H. F., *Democracy—the Threshold of Freedom* (New York, 1948).
   Merriam, C. E., Gosnell, H. F., *The American Party System* (New York, 1940).
   Odegard, P. H., and Helms, E. A., *American Politics* (2nd ed. New York, London, 1947).

32. Cf. Agar's study, op. cit., which skilfully develops these features of the American system.

33. Interesting observations could be made in this connection on the emergence of novel features in various systems. The new and unusual has different chances in different group structures and different forms of group organization.

34. Cf. Fisher, Paul, 'Reparation Labor, A Preliminary Analysis,' *The Quarterly Journal of Economics* (May 1946), vol. LX, no. 3, pp. 313ff.
   Keynes, John Maynard, *The Economic Consequences of the Peace* (New York, 1920).

35. Agencies such as the Federal Communications Commission, emergency agencies such as the war labor boards under Presidents Wilson and Roosevelt in the United States, the Witley Councils in Great Britain after World War I, the 'Arbeitsgemeinschaft' between business leaders and trade-union leaders in Germany (1918) may be mentioned as segmental bodies serving such ends in limited areas.

36. Impressed by crises and uncertainties such as the abdication crisis in Great Britain, the camarilla influences surrounding President Hindenburg in 1932-3, or the uncertain outcome of presidential nominations in 'a smoke-filled room,' in case American parties have to choose 'a dark horse' candidate, the author is concerned with ways and means to guard against the uncertainties of either hereditary selection or such a postwar situation as Presidents Harding and Grant had to cope with, or the role of the presidency

during the eclipse of the Weimar Republic. There are notes to indicate that Karl Mannheim intended to elaborate the issue more fully. [Ed.]

37. This is not quite obvious in the light of modern investigations in the sociology of knowledge.

CHAPTER 7. FROM CUSTOM TO SOCIAL SCIENCE

1. Cf. Cook, Lloyd Allen, *Community Backgrounds of Education* (New York, 1938).

2. Cf. Allport, F. H., *Institutional Behavior* (Chapel Hill, 1933).

3. Cf. Waller, W., *The Sociology of Teaching* (New York, 1932), esp. part II, 'The School and the Community.'

4. Mannheim, Karl, *Diagnosis of Our Time* (London, 1943).

5. Cf. Muzafer, Sherif, *The Psychology of Social Norms* (New York, London, 1936). 'In the group situation the members of the group tend to structure the situation by converging toward a common norm in their judgments. If in the beginning of the experimental session they start with divergent judgments, in the course of the experiment they come together, the divergent one feeling uncertain and even insecure in the deviating position of his judgments. This convergence is not brought about instantly by the direct influence of one or two judgements on the other members of the group, it exhibits a temporal pattern. . . In short, when a group of individuals face a new instable situation and has no previously established interests or opinions regarding the situation, the result is not chaos; a common norm arises and the situation is structured in relation to the common norm. Once the common norm is established, later the separate individuals keep on receiving it in terms of the frame of reference which was once the norm of the group.' pp. 107, 111.

6. Hiller, E. T., *Principles of Sociology* (New York, London, 1933), p. 473.

7. Stanford Education Conference, *Social Education* (New York, 1939).

8. We hear, for instance, that with the increase of unemployment the proportion of adults to juveniles grows disturbingly. 'In 1850, there were only 889 adults over twenty for each 1000 youth under sixteen. This ratio was shifted until now there are more than 2100 adults for every 1000 youth, and if present trends continue this disproportion of adults to youth will increase. . . The area of work opportunities for youth has narrowed and the age at which youth begins work has constantly risen. The result of this situation is a tremendous increase in the number of adolescents remaining in school and an increasing gap between the time adolescents leave school and the time they secure jobs.' *Social Studies in General Education* (1938), pp. 99-105, cites for these figures Homer P. Rainey *et al.*, *How Fare American Youth?* (New York, 1937), pp. 41-2. A report to the American Council on Education.

Lindley, Betty and Ernest K., *A New Deal for Youth* (New York, 1939).

9. A note in the MS. reveals that the author had in mind elaborating two further examples: (a) planned group migration with choice as against emigration by infiltration; (b) social methods of dealing with delinquency.

10. Gruchy, Care de, *Creative Old Age* (San Francisco, 1946).

Martin, Lillien J., *A Handbook for Old Age Counsellors* (San Francisco, 1944).

Samson, Emily D., *Old Age in the New World* (London, 1944).

Simmons, Leo W., 'Attitudes toward Aging and the Aged: Primitive Societies,' *Journal of Gerontology* (Jan. 1946), vol. 1, no. 1, pp. 72-95.

11. Cf. Mannheim, Karl, *Man and Society* (New York, 1940), part III, 1, pp. 117ff.

12. On the terms 'social education' and 'educational sociology' cf. H. E. Barnes, H. and F. B. Becker, *Contemporary Social Theory* (New York, 1940), ch. 22, 'Some Contributions of Sociology to Education,' esp. pp. 793ff.

13. Cf. Cooley, C. H., *Social Organization* (New York, 1909, 1929).

Frank, L. K., 'Research in Child-Psychology, History and Prospect,' *Child Behavior and Development* by R. G. Barker *et al.* (New York, 1943).

Folsom, J. K., *The Family and Democratic Society* (New York, 1945).

Freud, A., and Burlingham, D., *Infants without Families. The Case for and against Residential Nurseries* (New York, 1944).

Glover, E., 'State Parentalism: Some Reflections on Present Tendencies,' *The New English Weekly* (23 March 1944).

Waller, Willard, *The Family* (New York, 1938).

Also the publications of L. K. Frank, Margaret Mead, and Kimball Young.

14. Cf. Schlesinger, R., *Changing Attitudes towards the Family in Soviet Russia* (London, 1948).

Heuss-Knapp, Elly, *Schmale Wege* (Stuttgart, Tuebingen, 1946). (Human interest stories documenting family difficulties under Nazism.)

Kirkpatrik, Clifford, *Nazi Germany: Its Women and Family Life* (Indianapolis, New York, 1938).

Mann, Erika, *School for Barbarians* (New York, 1938).

15. See Myrdal, Alva, *Nation and Family* (New York, London, 1941), esp. ch. v.

Glass, O. V., *Population: Policies and Movements in Europe* (Oxford, 1940).

16. Cf. Glover, E., 'State Parentalism. . .' loc. cit.

17. Ibid. and his *War, Sadism and Pacifism; Further Essays on Group Psychology and War* (London, 1946).

18. Cf. the publications of Lawrence K. Frank.

19. Cf. Golden, Anton S., and Rattenberg, Harold J., *The Dynamics of Industrial Democracy* (New York, London, 1942).

Mooney, James D., *The Principles of Organisation* (London, New York, 1939).

20. Mayo, Elton, *The Human Problem of an Industrial Civilization* (Boston, 1946).

21. Cf. note 53, ch. 5.

22. Cf. Cooley, C. H., op. cit.

23. Cf. Myrdal, Gunnar, *An American Dilemma. The Negro Problem and Modern Democracy* (New York, 1944).

24. Georg Simmel said many important things on this topic in his *Philosophie des Geldes* (Leipzig, 1900).

25. For the problem: How the old incentives to work are affected by our social security measures and what different countries have done to make up for this, cf. Gertrude Williams, *The Price of Social Security* (London, 1944).

26. *The Times* (19 Nov. 1942).

27. Freud, A., and Burlingham, D., op. cit., esp. p. 64 on toys inducing the desire for various gratifications.
    Murphy, L. B., *Social Behaviour and Child Personality, An Exploratory Study of Some Roots of Sympathy* (New York, 1937).
    Murray, Henry A., *et al.*, *Explorations in Personality* (New York, 1938).
    Young, Kimball, *Personality and Problems of Adjustment* (New York, 1944).

28. Cf. note 30, ch. 5.

29. Cf. Chadwick, H. M., *The Heroic Age* (Cambridge, 1926).

30. Cf. Klein, Viola, *The Feminine Character. The History of an Ideology* (London, 1946).
    Mead, Margaret, *Sex and Temperament* (New York, London, 1937).
    Thomas, W. I., *Sex and Society: Studies in the Social Psychology of Sex* (London, 1907).

31. *Britain and Her Birthrate* (London, 1945). (A report prepared by Mass-Observation for the Advertising Service Guild.)

32. Lindsay, A. D., Introduction to *Lectures on the Principles of Political Obligation*. (Reprinted from Thomas Hill Green's Philosophical Works, New York, 1948, vol. II.)

33. Cf. the anecdote quoted by Howard Becker, 'Sarcasso Iceberg: A Study in Cultural Lag and Institutional Disintegration,' *American Journal of Sociology* (Nov. 1928), vol. XXXIV, no. 3, pp. 498-9. 'In the latter part of the nineteenth century a *Landrat* conceived the rather startling notion of installing a water and sewage system in the village. . .' Under the influence of the Paulskirche Democracy he invited the peasants and burghers to a meeting but the proposal was unanimously rejected. Years later the *Landrat* was fiercely reproached by a villager. He reminded him that he had tried to persuade them. Whereupon the peasant retorted: 'Persuade? You should simply have compelled us, forced us!'

34. Cf. ch. 9, 'The Pattern of Democratic Personality,' I.

35. Cooley, Charles H., 'Personal Competition,' *Economic Studies* 4 (1899), pp. 78-183.
    Cf. May, M. A., Allport, Gordon, Murphy, Gardner, *et al.*, 'Memorandum on Research in Competition and Cooperation,' *Social Science Research Council* (April 1937) (New York).
    Mead, Margaret (ed.), *Cooperation and Competition among Primitive Peoples* (New York, 1937).

Murphy, G., *et al.* (eds.), *Experimental Social Psychology* (New York, 1937).

36. Waller, Willard, 'Rating and Dating Complex,' *American Sociological Review* (1937), vol. 2, pp. 727-34.

37. Cf. Bardin, S., *Pioneer Youth in Palestine* (New York, 1932).
Infield, H., *Cooperative Communities at Work* (New York, 1945).
——— *Cooperative Living in Palestine* (New York, 1944).
Revusky, A., *Jews in Palestine* (New York, 1936).
Sampter, J. (ed.), *Modern Palestine* (New York, 1933).
Stoloff, R., *Cooperatives and Collectives in Palestine* (New York, 1938).

38. May, M. A., and Doob, L. W., *Competition and Cooperation* (New York, 1937), p. 8.

39. 'The child who gets a little ego satisfaction from dominating and triumphing could also get a little ego satisfaction from being nice to everyone around,' Murphy, L. B., op. cit. p. 751.

40. This, of course, does not exclude cases where co-operation is combined with unequal distribution. In a hunting tribe, for instance, all the members may co-operate in securing the prey, but the booty may be divided according to a scheme which gives more to the people with higher prestige. Cf. Margaret Mead, *Cooperation and Competition. . .* op. cit.

41. See ch. 8, section 1.

CHAPTER 8. THE PATTERN OF DEMOCRATIC BEHAVIOR

1. This, of course, does not mean that we shall repeat our discussion of the social and psychological conditions for the emergence and development of behavior based upon such ideas.

2. Lasswell speaks of 'deference' in his *Analysis of Political Behaviour* (New York, 1948).

3. Anderson, H. H., 'Domination and Social Integration in the Behaviour of Kindergarten Children and Teachers,' *Genetic Psychology Monographs*, 21 (1939), pp. 287-385.

4. Piaget, J., *The Moral Judgement of the Child*, tr. by M. Gabain (London, 1932).

5. Read, Herbert, *Education through Art* (London, 1947).

6. Harding, D. W., 'The Custom of War and the Notion of Peace,' *Scrutiny* (1940), vol. IX, no. 3.
——— *The Impulse to Dominate* (London, 1941).

7. Cf. also Harding's article, loc. cit. pp. 207-8.

8. Cf. Parsons, Elsie C., *Fear and Conventionality* (New York, 1914). We may refer to the elaboration of ceremony in China under the rule of the Mandarins; to the place of etiquette in court society during the *ancien régime* of eighteenth-century France.

9. Cf. Harding's article, loc. cit.

Morley, John, *On Compromise* (London, 1891, 1923).

10. The confrontation of 'fanaticism' and 'enthusiasm' goes back to Lord Shaftesbury. Cf. Weiser, C. F., *Shaftesbury und das deutsche Geistesleben* (Leipzig, Berlin, 1916), pp. 130f., 270.

For a modern description of the fanatical attitude see Karl Jaspers, *Psychologie der Weltanschauungen* (3rd ed. Berlin, 1925), pp. 137-8.

11. Cf. Wilson, Logan, *The Academic Man* (New York, 1942).

Znaniecki, Florian, *The Social Role of the Man of Knowledge* (New York, 1940).

12. '. . . and it is the great merit of the liberal creed that it reduced the range of subjects on which agreement was necessary to one on which it was likely to exist in a society of free men,' Hayek, *Road to Serfdom* (London, 1944), p. 52.

13. See note 10 above.

14. In this connection new light is thrown on the philosophy of Plato and his followers who tend to conceive of essentials—of 'ideas'—as immutable entities. This tendency corresponds to a type of human experience that derives its pattern from a static world or at least wishes to stabilize the flow of events, even if this stabilization must be artificial. On the other hand, any philosophy that wants to understand an expanding world will have to emphasize the experience of dynamic elements against these efforts at stabilization.

15. As a matter of fact, the connection between punishment and free will is of comparatively recent origin. In primitive ages we find the belief that the evil-doer was motivated by the devil or an evil spirit and therefore must be punished. Cf. Thorndike, E. L., *Human Nature and the Social Order* (New York, 1940), p. 950; also Sutherland, E. H., op. cit. p. 335.

Mannheim, H., *Criminal Justice and Social Reconstruction* (London, 1946).

Reiwald, P., *Eroberung des Friedens* (Zurich, 1944).

Rusche, G., and Kirchheimer, Otto, *Punishment and Social Structure* (New York, 1939).

16. Friedlaender, K., op. cit. p. 365.

Young, Kimball, *Personality and the Problem of Adjustment* (New York, 1944), p. 354.

17. At later stages the response to these stimuli may become more conscious, and hence more selective, so that not every reward or punishment will meet with the desired response. See Miller, N. E., and Dollard, J., *Social Learning and Imitation* (London, 1945).

18. Murray, Henry A., et al., *Explorations in Personality* (New York, 1938), p. 190.

19. Mumford, Lewis, *The Condition of Man* (New York, 1945), esp. glossary.

20. '. . . It suggests that the problem of education in dealing with emotion is less that of suppression and rigid regulation and more that of organizing conditions to minimize violent reaction and to provide opportunities for the

reasonable working through of vital energies.' Prescott, D. A., *Emotion and the Educative Process*, American Council of Education (Washington, D.C., 1938), p. 59.

21. Rousseau, Jean-Jacques, *Émile* (Flammarion ed., Paris), vol. 1, pp. 80-81. Quoted by K. D. Benne, *A Conception of Authority* (New York, 1943), pp. 117f.

22. Fromm, Erich, *Escape from Freedom* (New York, 1941).

23. Cf. F. Moreno's ideas on spontaneity in his *Who Shall Survive?* (Washington, D.C., 1934).

24. A note in the MS. indicates that the author intended to elaborate further on progressive education. He mentions the following seven main ideas:

1. To organize the curriculum around *functional nuclei or purposes* rather than in terms of the traditional subject matter.
2. To organize large projects or *coherent units of work*, each of which involves planning. They would be concerned with *field organization, reading, manual work*, and *co-operative activity* to give scope to differential abilities of pupils that are socially significant and naturally integrating.
3. To substitute the satisfaction of *self-improvement* for those of competitive victory over others; to set up 'achievable goals.'
4. To recognize and use *individual differences* more realistically than has been done by conventional schools.
5. To encourage *creative self-expressive activity*.
6. To make the school genuinely enjoyable.
7. To time various activities and subject matter according to the normal development of interests with age; to offer material when the child is ready for it. [Ed.]

Cf. MacLean, M. S., 'Future Pattern of Education,' *The Educational Scene* (May 1937), p. 178, quoted by J. H. Folsom, *Youth, Family and Education* (Washington, D.C., 1944).

25. Green, T. H., *Collected Works* (London, 1885-8), vol. II, *The Principles of Political Obligation*.

26. Cf. Mannheim, Karl, *Man and Society* (New York, 1940), pp. 295ff., 299ff.; also *Ideology and Utopia* (New York, London, 1936).

27. Cf. MacIver, R. M., *Society, a Textbook of Sociology* (New York, 1937). Cooley, C. H., *Social Process* (New York, 1918).

28. Gurvitch, Georges, *Sociology of Law* (New York, 1942), p. 211. (Engl. ed. p. 166.)

29. Ibid. p. 215. (Engl. ed. p. 169.)

30. Young, Kimball, *Personality and Problems of Adjustment* (New York, 1944).

31. Cf. Honigsheim, Paul, 'The Roots of the Nazi Concept of the Ideal German Peasant,' *Rural Sociology* (March 1947), vol. 12, no. 1.
L'Houet, A., *Psychologie des Bauerntums* (3rd ed. Tuebingen, 1935).
Martini, Fritz, *Das Bauerntum im deutschen Schrifttum von den Anfaengen bis zum 16 Jahrhundert* (Halle, 1944).

Sorokin, P. A., and Zimmerman, C. C., *A Systematic Source Book in Rural Sociology* (Minneapolis, 1930-32).

Thomas, W. I., and Znaniecki, F., *The Polish Peasant in Europe and America* (Chicago, 1918-20).

Weber, Max, 'Capitalism and Rural Society in Germany,' *Essays in Sociology* (New York, 1946), pp. 363-85.

32. Margaret Mead gives an interesting example of 'undeveloped' property sense among Manus children, in her *Growing Up in New Guinea* (London, 1931), pp. 93f.

33. Cf. on pride of status, Logan Wilson, *Academic Man*, esp. parts II and III.

Hughes, E. C., 'Institutional Office and the Office,' loc. cit.

Merton, R. K., 'Social Structure and Anomie,' *American Sociological Review* (1938), vol. III.

Veblen, T., *The Higher Learning in America* (New York, 1918).

34. Blain, L., *Les Sentiments familiaux* (Paris, 1927).

Folsom, K., *The Family and Democratic Society* (New York, 1943).

Paulhan, F., *Les Transformations sociales des sentiments* (Paris, 1920).

35. For a full discussion of these changes see Myrdal, Alva, *Nation and Family* (New York, 1941).

Cf. also 'The American Family in World War II,' *The Annals* (Amer. Acad. Pol. Soc. Science) (Sept. 1943), vol. 229.

Kolb, William, 'Sociologically Established Family Norms and Democratic Values,' *Social Forces* (May 1948), vol. 26, no. 4, pp. 451-6.

36. Calhoun, Arthur W., *A History of the American Family from Colonial Times to the Present* (New York, 1945).

37. Myrdal, Alva, op. cit. p. 506.

38. Cf. 'Social Problems and Policies in Sweden,' *The Annals* (May 1938), vol. 197, esp. pp. 200-232.

Winter, Ella, *Red Virtue* (New York, 1933).

39. See note 10, ch. 7.

CHAPTER 9. THE PATTERN OF DEMOCRATIC PERSONALITY

1. Newcomb, Theodore M., and Hartley, Eugene L. (eds.), *Readings in Social Psychology* (New York, 1947).

See also bibliography in Mannheim, Karl, *Man and Society* (New York, 1940), esp. pp. 390ff.

Dollard, John, *Frustration and Aggression* (New Haven, 1939).

Fromm, Erich, *Escape from Freedom* (New York, 1941).

—— 'Individual and Social Origins of Neurosis,' *American Sociological Review* (1944), vol. IX.

Green, Arnold W., 'Sociological Analysis of Horney and Fromm,' *The American Journal of Sociology* (May 1946), vol. 51, no. 6, pp. 533-40.

Gurvitch, Georges, and Moore, Wilbert E. (eds.), *Twentieth Century Sociology* (New York, 1945).

Klein, Viola, *The Feminine Character: The History of an Ideology* (London, 1946).

Linton, Ralph (ed.), *The Science of Man in the World Crisis* (New York, 1945).

Mead, Margaret, *Sex and Temperament in Three Primitive Societies* (New York, 1935).

2. Weber, Max, *The Protestant Ethic and the Spirit of Capitalism*, tr. by Talcott Parsons (London, 1930).

—— 'The Protestant Sects and the Spirit of Capitalism,' *Essays in Sociology* (New York, 1946), pp. 302-22.

—— 'Confucianism and Taoism,' *Gesammelte Aufsaetze zur Religionssoziologie* (Tuebingen, 1920), vol. 1, pp. 512-36. (Forthcoming translation by H. H. Gerth, Glencoe, Ill.)

3. Hodges, H. A., *Wilhelm Dilthey: An Introduction* (New York, 1944).

Hoffmann, P. T., *Der Mittelalterliche Mensch* (Gotha, 1922).

Martin, Alfred W. von, *Sociology of the Renaissance* (New York, 1944, Stuttgart, 1932).

Mumford, Lewis, *The Condition of Man* (New York, 1945).

Strich, W., *Der Irrationale Mensch* (Berlin, 1928). Studien zur Systematik der Geschichte.

Tawney, R. H., *Religion and the Rise of Capitalism* (London, 1938).

Wieser, M., *Der sentimentale Mensch gesehen aus der Welt hollaendischer und deutscher Mystiker im 18 Jahrhundert* (Gotha, Stuttgart, 1924).

4. On patronage in politics, see White, Leonard D., 'Spoils System,' *Encyc. Soc. Sciences*, vol. XIV, pp. 301-5. On patronage in the arts, see Bukofzer, Manfred F., *Music in the Baroque Era* (New York, 1947), esp. pp. 404-11.

Dorian, Frederick, *The Musical Workshop* (New York, London, 1947), ch. v, 'Music Made to Order,' pp. 104-19.

Neumann, Carl, *Rembrandt* (Munich, 1922), vol. I, on the social position of the Dutch painters, pp. 121-30.

5. Cf. Mead, G. H., *Mind, Self, and Society* (Chicago, 1934).

—— *Philosophy of the Act* (Chicago, 1938).

Kolb, William, 'A Critical Evaluation of Mead's "I" and "Me" Concepts,' *Social Forces* (March 1944), vol. 22, no. 3, pp. 291-6.

Scheler, Max, *Der Formalismus in der Ethik und die Materiale Wertethik* (Halle, 1927).

6. Cf. p. 201.

7. Cf. Becker, Howard, *German Youth* (New York, 1946).

Fromm, Erich, op. cit. ch. v, pp. 136-207.

Hemm, Ludwig, 'Die unteren Fuehrer in der HJ. Versuch ihrer psychologischen Tiefengliederung,' *Zeitschrift fuer angewandte Psychologie und Charakterkunde* (1940), Beiheft 87.

8. The following statement sums up what nontotalitarian progressive groups have learned from the past, and shows a new spirit at work: 'Throughout the world, leaders in government and in industry are more and more committed to a program of sustained full employment. This does not mean that everyone believes that perfection can be achieved. We shall fall short of the goal aimed at. There will be fluctuations in employment. But we are determined, through antidepression measures, to moderate these fluctuations. All modern governments are increasingly committed to expansionist developmental programs, to the promotion of rising standards of living and to the

creation of underlying conditions necessary for the attainment of full employment.

'A new attitude, moreover, is prevalent among the leading industrial countries with respect to the primary-producing and economically backward countries. In former times these retarded countries throughout the world were condemned to the position of economic colonies. They were mere appendages to the economies of the great industrial nations. Economic policies were as a matter of course directed toward the continuance of the status of economic colonialism. The industrially backward countries were expected to supply raw materials for the great countries and, in turn, to furnish a market for manufactured goods.

'There is a new outlook abroad in the world today. Now, everywhere the note is sounded that development, diversification and industrialization must be undertaken in the backward areas. We have come to realize that the future trade of the world cannot continue to run in the simplified terms of exchange of raw materials for finished manufactured products. Rather it must run in terms of highly diversified trade between countries with different skills and resources but each developed to the fullest possible extent. Large-scale developmental projects, industrialization to an extent that is economically feasible, and the diversification of agriculture, the development and improvement of human resources through improved health, nutrition and education, the promotion of a higher standard of living, rising productivity, and increased purchasing power—these are the new world economic goals. They promise a more stable economy and better living standards everywhere.' A. H. Hansen, *America's Role in the World Economy* (New York, 1945), pp. 19-20.

9. The status-ridden character of present-day American society has been most thoroughly investigated by W. Lloyd Warner and Paul S. Lunt in *The Status System of a Modern Community* (New Haven, 1942), vol. 2, Yankee City Series.

Similar studies were done by

Clayton, Horace, and Drake, St. Clair, *Black Metropolis* (New York, 1945).

Dollard, John, *Caste and Class in a Southern Town* (New York, 1937).

Powdermaker, Hortense, *After Freedom* (New York, 1939).

Frazier, E. Franklin, *The Negro Family in the United States* (Chicago, 1939), locates different family patterns in the context of status and income differentials.

Hughes, Everett, *French Canada in Transition* (Chicago, 1943), and *The Social Systems of American Ethnic Groups* by Leo Srole (New Haven, 1946), trace the interrelations between ethnic and class differences.

Warner, W. Lloyd, Havighurst, R. J., Loeb, Martin B., *Who Shall Be Educated? The Challenge of Unequal Opportunities* (New York, 1944), analyzes the functioning of the schools in the status system of the United States.

West, James (Carl Withers), *Plainville U.S.A.* (New York, 1945).

Zorbaugh, Harvey Warren, *The Gold Coast and the Slum* (Chicago, 1929).

For a brief but incisive review of recent American literature, see Edward Shils, *The Present State of American Sociology* (Glencoe, Ill., 1948), on 'Class Stratification,' pp. 12-25.

On the German status structure see

Gerth, Hans H., 'Germany on the Eve of Occupation,' *Problems of the*

Post War World, A Symposium on Post War Problems, ed. by Thomas C. T. McCormick (New York, London, 1945), pp. 391-439.

Parsons, Talcott, 'The Problem of Controlled Institutional Change, An Essay on Applied Social Science,' *Psychiatry* (February 1945), vol. 8, no. 1.

Weber, Max, 'Capitalism and Rural Society in Germany'; 'National Character and the Junkers'; 'Bureaucracy'; 'Class, Status, Power,' *Essays in Sociology* (New York, 1946).

For the status image of the German peasant see

Honigsheim, Paul, 'The Roots of the Nazi Concept of the Ideal German Peasant,' *Rural Sociology* (March 1947), vol. 12, no. 1, pp. 3-21. (Extensive bibliography.)

For Great Britain see

Abshagen, K. H., *King, Lords, and Gentlemen,* op. cit.

Dibelius, Wilhelm, *England,* tr. by M. A. Hamilton, Introduction by A. D. Lindsay (New York, 1930) (4th ed. Stuttgart, 1925).

10. Hiller, E. T., *Principles of Sociology* (New York, London, 1933), p. 226.

Cooley, C. H., 'Personal Competition, Its Place in the Social Order and Effect upon Individuals; with Some Considerations on Success,' *Economic Studies* (April 1899), vol. IV, no. 2. Section VII on Restlessness, Insecurity, and Strain, pp. 157-63.

11. The following statement aptly expresses the idea that freedom is compatible with guidance: 'Thus, though the personality has to choose its own way of developing, we can at the same time help it to choose. This paradox is identical with that of the botanist who has to let the plant grow in its own way but at the same time can produce, under controlled conditions, plants of great beauty and ruggedness which do not know how to produce themselves in certain climatic and geographical zones. The possibilities for self-creation are infinite, provided the environment is infinitely friendly for such purposes; but since the environment is far from infinitely friendly, the experimenter, considering both the organism and the world, permits free growth along certain lines by removing barriers.' Gardner Murphy, speaking about Moreno, in his *Experimental Social Psychology* (New York, London, 1937), p. 316.

12. Lukacs, Georg, 'Die Verdinglichung und das Bewusstsein des Proletariats,' *Geschichte und Klassenbewusstsein: Studien ueber Marxistische Dialektik* (Berlin, 1923), pp. 94-228.

Rosenberg, Harold, 'The Resurrected Romans,' *Kenyon Review* (Autumn 1948), vol. X, no. 4, pp. 602-20; the first of a series of essays on Marx's drama of history.

13. Marx-Engels, *Der historische Materialismus Frühschriften,* ed. by Mayer and J. P. Landshut (Leipzig, 1932), p. 325.

14. Ibid.

15. Ibid. p. 357.

16. Ibid. pp. 326, 359f.

17. Mead, G. H., *Mind, Self, and Society* (Chicago, 1934), pp. 186f.

18. Ibid. p. 188. Cf. a parallel statement of Karl Marx in *Frühschriften,* p. 328.

19. Mead, *Mind, Self, Society*, p. 222.

20. Ibid. p. 224, note.

21. 'A man's social Self is the recognition which he gets from his mates. We are not only gregarious animals liking to be in the sight of our fellows, but we have an innate propensity to get ourselves noticed, noticed favorably, by our kind. . . Properly speaking, a man has as many social selves as there are individuals who recognize him and carry an image of him in their mind.' William James, *The Principles of Psychology* (New York, 1890), vol. I, pp. 293f.

22. 'In some respects, of course, we can determine what that self is going to do. We can accept certain responsibilities in advance. One makes contracts and promises, and one is bound by them. . . In the duties of what we call rational conduct, in adjusting ourselves to a world in which the laws of nature and of economics and of political systems obtain, we can state what is going to happen and take over the responsibility for the thing we are going to do, and yet the real self that appears in that act awaits the completion of the act itself. Now, it is this living act which never gets directly into reflective experience. It is only after the act has taken place that we can catch it in our memory and place it in terms of that which we have done. It is that "I" which we may be said to be continually trying to realize, and to realize through the actual conduct itself. One does not ever get it fully before himself.' G. H. Mead, op. cit. p. 203.

Kolb, William, 'A Critical Evaluation of Mead's "I" and "Me" Concept,' loc. cit.

23. Young, Kimball, *Personality and the Problems of Adjustment* (New York, 1944), pp. 164-87.

24. Hallowell, John H., *The Decline of Liberalism as an Ideology with Particular Reference to German Politico-Legal Thought* (Berkeley, Los Angeles, 1943).

25. Cooley, Charles H., in his *Social Organization, A Study of the Larger Mind* (New York, 1929), raises some good points about the dangers of over-conventionalization. See ch. xxx, 'Formalism and Disorganization.'

Parsons, Elsie Worthington (Clews), *Fear and Conventionality* (New York, 1914).

CHAPTER 10. EDUCATION AS GROUNDWORK

1. Warner, W. Lloyd, Havighurst, R. J., and Loeb, M. B., *Who Shall Be Educated?* (New York, 1944), p. 55.

2. Hiller, E. T., *Principles of Sociology* (New York, London, 1933), p. 619.

3. Ibid. p. 618.

4. The problems the author had in mind while writing the rest of this chapter are summarized in a note attached to the manuscript:
  1. What shall be the content of the higher ferment?
  2. It is understanding the leading ideas of one's own age (Ortega y Gasset).

3. Man's place in Nature, but even more in Society—Human Nature and its plasticity—Conditions of the formation of Man.

4. Systems of *Weltanschauung*.

5. Responsibility for common tasks.

6. Educational groundwork for the social transformation of Man.

7. Separation of ideas on which we need to agree from controversial ones. [Ed.]

5. Cf. Counts, C. S., *Dare the Schools Build a New Social Order?* (New York, 1932).
   Kähler, A., and Hamburger, E., *Education for an Industrial Age* (New York, 1948).

6. *The Purpose and Content of the Youth Service* (London, 1943); a report of the Youth Advisory Council appointed by the Minister of Education in 1943.
   Industry and Education, A Statement (Nuffield College, Oxford, 1943), puts similar modern emphasis on continuity of education and proposes to integrate technical education into the scheme of education.

7. Op. cit. p. 15.

8. Cf. Durant, Ruth, *Watling: A Survey of Social Life on a New Housing Estate* (London, 1939).
   —— 'Social Aspects of Town Planning,' *Architectural Review* (March 1945).
   Community Centres Circular (London). Red Paper by the Ministry of Education.

9. Pearse, Innes H., and Crocker, Lucy H., *The Peckham Experiment. A Study in Living Structure of Society* (London, 1943).

10. Cf. Jacob L. Moreno's concept of spontaneity in *Who Shall Survive?* (Washington, D.C., 1934), p. 710.

11. *The Purpose and Content of Youth Service*, op. cit. p. 15.

12. Counts, C. S., op. cit.
    The report of the Nuffield College on 'Industry and Education,' op. cit., rightly says: '. . . it must be clearly understood that the main purpose of day-time continued education is not vocational but an extension of general education beyond the statutory leaving age and the provision of a much-needed bridge between school and adult education.' p. 10.

13. Tawney, R. H., *Education: The Task Before Us* (London, n.d.), p. 5.

14. Hodges, H. A., *Wilhelm Dilthey: An Introduction* (New York, London, 1944).

15. *Industry and Education*, op. cit. p. 26.

16. Ibid. p. 27.

17. Ortega y Gasset, José, *The Mission of the University*, tr. with an Introduction by Howard Lee Nostrand (Princeton, 1944; London, 1946).
    Cf. also the following Princeton University Press publications on related topics:
    The Meaning of the Humanities, 5 essays by various authors (1938).

Foerster, Norman, *et al.*, *The Humanities after the War* (1944).

Stroyer, Joseph R., *et al.*, *The Interpretation of History* (1945).

Other valuable contributions to the problem of the University in our Age are:

Carr-Saunders, H., 'The Function of Universities in the Modern World,' *The Sociological Review* (1940), vol. 32.

Etudiants à la recherche de leur université, Institut International de Cooperation Intellectuelle (Paris, 1938).

Flexner, Abraham, *Universities, American, English, German* (New York, 1944), Second Educational Conference, 15 April 1944.

Hutchins, R. M., *The Higher Learning in America* (New Haven, 1936).

Jaeger, Werner, *Stellung und Aufgaben der Universitaet in der Gegenwart* (Berlin, 1924), and Jaspers, Karl, *Die Idee der Universitaet* (Berlin, 1925), are two able presentations of the conservative view during the Weimar Republic; see also Jaspers' *Vom lebendigen Geist der Universitaet* (Heidelberg, 1946).

Millet, Fred B., *The Rebirth of Liberal Education* (New York, 1945).

Nash, Arnold S., *The University and the Modern World: An Essay in the Social Philosophy of University Education* (London, 1945).

Simon, Sir Ernest, *The Development of Political Universities* (London, 1945).

Truscott, Bruce, *Redbrick University* (London, 1943).

——— *Redbrick and the Vital Days* (London, 1945).

18. Cf. Mannheim, Karl, *Die Gegenwartsaufgaben der Soziologie* (Tuebingen, 1932).

As early as 1932-3 Professor Adolph Lowe and I arranged such interdepartmental courses and especially a joint seminar at the University of Frankfurt. On the underlying concept of a university cf. Lowe, Adolph, 'Das gegenwaertige Bildungsproblem der deutschen Universitaet,' *Die Erziehung*, vol. VII, no. 1.

Lowe, Adolph, *Universities in Transformation* (London, 1940).

See also Adams, Charles C., *Selected References on the Relation of Science to Modern Life* (Albany, 1940).

Clarke, F., *Freedom in the Educative Society* (1948).

Linton, Ralph (ed.), *The Science of Man in the World Crisis* (New York, 1945).

Lynd, Robert S., *Knowledge for What? The Place of Social Science in American Culture* (Princeton, 1939).

Young, Kimball, 'The Need of Integration of Attitudes among Scientists,' *Science Monthly* (1924), vol. 18, pp. 291-305.

19. Cf. as an early attempt Gray, G. W., *Education on an International Scale* (New York, 1941).

20. Chapman, Guy, *Culture and Survival* (London, 1940).

Hartnacke, W., and Wohlfahrt, E., *Geist und Torheit auf Primanerbänken* (Dresden, 1934).

——— *Bildungswahn-Volkstod* (Munich, 1932).

Leybourne and White, *Education and the Birth Rate* (London, 1940).

National Union of Teachers, *The Service of Youth* (1940).

21. Orr, Sir John Boyd, *Food, Health, and Income: Report on a Survey of Adequacy of Diet in Relation to Income* (London, 1936).

Gray, J. L., *The Nation's Intelligence* (London, 1936), p. 136.

——— and Moshinsky, Pearl, 'Ability and Opportunity in English Education,' *The Sociological Review* (April 1935), vol. 27, no. 2.

22. Kobler, Frank J., 'Cultural Differences in Intelligence,' *The Journal of Social Psychology* (1943), vol. 18, pp. 279-303; also pp. 295, 297.

23. Gray, J. L., *The Nation's Intelligence*, op. cit. p. 140.

24. Ichheiser rightly emphasizes that disturbances in action (*apraxie*) can be due first to personal shortcomings, second to hindrances in the objective fields of action, and third (the most important factor) to the consciousness of such hindrances. This 'preconception' (Jackson) of what is feasible or impossible greatly influences our ability and through it our whole personality. Gustav Ichheiser, 'Zur Psychologie des Nichtkoennens,' *Archiv fuer die Gesamte Psychologie* (1934), vol. 92, pp. 358-63.

25. Wittlin, Alma, *The Museum* (London, forthcoming).

The New Jersey Library established 'teen age corners.' Daily attendance and the number of books borrowed has increased considerably. *The New York Times* (28 May 1949), p. 12.

26. Cf. Farrell, James T., 'The Fate of Writing in America,' *New Directions* 9 (New York, 1946).

Heine, Patricke Johns, and Gerth, H. H., 'Values in Mass Periodical Fiction, 1921-1940,' *The Public Opinion Quarterly* (Spring 1949), pp. 105-13.

Waples, Douglas, Berelson, B., Bradshaw, F. R., *What Reading Does to the People* (Chicago, 1940).

27. Dewey, John, *Democracy and Education* (New York, 1916).

28. Naumann, H., *Grundzuege der deutschen Volkskunde* (2nd ed. Leipzig, 1929).

29. Cf. ch. 3, note 33.

CHAPTER 11. WORK AND LEISURE

1. One of the major sociological controversies of recent decades has turned on work incentives and the rise of Capitalism in the Western world. Max Weber (*The Protestant Ethic and the Spirit of Capitalism*, tr. by Talcott Parsons, New York, 1930, and 'The Protestant Sects and the Spirit of Capitalism,' in *From Max Weber: Essays in Sociology*, tr. by H. H. Gerth and C. Wright Mills, New York, 1946) attached great weight to the economic ramifications of the Protestant ethic, especially in its Calvinist form. His critical opponents, Brentano, Robertson, and Tawney notably, without distinguishing sharply between different types of Capitalism, trace capitalist behavior back to the Catholic Middle Ages, and point more definitely to nonreligious influences.

Cf. Brentano, Lujo, *Der Wirtschaftende Mensch in der Geschichte* (Leipzig, 1923).

Calverton, V. F., *The Passing of the Gods* (New York, 1934).

——— *The Awakening of America* (New York, 1939).

Parsons, Talcott, and Robertson, H. M., 'Max Weber and His School,' *Journal of Political Economy* (Oct. 1935), vol. XLIII.

Robertson, H. M., *The Rise of Economic Individualism* (Cambridge Studies in Economic History, 1935).

Schulze-Gaevernitz, G. v., 'Die geistigen Grundlagen der angelsächsischen Weltherrschaft,' *Archiv für Sozialwissenschaft und Sozialpolitik* (1926-7), vols. 56-8.

Sée, Henri, *Les Origines du capitalisme moderne* (Paris, 1940).

Sombart, Werner, *Der moderne Kapitalismus* (Munich, Leipzig, 1928).

Tawney, R. H., *Religion and the Rise of Capitalism* (Penguin ed. London, 1937). (With an interesting new Preface.)

For a good summary of the whole controversy and literature, cf. Fischoff, Ephraim, 'The Protestant Ethic and the Spirit of Capitalism, the History of a Controversy,' *Social Research* (Feb. 1944), vol. XI.

For a good illustration of the role of 'money making' as a major work incentive in contemporary America, cf. Lynd, R. S., *Middletown* (New York, 1929), ch. VIII, 'Why Do They Work So Hard?'

2. The Judaic-Christian concept of work as punishment for original sin was to a large extent determined by the prevailing heavy work and slavery. Actually the negative concept was always surpassed by an affirmation of work as creation.

3. Henry de Man's *Joy in Work* (London, 1929) is based on essays of student-workers at Frankfort-on-the-Main. Considering the special mentality of this very small group and their unrepresentativeness of German labor, one should be careful in generalizing from his highly interesting material.

Jacks, L. P., *My Neighbour the Universe, a Study in Human Labour* (New York, 1929).

Masaryk, T. G., *The Ideals of Humanity and How to Work* (London, 1938).

Maurois, André, *The Art of Living* (New York, London, 1940), ch. VI, 'The Art of Working.'

4. Bücher, Karl, *Industrial Revolution* (New York, 1912).

Herkner, Heinrich, *Die Arbeitsfreude in Theorie und Praxis der Volkswirtschaft* (1905).

——— 'Arbeit und Arbeitsteilung,' *Grundriss der Sozialoekonomik* (Tuebingen, 1923), section II, part I.

Levasseur, E., *Histoire des 'classes ouvrières avant* 1789 (2nd ed., 1900), vol. I.

Michels, Roberto, 'Wirtschaft und Rasse,' *Grundriss der Sozialoekonomik*.

Riehl, W. H., *Die deutsche Arbeit* (1861).

Ruskin, John, *Stones of Venice*, vol. II, ch. VI.

Sombart, Werner, *Der moderne Kapitalismus*, op. cit. vol. I, pp. 193-4. Sombart romanticizes handicraftwork and its product as the 'faithful document of its creator's personality.'

5. Cf. Weber, Max, 'Hinduismus und Buddhismus,' *Gesammelte Aufsaetze zur Religionssoziologie* (Tuebingen, 1921), vol. II, esp. pp. 176ff.

6. Studies in 'industrial sociology' have shown that output in a factory does not depend exclusively on the wage level of the worker no matter what the 'incentive system' of pay. The social setting of factory work, heightened feelings of status, the worker's feeling of participation in relevant decisions of management and concomitant psychological states influence

output significantly. Hence, management in capitalist society realizes—at least theoretically and in the case of its most enlightened representatives—the fallacy of dissecting the employee as *homo economicus*. Social relations in and outside of the factory greatly influence attitudes toward work.

Bell, Daniel, 'Adjusting Men to Machines,' *Commentary* (Jan. 1947), vol. III, no. 1, gives a critical evaluation of recent American literature in industrial sociology.

Franzen-Hellersberg, Elizabeth, *Das Leben der Jugendlichen Arbeiterin* (Tuebingen, 1932). An exemplary nonstatistical inquiry in the maturation problems and attitudes toward home life, work, fellow workers, superiors, etc. of unorganized and not 'class conscious' working women.

Gardener, Burleigh B., and Whyte, William F., 'Methods for the Study of Human Relations in Industry,' *American Sociological Review* (1946), vol. II, pp. 500-512.

7. Lange-Eichbaum, W., *Genie, Irrsinn, Ruhm* (2nd ed. 1935). (Extensive bibliography.)

MacDonald, William, *The Intellectual Worker and His Work* (New York, 1924).

Mayo, P. E., *The Social Problems of an Industrial Civilization* (Cambridge, 1945).

Merton, Robert K., *Science, Technology and Society in 17th Century England* (Bruges, 1938).

Moore, Wilbert, *Industrial Relations and the Social Order* (New York, 1946), ch. XIII, 'The Worker and the Machine.' (The outstanding textbook in industrial sociology with extensive bibliographies.)

Roethlisberger, F. J., and Dickson, W. J., *Management and the Worker* (Cambridge, 1941).

Whitehead, T. N., *Leadership in a Free Society* (Cambridge, 1937).

Wilson, Logan, *The Academic Man* (New York, 1942).

Zilsel, Edgar, *Die Entstehung des Geniebegriffes* (Tuebingen, 1926).

Znaniecki, Florian, *The Social Role of the Man of Knowledge* (New York, 1940).

Zweig, F., *Labour, Life and Poverty* (London, 1948).

8. Cf. Weber, Max, 'Bureaucracy,' *Essays in Sociology,* op. cit. pp. 196-244.

9. Cf. the wartime article, 'No One Works Just for Money,' by Lord Londonderry, K.G., in *Rotarian* (Dec. 1944), 65, 29.

10. Kotschnig, W. M., *Unemployment in the Learned Professions* (New York, London, 1937), esp. pp. 283-6.

11. This problem has not lost its significance since the war, at least not in England. Under the heading 'Will Graduates Be Unemployed?' London's *Economist* put the following questions: 'Will there be a sudden slump in the prestige of university education next summer, because of a steep increase in unemployment among young graduates? Are too many art students passing through the universities? Does a university education stimulate excessive hopes in the hearts of its beneficiaries? What can be done to persuade young men and women from the university to go willingly into business, and business to take more art students?' *The Economist* (20 Dec. 1947).

12. Hartshorne, E. Y., *The German Universities and National Socialism* (Cambridge, 1937).

For figures on the social composition of the German students from 1928-1934-5, cf. H. H. Gerth, 'Germany on the Eve of Occupation,' in *Problems of the Post War World*, ed. by T. C. McCormick (New York, 1945), p. 423. Under Nazism the student body of the then twenty-five state universities was cut by two-thirds, from 130,000 students in 1932 to 40,000 students in 1935. Before the war shortages of professional men existed in such war-essential skill groups as doctors, engineers, and teachers. The Nazi party under the pressure of the army command reversed its line in the winter 1936-37. Professions were ballyhooed; Hitler Youth guards were placed in front of monuments honoring medical men like Robert Koch; his tragic life was presented on the screen. Engineers were celebrated in historical essays in the daily press, and youth was held to pay deference to their teachers.' p. 422.

13. Cf. conclusion No. 18 of the Nuffield Report on 'Industry and Education, stressing 'that all possible steps should be taken to raise the quality of entrants to apprenticeships in the skilled manual crafts and to remove the bias of the educational system against entry into manual occupations. That is of the greatest importance to raise the prestige of high manual skill.' pp. 33-4.

'In order to secure a contented labor force of high productive and personal quality, it is essential to do everything possible to avoid a sense of thwartedness developing among those who have no prospect of rising through craftsmanship and higher vocational training in their specific jobs. This requires the widest possible opening of the opportunities for higher cultural education.' Ibid. pp. 13-14.

14. Jacks, L. P., *Responsibility and Culture* (New Haven, 1924), 'Labor and Leisure.'
———*Education through Recreation* (New York, 1932).
Mumford, Lewis, *Technique and Civilization* (New York, 1934).
Russell, Bertrand, *In Praise of Idleness* (1935).
Todd, A. J., *Industry and Society* (New York, 1933), ch. xiv, 'Hours and Leisure.'
L. P. Jacks presents a different concept of labor and leisure. Whereas Russell sees labor and leisure as opposites, Jacks views them as two different kinds of activities. Russell wishes to reduce labor to gain leisure, whereas Jacks proposes to raise labor to higher levels.
Cf. also Veblen, Thorstein, *The Theory of the Leisure Class: An Economic Study of Institutions* (New York, 1935).
———'The Instinct of Workmanship and the Irksomeness of Labour,' *American Journal of Sociology* (1898), vol. iv.

15. Bücher, G. Karl, *Arbeit und Rhythmus* (Leipzig, 1899).

16. For a description of leisure-time activities in an average community of contemporary America see Robert Lynd, *Middletown*, ch. iv, 'Using Leisure.' Lynd shows that leisure-time activities become more standardized with greater organization.
Durant, Henry, *The Problem of Leisure* (London, 1938).
Steiner, Jesse, *Americans at Play* (New York, 1933).
Encyclopedia of the Social Sciences, 'Amusements,' 'Sports,' 'Motion pictures,' 'Radio,' 'Football.'

17. Huizinga, J., *Homo Ludens* (Harlem, 1938).

18. Cf. Adorno, T. Wiesengrund, 'On Popular Music,' *Studies in Philosophy and Social Science* (New York, 1941), vol. IX, no. 1.

Dale, Edgar, *The Content of Motion Pictures* (New York, 1932).

Doob, L. W., *Public Opinion and Propaganda* (New York, 1948).

Eisler, Hans, *Composing for the Films* (New York, 1948).

Farrell, James T., 'The Fate of Writing in America,' in *Literature and Morality* (New York, 1946).

Hart, Hornell, 'Changing Attitudes and Interests,' *Recent Social Trends in the United States* (New York, 1933).

Rosten, Leo C., *Hollywood, the Movie Colony, the Movie Makers* (New York, 1941).

Schuecking, L. L., *The Sociology of Literary Taste* (London, 1942).

Smith, B., Lasswell, H., and Casey, R., *Propaganda, Communication, and Public Opinion* (Princeton, 1946).

Waples, Douglas, *What People Want to Read About* (Chicago, 1931).

19. Good material for this approach in the Soviet Union is given by John Somerville, *Soviet Philosophy* (New York, 1946).

For Germany the transformation of the 'Youth Movement' into the Hitler Youth is especially telling. Cf. Howard Becker, *German Youth Bond or Free?* (New York, 1947).

Cf. also Kris, Ernst, and Speier, Hans, *German Radio Propaganda* (New York, 1944).

Kracauer, Siegfried, *From Caligari to Hitler* (Princeton, 1948).

Sington, D., and Weidenfeld, A., *The Goebbels Experiment* (New Haven, 1943).

20. Cf. in this context Reich, W., *The Sexual Revolution towards a Self-Governing Character Structure* (New York, 1945).

——— *Character Analysis* (New York, 1945).

21. Cf. Russell, B., *In Praise of Idleness*, p. 20. 'The idea that the poor should have leisure has always been shocking to the rich.'

22. Cf. Friedländer, K., *The Psychoanalytic Approach to the Treatment of Delinquency* (London, 1947).

23. Cf. Read, Herbert, *Education through Art* (London, 1943).

24. Cf. Hammond, J. L., 'The Growth of Common Enjoyment,' L. T. Hobhouse Memorial Trust Lecture, no. 31 (London, 1937). According to Hammond only the Romanized countries developed patterns of communal leisure. In Great Britain community recreation has been unorganized since this country remained outside that sphere. Cf. also Thomson, D. C., *Radio Is Changing Us* (London, 1937), p. 32.

25. For further literature about leisure see the bibliography in Karl Mannheim, *Man and Society* (New York, 1940), pp. 437ff.

CHAPTER 12. THE DISCIPLINE OF FREEDOM

1. The following list of references may serve as background for the present chapter:

Angell, N., *Why Freedom Matters* (New York, 1918).

CC

Anshen, R. N. (ed.), *Freedom Its Meaning* (New York, 1940).

'Aspects of Freedom,' *Spectator*, vol. 155, pp. 852-4.

Cecil, H., *Liberty and Authority* (1910).

Croce, B., *La teoria della liberta* (nuova ed. Bari, 1945).

Heimann, E., *Freedom and Order* (New York, 1947).

Hobson, J. A., 'Democracy, Liberty, Force,' *Hibbert Journal* vol. 34, pp. 35-44.

Ingersoll, R. G., *Human Liberty* (1884).

Knight, F. H., 'Meaning of Freedom,' *Ethics*, vol. 52, pp. 86-109.

Laski, H. L., 'Liberty,' *Encyc. Soc. Sciences*, vol. IX.

Lee, A., 'Authority and Freedom,' *London Quarterly Review*, vol. 163, pp. 492-500.

Malinowski, B., *Freedom and Civilization* (New York, 1944), part III, ch. I, II, III.

Mann, Thomas, *Das Problem der Freiheit* (Stockholm, 1939).

Maritain, Jacques, *Freedom in the Modern World* (New York, 1936).

2. Gre, G. de, 'Freedom and the Social Structure,' *American Sociological Review*, vol. II, pp. 529-36.

Cooley, C. H., *Social Organization* (New York, 1929).

3. For bibliographical references see Karl Mannheim, *Man and Society* (London, New York, 1940), pp. 453-4. For additional formulations, see Coover, J. E., *Formal Discipline from the Standpoint of Experimental Psychology* (Princeton, 1916).

Hubert, R., *Le Principe d'autorité dans l'organisation démocratique* (Paris, 1926).

Michels, Roberto, 'Authority,' *Encyc. Soc. Sciences*.

Samuel, H. L., *Persuasion of Force* (London, 1947).

Sturzo, L., 'Authority and Democracy,' *Dublin Review*, vol. 210, pp. 151-63.

4. See ch. 3.

5. See Read, H., *The Philosophy of Anarchism* (London, 1943).

6. Martin Buber, quoted by Herbert Read in *Education Through Art* (London, 1943), p. 282.

7. See Robins, J. J., and Heckscher, G., 'Constitutional Theory of Autonomous Groups,' *Journal of Politics*, vol. 3, pp. 3-28.

8. Cf. Pape, L. M., 'Some Notes on Democratic Freedom: Democratic and Totalitarian Concepts in the Problem of Freedom and Restraint,' *Ethics*, vol. 51, pp. 349-55.

See also Mannheim, Karl, *Man and Society*, pp. 445-6, 453-4.

9. Ibid. part III ('Crisis, Dictatorship, War').

10. Ibid. (Extensive bibliography.) Also the following references:

Cohen, M. R., *The Faith of a Liberal* (New York, 1946), 'Freedom: Its Meaning.'

Garnett, A. C., 'Liberalism as a Theory of Human Nature,' *Journal of Social Philosophy*, vol. 7, pp. 127-41.

Hobhouse, L. T., *Liberalism* (London, 1911).

Jordan, E., 'False Principle of Liberalism,' *International Journal of Ethics*, vol. 46, pp. 276-91.

Kallen, H. M., *The Liberal Spirit* (Ithaca, 1948).

Montagne, W. P., 'Democracy as Liberalism: Its Hypocrisy and Futility,' *International Journal of Ethics*, vol. 45, pp. 143-6.

11. For a presentation of some similar ideas see F. Camper, 'Hayek's *Road to Serfdom*,' *Enquiry*, vol. 2, no. 3, pp. 22-4; also F. W. Coker's *Democracy, Liberty, Property* (New York, 1942).

12. See Lauterbach, A. T., *Economic Security and Individual Freedom* (Ithaca, 1948).

13. Leibholz, G., 'Two Types of Democracy,' *Hibbert Journal*, vol. 44, pp. 35-44.

14. *Authority and the Individual* (Cambridge, 1936). (Harvard Tercentenary Conference of Arts and Sciences, Cambridge.)

15. See part II, ch. 3, II.

16. Cf. Plamenatz, J. P., *Consent, Freedom and Political Obligation* (London, 1938).

17. Heimann, E., 'Industrial Society and Democracy,' *Social Research*, vol. 12, pp. 43-59.

18. For a previous discussion of 'Freedom and Planning,' see Karl Mannheim, *Man and Society*, 'Planning for Freedom,' pp. 385-8.

Also see Benn, E., 'Death-bed of the Nation? Is Freedom To Be Planned Away?' *Quarterly Review*, vol. 283, pp. 129-38.

Corey, L., 'Economic Planning without Statism; Planning in the Framework of Liberty,' *Commentary*, vol. 4, pp. 137-47.

Cummings, H. S., *Liberty under Law and Administration* (New York, 1934).

Keirstead, B. S., 'Liberty and a Planned Economy,' *Canadian Journal of Economics and Political Science*, vol. 11, pp. 281-5.

Madariaga, S. de, *Anarchie ou hierarchie* (3rd ed. Paris, 1936).

Mitrany, D., 'Political Consequences of Economic Planning,' *Sociological Review*, vol. 27, pp. 2-4.

Renner, K., *Demokratie und Bureaukratie* (Wien, 1946).

Rosenfarb, J., *Freedom and the Administrative State* (New York, 1948).

Smith, T. V., 'Political Liberty Today: Is It Being Restricted or Enlarged by Economic Regulation?' *American Political Science Review*, vol. 31, pp. 12-27.

Spinelli, A., 'Dawn or Dusk of Democracy,' tr. by A. O. Hirschman and S. Hirschman, *Social Research*, vol. 14, pp. 222-43.

Tawney, R. H., 'English Politics Today: We Mean Freedom,' *Review of Politics*, vol. 8, pp. 223-39.

Tugwell, R. G., 'Directive: Need for a New Philosophy of Governmental Powers,' *Journal of Social Philosophy*, vol. 7, pp. 5-36.

19. Kotschnig, W., *Unemployment in the Learned Professions* (New York, London, 1937). See part II particularly.

20. 'The principle means adopted by the new agricultural policy were the organization of the various markets by means of compulsory associations

whose functions are adapted to the temporary requirements of the market, subsidies, and encouragement of consumption by graded prices and advertising campaigns. . . No general plan was drawn up and systematically pursued.' Reventlow, Hedwig Ide, 'Die Entwicklung des britischen Agrarschutzes,' *Berichte über Landwirtschaft* (Berlin, 1937), p. 131.

'Farmers in the Modern World,' *Agricultural Yearbook* 1940, ed. by Henry A. Wallace (Washington, D.C., 1940).

Lamartine, Paul Yates, *Food Production in Western Europe: An Economic Survey of Agriculture in Six Countries* (New York, London, 1940), esp. the concluding chapter, 'The Planning of Agriculture,' pp. 551ff. (The report of an inquiry organized by Viscount Astor and B. Seebohm Rowntree with a Foreword by Sir William Beveridge.)

21. See content studies of hero models such as:

Dale, Edgar, *The Content of Motion Pictures* (New York, 1933).

Heine, Patricke Johns, and Gerth, H. H., 'Values in Mass Periodical Fiction,' *Public Opinion Quarterly* (Spring 1949), pp. 105-13.

Rosten, Leo C., *Hollywood, the Movie Colony, the Movie Makers* (New York, 1941).

CHAPTER 13. THOUGHT, PHILOSOPHY, RELIGION, AND THE INTEGRATION OF THE SOCIAL ORDER

1. On the conservative function of priesthood in the modern world see Max Weber, *Wirtschaft und Gesellschaft* (Tuebingen, 1925), ch. XI, 'Staat und Hierokratie,' pp. 807f. For a discussion of value conflicts between religion and various types of rationalizing processes see *From Max Weber: Essays in Sociology*, tr. by H. H. Gerth and C. Wright Mills (New York, 1946), ch. XIII, 'Religious Rejections of the World and Their Directions,' pp. 323-59. For a suggestive criticism of Max Weber by a religious socialist see Gerhard E. O. Meyer, 'The Religious Socialist in the World Crisis,' *The Journal of Liberal Religion* (Chicago, Winter and Spring 1942), vol. III, nos. 3 and 4.

Cf. also Jaspers, Karl, *Der Philosophische Glaube* (Munich, 1948).

Niebuhr, Reinhold, *Christianity and Power Politics* (New York, 1941).

—— *Moral Man and Immoral Society* (New York, 1932).

—— *The Nature and Destiny of Man* (New York, 1941).

Philip, André, *Le Christianisme et la paix* (Paris, 1933).

Wach, Joachim, *Sociology of Religion* (Chicago, 1944). (Comprehensive bibliographies.)

2. Burke, Edmund, *Reflections on the French Revolution*.

3. Cf. ch. 5, section VII, 3.

4. See Karl Jaspers' analyses in his *Psychologie der Weltanschauungen* (Berlin, 1925), esp. his concept of 'Gehause,' pp. 304-26. See also Walter Lippmann's concept of 'stereotypes' in his *Public Opinion* (New York, 1922; Pelican, 1946), part III, pp. 59-127.

5. Cf. Durkheim's distinction between 'organic' and 'mechanical' solidarity, *The Division of Labor in Society* (New York, 1933).

6. Ackerknecht, Erwin H., 'Psychopathology, Primitive Medicine and Primitive Culture,' *Bulletin of the History of Medicine* (June 1943), vol. XIV, no. 1, esp. pp. 30-35.

Merton, Robert K., 'The Sociology of Knowledge,' *Twentieth Century Sociology*, ed. by Gurvitch and Moore (New York, 1945), pp. 369f.

Plessner, Hellmuth, *Das Schicksal des deutschen Geistes im Ausgang seiner bürgerlichen Epoche* (Zurich, 1935), esp. pp. 120-34.

7. Quoted by F. Zweig, *The Planning of Free Societies* (London, 1942), p. 242.

8. Cf. the observations of young Marx on 'bourgeois morality,' Marx-Engels, *Gesamtausgabe*, 1st section, vol. 5, pp. 162, 163.

9. Fromm, Erich, *Escape from Freedom* (New York, 1941).

Index

Q

The International Library of
Sociology
and Social Reconstruction

Edited by W. J. H. SPROTT
Founded by KARL MANNHEIM

ROUTLEDGE & KEGAN PAUL
BROADWAY HOUSE, CARTER LANE, LONDON, E.C.4

CONTENTS

PRINTED IN GREAT BRITAIN BY HEADLEY BROTHERS LTD
109 KINGSWAY LONDON WC2 AND ASHFORD KENT

GENERAL SOCIOLOGY

Brown, Robert. Explanation in Social Science. *208 pp. 1963. (2nd Impression 1964.) 25s.*

Gibson, Quentin. The Logic of Social Enquiry. *240 pp. 1960. (2nd Impression 1963.) 24s.*

Homans, George C. Sentiments and Activities: Essays in Social Science. *336 pp. 1962. 32s.*

Isajiw, Wsevelod W. Causation and Functionalism in Sociology. *About 192 pp. 1968. 25s.*

Johnson, Harry M. Sociology: a Systematic Introduction. *Foreword by Robert K. Merton. 710 pp. 1961. (4th Impression 1964.) 42s.*

Mannheim, Karl. Essays on Sociology and Social Psychology. *Edited by Paul Keckskemeti. With Editorial Note by Adolph Lowe. 344 pp. 1953. (2nd Impression 1966.) 32s.*

Systematic Sociology: An Introduction to the Study of Society. *Edited by J. S. Erös and Professor W. A. C. Stewart. 220 pp. 1957. (3rd Impression 1967.) 24s.*

Martindale, Don. The Nature and Types of Sociological Theory. *292 pp. 1961. (3rd Impression 1967.) 35s.*

Maus, Heinz. A Short History of Sociology. *234 pp. 1962. (2nd Impression 1965.) 28s.*

Myrdal, Gunnar. Value in Social Theory: A Collection of Essays on Methodology. *Edited by Paul Streeten. 332 pp. 1958. (2nd Impression 1962.) 32s.*

Ogburn, William F., and **Nimkoff, Meyer F.** A Handbook of Sociology. *Preface by Karl Mannheim. 656 pp. 46 figures. 35 tables. 5th edition (revised) 1964. 40s.*

Parsons, Talcott, and **Smelser, Neil J.** Economy and Society: A Study in the Integration of Economic and Social Theory. *362 pp. 1956. (4th Impression 1967.) 35s.*

Rex, John. Key Problems of Sociological Theory. *220 pp. 1961. (4th Impression 1968.) 25s.*

Stark, Werner. The Fundamental Forms of Social Thought. *280 pp. 1962. 32s.*

FOREIGN CLASSICS OF SOCIOLOGY

Durkheim, Emile. Suicide. A Study in Sociology. *Edited and with an Introduction by George Simpson. 404 pp. 1952. (4th Impression 1968.) 35s.*

Socialism and Saint-Simon. *Edited with an Introduction by Alvin W. Gouldner. Translated by Charlotte Sattler from the edition originally edited with an Introduction by Marcel Mauss. 286 pp. 1959. 28s.*

Professional Ethics and Civic Morals. *Translated by Cornelia Brookfield. 288 pp. 1957. 30s.*

Gerth, H. H., and **Mills, C. Wright.** From Max Weber: Essays in Sociology. *502 pp. 1948. (6th Impression 1967.) 35s.*

Tönnies, Ferdinand. Community and Association. *(Gemeinschaft und Gesellschaft.) Translated and Supplemented by Charles P. Loomis. Foreword by Pitirim A. Sorokin. 334 pp. 1955. 28s.*

SOCIAL STRUCTURE

Andreski, Stanislaw. Military Organization and Society. *Foreword by Professor A. R. Radcliffe-Brown. 226 pp. 1 folder. 1954. Revised Edition 1968. 35s.*

Cole, G. D. H. Studies in Class Structure. *220 pp. 1955. (3rd Impression 1964.) 21s.*

Coontz, Sydney H. Population Theories and the Economic Interpretation. *202 pp. 1957. (2nd Impression 1961.) 25s.*

Coser, Lewis. The Functions of Social Conflict. *204 pp. 1956. (3rd Impression 1968.) 25s.*

Dickie-Clark, H. F. Marginal Situation: A Sociological Study of a Coloured Group. *240 pp. 11 tables. 1966. 40s.*

Glass, D. V. (Ed.). Social Mobility in Britain. *Contributions by J. Berent, T. Bottomore, R. C. Chambers, J. Floud, D. V. Glass, J. R. Hall, H. T. Himmelweit, R. K. Kelsall, F. M. Martin, C. A. Moser, R. Mukherjee, and W. Ziegel. 420 pp. 1954. (4th Impression 1967.) 45s.*

Kelsall, R. K. Higher Civil Servants in Britain: From 1870 to the Present Day. *268 pp. 31 tables. 1955. (2nd Impression 1966.) 25s.*

König, René. The Community. *224 pp. 1968. 25s.*

Lawton, Dennis. Social Class, Language and Education. *192 pp. 1968. 21s.*

Marsh, David C. The Changing Social Structure in England and Wales, 1871-1961. *1958. 272 pp. 2nd edition (revised) 1966. (2nd Impression 1967.) 35s.*

Mouzelis, Nicos. Organization and Bureaucracy. An Analysis of Modern Theories. *240 pp. 1967. 28s.*

Ossowski, Stanislaw. Class Structure in the Social Consciousness. *210 pp. 1963. (2nd Impression 1967.) 25s.*

SOCIOLOGY AND POLITICS

Barbu, Zevedei. Democracy and Dictatorship: Their Psychology and Patterns of Life. *300 pp. 1956. 28s.*

Crick, Bernard. The American Science of Politics: Its Origins and Conditions. *284 pp. 1959. 32s.*

Hertz, Frederick. Nationality in History and Politics: A Psychology and Sociology of National Sentiment and Nationalism. *432 pp. 1944. (5th Impression 1966.) 42s.*

Kornhauser, William. The Politics of Mass Society. *272 pp. 20 tables. 1960. (2nd Impression 1965.) 28s.*

Laidler, Harry W. History of Socialism. Social-Economic Movements: An Historical and Comparative Survey of Socialism, Communism, Co-operation, Utopianism; and other Systems of Reform and Reconstruction. *New edition in preparation.*

Lasswell, Harold D. Analysis of Political Behaviour. An Empirical Approach. *324 pp. 1947. (4th Impression 1966.) 35s.*

Mannheim, Karl. Freedom, Power and Democratic Planning. *Edited by Hans Gerth and Ernest K. Bramstedt. 424 pp. 1951. (2nd Impression 1965.) 35s.*

Mansur, Fatma. Process of Independence. *Foreword by A. H. Hanson. 208 pp. 1962. 25s.*

Martin, David A. Pacificism: an Historical and Sociological Study. *262 pp. 1965. 30s.*

Myrdal, Gunnar. The Political Element in the Development of Economic Theory. *Translated from the German by Paul Streeten. 282 pp. 1953. (4th Impression 1965.) 25s.*

Polanyi, Michael. F.R.S. The Logic of Liberty: Reflections and Rejoinders. *228 pp. 1951. 18s.*

Verney, Douglas V. The Analysis of Political Systems. *264 pp. 1959. (3rd Impression 1966.) 28s.*

Wootton, Graham. The Politics of Influence: British Ex-Servicemen, Cabinet Decisions and Cultural Changes, 1917 to 1957. *316 pp. 1963. 30s.*

Workers, Unions and the State. *188 pp. 1966. (2nd Impression 1967.) 25s.*

FOREIGN AFFAIRS: THEIR SOCIAL, POLITICAL AND ECONOMIC FOUNDATIONS

Baer, Gabriel. Population and Society in the Arab East. *Translated by Hanna Szöke. 288 pp. 10 maps. 1964. 40s.*

Bonné, Alfred. State and Economics in the Middle East: A Society in Transition. *482 pp. 2nd (revised) edition 1955. (2nd Impression 1960.) 40s.*

Studies in Economic Development: with special reference to Conditions in the Under-developed Areas of Western Asia and India. *322 pp. 84 tables. 2nd edition 1960. 32s.*

Mayer, J. P. Political Thought in France from the Revolution to the Fifth Republic. *164 pp. 3rd edition (revised) 1961. 16s.*

Trouton, Ruth. Peasant Renaissance in Yugoslavia 1900-1950: A Study of the Development of Yugoslav Peasant Society as affected by Education. *370 pp. 1 map. 1952. 28s.*

CRIMINOLOGY

Ancel, Marc. Social Defence: A Modern Approach to Criminal Problems. *Foreword by Leon Radzinowicz. 240 pp. 1965. 32s.*

Cloward, Richard A., and Ohlin, Lloyd E. Delinquency and Opportunity: A Theory of Delinquent Gangs. *248 pp. 1961. 25s.*

Downes, David M. The Delinquent Solution. A Study in Subcultural Theory. *296 pp. 1966. 42s.*

Dunlop, A. B., and McCabe, S. Young Men in Detention Centres. *192 pp. 1965. 28s.*

Friedländer, Kate. The Psycho-Analytical Approach to Juvenile Delinquency: Theory, Case Studies, Treatment. *320 pp. 1947. (6th Impression 1967.) 40s.*

Glueck, Sheldon and **Eleanor.** Family Environment and Delinquency. *With the statistical assistance of Rose W. Kneznek. 340 pp. 1962. (2nd Impression 1966.) 40s.*

Mannheim, Hermann. Comparative Criminology: a Text Book. *Two volumes. 442 pp. and 380 pp. 1965. (2nd Impression with corrections 1966.) 42s. a volume.*

Morris, Terence. The Criminal Area: A Study in Social Ecology. *Foreword by Hermann Mannheim. 232 pp. 25 tables. 4 maps. 1957. (2nd Impression 1966.) 28s.*

Morris, Terence and **Pauline,** assisted by **Barbara Barer.** Pentonville: A Sociological Study of an English Prison. *416 pp. 16 plates. 1963. 50s.*

Spencer, John C. Crime and the Services. *Foreword by Hermann Mannheim. 336 pp. 1954. 28s.*

Trasler, Gordon. The Explanation of Criminality. *144 pp. 1962. (2nd Impression 1967.) 20s.*

SOCIAL PSYCHOLOGY

Barbu, Zevedei. Problems of Historical Psychology. *248 pp. 1960. 25s.*

Blackburn, Julian. Psychology and the Social Pattern. *184 pp. 1945. (7th Impression 1964.) 16s.*

Fleming, C. M. Adolescence: Its Social Psychology: With an Introduction to recent findings from the fields of Anthropology, Physiology, Medicine, Psychometrics and Sociometry. *288 pp. 2nd edition (revised) 1963. (3rd Impression 1967.) 25s. Paper 12s. 6d.*
The Social Psychology of Education: An Introduction and Guide to Its Study. *136 pp. 2nd edition (revised) 1959. (4th Impression 1967.) 14s. Paper 7s. 6d.*

Halmos, Paul. Towards a Measure of Man: The Frontiers of Normal Adjustment. *276 pp. 1957. 28s.*

Homans, George C. The Human Group. *Foreword by Bernard DeVoto. Introduction by Robert K. Merton. 526 pp. 1951. (7th Impression 1968.) 35s.*
Social Behaviour: its Elementary Forms. *416 pp. 1961. (2nd Impression 1966.) 32s.*

Klein, Josephine. The Study of Groups. *226 pp. 31 figures. 5 tables. 1956. (5th Impression 1967.) 21s. Paper, 9s. 6d.*

Linton, Ralph. The Cultural Background of Personality. *132 pp. 1947. (7th Impression 1968.) 16s.*

Mayo, Elton. The Social Problems of an Industrial Civilization. With an appendix on the Political Problem. *180 pp. 1949. (5th Impression 1966.) 25s.*

Ottaway, A. K. C. Learning Through Group Experience. *176 pp. 1966. 25s.*

Ridder, J. C. de. The Personality of the Urban African in South Africa. A Thematic Apperception Test Study. *196 pp. 12 plates. 1961. 25s.*

Rose, Arnold M. (Ed.). Human Behaviour and Social Processes: an Interactionist Approach. *Contributions by Arnold M. Rose, Ralph H. Turner, Anselm Strauss, Everett C. Hughes, E. Franklin Frazier, Howard S. Becker, et al. 696 pp. 1962. 70s.*

Smelser, Neil J. Theory of Collective Behaviour. *448 pp. 1962. (2nd Impression 1967.) 45s.*

Stephenson, Geoffrey M. The Development of Conscience. *128 pp. 1966. 25s.*

Young, Kimball. Handbook of Social Psychology. *658 pp. 16 figures. 10 tables. 2nd edition (revised) 1957. (3rd Impression 1963.) 40s.*

SOCIOLOGY OF THE FAMILY

Banks, J. A. Prosperity and Parenthood: A study of Family Planning among The Victorian Middle Classes. *262 pp. 1954. (2nd Impression 1965.) 28s.*

Burton, Lindy. Vulnerable Children. *about 272 pp. 1968. 35s.*

Gavron, Hannah. The Captive Wife: Conflicts of Housebound Mothers. *190 pp. 1966. (2nd Impression 1966.) 25s.*

Klein, Josephine. Samples from English Cultures. *1965. (2nd Impression 1967.)*
  1. Three Preliminary Studies and Aspects of Adult Life in England. *447 pp. 50s.*
  2. Child-Rearing Practices and Index. *247 pp. 35s.*

Klein, Viola. Britain's Married Women Workers. *180 pp. 1965. 28s.*

McWhinnie, Alexina M. Adopted Children. How They Grow Up. *304 pp. 1967. (2nd Impression 1968.) 42s.*

Myrdal, Alva and Klein, Viola. Women's Two Roles: Home and Work. *238 pp. 27 tables. 1956. Revised Edition 1967. 30s. Paper 15s.*

Parsons, Talcott and Bales, Robert F. Family: Socialization and Interaction Process. *In collaboration with James Olds, Morris Zelditch and Philip E. Slater. 456 pp. 50 figures and tables. 1956. (2nd Impression 1964.) 35s.*

THE SOCIAL SERVICES

Ashdown, Margaret and Brown, S. Clement. Social Service and Mental Health: An Essay on Psychiatric Social Workers. *280 pp. 1953. 21s.*

Goetschius, George W. Working with Community Groups. *About 256 pp. 1968. about 35s.*

Goetschius, George W. and Tash, Joan. Working with Unattached Youth. *416 pp. 1967. 40s.*

Hall, M. Penelope. The Social Services of Modern England. *416 pp. 6th edition (revised) 1963. (2nd Impression with a new Preface 1966.) 30s.*

Hall, M. P., and Howes, I. V. The Church in Social Work. A Study of Moral Welfare Work undertaken by the Church of England. *320 pp. 1965. 35s.*

Heywood, Jean S. Children in Care: the Development of the Service for the Deprived Child. *264 pp. 2nd edition (revised) 1965. (2nd Impression 1966.) 32s.*

An Introduction to Teaching Casework Skills. *190 pp. 1964. 28s.*

Jones, Kathleen. Lunacy, Law and Conscience, 1744-1845: the Social History of the Care of the Insane. *268 pp. 1955. 25s.*

Mental Health and Social Policy, 1845-1959. *264 pp. 1960. (2nd Impression 1967.) 28s.*

Jones, Kathleen and **Sidebotham, Roy.** Mental Hospitals at Work. *220 pp. 1962. 30s.*

Kastell, Jean. Casework in Child Care. *Foreword by M. Brooke Willis. 320 pp. 1962. 35s.*

Nokes, P. L. The Professional Task in Welfare Practice. *152 pp. 1967. 28s.*

Rooff, Madeline. Voluntary Societies and Social Policy. *350 pp. 15 tables. 1957. 35s.*

Shenfield, B. E. Social Policies for Old Age: A Review of Social Provision for Old Age in Great Britain. *260 pp. 39 tables. 1957. 25s.*

Timms, Noel. Psychiatric Social Work in Great Britain (1939-1962). *280 pp. 1964. 32s.*

Social Casework: Principles and Practice. *256 pp. 1964. (2nd Impression 1966.) 25s. Paper 15s.*

Trasler, Gordon. In Place of Parents: A Study in Foster Care. *272 pp. 1960. (2nd Impression 1966.) 30s.*

Young, A. F., and **Ashton, E. T.** British Social Work in the Nineteenth Century. *288 pp. 1956. (2nd Impression 1963.) 28s.*

Young, A. F. Social Services in British Industry. *about 350 pp. 1968. about 45s.*

SOCIOLOGY OF EDUCATION

Banks, Olive. Parity and Prestige in English Secondary Education: a Study in Educational Sociology. *272 pp. 1955. (2nd Impression 1963.) 32s.*

Bentwich, Joseph. Education in Israel. *224 pp. 8 pp. plates. 1965. 24s.*

Blyth, W. A. L. English Primary Education. A Sociological Description. *1965. Revised edition 1967.*

1. Schools. *232 pp. 30s.*
2. Background. *168 pp. 25s.*

Collier, K. G. The Social Purposes of Education: Personal and Social Values in Education. *268 pp. 1959. (3rd Impression 1965.) 21s.*

Dale, R. R., and **Griffith, S.** Down Stream: Failure in the Grammar School. *108 pp. 1965. 20s.*

Dore, R. P. Education in Tokugawa Japan. *356 pp. 9 pp. plates. 1965. 35s.*

Edmonds, E. L. The School Inspector. *Foreword by Sir William Alexander. 214 pp. 1962. 28s.*

Evans, K. M. Sociometry and Education. *158 pp. 1962. (2nd Impression 1966.) 18s.*

Foster, P. J. Education and Social Change in Ghana. *336 pp. 3 maps. 1965. (2nd Impression 1967.) 36s.*

Fraser, W. R. Education and Society in Modern France. *150 pp. 1963. 20s.*

Hans, Nicholas. New Trends in Education in the Eighteenth Century. *278 pp. 19 tables. 1951. (2nd Impression 1966.) 30s.*

Comparative Education: A Study of Educational Factors and Traditions. *360 pp. 3rd (revised) edition 1958. (4th Impression 1967.) 25s. Paper 12s. 6d.*

Hargreaves, David. Social Relations in a Secondary School. *240 pp. 1967. 32s.*

Holmes, Brian. Problems in Education. A Comparative Approach. *336 pp. 1965. (2nd Impression 1967.) 32s.*

Mannheim, Karl and **Stewart, W. A. C.** An Introduction to the Sociology of Education. *206 pp. 1962. (2nd Impression 1965.) 21s.*

Musgrove, F. Youth and the Social Order. *176 pp. 1964. 21s.*

Ortega y Gasset, José. Mission of the University. *Translated with an Introduction by Howard Lee Nostrand. 86 pp. 1946. (3rd Impression 1963.) 15s.*

Ottaway, A. K. C. Education and Society: An Introduction to the Sociology of Education. *With an Introduction by W. O. Lester Smith. 212 pp. Second edition (revised). 1962. (5th Impression 1968.) 18s. Paper 10s. 6d.*

Peers, Robert. Adult Education: A Comparative Study. *398 pp. 2nd edition 1959. (2nd Impression 1966.) 42s.*

Pritchard, D. G. Education and the Handicapped: 1760 to 1960. *258 pp. 1963. (2nd Impression 1966.) 35s.*

Simon, Brian and **Joan** (Eds.). Educational Psychology in the U.S.S.R. *Introduction by Brian and Joan Simon. Translation by Joan Simon. Papers by D. N. Bogoiavlenski and N. A. Menchinskaia, D. B. Elkonin, E. A. Fleshner, Z. I. Kalmykova, G. S. Kostiuk, V. A. Krutetski, A. N. Leontiev, A. R. Luria, E. A. Milerian, R. G. Natadze, B. M. Teplov, L. S. Vygotski, L. V. Zankov. 296 pp. 1963. 40s.*

SOCIOLOGY OF CULTURE

Eppel, E. M., and **M.** Adolescents and Morality: A Study of some Moral Values and Dilemmas of Working Adolescents in the Context of a changing Climate of Opinion. *Foreword by W. J. H. Sprott. 268 pp. 39 tables. 1966. 30s.*

Fromm, Erich. The Fear of Freedom. *286 pp. 1942. (8th Impression 1960.) 25s. Paper 10s.*

The Sane Society. *400 pp. 1956. (3rd Impression 1963.) 28s. Paper 12s. 6d.*

Mannheim, Karl. Diagnosis of Our Time: Wartime Essays of a Sociologist. *208 pp. 1943. (8th Impression 1966.) 21s.*

Essays on the Sociology of Culture. *Edited by Ernst Mannheim in co-operation with Paul Kecskemeti. Editorial Note by Adolph Lowe. 280 pp. 1956. (3rd Impression 1967.) 28s.*

Weber, Alfred. Farewell to European History: or The Conquest of Nihilism. *Translated from the German by R. F. C. Hull. 224 pp. 1947. 18s.*

SOCIOLOGY OF RELIGION

Argyle, Michael. Religious Behaviour. *224 pp. 8 figures. 41 tables. 1958. (3rd Impression 1965.) 25s.*

Knight, Frank H., and **Merriam, Thornton W.** The Economic Order and Religion. *242 pp. 1947. 18s.*

Stark, Werner. The Sociology of Religion. A Study of Christendom.
Volume I. Established Religion. *248 pp. 1966. 35s.*
Volume II. Sectarian Religion. *368 pp. 1967. 40s.*
Volume III. The Universal Church. *464 pp. 1967. 45s.*

Watt, W. Montgomery. Islam and the Integration of Society. *320 pp. 1961. (3rd Impression 1966.) 35s.*

SOCIOLOGY OF ART AND LITERATURE

Beljame, Alexandre. Men of Letters and the English Public in the Eighteenth Century: 1660-1744, Dryden, Addison, Pope. *Edited with an Introduction and Notes by Bonamy Dobrée. Translated by E. O. Lorimer. 532 pp. 1948. 32s.*

Misch, Georg. A History of Autobiography in Antiquity. *Translated by E. W. Dickes. 2 Volumes. Vol. 1, 364 pp., Vol. 2, 372 pp. 1950. 45s. the set.*

Schücking, L. L. The Sociology of Literary Taste. *112 pp. 2nd (revised) edition 1966. 18s.*

Silbermann, Alphons. The Sociology of Music. *Translated from the German by Corbet Stewart. 222 pp. 1963. 28s.*

SOCIOLOGY OF KNOWLEDGE

Mannheim, Karl. Essays on the Sociology of Knowledge. *Edited by Paul Kecskemeti. Editorial note by Adolph Lowe. 352 pp. 1952. (3rd Impression 1964.) 35s.*

Stark, W. America: Ideal and Reality. The United States of 1776 in Contemporary Philosophy. *136 pp. 1947. 12s.*
The Sociology of Knowledge: An Essay in Aid of a Deeper Understanding of the History of Ideas. *384 pp. 1958. (3rd Impression 1967.) 36s.*
Montesquieu: Pioneer of the Sociology of Knowledge. *244 pp. 1960. 25s.*

URBAN SOCIOLOGY

Anderson, Nels. The Urban Community: A World Perspective. *532 pp. 1960. 35s.*

Ashworth, William. The Genesis of Modern British Town Planning: A Study in Economic and Social History of the Nineteenth and Twentieth Centuries. *288 pp. 1954. (3rd Impression 1968.) 32s.*

Bracey, Howard. Neighbours: On New Estates and Subdivisions in England and U.S.A. *220 pp. 1964. 28s.*

Cullingworth, J. B. Housing Needs and Planning Policy: A Restatement of the Problems of Housing Need and "Overspill" in England and Wales. *232 pp. 44 tables. 8 maps. 1960. (2nd Impression 1966.) 28s.*

Dickinson, Robert E. City and Region: A Geographical Interpretation. *608 pp. 125 figures. 1964. (5th Impression 1967.) 60s.*
The West European City: A Geographical Interpretation. *600 pp. 129 maps. 29 plates. 2nd edition 1962. (3rd Impression 1968.) 55s.*
The City Region in Western Europe. *320 pp. Maps. 1967. 30s. Paper 14s.*

Jennings, Hilda. Societies in the Making: a Study of Development and Redevelopment within a County Borough. *Foreword by D. A. Clark. 286 pp. 1962. (2nd Impression 1967.) 32s.*

Kerr, Madeline. The People of Ship Street. *240 pp. 1958. 23s.*

Mann, P. H. An Approach to Urban Sociology. *240 pp. 1965. (2nd Impression 1968.) 30s.*

Morris, R. N., and **Mogey, J.** The Sociology of Housing. Studies at Berinsfield. *232 pp. 4 pp. plates. 1965. 42s.*

Rosser, C., and **Harris, C.** The Family and Social Change. A Study of Family and Kinship in a South Wales Town. *352 pp. 8 maps. 1965. (2nd Impression 1968.) 45s.*

RURAL SOCIOLOGY

Haswell, M. R. The Economics of Development in Village India. *120 pp. 1967. 21s.*

Littlejohn, James. Westrigg: the Sociology of a Cheviot Parish. *172 pp. 5 figures. 1963. 25s.*

Williams, W. M. The Country Craftsman: A Study of Some Rural Crafts and the Rural Industries Organization in England. *248 pp. 9 figures. 1958. 25s. (Dartington Hall Studies in Rural Sociology.)*
The Sociology of an English Village: Gosforth. *272 pp. 12 figures. 13 tables. 1956. (3rd Impression 1964.) 25s.*

SOCIOLOGY OF MIGRATION

Eisenstadt, S. N. The Absorption of Immigrants: a Comparative Study based mainly on the Jewish Community in Palestine and the State of Israel. *288 pp. 1954. 28s.*

Humphreys, Alexander J. New Dubliners: Urbanization and the Irish Family. *Foreword by George C. Homans. 304 pp. 1966. 40s.*

SOCIOLOGY OF INDUSTRY AND DISTRIBUTION

Anderson, Nels. Work and Leisure. *280 pp. 1961. 28s.*

Blau, Peter M., and **Scott, W. Richard.** Formal Organizations: a Comparative approach. *Introduction and Additional Bibliography by J. H. Smith. 326 pp. 1963. (2nd Impression 1964.) 28s. Paper 15s.*

Eldridge, J. E. T. Industrial Disputes. Essays in the Sociology of Industrial Relations. *about 272 pp. 1968. 40s.*

Hollowell, Peter G. The Lorry Driver. *272 pp. 1968. 42s.*

Jefferys, Margot, with the assistance of Winifred Moss. Mobility in the Labour Market: Employment Changes in Battersea and Dagenham. *Preface by Barbara Wootton. 186 pp. 51 tables. 1954. 15s.*

Levy, A. B. Private Corporations and Their Control. *Two Volumes. Vol. 1, 464 pp., Vol. 2, 432 pp. 1950. 80s. the set.*

Liepmann, Kate. Apprenticeship: An Enquiry into its Adequacy under Modern Conditions. *Foreword by H. D. Dickinson. 232 pp. 6 tables. 1960. (2nd Impression 1960.) 23s.*

Millerson, Geoffrey. The Qualifying Associations: a Study in Professionalization. *320 pp. 1964. 42s.*

Smelser, Neil J. Social Change in the Industrial Revolution: An Application of Theory to the Lancashire Cotton Industry, 1770-1840. *468 pp. 12 figures. 14 tables. 1959. (2nd Impression 1960.) 42s.*

Williams, Gertrude. Recruitment to Skilled Trades. *240 pp. 1957. 23s.*

Young, A. F. Industrial Injuries Insurance: an Examination of British Policy. *192 pp. 1964. 30s.*

ANTHROPOLOGY

Ammar, Hamed. Growing up in an Egyptian Village: Silwa, Province of Aswan. *336 pp. 1954. (2nd Impression 1966.) 35s.*

Crook, David and **Isabel.** Revolution in a Chinese Village: Ten Mile Inn. *230 pp. 8 plates. 1 map. 1959. 21s.*
The First Years of Yangyi Commune. *302 pp. 12 plates. 1966. 42s.*

Dickie-Clark, H. F. The Marginal Situation. A Sociological Study of a Coloured Group. *236 pp. 1966. 40s.*

Dube, S. C. Indian Village. *Foreword by Morris Edward Opler. 276 pp. 4 plates. 1955. (5th Impression 1965.) 25s.*
India's Changing Villages: Human Factors in Community Development. *260 pp. 8 plates. 1 map. 1958. (3rd Impression 1963.) 25s.*

Firth, Raymond. Malay Fishermen. Their Peasant Economy. *420 pp. 17 pp. plates. 2nd edition revised and enlarged 1966. (2nd Impression 1968.) 55s.*

Gulliver, P. H. The Family Herds. A Study of two Pastoral Tribes in East Africa, The Jie and Turkana. *304 pp. 4 plates. 19 figures. 1955. (2nd Impression with new preface and bibliography 1966.) 35s.*
Social Control in an African Society: a Study of the Arusha, Agricultural Masai of Northern Tanganyika. *320 pp. 8 plates. 10 figures. 1963. 35s.*

Hogbin, Ian. Transformation Scene. The Changing Culture of a New Guinea Village. *340 pp. 22 plates. 2 maps. 1951. 30s.*

Ishwaran, K. Shivapur. A South Indian Village. *about 216 pp. 1968. 35s.*
Tradition and Economy in Village India: An Interactionist Approach. *Foreword by Conrad Arensburg. 176 pp. 1966. 25s.*

Jarvie, Ian C. The Revolution in Anthropology. *268 pp. 1964. (2nd Impression 1967.) 40s.*

Jarvie, Ian C. and Agassi, Joseph. Hong Kong. A Society in Transition. *about 388 pp. 1968. 56s.*

Little, Kenneth L. Mende of Sierra Leone. *308 pp. and folder. 1951. Revised edition 1967. 63s.*

Lowie, Professor Robert H. Social Organization. *494 pp. 1950. (4th Impression 1966.) 42s.*

Maunier, René. The Sociology of Colonies: An Introduction to the Study of Race Contact. *Edited and translated by E. O. Lorimer. 2 Volumes. Vol. 1, 430 pp. Vol. 2, 356 pp. 1949. 70s. the set.*

Mayer, Adrian C. Caste and Kinship in Central India: A Village and its Region. *328 pp. 16 plates. 15 figures. 16 tables. 1960. (2nd Impression 1965.) 35s.*
Peasants in the Pacific: A Study of Fiji Indian Rural Society. *232 pp. 16 plates. 10 figures. 14 tables. 1961. 35s.*

Smith, Raymond T. The Negro Family in British Guiana: Family Structure and Social Status in the Villages. *With a Foreword by Meyer Fortes. 314 pp. 8 plates. 1 figure. 4 maps. 1956. (2nd Impression 1965.) 35s.*

DOCUMENTARY

Meek, Dorothea L. (Ed.). Soviet Youth: Some Achievements and Problems. *Excerpts from the Soviet Press, translated by the editor. 280 pp. 1957. 28s.*

Schlesinger, Rudolf (Ed.). Changing Attitudes in Soviet Russia.

1. The Family in the U.S.S.R. *Documents and Readings, with an Introduction by the editor. 434 pp. 1949. 30s.*

2. The Nationalities Problem and Soviet Administration. Selected Readings on the Development of Soviet Nationalities Policies. *Introduced by the editor. Translated by W. W. Gottlieb. 324 pp. 1956. 30s.*

13

Reports of the Institute of Community Studies

(Demy 8vo.)

Cartwright, Ann. Human Relations and Hospital Care. *272 pp. 1964. 30s.*
Patients and their Doctors. A Study of General Practice. *304 pp. 1967. 40s.*

Jackson, Brian. Streaming: an Education System in Miniature. *168 pp. 1964. (2nd Impression 1966.) 21s. Paper 10s.*
Working Class Community. Some General Notions raised by a Series of Studies in Northern England. *192 pp. 1968. 25s.*

Jackson, Brian and **Marsden, Dennis.** Education and the Working Class: Some General Themes raised by a Study of 88 Working-class Children in a Northern Industrial City. *268 pp. 2 folders. 1962. (4th Impression 1968.) 32s.*

Marris, Peter. Widows and their Families. *Foreword by Dr. John Bowlby. 184 pp. 18 tables. Statistical Summary. 1958. 18s.*
Family and Social Change in an African City. A Study of Rehousing in Lagos. *196 pp. 1 map. 4 plates. 53 tables. 1961. (2nd Impression 1966.) 30s.*
The Experience of Higher Education. *232 pp. 27 tables. 1964. 25s.*

Marris, Peter and **Rein, Martin.** Dilemmas of Social Reform. Poverty and Community Action in the United States. *256 pp. 1967. 35s.*

Mills, Enid. Living with Mental Illness: a Study in East London. *Foreword by Morris Carstairs. 196 pp. 1962. 28s.*

Runciman, W. G. Relative Deprivation and Social Justice. A Study of Attitudes to Social Inequality in Twentieth Century England. *352 pp. 1966. (2nd Impression 1967.) 40s.*

Townsend, Peter. The Family Life of Old People: An Inquiry in East London. *Foreword by J. H. Sheldon. 300 pp. 3 figures. 63 tables. 1957. (3rd Impression 1967.) 30s.*

Willmott, Peter. Adolescent Boys in East London. *230 pp. 1966. 30s.*
The Evolution of a Community: a study of Dagenham after forty years. *168 pp. 2 maps. 1963. 21s.*

Willmott, Peter and **Young, Michael.** Family and Class in a London Suburb. *202 pp. 47 tables. 1960. (4th Impression 1968.) 25s.*

Young, Michael. Innovation and Research in Education. *192 pp. 1965. 25s.*

Young, Michael and **McGeeney, Patrick.** Learning Begins at Home. A Study of a Junior School and its Parents. *about 128 pp. 1968. about 18s. Paper about 8s.*

Young, Michael and **Willmott, Peter.** Family and Kinship in East London. *Foreword by Richard M. Titmuss. 252 pp. 39 tables. 1957. (3rd Impression 1965.) 28s.*

14

The British Journal of Sociology. *Edited by Terence P. Morris. Vol. 1, No. 1, March 1950 and Quarterly. Roy. 8vo., £2 10s. annually, 15s. a number, post free. (Vols. 1-16, £6 each; Vol. 17, £2 10s. Individual parts 37s. 6d. and 15s. respectively.)*

All prices are net and subject to alteration without notice

1267 H.B.